Health and Long-Term Care
Financing for Seniors

Huebner School Series

H. King McGlaughon, Jr., Editor

Huebner School Series

Health and Long-Term Care Financing for Seniors

Second Edition

Burton T. Beam, Jr.
Thomas P. O'Hare

This course is included in the CASL™ curriculum

The American College Press/*Bryn Mawr, Pennsylvania*

This publication is designed to provide accurate and authoritative information about the subject covered. While every precaution has been taken in the preparation of this material, the authors and The American College assume no liability for damages resulting from the use of the information contained in this publication. The American College is not engaged in rendering legal, accounting, or other professional advice. If legal or other expert advice is required, the services of an appropriate professional should be sought.

To
Evelyn Rice
for all her work on this
and my other books
BTB

To my children,
Brian, Carolyn,
and Michelle
TPO'H

About the Authors

Burton T. Beam, Jr., CPCU, CLU, ChFC, CASL, is associate professor of insurance at The American College. Mr. Beam did his undergraduate work at the University of Oregon and holds graduate degrees from that institution and the University of Pennsylvania. Prior to joining The American College, Mr. Beam was on the faculties of the University of Florida and the University of Connecticut. He has written extensively in the area of group insurance and has had articles published in several professional journals, including *Health Insurance Underwriter, Benefits Quarterly,* and *Journal of the American Society of CLU & ChFC.* He is also author of *Group Benefits: Basic Concepts and Alternatives,* and coauthor of *Fundamentals of Insurance Planning, Health and Long-Term Care Financing for Seniors,* and *Employee Benefits,* a textbook used at many colleges and universities. Mr. Beam is an assistant editor of the *Journal of Financial Service Professionals.* He is a member of the National Association of Health Underwriters, the CPCU Society, and the Society of Financial Service Professionals.

Thomas P. O'Hare, STB, MBA, HIA, is an adjunct professor of insurance at The American College. He received his BA and STB degrees from the University of St. Mary of the Lake, Mundelein, Illinois, and his MBA from Loyola University of Chicago. Prior to joining The American College, Mr. O'Hare served in leadership positions with the Health Insurance Association of America (HIAA) in both Chicago and Washington, D.C. Most recently as vice president of membership and special programs and director of insurance education, he led the revision and update of HIAA's education curriculum, including the establishment of the Managed Healthcare Professional (MHP) designation program and the creation of the course material to support it. He previously worked for the American Hospital Association in Chicago, where he was a hospital payment/reimbursement specialist with responsibilities for membership consulting on regulatory compliance. Mr. O'Hare is author of *Individual Medical Expense Insurance* and coauthor of *Health and Long-Term Care Financing for Seniors.* He is also a member of the National Association of Health Underwriters.

Contents

Preface

Over the last few years, seniors have become increasingly concerned about financing medical expenses and long-term care. This concern is justified as the percentage of retirement income devoted to health care continues to increase, rising from 16 percent of income in 2000 to an estimated 35 percent in 2030 according to the Center for Retirement Research at Boston College.

Without significant assets or adequate insurance, seniors will be unable to maintain their hoped-for standard of living and may have to rely on public assistance to meet their basic health care needs. On the other hand, adequate planning for health care needs during retirement will enable seniors to have a better quality of life, both from a physical and financial standpoint.

In the second edition of this book, we maintain our focus on the ways medical expenses and long-term care can be financed. The emphasis continues to be on insurance—private and government. Both types of insurance have undergone significant changes in recent years as a result of such factors as tax legislation, regulatory changes at the federal and state levels, new types of care and care settings, cost escalation, and the competitive pressures of the marketplace. Changes now encompass the rapid development of new forms of consumer-directed health plans, the 2006 implementation of the Medicare prescription drug program, and the 2006 enactment of the Deficit Reduction Act. The second edition presents current information on those changes and their effects.

Our overall objective, however, is quite broad. It is to write a book that helps readers better meet their own health care needs as well as the needs of their clients and families. To accomplish this goal, we focused on explaining and describing the following:

- the components of health care and the settings in which they can be provided
- the types of caregivers
- employment-related medical expense coverage, both before and after Medicare eligibility
- principal policies of individual medical expense insurance, including managed care
- consumer-directed health care plans for older clients
- interim, supplemental, and ancillary medical expense policies

- Medicare, including the effects of the Medicare Prescription Drug, Improvement, and Modernization Act (MMA)
- Medicare supplements, including the effects that MMA has on them
- the need for long-term care protection and the use of personal resources other than insurance to meet long-term care needs
- the development of long-term care insurance and characteristics of today's long-term care insurance policies
- underwriting of health insurance and how coverage can be obtained for the unhealthy
- Medicaid and other federal programs to provide health insurance protection

Although the main impetus for writing this book is its use in The American College's CASL (Chartered Advisor for Senior Living) designation, we believe the book will be of value to consumers, insurance agents, financial planners, and anyone else who deals with seniors.

We would like to thank the many persons who assisted us with this second edition, beginning with our students, who are an ongoing source of constructive comments. In particular, we recognize those individuals whose efforts improved our text material on long-term care insurance:

- John R. Boni, RHU, Physicians Mutual Insurance Company
- Nancy P. Morith, CLU, CSA, NP Morith, Inc.
- John C. Parker, RHU, LTCP, Parker Agency

We also thank our colleagues at The American College for their encouragement and support, including Virginia Webb and her library staff for their help in providing resources and responding to our research requests. As with all of The College's textbooks, this second edition is possible only with the enormous dedication of the people involved in the production process. We owe a particular debt of gratitude to Evelyn Rice for her patience in typing and retyping our many drafts and to Keith de Pinho for his superb and thorough editing.

We as authors, however, have the ultimate responsibility for providing you with the best book possible, and we have tried to do that. It is foolish to believe that any book is perfect. Please take some time to give us your constructive comments on how we can improve future editions. Remember that future readers may someday be advising you and your family about health care financing!

Health and Long-Term Care Financing for Seniors

1

Introduction to Health Care Financing

Chapter Outline

Many seniors fail to realize the magnitude of their future health care costs. Yet health care represents one of the largest expenses in retirement, and these costs will continue to grow as life expectancy increases for retirees. Some of the reasons for these high costs are based on factors related to age:

- Health problems increase with age, as does the time to recover from medical problems.
- Seniors are hospitalized more frequently and for longer periods than are younger persons.
- Seniors are more likely to be injured in accidents than are younger adults.
- Seniors are more likely than other groups of the population to have chronic conditions that require expensive and ongoing treatment.

Proper planning for health care expenses improves the quality of life during retirement, lessens a senior's financial worry about paying health care expenses, and allows a senior to meet such future financial goals as creating an estate for heirs or contributing to a grandchild's education fund.

Many seniors are shocked when they realize that Medicare will not fully cover their health care expenses after retirement, particularly long-term care costs. Recent statistics from the Employee Benefits Research Institute (EBRI) show that an individual needs to have significant resources prior to retirement to pay for medical expenses during retirement. These resources are necessary to pay premiums for Medicare and insurance policies as well as to pay for expenses that are not reimbursed by either of these sources. EBRI estimates that if medical costs rise at an annual rate of 10 percent, a person will need at least $90,000 at age 65 to finance medical care expenses until age 80, $206,000 until age 90, and $376,000 until age 100[1]. Of course, these figures increase if an individual retires at an earlier age, and they become even more dramatic when they are doubled for an older couple. These figures are also significantly larger when long-term care costs are considered. With minor exceptions, Medicare and medical expense policies do not cover these costs. Nursing home fees now average over $62,000 per year for semiprivate accommodations, and premiums for long-term care insurance are often several thousand dollars a year.

Another recent study indicates that medical costs will consume an annual amount equal to 20 percent of postretirement income for persons over age 65 if they have no subsidy from a former employer for these costs. Even with a generous employer subsidy, at least 5 percent of postretirement income will go to medical care.[2]

The purpose of this book is to examine the ways a senior can finance medical care and long-term care after retirement. With the exception of some very affluent people, this will require some type of health insurance protection through private insurance and/or government programs. However, even with very comprehensive protection, seniors will still have to finance some health care costs from other resources.

It is always difficult to define exactly what the term *senior* means. For purposes of this book, the authors assume it means someone who has retired, even though retirement can take place at almost any age. The needs for medical expense coverage are the same for a retiree at any age. However, the resources to meet these needs depend largely on whether an individual is eligible for Medicare or not. The types of resources required to meet long-term care needs are similar at all ages.

PLAN OF THIS BOOK

Chapter 1 lays the groundwork for an in-depth discussion of medical expense and long-term care financing for seniors by briefly describing the components of health care needs, the settings in which these needs can be met, and the caregivers who provide the care. The chapter continues with a discussion of the regulatory environment for medical expense and long-term care insurance and the issues surrounding the suitability of various products and policy provisions. The chapter concludes with a discussion of some of the issues about financing health care that confront seniors.

Chapters 2 through 6 are devoted to medical expense coverage prior to Medicare eligibility. Chapter 2 looks at the coverage that continues as a result of a prior employment relationship and includes employer-provided postretirement protection and COBRA continuation.

Chapter 3 focuses on the types of principal insurance policies that are available in the individual marketplace. These vary from traditional indemnity policies to managed care plans, such as preferred-provider organizations (PPOs) and health maintenance organizations (HMOs). These policies may be the basis for consumer-directed health insurance plans, which are described in chapter 4. Such plans include health savings accounts (HSAs).

Not everyone is healthy enough to meet the normal underwriting requirements of insurance companies or managed care organizations and to qualify for insurance protection. However, federal laws and state insurance pools may be mechanisms for many of these people to obtain coverage. Underwriting and the alternatives when a person is unhealthy are described in chapter 5.

Principal policies of medical expense insurance may not fully meet the needs of all persons. If an individual travels, he or she might need an international travel policy. Some persons may want a supplemental policy for critical illnesses. Still other persons may see a need for dental insurance. Chapter 6 looks at a wide variety of interim, supplemental, and ancillary medical expense policies.

At age 65, most Americans are eligible for Medicare. Chapter 7 is devoted to eligibility for benefits, a description of the available benefits—which now includes prescription drugs—and the issues surrounding its financing. Medicare has gaps and does not fully cover the medical expenses of many retirees. Chapter 8 addresses ways in which many retirees obtain coverage to fill some of these gaps.

Unfortunately, not everyone can afford medical expense coverage, even the premiums for the heavily subsidized Medicare program. However, insurance protection may be available from various other government programs, including Medicaid and veterans' benefits. These government programs for specific groups of individuals—which may provide both medical expense and long-term care benefits—are described in chapter 9.

Chapters 10 through 18 of the book focus on financing long-term care. Whereas medical expense needs are financed primarily by insurance, long-term care needs may also be met in a variety of other ways.

Chapter 10 looks at the reason why there is a growing need for long-term care. Chapter 11 describes the variety of settings in which such care might be received.

Most individuals have noninsurance resources to meet some of their long-term care needs. These may include assets, income, and family support. Chapter 12 addresses these personal resources.

In most cases, an individual or couple will have a need for long-term care insurance. Its development is traced in chapter 13. Chapter 14 describes its characteristics and chapter 15 is devoted to its underwriting. Chapter 16 looks at consumer attitudes about long-term care insurance and the decisions consumers have to make.

Some individuals have long-term care insurance as a result of prior employment or are eligible for coverage from an employer-provided plan of a relative. Group insurance, as well as hybrid long-term care insurance products, is discussed in chapter 17.

The federal government recognizes the need for long-term care insurance. Not only does the federal government make coverage available to its own employees, but it also supports other efforts to increase the sale of long-term care insurance. This government support is described in chapter 18, the final chapter of this book.

COMPONENTS OF HEALTH CARE NEEDS

There are many components of health care needs, not all of which are met or fully met with insurance products. These components include maintaining wellness, medical care, and long-term care.

Maintaining Wellness

wellness

Although most health care needs arise from poor health, they also include the need to prevent poor health. Many of these needs fall into the category of *wellness*, which can best be defined as the state of being in good health. Wellness can eliminate or minimize future health care costs. There is plenty of scientific evidence to show that lifestyle affects the need for health care. People who maintain a proper weight, exercise, avoid tobacco, and drink moderately are less likely to incur medical expenses. When they do require health care, the severity of their illnesses and recovery time are often less than people who lead less healthy lifestyles. Although lifestyle decisions are beyond the scope of this book, they are an important element in maintaining good health and controlling health care costs.

Other types of wellness care fall into the category of preventive medicine because the services of medical professionals are involved. These include regular physical examinations and medical screening, particularly for conditions that are often easily treatable at reasonable cost if discovered early. Such checkups include tests for high blood pressure, high cholesterol, osteoporosis, diabetes, and breast, cervical, colon, and prostate cancer. There is also ample evidence that many groups of people, including seniors, benefit from annual immunizations for flu and pneumonia. These immunizations not only prevent sickness, they also prevent many deaths.

Historically, medical insurance policies focused on providing benefits for the results of accidents and sickness; they did not provide benefits for wellness care. Over the years, this has changed as many insurance policies—particularly those of managed care organizations—now provide an assortment of benefits for preventive medicine. Some policies also include benefits for such wellness activities as smoking cessation and substance abuse programs.

Medical Care

A second category of health care needs arises from the cost of medical care, which has the potential to bankrupt any American who does not have some type of medical expense insurance that covers catastrophic claims. There is a tendency to think of medical costs as the charges arising from stays in hospitals or other medical facilities, outpatient surgery, diagnostic tests, visits to doctors' offices, and prescription drugs. Most seniors have protection for these types of expenses, with the possible exception of prescription drugs. However, the major source of protection for those over 65 is Medicare, and its benefits are subject to certain limitations, as explained in chapter 7.

Medical care also includes treatment for dental problems. For some seniors, dental costs are a major expense that is often uninsured. Even when dental insurance is available, annual benefits are relatively modest in relation to the potential cost of treating major dental disorders.

The costs of prescription glasses, hearing aids, and orthopedic shoes and inserts are another category of expenses that arise from medical care. Many seniors need these devices but must pay for them from their own resources because Medicare and many private insurance policies exclude these expenses from coverage.

Another consequence that can result from medical care is the necessity for personal assistance during a period of recovery. After outpatient surgery or discharge from a hospital, for example, a person of any age may require help preparing meals, getting dressed, or bathing while he or she recovers at home. As people age, they are less able to take care of themselves in such situations and have longer recovery periods. Medical insurance usually does not cover this type of care. Even if a person has long-term care insurance, this type of home-health care is typically subject to waiting periods of 60 to 90 days. As a result, a spouse, a child, or a friend often renders such care. Health care professionals can also be hired to perform these services.

Example: Jean, a retired widow aged 74, broke both arms when she fell off a ladder while painting her house. During the next 2 months while both arms are in casts, Jean will need help to care for herself and to clean her home. She was surprised when she found out that home health care under Medicare did not pay for this type of assistance. Jean's children do not live nearby, but she is fortunate to have good friends who will occasionally help her by preparing meals she can heat up for dinner and by taking her to doctor and hair-dressing appointments. However, she does not feel she can ask them to assist her on a regular basis to get dressed and bathed in the morning, to prepare break-fast, to walk her dog, to clean her house, or to do her laundry. Consequently, she has hired a home-health aide to come in for a few hours each morning and a cleaning person to come in one afternoon a week. She estimates this expense to be about $650 per week.

The inability to earn a living is another serious consequence associated with medical care. Although the importance of disability income insurance is beyond the scope of this book on the health care needs of retirees, its importance for preretirees should not be overlooked. In addition, it should be pointed out that some people will continue to work part-time during "retirement" and a medical condition may make it impossible for them to perform this work.

Long-Term Custodial Care

As individuals age, there is an increasing probability that they will have chronic medical conditions, including normal frailties of aging, that will make them unable to care for themselves. Although they may need varying degrees of skilled medical care, their primary need is for custodial care on a long-term basis to help them with activities of daily living (ADLs). Some seniors may still be able to live independently and need minimal assistance; other seniors need around-the-clock care. Medicare and private medical expense insurance policies largely exclude custodial care, which may cost tens of thousands of dollars per year. Some seniors have planned their retirement finances so that long-term care insurance and/or personal resources will meet these costs. Other seniors will need to rely on family or public assistance.

Example 1:   Shirley is no longer able to drive or write checks because of macular degeneration. However, she is still able to remain in her long-time home, but needs some assistance. She has friends who take her grocery shopping on a regular basis and often take her other places when their schedules allow. If friends are unavailable, she calls a taxi. Shirley has also hired an elder-care specialist who comes in once a week for an hour or two, goes through her mail, tells her what it is about, and prepares checks to pay bills.

Example 2:   Bill and Claire have been married for over 60 years. Bill had been caring for Claire, whose activities are limited by arthritis. Bill recently had a stroke and needs almost continuous care, which Claire cannot provide. Their doctor has told their children that Bill should be in a nursing home and that Claire should either move in with one of them or enter an assisted-living facility.

SETTINGS FOR HEALTH CARE

Health care can be provided in many settings. To some extent, these settings depend on whether the need is for medical care or long-term care. In addition, insurance (both private and government) may provide benefits if care is received in some settings but not if it is received in other settings.

care continuum   Health care settings form a *care continuum*, along which the level of care ranges from less intensive to more intensive. However, seniors may move along this continuum in different ways and use different care settings at different times. In some cases, the need for care will cease. In many cases, the need for care will continue but be provided in different settings.

The care continuum is commonly discussed as it applies to long-term care, and chapter 11 of this book addresses this topic in detail. But there is also a care continuum for medical care. For many persons, medical care is received while they are still living at home. This care may be self-care, such as taking medicines or changing dressings. It also includes care provided in doctors' offices and other locations, such as diagnostic facilities and outpatient surgical centers. At the other extreme, care is often received in hospitals. In between these two extremes, care may be received in skilled-nursing facilities and in hospices. Coverage for care in these settings, as well as home health care, was pioneered by Medicare and is discussed more thoroughly in chapter 7. However, medical expense insurance for persons under age 65 often provides similar benefits.

Example 1:	Joan was hospitalized after suffering a stroke. Following her discharge, she spent 2 months in a skilled-nursing facility for rehabilitative treatment and then returned home. Her Medicare coverage paid for continued rehabilitative and medical care after she returned home. However, she also needed further assistance to perform her daily activities and to care for herself. After 3 more months, she and her family decided that the proper care setting was an assisted-living facility.
Example 2:	Charles needed health care because of a severe hip problem. Although he was able to care for himself, he needed pain medication, which was prescribed by his doctor. Finally, Charles decided that it was wise to enter a hospital and have a hip replacement. After therapy in a rehabilitation hospital and at home, Charles is now fully recovered and living at home without needing health care.

CAREGIVERS

Just as settings for care vary, so do providers of care. Some care, particularly long-term care, often is provided voluntarily by persons without training in health care. These include family members and friends, as well as volunteers from churches, charities, and community groups. Many licensed professionals also earn their livings by providing health care services. These include physicians, nurses, therapists, social workers, and dieticians. Long-term care for seniors is also often provided by nonlicensed personnel, such as homemakers, companions, and chore workers.

Medical expense insurance policies generally require that care be received from licensed health care professionals. Long-term care insurance policies, however, usually pay benefits for care received from a broader spectrum of care providers.

The various types of health care providers are discussed where appropriate in later chapters of this book.

Example: Clarissa still lives in her own home, but her health is declining. She sees doctors regularly for a variety of ailments but is not always able to remember their instructions or when to take her medications. As a result, her family visits her regularly to administer her medications, which include insulin injections. When they are on vacation, they arrange for a nurse from a home health agency to perform these duties. Clarissa also has a chore worker who comes in three mornings a week to clean her house and do laundry.

REGULATION OF PRIVATE INSURANCE

An understanding of private health insurance requires a basic knowledge of insurance regulation. For the most part, insurance regulation is conducted by the states, but at the same time a number of federal laws and regulations are applicable to health insurance. All types of insurance are subject to regulation. However, health insurance is arguably the most heavily regulated type of insurance. One of the reasons for this regulation is past abuses by some insurers and agents when dealing with vulnerable older clients, who have been subject to less-than-ethical sales practices.

Health insurance is stringently regulated because it protects a truly irreplaceable value—personal health and well being. Health insurance plays a traditional insurance role when it covers financial loss incurred by the expense of health insurance services. But it has assumed a much greater role as a major source of payment of health care services and as a crucial means for access to these services.

The following discussion looks at both state and federal regulation, which may overlap. In some cases, both types of regulation may apply and insurers must design policies that meet both sets of regulations. In other cases, particularly when employer-provided coverage is involved, federal regulation may preempt state law. In still other cases, federal regulation applies only if there is either no state regulation or no regulation that meets specified standards.

Whether state or federal regulation is involved, regulation may come from three sources:

- legislatures
- regulators
- courts

Legislation is the foundation of insurance law because state legislatures and Congress pass laws that pertain to insurance. The actual enforcement of these laws is given to regulatory bodies that often have considerable leeway to interpret them and do so by issuing regulations that must be followed. At the state level, this regulatory body is usually the state insurance department, although regulation of health maintenance organizations may be carried out by a different agency, such as the state health department. At the federal level, it may be one of several agencies, such as the Department of Labor, the Internal Revenue Service, or the Centers for Medicare & Medicaid Services.

The courts are often involved in insurance in two primary ways. First, they may declare laws unconstitutional or overrule regulations as being beyond the scope of the regulatory agency. Second, they may be called on to resolve disputes between insurers and their insureds.

State Regulation

National Association of Insurance Commissioners (NAIC)

State regulation of health insurance falls into several categories. While the categories are the same in all states, the type and extent of regulation varies among the states and significant variations often exist. There is a great degree of uniformity, however, primarily as a result of the *National Association of Insurance Commissioners (NAIC)*. The NAIC is a voluntary association of all insurance commissioners that has as its goal the promotion of uniformity in legislation and administrative rules affecting insurance. It has developed many model laws and regulations, which states and insurance commissioners may or may not adopt. Numerous states have adopted many of them but sometimes with modifications.

State regulation falls into the following major categories:

- licensing
- financial standards
- policy forms
- mandated benefits
- market conduct
- access and affordability
- premium rates
- renewability
- policyowner complaints

Licensing

Every state requires the licensing of insurance companies that sell insurance in the state. The primary objective of insurer licensing is to evaluate whether the company can provide the coverage it promises to its insureds. When licensing an insurer, the states look at the insurer's financial strength as well as its management and business practices. For example, a new company owned or managed by persons who had been convicted of defrauding clients in past business ventures would most likely be denied a license.

Although most agents and applicants for insurance have little reason to suspect it, a very small number of organizations have been known to sell insurance without a license. It is always wise to make sure that one is dealing with an insurer authorized to do business within the state. If there is any doubt, call the state insurance department. Note that many states impose penalties on agents who sell insurance from unauthorized insurers.

Financial Standards

In addition to its financial strength at the time a company is licensed, a state is concerned with the insurer's ongoing financial viability. To guarantee this financial strength, there are regulations regarding investment practices and the maintenance of reserves for claims and other contingencies.

Even when regulation is very good, some insurers encounter financial difficulties and are unable to meet their obligations to insureds. In such situations, state insurance departments will step in and attempt to rehabilitate the insurer and possibly liquidate it. In some cases, a block of business may be taken over by another insurer and coverage will continue, although premiums might be increased. In other cases, the insurance coverage will **guaranty funds** cease. However, existing claims are almost always paid by state *guaranty funds*. These funds are established by state law for paying the claims of insolvent insurers and are typically financed by assessments of other insurers that are licensed in the state.

Although there is no perfect way to evaluate the future strength of an insurer, a potential insured can look at the ratings of one or more of the independent organizations that evaluate insurers. These organizations are discussed in more detail in chapter 16.

Policy Forms

policy form A *policy form* is a standardized contract that an insurer offers to its policyowners. In some states, an insurer may have to actually file these forms with the insurance commissioner's office. In almost all states, however, policies must follow prescribed formats and define specified terms. For example, a state may dictate the order in which provisions are presented in a policy and the size of type that must be used. Gone are the days when exclusions were printed in such small type that even people with excellent eyesight would have trouble reading them. And exclusions must be conspicuously labeled as such. There must also be separate and clearly identified paragraphs with respect to preexisting conditions and policy limitations.

States also have standards for defining many of the terms used in health insurance policies. Examples include hospital, accident, sickness, preexisting condition, physician, nurse, mental and nervous disorder, convalescent nursing care, and home health care.

Laws also require that certain provisions be contained in policy forms and prohibit the use of other provisions. Other provisions may be optional on the part of the insurer, but if they are used they must adhere to specified standards. Some of these optional provisions are mentioned under this heading, but other provisions mentioned later also fall into the broad category of regulation of policy forms.

Examples of required provisions include the following:

entire contract provision

- *entire contract provision.* This provision states that only those items actually included in the policy, including any riders or attachments, are part of the contract of insurance. A change in the policy is not valid until approved by an executive officer of the insurance company and an appropriate endorsement is attached to the policy. An agent does not have authority to change the policy or waive any of its provisions.

  This provision is advantageous to both the insured and the insurer because it limits the contract's terms to the contents of the written policy. Representations made in the application also bind the insured when a copy of the application is made part of the policy—which it usually is.

- *time limit on certain defenses and the incontestable clause.* The time limit provision restricts an insurer's right to rescind or void a policy because of nonfraudulent misstatements to 2 years (3 years in some states). However, if the misstatements were fraudulent, meaning that they were intended to deceive the insurer and would have caused the insurer to take a materially different action if the truth had been known, the time limit provision does not apply. The intent to defraud is difficult to prove.

incontestable clause

  The *incontestable clause*, which may be used in some policies, is an alternative to the time limit provision. This clause not only limits an insurer's right to contest the policy to 2 years (3 years in some states), but it also makes the policy fully incontestable with respect to any misstatement made by the insured on the application.

grace period

- *grace period.* This provision gives an insured a specific number of days or grace period beyond the due date to pay each premium. During this grace period, the premium can be paid and the policy maintained in force. States usually require a 31-day grace period for most policies.

reinstatement provision

- *reinstatement provision.* If a premium is not paid before the end of the grace period, coverage ceases. This provision sets forth the procedures for allowing the insured to apply for reinstatement of the policy and affording the insurer the opportunity to reevaluate the insured's acceptability for coverage.

  If an insurer (or the insurer's agent) accepts a premium without requiring an application for reinstatement, the policy is automatically reinstated upon receipt of the premium. If the insurer does require an application and issues a conditional receipt for money paid with such an application, it has 45 days to decide whether or not to accept the risk again. If it fails to notify the insured within 45 days that the application has been declined, the policy is reinstated automatically at the conclusion of such period.

  Upon the date of reinstatement of a medical expense policy, the policy initially covers only accidental injuries. Coverage for losses due to sickness is restored 10 days after reinstatement. The 10-day delay for coverage of sickness is designed to avoid claims for illnesses in existence at the time of reinstatement.

- *claims provisions.* The following provisions deal with the filing and payment of claims:
  - *notice of claim.* Written notice must be given to the insurer within 20 days of loss or as soon as is reasonably possible.
  - *claims form.* The insurer must supply forms within 15 days after the insured gives notice of claim.
  - *proofs of loss.* Depending on the type of health insurance policy, the insured usually has anywhere from 90 days to one year to file a formal proof of loss with the insurer.
  - *time of payment of claims.* Claims must be paid promptly.
  - *payment of claims.* Benefits must be paid to the insured, to a policy beneficiary, or with the insured's permission to the person or institution rendering services.

- *physical examinations and autopsy.* This provision gives an insurer the right to have the insured examined at its own expense while a claim is pending. The examination provides the insurer with an independent opinion as to the extent of loss or impairment. In the case of death, the provision also permits an insurer to have an autopsy performed where it is not forbidden by law, but insurers rarely request an autopsy in the case of health insurance claims.

- *legal actions.* Under this provision, the policy states that the insured must wait at least 60 days after submitting proof of loss before starting legal action against the insurer. Furthermore, it prohibits the insured from bringing legal action more than 3 years after proof is required.

This provision protects the insurer against untimely lawsuits begun before it has a reasonable opportunity to investigate the claim. The provision also allows the insurer to consider claims closed 3 years after the final action. The 3-year limit is usually shorter than the statutory limit on contract actions in general, which in some states is 5 or 6 years.

Some of the optional provisions that an insurer may include in various types of health insurance policies include the following:

- *misstatement of age.* If the insured's age has been misstated, all benefits payable under the policy shall be at a level that the premium paid would have purchased at the correct age. In health expense insurance policies, this provision may allow the payment of the additional premium at the correct age if the insured understated the age but remains eligible for coverage. If the covered person is ineligible for coverage at the correct age, then the misapplied coverage shall be rescinded and any applicable premium refunded.
- *insurance with other insurers.* Insurers sometimes attempt to lessen the possibility of claimants profiting from insurance by including "other insurance" provisions. Such provisions allow an insurer in the presence of valid coverages with other insurers to limit its payment responsibility to a proportionate amount of the insured's allowable benefits for medical services under its policy during the benefit period. Other valid coverage may include basic hospital, basic medical-surgical, or major medical benefits under group and individual and family coverage.
- *conformity with state statute.* This provision specifies that any policy provision which, on its effective date, is in conflict with the statutes of the state in which the insured resides is made to conform to the minimum requirements of such statutes.

Mandated Benefits

mandated benefits

Every state has passed laws that are known collectively as *mandated benefits* because they require that medical expense policies contain coverage requirements for certain populations, providers, alternative care settings, specific conditions, diagnostic tests and exams, treatments, and services and products. These mandates have proliferated over the last four decades from fewer than 100 in the 1960s to over 1,000 today. While some of these statutes initially affected only group insurance, they now typically apply to individual policies also.

For consumers, mandated benefits present issues of affordability and equity. State-mandated benefit laws are estimated to increase health insurance premiums from 4 to 13 percent. To the extent these increases make medical insurance less affordable, the number of individuals without medical insurance is increased.

Mandated benefits challenge an insurer's ability to remain price competitive and profitable. The extent of the challenge from any specific mandated benefit or set of benefits varies significantly by company due to the unique mix of products, insured populations, market share, and claims expense experience specific to each company's book of business. Many of these benefits can easily lead to very expensive claims that can create significant losses for affected companies. The more recent rise of *mandated option laws,* which allow insurers to offer mandated benefits for purchase at the consumer's option, permits policies to be issued without mandates. Optional benefits are often difficult to price appropriately because they may also be expensive and are likely to be purchased by individuals who are more likely to use them than the general insured population (adverse selection). While that approach has the advantage of keeping basic coverage more affordable, it may further aggravate a company's loss situation. Just as each insurer carefully includes in each contract the provisions required by the state in which it is to be sold, each insurer also thoroughly evaluates the continued viability of its medical expense products in each market.

mandated option laws

The range of enacted mandates is quite extensive and may be categorized according to the object of the benefits they require:

Populations. Historically, the most common populations singled out for mandated benefits are newborn and handicapped children. Most seniors are unlikely to have newborn children, but some seniors are caring for handicapped children. Family policies ordinarily set an age limit (such as 19 or 23) at which dependent children's coverage stops. In states that have adopted the handicapped children provision, this age limit does not apply to any dependent child who is mentally or physically unable to earn her or his own living.

Provider Recognition. Many states have passed statutes requiring that insurers recognize the services of specified providers as long as they are acting within the scope of their licenses and the service is covered by the policy. Insurers do not necessarily have to spell out in their policies all of the types of providers whose services are covered. Policy definitions of such terms as "duly licensed physician" or "duly qualified physician" indicate that the insurer recognizes every type of provider licensed by the state. These requirements, however, do not preclude benefit limitations for specific services. Frequently identified providers include chiropractors, dentists, naturopaths, optometrists, and psychologists.

Alternative Care Settings. To encourage methods of treatment that are less costly than hospital confinement, some states require that basic hospital expense and major-medical policies provide coverage for a freestanding surgical facility or "surgicenter"—that is, a place where outpatient surgery is performed but which is not part of a hospital. A growing number of states also require coverage for home health care services (such as the services of a visiting nurse).

Conditions. Many state legislatures have passed statutes requiring coverage for specified conditions. In some states, the identified condition must be covered just like any other illness, although in other states these statutes permit more limited coverage. Some of the more common specific condition mandates include alcoholism, chemical dependency, congenital defects, Lyme disease, mental illness, and temporomandibular joint (TMJ) syndrome.

Diagnostic Tests and Exams. Increased interest in preventive health care services has stimulated mandates for certain diagnostic tests. Among the more common examples are colon cancer exams, mammograms, osteoporosis screenings, prostate exams, ovarian cancer screenings, and pelvic exams.

Treatments. Perhaps the largest category of benefit mandates is specific treatments. They often include acupuncture, autologous bone marrow treatments, cosmetic surgery, dental services for disabled insureds, experimental drugs, human organ transplants, immunizations, investigational therapies for cancer, mastectomy hospital stays, mental health or substance abuse hospital stays, occupational therapy, and physical therapy.

Services and Products. In addition to treatments, a number of health-related services and products are also the subject of mandates. Examples include diabetes self-management training and equipment as well as marriage and pastoral counseling.

Market Conduct

All states have standards aimed at the market conduct of insurers. These standards relate to many aspects of health insurance marketing and operations, including advertisements, claims settlement practices, unfair discrimination, conduct of agents, a free-look period, replacement of insurance, and privacy protection.

Advertising. The purpose of advertising standards is to provide the insurance-buying public with an accurate, clear, and truthful presentation and description of insurance products in both the advertising media and the material issued and/or used by agents and insurers. That purpose is achieved through standards that prevent unfair, deceptive, and misleading advertising. Because advertising can occur after a policy sale, the definition extends to material that accompanies a policy when it is delivered and material used in the solicitation of renewals and reinstatements.

The standards specify required information as well as the methods of its disclosure in form and content. Required information must be conspicuous with a prominent arrangement of text and captions. Advertisements must fairly and accurately describe benefits and premium payable. The standards also specifically prohibit deceptive and exaggerated words and phrases, enumerate the conditions under which examples and illustrations may be given, and establish acceptability criteria for testimonials and statistics relating to the insurer or policy used in advertising. The manner in which an insurer identifies itself to the public is delineated. The insurer's areas of licensed operation must be disclosed. No advertisements may make disparaging comparisons of other insurers, their products, or their methods.

The most extensive requirements are applied to advertising that constitutes an *invitation to contract;* they go well beyond fair and accurate descriptions and avoidance of misleading statements. An advertisement that is an invitation to contract must disclose:

- exceptions, reductions, and limitations affecting the basic provisions of the policy
- the amount of any deductible or the percentage of any coinsurance factor
- the extent to which any loss is not covered if the cause of the loss is traceable to a condition existing prior to the effective date of the policy
- provisions relating to renewability, cancelability, and termination

Each insurer is required to maintain a complete file of all its advertising materials. This file is subject to inspection by the insurance department. A few states also require the filing of certain advertisements with the department.

Claims Settlement Practices. An insurer's practices in paying claims represent a major source of insured and claimant dissatisfaction and can be an area of abuse because of unfamiliarity with all of the technical details of the insurance contract. Therefore, states have imposed regulations aimed at eliminating unfair claim settlement practices.

Some of the practices regarded as unfair include the following:

- misrepresenting pertinent facts or policy provisions that have a bearing on the claim
- failing to act promptly in answering claimants' correspondence regarding paying or denying claims, or delaying payment by requiring submission of several forms with substantially the same information
- refusing to pay a claim without conducting a reasonable investigation based on all available information
- attempting to settle a claim on the basis of an application altered without the insured's knowledge and consent
- making a claim payment not accompanied by a statement setting forth the coverage under which payment is being made
- failing to explain the basis for denying a claim
- forcing the insured to start legal action to collect an amount due
- attempting to pay less than a reasonable person would expect to collect, considering the printed advertising material furnished at the time of application
- holding up payment that is clearly due under one policy provision in order to influence settlement under other provisions

Some states go further and spell out limits in terms of a specific number of days in which the insurer must acknowledge a claim, furnish claim forms, answer a claimant's correspondence, and pay or deny a claim. If an investigation is necessary, the insurer must notify the claimant within a given time and must periodically inform the insured of the reason for any continuing delay. In an increasing number of states, the insurer must pay the claimant interest on amounts that are due but not paid within a certain number of days.

Unfair Discrimination. Most states prohibit "unfair discrimination" between individuals of the same class and essentially the same hazard. Such regulations limit the insurer's ability to decline coverage and to underwrite and rate individuals applying for or seeking to renew their health insurance. Specific regulations deal with several topics, including gender and marital status, blindness, physical or mental impairment, and AIDS. The following are common regulations:

- *regulation to eliminate unfair gender discrimination.* This regulation prohibits insurers from denying availability of coverage or restricting any term, condition, or type of coverage on the basis of gender or marital status. In most states the purpose of this regulation is to enforce a standard of equal access, not to impose uniformity in premium rates. Therefore, insurers are allowed to use gender-distinct rates for individual insurance products.

- *regulation on the basis of blindness or partial blindness.* This regulation prohibits actions by an insurer based solely on an applicant's blindness or partial blindness. The actions prohibited include: refusing to insure or refusing to continue to insure; limiting the amount or kind of coverage available; and charging a different rate for the same coverage.

- *unfair discrimination in life and health insurance on the basis of physical or mental impairment.* This regulation applies to unfair discrimination among individuals in the same class on the basis of physical or mental impairment with respect to (1) issuance and renewal of coverage, (2) the amount, extent, or kind of coverage, and (3) rates. However, different treatment of applicants and insureds is allowed if that different treatment is based on sound actuarial principles or it is related to actual or anticipated experience. While such treatment could be called discrimination, it is not "unfair" discrimination under the regulation.

- *guidelines outlining minimum standards for insurance application questions and underwriting relating to AIDS.* Many states have guidelines that outline minimum standards for insurance application questions relating to acquired immunodeficiency syndrome (AIDS) and the underwriting of persons with AIDS. An insurer must refrain from asking questions designed to elicit information about an individual's sexual orientation or preference. Information about sexual orientation cannot be used in the underwriting process and is not to influence the decision on whether an individual is considered insurable. For the most part, insurers are permitted to ask questions of a strictly medical nature, such as whether an individual had been diagnosed or treated for the human immunodeficiency virus (HIV) or AIDS.

Conduct of Agents. States also have laws that prohibit fraudulent and unethical acts of agents and brokers. The regulations exact fines and, more importantly, suspend or revoke licenses as penalties for violations. Examples of such unfair practices include:

rebating

- *rebating.* This is the return of any part of the premium to the policyowner by the insurer or agent as a price-cutting sales inducement.

twisting

- *twisting.* This is a special form of misrepresentation in which an agent may induce the policyowner to cancel disadvantageously the contract of another insurer in order to take out a new contract.

misappropriation

- *misappropriation*. This occurs when an agent unlawfully keeps funds belonging to others.
- *commingling of funds*. This is prevented in some states by requiring a separate bank account for the agent's premium funds.
- *misleading advertising*. Many regulators restrain this practice by requiring full and fair information in advertisements by insurers and agents.

free-look period

Free-Look Period. Policyowners must be given a period of time—called a *free-look period*—to return a health insurance policy and have the premium refunded if, after examination of the policy, the policyowner is not satisfied for any reason. In most states, this period of time is 30 days, but a few states have 10-day periods for some medical expense policies.

Policy Replacement. Application forms must include questions as to whether the policy is intended to replace any other health insurance in force. If so, the applicant must be given a notice warning that preexisting conditions possibly covered by the old policy may not be covered by the new one. The notice advises the insured to consult the previous insurer or its agent before terminating the old coverage. The insured is also warned to be certain that the questions on the application are answered truthfully and completely, because any misrepresentation in the application may result in recision of the policy.

Privacy Protection. Most states have privacy protection regulations. Although not targeted directly at health insurance, these regulations are relevant because of the personal information gathered in the health insurance contract and claims processes. They often include the following features:

- *restrictions* designed to minimize intrusiveness—in particular, pre-text interviews (interviews in which the investigator's purpose is not disclosed).
- *a mechanism* to enable people to find out what information is being or has been collected about them. Before gathering information, the insurer must notify the individual that personal information may be gathered from, and disclosed to, other parties and that he or she has a right to obtain access to the information and to make corrections to it. On request, the individual may obtain a more detailed description of the types of information to be sought, the parties from whom it is to be sought, and the method of investigation to be used.
- *prescribed procedures* for granting the individual access to the information, permitting corrections, or including explanatory information.
- *safeguards* to limit disclosure of information. These safeguards include prescribed authorization forms, specific time limits for the use of authorizations (usually 30 months in the case of an authorization obtained for

underwriting purposes and the duration of the claim when the authorization is used for claim investigation), and rules severely restricting further dissemination of information without the insured's specific consent.

- *notification* of adverse underwriting decisions. Insurers are required to notify individuals of the reasons for an adverse underwriting decision and of the procedures for obtaining more detailed information about the decision.

Access and Affordability

Most states have used their regulatory authority to improve access and affordability in the individual medical expense insurance market primarily (though not exclusively) for people with previous health problems. More than a dozen states require guaranteed issue of one or more products to all applicants. Approximately 20 states have passed legislation limiting variations in premium rates or the use of such factors as health status, claims experience, age, or gender in determining rates for individuals. More than 20 states also limit the use of preexisting-conditions exclusions. However, some states allow insurers to issue a rider that excludes coverage for identified conditions (such as heart problems) for the duration of the policy.

In addition to direct individual product regulation, 34 states have high-risk health insurance plans that offer comprehensive medical expense benefits to uninsurable individuals. State high-risk health insurance plans are discussed in chapter 5.

Premium Rates

Health insurance is difficult to price. Despite regulations, benefit provisions are not totally standardized, although benefits do fall into certain patterns. Actuaries (the persons who determine insurance prices) base premiums largely on the average loss experience for similar benefits in the past. At the same time, they must anticipate future changes in the cost and utilization of covered services. In projecting future costs, actuaries evaluate inflationary trends observable in the most recent periods.

Each insurer develops its own rates, and most states require insurers to file these rates with the insurance department. States typically require that certain types of medical insurance policies have a specified loss ratio, which is the aggregate percentage of the overall premiums received (such as 60 percent) returned to insureds in the form of benefits paid. States require a statement describing the anticipated loss ratio for the policy form in question and may also require an actuarial memorandum showing how the rates were developed. Commissioners reject policy form submissions if they conclude that the benefits provided are unreasonable in relation to the premium.

Each year insurers are required to file loss ratio information with the insurance department for each policy form being used. The loss ratio shows the premium-dollar percentage used to pay claim benefits and gives commissioners the opportunity to check the experience. If they find that the loss ratio on a given policy form is unreasonably low, they may question the insurer for clarification. In addition, a growing number of states now have complex and detailed requirements for rate analysis and for maintaining and reporting claim experience.

It is sometimes necessary for insurers to revise their rate tables when they find themselves paying out more in claims than they anticipated. This situation has arisen, especially in medical expense coverages, as a result of escalating hospitals' and physicians' charges and increased utilization of services. In filing for a rate increase, insurers are usually required to report their claims and premiums for the past few years on the policy form and give evidence that adverse experience is likely to continue.

Renewability

guaranteed renewable

Health insurance policies usually are written for a period of one year, and the states determine whether the policyowner has the right to continue coverage for an additional period. In most cases, coverage must be *guaranteed renewable*. This means that the policyowner must be given the right to renew the policy. However, the insurer is allowed to change the premium rate at time of renewal and often does as a result of claims experience. The increased rates must apply to all policyowners in a given class of business and cannot be applied on an individual basis.

Policyowner Complaints

Dealing with policyowner complaints is an important function of the state insurance departments. Even with the best intentions and efforts, no insurance company can avoid some policyowner dissatisfaction. This is inherent in the technical nature of the insurance contract. Furthermore, considerable time often elapses after the original sale of the policy before a claim occurs. The claimant's understanding of the policy provisions may have become blurred. In the case of health insurance, the somewhat more subjective nature of the risk increases the possibility of misunderstanding. Consequently, most insurance departments report more complaints arising from health insurance than from most other lines of insurance.

The first step an insurance department takes in processing a complaint is to ask the insurer to state the reasons for its position. The insurer's reply usually satisfies the department that the insurer's position is correct. On the other hand, the department sometimes learns of some fact unknown to the insurer, or it has some other basis for asking the insurer to reconsider its position. Most often, differences of opinion between the department and the insurer are resolved. However, in relatively rare instances where the issue has broad implications, the department may require the insurer to attend a hearing on the matter. If a violation of the law is found to have occurred, the department can impose penalties.

In recent years, most states have enacted laws or regulations that provide for an independent, external review of certain types of benefit decisions, particularly those involving the denial of benefits because a treatment was not medically necessary or because it was experimental.

Federal Regulation

Federal regulations also affect the private health insurance products that provide protection to seniors. The discussion here and in later chapters includes ERISA, HIPAA, the Women's Health and Cancer Rights Act, Medicare supplement legislation, and the Internal Revenue Code.

ERISA

ERISA

In 1974, Congress passed the Employee Retirement Income Security Act, commonly known as *ERISA*. The purpose of ERISA was largely to protect and regulate retirement plans. However, many of the act's provisions also apply to other employee benefit plans of employers. ERISA clearly affects seniors who are still actively employed and who have health insurance coverage under plans provided by their employers. However, seniors may also be covered under these plans as retirees. For example, many employees are eligible to continue employer-provided coverage for a limited period of time after termination of employment for any reason, including retirement. Such COBRA continuation is discussed in detail in chapter 2. Other employees have employer-provided coverage made available to them until age 65 or even for life.

A detailed discussion of ERISA is left for books on employee benefits, but a few comments are made here. First, while state regulation applies to insurance contracts, ERISA applies to benefit plans whether they are insured or not. Because many employees are covered under self-funded plans, this gives them many of the same protections that are provided by state regulation. Second, ERISA does not apply to individual health insurance policies purchased by seniors.

Third, ERISA for the most part does not affect a state's regulation of insurance contracts sold in that state. However, in most other cases, it preempts any state regulation of employee benefit plans. This is one reason that many employers have turned to self-funding of medical expense benefits. Without using insurance contracts, employers do not have to provide the mandated benefits that must be contained in insurance contracts and they have fewer administrative burdens if they operate in several states. ERISA also results in many disputes involving employee benefits being moved from state to federal jurisdiction, where awards for noneconomic damages (such as pain and suffering) are generally not available.

HIPAA

HIPAA

In 1996, Congress enacted the Health Insurance Portability and Accountability Act, usually referred to as *HIPAA*. The primary motivation for HIPAA was to address the problem of employees losing medical expense coverage after they changed or terminated employment. The effect of HIPAA on the availability of coverage for seniors after retirement is discussed in chapter 5.

HIPAA also affects individual medical expense insurance in other ways. Unless a state has some mechanism for insuring the unhealthy, HIPAA requires health insurers to renew medical expense policies that fit the category of the principal policies described in chapter 3. However, there is no federal regulation of the premiums that can be charged at renewal. It should be pointed out that the HIPAA renewability rules do not apply to long-term care insurance policies or to ancillary or supplemental medical insurance policies.

In addition, HIPAA contains regulations that apply to the privacy of health insurance information. The regulations are similar to those adopted by many states but do not override state laws if they contain stricter provisions.

Women's Health and Cancer Rights Act

With a few exceptions, federal law does not mandate benefits that a medical expense insurance policy must include. One of these exceptions is the provisions of the Women's Health and Cancer Rights Act. Any policy that provides medical and surgical benefits for mastectomy must also provide coverage for the following:

- reconstruction of the breast on which the mastectomy was performed
- surgery and reconstruction of the other breast to maintain a symmetrical appearance
- prostheses and physical complications of all stages of mastectomy, including lymphedemas

Prior to the act's taking effect, such services or items were often not covered because of exclusions, particularly exclusions that applied to cosmetic surgery. Benefits can be subject to deductibles and coinsurance provisions as long as they are consistent with those provided for other procedures under the plan or policy.

Medicare Supplement Legislation

Medicare supplement insurance in the individual marketplace became directly subject to federal regulation in 1990, when Congress directed the NAIC to develop a group of standard Medicare supplement policies. Congress mandated several other features, including a 6-month open enrollment period, limited preexisting-conditions exclusions, a prohibition on the sale of duplicate coverage, increased loss ratios, and guaranteed renewability. The specific features of these regulated policies are discussed in chapter 8.

Internal Revenue Code

The Internal Revenue Code affects health insurance in many ways. It affects affordability in that health insurance expenses, including insurance premiums, may be deductible for income tax purposes. In some cases, this deductibility is contingent on an insurance policy containing specific provisions.

Benefits received from a medical expense policy are not taxable to an individual except to the extent they exceed any medical expenses incurred. In addition, an individual is allowed to deduct most medical and dental expenses for which no reimbursement was received as long as the individual itemizes deductions. The deduction, however, is limited to expenses that exceed 7.5 percent of the person's adjusted gross income. Information on the deductibility of medical expenses can be found on the IRS Web site, www.irs.gov.

The situation is somewhat different for long-term care insurance. Although many long-term care expenses can be deducted as medical expenses, there are limitations on the deductibility of premiums—both with respect to amount and the provisions that must be contained in a policy for which a deduction is allowed. These rules for long-term care insurance policies are discussed in chapter 13.

ISSUES

There are many issues involving the financing of health care for seniors, and they are discussed at appropriate points throughout the course. However, mention of two of these issues is made at this point—dealing with seniors and suitability. In addition, the issue of advance medical directives is mentioned.

Dealing with Seniors

Dealing with seniors can often be more difficult than dealing with younger persons. It is a fact that as people age they may have diminished physical and mental capacity. Although many seniors are in excellent health, some seniors have such conditions as poor hearing, poor eyesight, and cognitive impairments. This presents challenges to agents selling policies, medical professionals providing services, and seniors and their families.

In dealing with seniors, it is important to ascertain what their medical conditions might be. Poor hearing may call for more distinct, slower, and louder speech. However, speaking this way to a senior who is not hard of hearing may be viewed as insulting. Because of eyesight problems, many advertisements and insurance policies for seniors are printed in larger type than may have been used for younger persons.

Seniors with cognitive impairments may have difficulty understanding insurance presentations or their health insurance policies. They may also have difficulty understanding the claims process when they receive medical care. They may not remember that premiums have to be paid. And worst of all, they may be unable to follow health care instructions, such as when to take medications.

For agents and health care professionals, understanding the aging process and how they must deal with seniors of varying ages is of utmost importance. In addition, seniors and their families need to be aware that seniors may need assistance in their financial affairs. In many cases, family members or friends help seniors make financial decisions, pay bills, file claims, and follow doctors' orders. In other cases, professionals who specialize in offering such services perform these tasks. Unfortunately, seniors may be unaware that they need this help or be unwilling to ask for or accept it.

While it is beyond the scope of this book, seniors, their family members, and anyone who deals with seniors should obtain information about the aging process. Information can be found by surfing the Internet or reading books on the subject. For readers who are using this book as part of the Chartered Advisor for Senior Living (CASL) designation program of The American College, this topic is the focus of one of the program's courses—HS 350 Understanding the Older Client.

Suitability

suitability

When making decisions about health care financing, individuals must find solutions that are appropriate for their needs and wants. This process is often referred to as *suitability*, and it is of great importance to insurers, financial planners, and regulators. In fact, many of the regulatory requirements mentioned earlier have suitability as an objective.

Suitability involves an understanding of alternative financing mechanisms by everyone involved—consumers, agents, financial planners, attorneys, health care professionals, and families who assist seniors in making decisions. A major objective of this book is to educate readers about these decisions, and suitability is discussed throughout. However, a few examples are presented here to highlight some of the types of suitability decisions that must be addressed.

The first decision in the suitability process usually is to determine the needs and wants of seniors, and these needs and wants vary among seniors even if they are in similar financial positions.

Example:	Larry and Harry are twin brothers who recently sold their successful business and retired. Each has sufficient assets to live very well during retirement. Larry and his wife want to leave their hard-earned assets to their children and do not want the assets depleted by health care expenses. They are willing to pay the premiums for medical expense and long-term care insurance policies that will pay virtually all health care expenses that might occur. Harry and his wife, on the other hand, feel their children can take care of themselves. They are satisfied with medical expense policies that have high deductibles and feel that their accumulated assets are more than adequate to finance any long-term care needs.

Even though seniors may have different opinions about how to finance health care needs, it is important that they understand the magnitude of their potential health care expenses and the benefits that available insurance products will provide.

Example:	When Harry and his wife (from the previous example) approached their financial planner for advice about investing the assets from the sale of the business, the planner determined that they underestimated the potential magnitude of long-term care costs, particularly if they both were in nursing homes. She also pointed out that these costs could be even higher if they wanted home health care. As a result, Harry and his wife decided to purchase a long-term care policy to finance a portion of future long-term care expenses.

Even when health care needs are understood, there may be alternative ways to meet these needs, and some alternatives may be more desirable to some seniors than other alternatives.

Example:	When Gail and her husband Charles became eligible for Medicare, they were made aware that they could either elect coverage under the original Medicare program or under a Medicare Advantage plan. The Medicare Advantage plan available to them provides broader coverage than the original Medicare program and is the least expensive alternative because it eliminates the need to purchase a Medicare supplement policy. However, it is an HMO that limits the physicians that they can use. This fact does not bother Gail, but Charles has several health problems and wants to be able to see the physician of his choice. After thoroughly considering the alternatives, Gail elected the Medicare Advantage plan, and Charles elected original Medicare and purchased a Medicare supplement policy.

Suitability also involves consideration of the cost of varying financing alternatives today and in the future.

Example 1:	Ruth recently retired and has a very limited income and few assets. She is aware that long-term care is a potential future expense that might arise. When she inquires about a policy, she discovers that there is no way she can afford the premium, even for a policy with modest benefits. As a result, she realizes that her method of financing long-term care expenses will be to rely on Medicaid if the need arises.
Example 2:	Karen and Jack, both in their early 60s and still working, decided to purchase long-term care insurance. They were surprised by the premium for the benefits they told their insurance agent they would like. Even though they can afford the premium today, they are concerned about being able to afford the policy after retirement, particularly if the premium

increases. Their insurance agent was able to suggest alternative benefits that made the policy better fit their future financial circumstances.

Advance Medical Directives

One final topic seems appropriate to briefly mention in this chapter, even though it is not covered in this book. When the financing of health care expenses is discussed, the issue of advance medical directives may arise. In most cases, an individual is able to make decisions about his or her medical care. However, this is often not true if a person is near death or incapacitated. As a result, advance medical directives have evolved. These usually consist of a living will and a durable medical power of attorney. A **living will** *living will* addresses what should be done when a person is clearly in a terminal medical condition. A *durable medical power of attorney* is a document that appoints someone else to make decisions about health care in the event of medical incapacity.

living will

durable medical power of attorney

Seniors should make themselves aware of these legal documents. Insurance agents, financial planners, and health care professionals should mention them to clients when appropriate and let them know where they can find more information. These documents are described on various Web sites, and blank documents can be obtained there or from various other sources. However, these documents differ from state to state, and often require making several alternative choices. Therefore, it is usually advisable to consult an attorney or other professional who specializes in preparing the documents.

For readers in the CASL designation program, these documents are discussed in detail in HS 330 Fundamentals of Estate Planning.

NOTES

1. "Retirees Often Fail to Save Enough for Health Costs," *The Wall Street Journal,* May 13, 2004.
2. Hewitt Associates, *Total Retirement Income at Large Companies,* 2004.

Employment-Related Medical Expense Coverage

Chapter Outline

Many persons retire prior to the time they will be eligible for Medicare at age 65. Until that time, they need some form of protection against the financial consequences of medical bills. In many cases, this protection is available as a result of their prior employment. In some cases, this coverage may also be available to spouses of deceased employees or to spouses who are still under age 65 after retired employees are eligible for Medicare.

The chapter first looks at the circumstances under which employer-provided medical expense coverage may cease prior to Medicare eligibility. The majority of the chapter is then devoted to the three ways that employment-related medical expense coverage might continue:

- as a result of COBRA continuation
- as a result of employer practices that continue coverage for retirees, dependents, survivors, and others
- as a result of a conversion policy

When employment-related medical expense coverage is not available or ceases, retirees under age 65 typically are eligible for individual coverage without evidence of insurability in the private insurance market as a result of HIPAA. The availability of this coverage is discussed in chapter 5.

One additional topic that is covered in this chapter is actually an issue that faces many retirees. What effect does managed care have on the ability to continue coverage if a retiree moves out of the service area of the managed care plan?

TERMINATION OF EMPLOYER-PROVIDED COVERAGE

In the absence of any plan provisions or laws to the contrary, employer-provided medical expense coverage ceases for an employee when employment terminates for any reason. Coverage may also terminate when an employee is no longer eligible under a medical expense plan, even though the employee may still be working.

Example:	Gerald decided to semi-retire at age 60. At that time, he continued to work part-time for the employer that had employed him for the last 30 years. Eligibility under the employer's medical expense plan, however, requires that an employee work full time, and the plan does not provide benefits for retirees. Gerald needs to obtain medical expense coverage from some source until he is eligible for Medicare.

Medical expense coverage for dependents usually ends when coverage on an employee ceases for any reason, including death. Coverage may also cease because an older person is no longer a dependent, often because of divorce.

Example 1:	At age 59, George was widowed when his wife died of cancer. He is self-employed and has always been covered under his wife's medical expense plan. His coverage terminated at the end of the month following his wife's death.

Example 2:   Coral has spent her life as a homemaker and has had coverage under her husband's medical expense plan. When she was 61, her husband announced that he wanted a divorce. At the time of the divorce, her medical expense coverage ceased under her former husband's plan.

As the following discussion will show, employer-provided coverage may continue in situations like these, at least for a period of time.

CONTINUATION OF COVERAGE UNDER COBRA

COBRA   A federal law known as *COBRA* (because it was part of the Consolidated Omnibus Budget Reconciliation Act of 1985) requires that group health plans allow employees and certain beneficiaries to extend their current health insurance coverage at group rates for up to 36 months following a "qualifying event" that results in the loss of coverage for a "qualified beneficiary." In most cases, the continuation of employer-provided coverage is the most cost-effective method for employees under age 65 to obtain medical expense coverage. However, the duration of the coverage is limited.

The term *group health plan* as used in the act is broad enough to include medical expense plans, dental plans, vision care plans, and prescription drug plans, regardless of whether benefits are self-insured or provided through other entities, such as insurance companies, HMOs, or PPOs. Long-term care and disability income coverages are not included in the definition of group health plan and are not subject to COBRA.

COBRA also applies to voluntary (employee-pay-all) group health plans as long as an employee would not be able to receive the coverage at the same cost if the employment relationship ended. COBRA does not apply if the voluntary plan has a portability provision whereby an employee can continue the coverage on an individual basis at no increase in cost.

Certain church-related plans and plans of the federal government are exempt from COBRA, but the act applies to all other employers who had the equivalent of 20 or more full-time employees on a typical business day during the preceding calendar year. For example, an employer who has 10 full-time and 16 half-time employees throughout the year has the equivalent of 18 full-time employees and is not subject to COBRA.

Failure to comply with the act results in an excise tax of up to $100 per day for each person denied coverage. The tax can be levied on the employer as well as on the entity (such as an insurer or HMO) that provides or administers the benefits. In addition, employers face a significant liability risk if they fail to notify qualified beneficiaries about the availability of

COBRA coverage. There have been legal judgments under which employers have been required to pay uninsured claims that would have been covered if a qualified beneficiary had known about COBRA and elected coverage.

Qualified Beneficiaries

qualified beneficiary   Since the passage of COBRA, a *qualified beneficiary* has been defined as any employee, or the spouse or dependent child of the employee, who on the day before a qualifying event was covered under the employee's group health plan. The Health Insurance Portability and Accountability Act (HIPAA) expanded the definition to include any child who is born to or placed for adoption with the employee during the period of COBRA coverage. This change gives automatic eligibility for COBRA coverage to the child as well as the right to have his or her own election rights if a second qualifying event occurs. Although this change will have no effect on most older COBRA beneficiaries, there are circumstances in which it is applicable. For example, a grandparent may adopt a grandchild after the child's parents are killed in an accident.

Qualifying Events

qualifying event   Under COBRA, each of the following is a *qualifying event* if it results in the loss of medical expense coverage by a qualified beneficiary:

- the death of the covered employee
- the termination of the employee for any reason except gross misconduct. This includes quitting, retiring, or being fired for anything other than gross misconduct.
- a reduction of the employee's hours so that the employee or dependent is ineligible for coverage
- the divorce or legal separation of the employee and his or her spouse
- for spouses and children, the employee's eligibility for Medicare
- a child's ceasing to be an eligible dependent under the plan

The act specifies that a qualified beneficiary is entitled to elect continued coverage without providing evidence of insurability. The beneficiary must be allowed to continue coverage identical to that available to employees and dependents to whom a qualifying event has not occurred. Coverage for persons electing COBRA continuation can be changed when changes are made to the plan covering similarly situated active employees and their dependents. In addition, a qualified beneficiary who moves out of an area served by a region-specific plan must be given the right to change coverage if the employer is able to provide coverage under another of its existing plans.

Example 1:	Herb and his wife Susan are covered by his employer's medical expense plan, under which 200 employees are insured. Herb plans to retire next year when he and Susan will be aged 64 and 62, respectively. They will both then be eligible for COBRA coverage for a maximum of 18 months. If they elect COBRA, Herb's coverage will cease upon his entitlement to Medicare at age 65. Susan's coverage will continue for the full 18 months, at which time she will need to find another source for her medical expense protection until she turns age 65.
Example 2:	Diane and her husband Michael have decided to retire prior to age 65. Each is covered only by the medical expense plan of his or her own employer. Michael's employer, however, has only 15 employees, and therefore he will not be eligible for COBRA continuation. In addition, he will not be eligible for COBRA coverage under his wife's medical expense plan because his retirement will not result in a loss of coverage under that plan. An option they might consider prior to retirement is for him to drop his coverage and to have Diane add him as a dependent to her policy. Then when she retires, they both will be eligible for COBRA continuation under her plan.

Length of Coverage

Each qualified beneficiary must be allowed to continue coverage from the qualifying event until the earliest of the following:

- 18 months for employees and dependents when the employee's employment has terminated or coverage has been terminated because of a reduction in hours. This period is extended to 29 months for a qualified beneficiary if the Social Security Administration determines that the beneficiary was or became totally disabled at any time during the first 60 days of COBRA coverage.
- 36 months for other qualifying events
- the date the plan terminates for all employees
- the date the coverage ceases because of a failure to make a timely payment of premium for the qualified beneficiary's coverage. COBRA regulations prohibit a plan from discontinuing coverage

because a payment is short by an insignificant amount, which is defined as the lesser of $50 or 10 percent of the amount due. The plan must either accept the amount received as satisfying the plan's payment requirement, or it must notify the beneficiary of the amount of the deficiency and grant a reasonable time for,it to be paid.

- the date the qualified beneficiary subsequently becomes entitled to Medicare or becomes covered (as either an employee or dependent) under another group health plan, provided the group health plan does not contain an exclusion or limitation with respect to any preexisting condition. If the new plan does not cover a preexisting condition, the COBRA coverage can be continued until the earlier of (1) the remainder of the 18- or 36-month period or (2) the time when the preexisting-conditions provision no longer applies. Note that COBRA coverage is not affected by entitlement to benefits under Medicare or coverage under another group plan if this entitlement or coverage existed at the time of the qualifying event.

If a second qualifying event (such as the death or divorce of a terminated employee) occurs during the period of continued coverage, the maximum period of continuation is 36 months.

Example: Fritz elected COBRA continuation coverage for himself and his wife Edna when he retired at age 61. At his death 15 months later, a second qualifying event occurred for Edna. The normal period of COBRA continuation resulting from the death of an employee is 36 months. However, because Edna has already had COBRA coverage for 15 months, the second qualifying event extends her coverage period for an additional 21 months.

At the termination of continued coverage, a qualified beneficiary must be offered the right to convert to an individual insurance policy if a conversion privilege is generally available to employees under the employer's plan.

Notification of COBRA Rights

Notification of the right to continue coverage must be made at two times by a plan's administrator. First, when a plan becomes subject to COBRA or when a person becomes covered under a plan subject to COBRA, notification must be given to an employee as well as to his or her spouse, generally within 90 days. A single letter to the employee and spouse satisfies this requirement as long as they reside at the same location. Second, when a qualifying event occurs, the employer must notify the plan administrator, who then must notify all qualified beneficiaries within 14 days. In general, the employer has 30 days to notify the plan administrator. However, an employer may not know of a qualifying event if it involves divorce, legal separation, or a child ceasing to be eligible for coverage. In these circumstances, the employee or family member must notify the employer within 60 days of the event, or the right to elect COBRA coverage is lost. The time period for the employer to notify the plan administrator begins when the employer is informed of the qualifying event, as long as this occurs within the 60-day period.

Recent changes to COBRA rules also require plan administrators to provide notification to qualified beneficiaries in two other circumstances. First, if a plan beneficiary receives a notice of a qualifying event and the qualified beneficiary is ineligible for COBRA coverage, the plan administrators must explain why the qualified beneficiary is not entitled to coverage. Second, if COBRA coverage is terminated before the end of the maximum duration, the plan administrator must explain when and why the coverage is being terminated and inform the qualified beneficiary of any available rights to other coverage.

COBRA Elections

The continuation of coverage is not automatic; a qualified beneficiary must elect it. The election period starts on the date of the qualifying event and may end not earlier than 60 days after actual notice of the event to the qualified beneficiary by the plan administrator. Once coverage is elected, it is effective retroactively to the date coverage would otherwise have ceased, and the beneficiary has 45 days to pay the premium for the period of coverage prior to the election.

COBRA Premiums

Under COBRA, the cost of the continued coverage may be passed on to the qualified beneficiary, but the cost cannot exceed 102 percent of the cost to the plan for the period of coverage for a similarly situated active employee to whom a qualifying event has not occurred. The extra 2 percent is supposed to cover the employer's extra administrative costs. (The one exception to this rule occurs for months 19 through 29 if an employee is disabled, in which case the premium can then be as high as 150 percent.) Qualified beneficiaries must have the option of paying the premium in monthly installments. In addition, there must be a grace period of at least 30 days for each installment.

It is important to point out that an employer can charge less than 102 percent for COBRA continuation and may even pay the full premium for a period of time as part of a severance or early-retirement package.

Example:	Clark, aged 62, recently accepted an early-retirement package from his employer. He has decided to elect COBRA coverage. Prior to retirement, he paid $100 per month toward his medical expense coverage, and his employer paid the remaining $400 of the $500 total premium. The employer can charge him a COBRA premium of up to $510 (102 percent of $500). However, as part of the early-retirement package, his COBRA premium will only be $100, or the same amount of his contribution while employed.

COBRA has resulted in significant extra costs for employers. Precise statistics are difficult to obtain, but one insurer indicates that coverage is elected by approximately 20 percent of those persons who are entitled to a COBRA continuation. The length of coverage averages almost 1 year for persons eligible for an 18-month extension and almost 2 years for persons eligible for a 36-month extension. Although significant variations exist among employers, claim costs of persons with COBRA coverage generally run about 150 percent of claim costs for active employees and dependents. Moreover, administrative costs are estimated to be about $20 per month for each person with COBRA coverage.

Is COBRA Coverage Worth the Cost?

In most cases, continuation of coverage under COBRA is the most cost-effective way for an older former employee to obtain medical expense coverage for as long as it lasts. However, circumstances vary, and the other alternatives that are mentioned in this and later chapters need to be explored as well.

As a result of the federal Age Discrimination in Employment Act, older employees who are actively working cannot be required to contribute more to the cost of their medical expense coverage that younger employees contribute. In addition, most insurers charge an employer a set rate for each employee. This rate is usually determined for a period of time and is based on the mix of employees by such factors as age, gender, marital status, and number of dependents. However, once determined, it is the rate for all employees regardless of age. The result is an average rate that is usually significantly below what an older person would pay for identical coverage in the individual marketplace, where rates are a function of age.

Many employers base the COBRA premium on this insurance rate. However, the Age Discrimination in Employment Act does not apply to retired employees, and employers can have COBRA premiums that are based on age as long as these rates can be actuarially justified. Even if an employer uses this approach, the COBRA coverage is still often less expensive than individual coverage because of the economies of scale that accompany employer-provided group insurance arrangements. In some cases, however, an individual policy may cost less.

Example 1: Harry, who is single, decided to retire at age 62. His employer currently pays an insurance premium of $400 per month for each actively working single employee. The employer has set the monthly COBRA premium at 102 percent of this amount, or $408. The least expensive comparable coverage Harry can find in the individual marketplace has a monthly premium of $500. Therefore, COBRA continuation is less expensive than an individual policy. However, Harry will need to find alternative coverage in 18 months when COBRA coverage is no longer available.

Example 2: Harry lives with his twin brother, Larry, who has also decided to retire. Larry works for a different employer, but the cost of the medical expense coverage for Larry's employer is also $400 for each actively working single employee. Larry's employer has determined that the monthly cost of coverage is actually $550 for an employee aged 55–64 when determined on an actuarial basis. Therefore, Larry's COBRA premium will be $561. In Larry's case, the individual coverage at $500 per month is the least expensive alternative.

One final point worth mentioning involves comparing COBRA coverage with coverage available in the individual marketplace. In many cases employer-provided coverage includes more comprehensive benefits than individually purchased coverage. As a result, any comparison of the two should look at benefits as well as cost. In addition, a retiree who is in good health and who is willing to assume higher deductibles and copayments can often find individual coverage that is less expensive than COBRA continuation.

State COBRA Laws

Some states have continuation laws for insured medical expense plans that require coverage to be made available in situations not covered by COBRA. These laws are often referred to as state COBRA laws or mini-

COBRA laws. One example is coverage for employees of firms with fewer than 20 employees; another is coverage for periods longer than those required by COBRA.

It should be noted that these state laws do not apply to self-funded plans. Such plans, which insure about one-half of the country's workers and their families, are exempt from state legislation of this type because of ERISA.

CONTINUATION OF COVERAGE IN ADDITION TO COBRA

Even before the passage of COBRA, it was becoming increasingly common for employers (particularly large employers) to continue group insurance coverage for certain employees—and sometimes their dependents—beyond the usual termination dates. Obviously, when coverage is continued now, an employer must at least comply with COBRA. However, an employer can be more liberal than COBRA by paying all or a portion of the cost, providing continued coverage for additional categories of persons, or continuing coverage for a longer period of time.

Retired Employees

Although not required to do so by the Age Discrimination in Employment Act, some employers continue coverage on "retired" employees. The definition of retired varies among employers and is usually spelled out clearly in the plan document of the employer's medical expense plan as well as the benefit handbook given to employees. In some cases, an employee will be eligible for retiree coverage if he or she retires after the date on which retirement benefits are available under a defined-benefit pension plan. In other cases, eligibility may be contingent upon attainment of certain age and years of service. Other variations are also found.

Example: The Hayes Corporation provides retiree medical expense coverage to employees who have retired from full-time employment as long as an employee (1) is at least age 62, (2) has a minimum of 10 years of service with the corporation, and (3) has a combination of age and service at time of retirement that totals at least 75.

It should be pointed out that retiree medical expense coverage may be made available to all employees or limited to certain classes of employees, such as executives.

The subject of retiree benefits has become a major concern to employers since the Financial Accounting Standards Board (FASB) phased in new rules between 1993 and 1997 for the accounting of postretirement benefits other than pensions. These rules require that employers do the following:

- recognize the present value of future retiree medical expense benefits on the firm's balance sheet with other liabilities
- record the cost for postretirement medical benefits in the period when an employee performs services. This is comparable to the accounting for pension costs.
- amortize the present value of the future cost of benefits accrued prior to the new rules

These rules are in contrast to the long-used previous practice of paying retiree medical benefits or premiums out of current revenue and recognizing these costs as expenses when paid. Although the rules are logical from a financial accounting standpoint, the effect on employers has been significant. Employers that immediately recognized the liability had to show reduced earnings and net worth. Firms that amortized the liability (often because immediate recognition would wipe out net worth) will be affected for years to come.

The FASB rules, along with the increasing cost of medical expense coverage, have resulted in two major changes by employers. First, many employers have reduced or eliminated retiree benefits or are considering such a change. Since 1993, the number of private employers providing coverage to early retirees has dropped from about 45 percent to 25 percent, and the number of employers providing coverage after Medicare eligibility has declined from about 40 percent to 20 percent. (These percentages are 6 or 7 percent higher if government employees are included.) However, there are legal uncertainties as to whether benefits that have been promised to retirees can be eliminated or reduced. Some employers also feel that there is a moral obligation to continue these benefits. As a result, many employers are not altering plans for current retirees or active employees who are eligible to retire. Instead, the changes apply to future retirees only. These changes, which seem to run the gamut, include the following:

- eliminating benefits for future retirees
- shifting more of the cost burden to future retirees by reducing benefits. Such a reduction may be accomplished by providing lower benefit maximums, covering fewer types of expenses, or increasing copayments.
- adding or increasing retiree sharing of premium costs after retirement

- shifting to a defined-contribution approach to funding retiree benefits. For example, an employer might agree to pay $5 per month toward the cost of coverage after retirement for each year of service by an employee. Thus, an employer would make a monthly contribution of $150 for an employee who retired with 30 years of service, but the employer would make a contribution of only $75 for an employee with 15 years of service. Many plans of this nature have been designed so that the employer's contribution increases with changes in the consumer price index, subject to maximum increases (such as 5 percent per year).
- encouraging retirees to elect benefits from managed care plans if they are not already doing so. With this approach, retirees are required to pay a significant portion of the cost if coverage is continued through a traditional indemnity plan.

A second change is that employers have increasingly explored methods to prefund the benefits. However, there are no alternatives for prefunding that are as favorable as the alternatives for funding pension benefits. One alternative is the use of a 501(c)(9) trust (or VEBA). Another alternative is to prefund medical benefits within a pension plan. A discussion of these alternatives—both of which are subject to limitations and administratively complex—is beyond the scope of this book.

Coverage before Medicare Eligibility

The majority of employers that provide postretirement medical expense coverage continue it for the life of an employee, but some employers provide coverage only until an employee is eligible for Medicare. Coverage is also frequently made available to spouses who were covered under the plan at time of retirement.

In most cases, retirees and their spouses have the same coverage that is available to active employees. Premium contributions are often identical to those made by active employees. However, this is a matter for the employer to determine, and the required contributions may be higher or lower. They may also be a function of the length of active employment.

Example: The Springfield Corporation continues medical expense coverage for retired employees and their spouses until Medicare eligibility. The spouse can be any age at the time of an employee's retirement. While both are under age 65, the required contribution is the same as the employee and spouse contribution for actively working employees. When either spouse reaches age 65, the other spouse can retain coverage by paying the contribution made by actively working single employees.

Coverage after Medicare Eligibility

When coverage is provided to employees or spouses after they reach age 65, it is often provided by either a Medicare carve-out or a Medicare supplement.

Medicare carve-out

With a *Medicare carve-out,* plan benefits are reduced to the extent that benefits are payable under Medicare for the same expenses. (Medicare may also pay for some expenses not covered by the group plan.)

| *Example:* | If Karen incurs $1,000 of covered expenses and is not eligible for Medicare, $720 in benefits is paid under her medical expense plan that has a $100 deductible and an 80 percent coinsurance provision. However, if she is eligible for Medicare, and if Medicare pays $650 for the same expenses, the employer's plan pays only $70, for a total benefit of $720. |

Some medical expense plans use a more liberal carve-out approach and reduce covered expenses (rather than benefits payable) by any amounts received under Medicare.

| *Example:* | In the previous example, the $650 paid by Medicare would be subtracted from the $1,000 of covered expenses, which would leave $350. After the deductible and coinsurance are applied to this amount, the employer's plan would pay $200, so Karen would receive a total of $850 in benefits, or $130 more than a person not eligible for Medicare. |

Medicare supplement

As an alternative to using a carve-out approach, some employers use a *Medicare supplement* that provides benefits for certain specific expenses not covered under Medicare. These include (1) the portion of expenses not paid by Medicare because of deductibles, coinsurance, or copayments, and (2) certain expenses excluded by Medicare, such as medical costs incurred in a foreign country. Such a supplement may or may not provide benefits similar to those available under a carve-out plan.

In the case of either a Medicare carve-out or Medicare supplement, there may also be a lifetime benefit maximum that is relatively low, such as $5,000 or $10,000.

Just as with coverage prior to Medicare eligibility, any required retiree contribution for the coverage is determined by the employer. In the most generous situations, the employer may pay the entire cost of the coverage and even pay the retiree's Part B Medicare premium. However, most plans are less generous.

Surviving Dependents

Coverage can also be continued for the survivors of deceased active employees and/or deceased retired employees. However, coverage for the survivors of active employees is not commonly continued beyond the period required by COBRA, and coverage for the survivors of retired employees may be limited to surviving spouses. In both instances, the continued coverage is usually identical to what was provided prior to the employee's death. It is also common for the employer to continue the same premium contribution level.

Disabled Employees

Medical expense coverage can be continued for an employee (and dependents) when he or she has a temporary interruption of employment, including one arising from illness or injury. Many employers also cover employees who have long-term disabilities or who have retired because of a disability. In most cases, this continuation of coverage is contingent on satisfaction of some definition of total (and possibly permanent) disability. When continuing coverage for disabled employees, an employer must determine the extent of employer contributions. For example, the employer may continue the same premium contribution as for active employees, although there is nothing to prevent a different contribution rate—either lower or higher.

Domestic Partners

It is becoming increasingly common for medical expense plans to provide benefits for domestic partners. Domestic partners do not meet the definition of a qualified beneficiary for purposes of COBRA. However, some employers provide domestic partners who have coverage under the employer's plan with continuation coverage that is similar or identical to what is available under COBRA.

In addition, such plans also usually treat domestic partners in the same manner as spouses for purposes of retiree coverage.

CONVERSION

conversion provision

Except when termination results from the failure to pay any required premiums, medical expense contracts often contain (and may be required to contain) a *conversion provision*. With such a provision, most covered persons whose group coverage terminates are allowed to purchase individual medical expense coverage without evidence of insurability and without any limitation of benefits for preexisting conditions. Covered persons have a specified number of days (typically 31) from the date of termination of the group coverage to exercise this conversion privilege, and coverage is then effective retroactively to the date of termination.

This conversion privilege is typically given to any employee who has been insured under the group contract (or under any group contract it replaced) for at least 3 months, and it permits the employee to convert his or her own coverage as well as any dependent coverage. In addition, a spouse or child whose dependent coverage ceases for any other reason may also be eligible for conversion (for example, a spouse who divorces or separates, and children who reach age 19).

State laws and insurance company practices vary with respect to the conversion provision and COBRA. In some cases, conversion is contingent upon an individual electing COBRA coverage and maintaining it for the maximum election period. At that time, a conversion policy is available. In other cases, a person who is eligible for both the conversion privilege and the right to continue the group insurance coverage under COBRA has two choices when eligibility for coverage terminates. He or she can either elect to convert under the provisions of the policy or elect to continue the group coverage under COBRA. If the latter choice is made, the COBRA rules specify that the person must again be eligible to convert to an individual policy within the usual conversion period (31 days) after the maximum continuation-of-coverage period ceases. In either situation, policy provisions may also make the conversion privilege available to persons whose coverage terminates prior to the end of the maximum continuation period. If the conversion option is elected, there are no COBRA rights if the conversion policy term terminates.

The provider of the medical expense coverage has the right to refuse the issue of a conversion policy to anyone (1) who is covered by Medicare or (2) whose benefits under the converted policy, together with similar benefits from other sources, would result in overinsurance according to the insurance company's standards. These similar benefits may be found in other coverages that the individual has (either group or individual coverage) or for which the individual is eligible under any group arrangement.

The use of the word *conversion* is often a misnomer. In actuality, a person whose coverage terminates is only given the right to purchase a contract on an individual basis at individual rates. Most Blue Cross–Blue Shield plans and some HMO plans offer a conversion policy that is similar or identical to the terminated group coverage. However, many insurance companies offer a conversion policy (or a choice of policies) that contains a lower level of benefits than existed under the group coverage.

Some plans offer a conversion policy that is written by another entity. For example, an HMO might enter into a contractual arrangement with an insurance company. In some cases, the HMO and insurance company are commonly owned or have a parent-subsidiary relationship.

Self-funded medical expense plans, which are exempt from state laws mandating a conversion policy, may still provide such a benefit. Rather than providing coverage directly to the terminated employee, an agreement is usually made with an insurance company to make a policy available.

Historically, the persons who elect to convert coverage have been relatively unhealthy, and the premiums for this coverage often reflect this fact. Older persons in good health can often find less expensive coverage in the individual marketplace. Persons in poor health may also find better and less expensive coverage by purchasing an individual policy under provisions of HIPAA. As a result, conversion is seldom used. However, it is an available option to explore and occasionally may be the best option.

EFFECT OF MANAGED CARE

At one time, most Americans had their medical expense coverage under traditional indemnity plans that allowed them to receive medical care from any provider in any location. The situation has changed dramatically over the past 30 years, and now most estimates indicate that over 90 percent of workers and their families have coverage under various types of managed care plans. One of the characteristics of managed care plans is provider networks. Under some medical expense plans, primarily health maintenance organizations (HMOs), care must be received from these providers. No benefits are paid if care is received outside the provider network, except in the case of emergencies. Under other plans, such as preferred-provider organization (PPOs), benefits are reduced—often substantially—when care is received from nonnetwork providers.

Many retirees relocate to other geographic locations, and the medical expense coverage they have under retiree plans or COBRA may be limited or unavailable.

Example 1:   Charlene and Jim both worked for an employer in Chicago. Their medical expense coverage was under an HMO that served Chicago and its suburbs. The coverage continued under a retiree plan when they retired at age 60. At age 62, they decided to move to California to be near their children and grandchildren and to get away from the Chicago winters. The HMO told them that they were no longer eligible for coverage because they did not live in the plan's service area.

Example 2:   When Bill retired from his job at a Philadelphia college at age 62, he and his wife started spending their summers in Maine. His retiree coverage was through a PPO that had the Philadelphia metro-politan area as its service area. Although the plan covered medical expenses incurred in Maine, none of the providers there are in the PPO's network. As a result, Bill and his wife are faced with the situation of being reimbursed for only about 50 percent of their medical expenses or returning to Philadelphia for care, where most of their medical expenses are paid in full.

Example 3:   When Jane retired at age 64, she elected COBRA coverage and expected to continue it until she was eligible for Medicare. When she moved to a retirement community 100 miles from her former home, she found herself outside the service area of the HMO and realized that she effectively had no coverage except in the case of a medical emergency. Her visits to a cardiologist and allergist were not covered because they were not network participants.

As these examples show, retirees must be aware of the effect of relocation, either permanently or part time on their medical expense coverage. As a general rule, most managed care plans will not continue to provide coverage if a member moves out of its service area. The exception to the rule is that they are required by federal law to continue COBRA coverage as long as a person is eligible. However, the rules regarding the use of network providers still apply, which limits the benefits available.

In the case of COBRA coverage, beneficiaries who move out of a plan's service area must be allowed to switch to another plan of the employer that will provide coverage in the new area of residence *if* the employer has another plan that provides coverage in that area. In many cases, there is no other plan. In other cases, the plan is an indemnity plan that has a significantly higher premium.

The only available option for many retirees is to purchase coverage in the individual marketplace. In almost all cases, some type of coverage is available, but its cost may be prohibitive, particularly if the retiree is in poor health. It is common for employers that provide retiree coverage to make a contribution to the cost of coverage when a retiree is faced with this situation.

Example: The cost to the Highlight Corporation for providing medical expense coverage to a retiree and spouse is currently $840 per month. The corporation and the retiree each pay 50 percent of this amount, or $420. The corporation's only plan does not provide coverage if a retiree moves out of its service area. In this case, the retiree is responsible for obtaining his or her own coverage, but the corporation will continue to pay 50 percent of the cost up to $420 per month. If a retiree can find coverage for $750, the corporation will pay $375. If a retiree or spouse is in poor health, and can only find coverage at a cost of $1,400, the corporation will pay $420.

3

Principal Policies of Individual Medical Expense Insurance

Chapter Outline

For many retired persons or those planning to retire, maintaining some form of employer-sponsored coverage discussed in the previous chapter may not be a viable option for them and/or their spouses and children. At some point, they are likely to seek medical expense insurance in the individual market or possibly from a group plan offered by an association. The reasons for this are varied.

Many retired persons are too young to be eligible for Medicare. Frequently, employer-financed coverage is not offered or has been cut back or eliminated. COBRA coverage might not be available or the maximum COBRA continuation period might have terminated. Conversion policies may offer less than desired protection. Retirees who are age 65 and older rely on Medicare for their principal medical expense coverage, but may need to obtain coverage for their spouses under age 65 and possibly dependent children.

OVERVIEW OF INDIVIDUAL COVERAGE

There are three categories of medical expense insurance in the private market that retirees may purchase: principal, supplemental, and ancillary.

principal medical expense insurance

- *Principal medical expense insurance* provides substantial benefits for the major portion of the medical expenses that a retiree and his or her family may incur. Most retirees and those planning for retirement as well as their advisors must give the major priority to securing a source for this coverage. The policies purchased may be of several types: major medical policies, high-deductible policies, HMO coverage, and interim insurance.

supplemental medical expense insurance

- *Supplemental medical expense insurance*, which falls into several categories, provides cash benefits for the direct, indirect, and/or personal expenses left unpaid when an illness or injury occurs. Many persons of all ages seek to enhance the protection provided by their principal medical insurance through supplemental policies. They pay benefits in addition to other forms of medical insurance.

ancillary medical expense insurance

- *Ancillary medical expense insurance* provides coverage and benefits for specific health care services that are usually outside the scope of or incidental to medical care, such as dental and vision services.

This chapter begins the discussion of principal medical expense policies that provide substantial benefits for the major portion of the expenses for needed health care services. These policies generally constitute the policyowner's or insured's[1] fundamental program of medical expense protection. Historically, principal policies usually were limited to hospital and physician services related to inpatient care and surgery with fixed or scheduled benefit limits. While an inpatient focus is still true for products that seek to maintain low premiums, most principal policies are typically more comprehensive. They include a broad array of additional services in hospital outpatient departments, ambulatory facilities (both surgical and nonsurgical), and doctors' offices as well as routine physicians' services, diagnostic tests, and therapies regardless of setting. Coverage for other services, such as emergency transport and outpatient prescription drugs, is frequently included as well.

Insurance companies, Blue Cross–Blue Shield plans, and managed care organizations offer principal policies of medical expense insurance in the individual market. Over time, the traditional differences between these types of organizations have tended to blur because of mergers, acquisitions, the creation of subsidiaries, and product evolution. Today, many managed care organizations still specialize in selling products that are associated with their particular legal form of being a preferred-provider organization (PPO) or health maintenance organization (HMO). However, most insurers and Blue Cross–Blue Shield plans sell traditional health insurance products as well as managed care plans, such as HMOs and PPOs.

Individuals and their advisors may identify the companies that are offering principal policies of medical expense coverage in a specific area by contacting the state department of insurance or searching the Internet.

Chapter 4 is devoted to consumer-directed medical expense plans, a topic that has received considerable attention as medical costs continue to rise. Consumer-directed plans give individuals increased choices and responsibilities with respect to the selection of their own medical expense coverage. These plans include health reimbursement arrangements (HRAs), flexible spending accounts (FSAs), health savings accounts (HSAs), and Archer medical savings accounts (MSAs).

Chapter 5 looks at underwriting. Underwriting is essential to providing insurance in the individual market, but can significantly affect the availability and cost of coverage for retirees who are usually at least 55 years of age and often have health problems. The chapter also addresses the issue of insuring the unhealthy by reviewing two often-related alternatives to obtain insurance for those who would otherwise be uninsurable: coverage under the provisions of the Health Insurance Portability and Accountability Act (HIPAA) and through state high-risk health insurance plans.

Chapter 6 describes the interim, supplemental, and ancillary medical insurance policies that may meet specific needs or desires of older clients.

THE EVOLUTION OF PRINCIPAL POLICIES

indemnity (fee-for-service) contract

Principal policies can take many forms. Until about 25 years ago, individual major medical insurance consisted almost totally of traditional *indemnity*, or *fee-for-service*, *contracts*. Under these policies, medical expenses were incurred and patients had considerable freedom in choosing providers of medical services. Claims were generally paid on the basis of charges billed by providers with few attempts to control costs. Beginning in the 1980s, and following what was occurring in the employer-provided market, insurers began to issue policies that contained elements of managed care. HMOs also became more likely to offer individual coverage.

This chapter continues with a description of the general nature of major medical policies. The chapter then looks at the ways traditional policies have been modified by managed care provisions, often including the use of preferred-provider networks. Finally, HMOs are discussed.

Today, the typical policy purchased for individual medical insurance is a PPO plan, which represents more than eight out of ten policies sold. Well over half of these policies have deductibles in the range of $1,000 to $3,000 with over three-quarters of them having a lifetime benefit maximum between $5 and $7.5 million.[2] Traditional major medical policies and HMO coverage are much less common.

MAJOR MEDICAL INSURANCE

Major medical policies are the foundation of most principal programs of individual medical expense insurance, including many managed care plans that are typically PPO plans. Even HMOs, especially those with a point of service (POS) option, incorporate major medical insurance features. In addition, many of the features and definitions included in major medical policies may also be found in the other forms of medical expense insurance discussed in chapters 4 and 6.

major medical insurance

Individual *major medical insurance* pays for *covered health care services* through a *benefit structure* based on (1) the payment of a *deductible* by the insured, (2) a plan payment of a *percentage of allowable charges (co-insurance)* with an *out-of-pocket limit*, and (3) *benefit maximums*.

An explanation of several of the above terms used in this definition forms the basis for understanding major medical insurance policies and indeed all types of medical expense policies, which share many of these same features.

Covered health care services may be limited to a core of services or may extend to a more comprehensive array.

Core Covered Services

All major medical programs provide at least a core of covered services for the treatment of illness and injury that focus largely, though not exclusively, on the inpatient setting. Programs that limit coverage to these core services are known as hospital/surgical major medical policies. The following is a typical list of core inpatient, outpatient, physicians', and other services.

Inpatient Services

Hospital inpatient services fall into two categories: room-and-board services and other inpatient services.

Room and Board. Room-and-board services typically consist of

- hospital room, meals, and the services normally provided to inpatients, including routine nursing care in a semiprivate (two-bed) room for a standard level of care; if a hospital has only private rooms, benefits do not exceed the most common semiprivate room rate in the area

- higher levels of medically necessary service requiring intensive care, coronary care, or interim care units, possibly subject to day or dollar maximums
- skilled-nursing home care for recovery within 30 days after and in lieu of a hospital inpatient stay, subject to day or dollar maximums

Other Services. Other inpatient benefits include additional medically necessary services and supplies furnished by a hospital for inpatient care, such as

- operating room
- drugs
- surgical dressings
- laboratory and radiology

Outpatient Services

Several types of services are covered on an outpatient basis to reduce the unnecessary use of more costly inpatient services. They usually include

- preoperative outpatient testing given in preparation for a scheduled inpatient admission (covered as part of the inpatient hospital stay, provided that it would have been eligible as a covered service if received as an inpatient)
- surgery performed in a hospital outpatient department or a free-standing surgical center and related diagnostic services rendered within 72 hours prior to the surgery
- outpatient chemotherapy and radiation therapy treatments
- emergency accident and illness care if hospital admission occurs as a result of the accident or the illness within 72 hours of the emergency care; sometimes care is eligible as a covered service without a subsequent admission but with a greater out-of-pocket payment

Physicians' Services

The following physicians' services are typically covered:

- surgery performed by a physician and any related diagnostic services received on the same day as the surgery
- anesthesia administered at the same time as a covered surgical procedure by a physician other than the operating surgeon or by a Certified Registered Nurse Anesthetist (CRNA)
- services provided by a physician who assists the operating surgeon in performing covered surgery, but only if a hospital intern or resident is not available

- inpatient visits in a hospital or skilled-nursing facility
- specialist consultations requested by the attending physician in a hospital or skilled-nursing facility
- reconstructive surgery (1) related to or following surgery for injury, trauma, infection, or disease, or (2) for the correction of birth abnormalities or congenital defects of a newborn child
- services that are associated with covered chemotherapy and radiation therapy
- services that are associated with covered emergency, accident, and illness care

Other Covered Services

Other covered services may include

- mammograms, Papanicolaou (Pap) smear tests, and associated office visits
- ambulance transportation in connection with a covered inpatient admission or covered emergency accident or illness
- initial prosthetic devices, special appliances, and surgical implants, to replace all or part of an organ or tissue

Comprehensive Covered Services

Major medical policies that extend coverage beyond the core services for the treatment of illness and injury listed above are called *comprehensive*. They provide a broad scope of covered services for outpatient, routine, and preventive care. Included among these additional covered services are the following:

- physician services for the diagnosis and treatment of sickness or injury in or out of the hospital
- routine outpatient X-ray and laboratory tests for diagnosis and treatment of sickness or injury
- outpatient prescription drugs and medicines dispensed by a pharmacist. However, under some policies, prescription drug coverage is an optional benefit that requires an additional premium.
- blood or blood plasma
- oxygen and rental of equipment for its administration
- inpatient and outpatient private-duty nursing authorized by a physician up to an annual maximum, such as 30 days
- rental of a wheelchair, hospital bed, or other durable equipment
- outpatient occupational, physical, or speech therapy services on an ambulatory basis

- home care
- outpatient and inpatient psychiatric care in licensed facilities other than acute-care hospitals
- treatment of alcoholism and substance abuse
- replacement of prosthetic devices
- hospice care
- routine preventive examinations and tests

Benefits for several of these additional covered services may be subject to separate maximums as listed in table 3-1 later in this chapter.

Benefit Structure

As indicated previously, the benefit structure for the specified covered services is based on (1) the payment of a deductible by the insured, (2) a plan payment of a percentage of allowable charges (coinsurance) with an out-of-pocket limit, and (3) benefit maximums.

Deductibles

deductible

Major medical benefits typically require a deductible. A *deductible* is the initial amount an insured must pay for covered services before the plan begins to pay its benefits. Insurers impose deductibles to avoid the cost of singly processing small initial claims and to give the insured a personal financial stake in obtaining less costly services, which would otherwise be subject only to a low patient out-of-pocket payment.

Thus, even though the services are covered, the insured must pay 100 percent of covered expenses up to the deductible amount. Charges for noncovered services and disallowed portions of charges for covered services do not count toward the satisfaction of the deductible. A deductible may be applied (separately or in combination) per service, person, or family. Typically, the deductible is incurred only once per person per benefit period (almost always one calendar year) for the expenses of most covered services in aggregate. This type of deductible is often referred to as an *all causes* deductible. Although major medical policy deductibles may range from $250 to $10,000, the average deductible amount in recently purchased policies is approximately $2,000.[3] A deductible may also be applied to each separate injury or episode of illness. Such a *per cause* deductible, however, is not common.

If a policy covers a family, the deductible applies separately to each covered person each year and any family member who meets his or her own deductible may begin to receive benefits. Most policies waive any remaining deductible amounts for all family members after a certain number of family members (usually two or three) have satisfied their individual deductibles. If two or more covered persons are injured in the same accident, only one deductible is usually applicable to the expenses arising from the accident.

Some policies contain a deductible carryover provision so that expenses in the last 3 months of the year used to meet that year's deductible are also used to meet the following year's deductible.

Separate deductibles often apply to specific services, as identified later in table 3-2, when other benefits are added to the policy.

Percentage of Allowable Charges (Coinsurance)

allowable charges

Allowable charges are the basis on which benefit payments are determined. Once a deductible is satisfied, the benefit payment is a specified percentage of the remaining allowable charge.

reasonable and customary (R&C) fees

Traditionally, under major medical policies, insurers determine allowable charges using *reasonable and customary (R&C) fees*. R&C fees are defined as the lesser of the provider's fee, the fee most often charged by the providers for the same service, or the fee most often charged for comparable services in the area by providers with similar training and experience. Insurers may define "area" to mean a metropolitan area (or section thereof), a county, or a larger area if needed to find a representative sample of provider fees for a comparable service or supply. If the charges for covered services exceed allowable charges, the unallowed amount becomes the insured's responsibility.

More recently, under PPO arrangements, the allowable charge is the fee negotiated with participating providers. If insureds use a participating provider, they are not responsible for the payment of any charges above the negotiated fee. However, the negotiated fees are often the allowable amount or charges paid to nonparticipating providers. As a result, insureds in a PPO arrangement who receive services from nonparticipating providers may be responsible for amounts charged above the negotiated levels rather than R&C levels, which are usually more generous.

coinsurance

The term *coinsurance* as used in this book refers to the percentage of allowable charges paid by a medical expense plan with the remaining percentage of such charges paid by the insured. Thus a policy with 80 percent coinsurance, sometimes referred to as an 80/20 policy, pays 80 percent of allowable charges for covered services, while the insured must pay the remaining 20 percent. The level or amount of the benefit paid by the insurance plan usually ranges from 50 percent to 90 percent, depending on the policy's terms, generally after the deductible has been satisfied. The coinsurance percentage is often the same for all covered medical services, but different percentages may be used for different services.

percentage participation

In some policies, the insured's percentage participation in paying allowable charges for covered services, such as 20 percent, is specified. As commonly used, a *percentage participation* refers to the percentage of covered medical expenses that is not paid by a medical expense policy and that the person receiving benefits must pay. Note that a percentage participation is sometimes referred to as a *copayment*, but this terminology usually implies a fixed dollar amount that the insured must pay for a covered service. A few insurers also refer to the percentage participation, rather than their portion of the benefit payment, as coinsurance.

copayment

Out-of-Pocket Limit

out-of-pocket limit

An *out-of-pocket limit* (also known as a *stop-loss limit*) is the maximum sum of all the percentage participation amounts paid by an insured after the receipt of benefits for covered services in a yearly benefit period. When this level is reached, the policy pays 100 percent of all subsequent allowable charges for the remainder of the calendar year. The average out-of-pocket limit across a spectrum of currently purchased policies ranges from $2,500 to approximately $5,000.[4] Under a family policy, the out-of-pocket limit is the total amount for all insureds covered under the policy. The family limit is usually set at two or three times the per person insured limit and can be satisfied by the accumulated expenses of one or more family members. The following expenses do not apply toward the out-of-pocket limit:

- disallowed charges for covered services (that is, above reasonable and customary or other limits)
- expenses incurred beyond separate covered service benefit maximums
- expenses for noncovered services
- benefit reductions or penalties for failure to use cost containment or other required procedures
- copayments (fixed dollar amounts for doctor's office visits and other outpatient services)

Under most policies, any deductibles paid are also not considered when determining the out-of-pocket limit. However, some policies do allow this amount to be considered.

Some insurers also explain the out-of-pocket limit as the level of allowable charges for covered services after which the policy's benefit increases to 100 percent of such charges. For example, the policy may state that after the insured pays the deductible, the coinsurance benefit is 80 percent of the next $10,000 of allowable charges for covered services; after that, the policy pays 100 percent of such charges up to the applicable benefit maximum.

Benefit Maximums

Major medical policies usually contain an aggregate maximum and separate covered service maximums that are designed to control plan cost, thereby maintaining affordability and stability in the product's premium price.

aggregate maximum

Aggregate Maximum. An *aggregate maximum* (often called a lifetime maximum) is the overall amount of benefits payable under the policy for all covered services on behalf of each insured as long as the policy is in force. These maximum amounts vary by policy and may range from $1 million to $8 million; while some policies may be unlimited, the average maximum is $5 million.[5] In the absence of any provision to the contrary, benefits paid reduce the aggregate maximum. However, policies often permit restoration of the aggregate maximum under certain conditions, such as the absence of claims for 2 consecutive calendar years. Some policies may impose a maximum per calendar year, such as $1 million, in addition to an aggregate (lifetime) maximum, such as $5 million.

separate service maximum

Separate Service Maximum. A *separate service maximum* (also called an internal limit) may apply to benefits for specific services, if covered, such as organ transplants, substance abuse and dependency, mental illness, home health care, skilled-nursing home care, infertility treatments, and private-duty nursing. Illustrative separate service benefit maximums are presented in table 3-1. Note that the services shown may not be covered in all policies. These maximums may be imposed per lifetime, per year, or per service or episode of service, and they may be expressed as dollar amounts or units of service. Although benefits remain subject to the overall aggregate (lifetime) maximum, charges that are incurred above the separate benefit maximums do not count toward the out-of-pocket limit. Applicable state law may inhibit an insurer's ability to implement these maximums.

Optional Coverages

Major medical policies sometimes have optional coverages for which an extra premium is charged. If the optional coverage is not elected, benefits are excluded. These optional coverages might include outpatient prescription drugs (if not otherwise covered), dental services, and maternity services. Benefits for maternity services may be of little value to most seniors. However, the benefit may be of significance if coverage is purchased for younger dependents. Table 3-2 is an example of the separate benefit structures that often apply to these optional coverages.

TABLE 3-1
Separate Service Benefit Maximums

Covered Services	Maximum*
Chemical abuse and dependency, inpatient and outpatient	$1,000 per year
Organ transplants and high-dose chemotherapy	$100,000 per benefit treatment period
Home health care	1 visit per day up to 60 per year
Hospice	30 inpatient days and $3,000 lifetime
Mental illness, inpatient and outpatient services	Combined maximum $10,000 lifetime
Inpatient services	30 days per year
Outpatient services	20 visits per year and 1 visit per week with 50 percent coinsurance up to $25 per visit
Private-duty nursing	30 days per year
Routine preventive examinations and tests	$150 per year
Skilled-nursing facility care	60 days per year
Manipulative treatment, heat treatment, and ultrasound	$1,000 per year

*All benefits are subject to the overall aggregate (lifetime) maximum.

Outpatient Prescription Drugs

Outpatient prescription drug benefits, while frequently provided under comprehensive major medical policies, may also be offered as an option. Deductibles, copayments, and coinsurance benefits are typically separate from those applicable to the overall plan, usually with no limit on out-of-pocket payments.

formulary

The prescription drug benefit is often administered by a third party, often known as a pharmacy benefit manager, and uses a formulary. The *formulary* is a list of drug products that are preferred for dispensing to covered persons when appropriate and contains both generic and brand-name drugs. A generic drug product is one that is chemically equivalent to a brand-name drug whose patent has expired. A brand-name drug is manufactured and marketed under a trademark or name by a specific drug manufacturer.

TABLE 3-2
Separate Benefit Structures for Optional Coverages

Optional Coverages	Benefit Structures*
Prescription drugs	Deductible: $100 to $1,000 depending on medical plan deductible selected Copayment for retail pharmacy: $10 generic or $25 brand-name formulary, and $40 nonformulary for 30-day supply** Copayment for mail-order supply: $20 generic or $50 brand-name formulary and $80 nonformulary for 90-day supply**
Dental	Deductible: $50 per person per year with no family deductible Coinsurance: 50% to 80% depending on the service Calendar maximum: $1,000 or $1,500
Maternity	Deductible: $1,000 Coinsurance: 80% after one or more years of coverage; 50% with less than one year of coverage

*Reasonable and customary limitations apply to all coinsurance levels; out-of-pocket amounts are not subject to any limits and do not contribute to the overall medical policy out-of-pocket limit.
**Coinsurance may also apply after deductible and copayment.

Today, most drug coverage has a three-tier copayment structure. The lowest copayment is for generic drugs, with brand-name drugs on the formulary requiring a higher amount, and nonformulary drugs requiring the highest copayment. Ordinarily, a generic drug is automatically substituted for a brand name if an equivalent is available, unless the doctor specifies "Dispense as written" on the prescription. The pharmacy plan usually limits a retail pharmacy prescription to a 30-day supply, although refills are covered. The plan's goal is to encourage the use of its lower-cost mail-order pharmacy, especially among insureds with chronic conditions and those who use maintenance drugs. Plans frequently suggest that when doctors first prescribe a drug that is to be taken for an extended or indefinite period, patients should request a 30-day prescription to be filled immediately at a network retail pharmacy. They should also request a second prescription for at least 90 days (with additional refills as appropriate) to be filled through the mail-order pharmacy. A financial incentive for the use of mail order is a lower copayment than would be the case if three 30-day supplies of the drug were obtained from the network retail pharmacy.

Prior approval is often needed before certain drugs will be dispensed. Those typically include high-cost drugs when there are often less expensive alternatives. However, these drugs are typically approved as long as a physician can justify their use.

Two techniques that are gaining wider use in prescription drug programs are a four-tier copayment structure and step therapy. With a four-tier copayment structure, there is a fourth tier for very expensive drugs. There is either a large copayment, which may be as high as $200 or $300 per prescription, or a high percentage participation, such as 25 or 50 percent. With step therapy, approval for higher-cost medications is contingent on an individual first trying lower-cost, often well-established, drugs to see if they are effective.

Unique Exclusions. Prescription drug programs contain many exclusions unique to this type of benefit and often include the following:

- coverage for prescription drug products for any amount that exceeds the supply limits
- drugs prescribed, dispensed, or intended for use while the covered person is in a hospital, skilled-nursing facility, or alternative facility
- experimental, investigational, or unproven services and medications; medications used for treatments and/or dosage regimens determined to be experimental
- drugs furnished or paid for by the government
- appetite suppressants and other weight-loss products
- compounded drugs not containing at least one ingredient requiring a prescription order or refill
- over-the-counter drugs that do not require a prescription by federal or state law before being dispensed and any drug that is therapeutically equivalent to an over-the-counter drug
- injectable drugs except when (1) self-administered as defined by the plan and (2) injected subcutaneously or intramuscularly
- durable medical equipment, including prescribed and nonprescribed outpatient supplies, other than specifically covered diabetic supplies
- replacement of a lost, stolen, broken, or destroyed prescription order or refill
- general and injectable vitamins, except prenatal vitamins, vitamins with fluoride, and B-12 injections
- prescription smoking-cessation products
- unit-dose packaging of prescription drug products
- progesterone suppositories
- medications for cosmetic purposes only
- prescription infertility drugs
- contraceptive drugs
- sexual dysfunction drugs

Dental Services

Coverage for preventive, basic, and major dental services is available, usually with a separate calendar-year deductible, varying coinsurance benefit levels depending on the services, and a separate calendar-year maximum. Dental benefit plan features are also explained in chapter 6 under ancillary benefits.

Maternity Services

A separate maternity option may be provided under individual medical expense policies (subject to state law) to cover the expenses of normal pregnancy, including prenatal and postpartum care, childbirth, and routine nursery care. Complications of pregnancy and treatment of sickness or injury of the newborn are covered whether or not there is an optional benefit for normal maternity care.

Range of Available Benefits

Major medical policies offer a complete range of benefit provisions. Policies that have benefit provisions in the lower ranges of available aggregate maximums and coinsurance but have higher deductibles and out-of-pocket limits (and therefore higher out-of-pocket expenses for the insured) are considered lower-option plans. Policies that have higher lifetime maximums and coinsurance but have lower deductibles and out-of-pocket limits (and therefore lower out-of-pocket expenses for the insured) are considered higher-option plans. Thus, major medical expense insurance that provides either a comprehensive or core program of covered services may also provide either a high or a more limited level of plan benefits, based on the same structural elements.

Table 3-3 provides a representative list of benefit provisions and available options. Many of these alternatives are offered by the same insurance company and indeed are frequently available in various combinations within the same policy form. Many individual major medical benefit provisions are quite similar to those available in the group insurance market.

Example: George is insured under a major medical policy with the following benefit features:

- $2 million aggregate (lifetime) maximum
- $500 individual annual deductible
- 80 percent coinsurance above the deductible
- $2,000 annual out-of-pocket limit

He incurs $60,000 in total medical expenses for the year, but $2,500 of these expenses is not allowable because they exceed reasonable and customary charges.

TABLE 3-3
Major Medical Policies and the Range of Available Benefit Features

Benefit	Available Features
Aggregate (lifetime) maximum	$1 million to $8 million
Deductible per calendar year	Individuals: $250, $500, $1,000, $1,500, $2,500, $5,000, $7,500, $10,000
	Family: 2 or 3 individual deductibles
Coinsurance percentage*	50; 80
Out-of-pocket limit per calendar year**	Individuals: $1,000, $1,500, $2,000, $2,500, $5,000, $7,000
	Family: 2 or 3 times the individual level

*Policy pays 100 percent of allowable charges for covered services with deductibles of $5,000 or higher.

**The out-of-pocket limit must be $5,000 or higher if the 50 percent coinsurance option is selected.

If George has no other medical expenses during the yearly benefit period, the policy pays $55,000.

Incurred medical expenses	$60,000
minus disallowed charges	(2,500)
Allowable expenses	$57,500
minus deductible	(500)
Amount subject to coinsurance	$57,000
minus insured's 20% participation up to out-of-pocket limit	(2,000)
Benefit payment	$55,000

This payment also reduces the remaining aggregate maximum benefit by $55,000.

Note that the percentage participation normally would be calculated as 20 percent of the amount subject to coinsurance. However, this amount ($11,400) exceeds the policy's out-of-pocket limit ($2,000), so the latter is used. The effect of the out-of-pocket limit is that the benefit payment exceeds 80 percent of allowable expenses after the deductible.

George is responsible for $5,000 of the expenses that is not included in the benefit payment. These expenses consist of the nonallowable expenses ($2,500), the deductible ($500), and the out-of-pocket amount at the limit ($2,000), which the insurer may display in a benefit summary as follows.

	Benefit Payment	George's Payment
Disallowed charges	$ 0	$ 2,500
Deductible	$ 0	$ 500
Coinsurance applied to the next $10,000	$ 8,000	$ 2,000
Remaining allowable charges	$47,000	$ 0
Total	$55,000	$ 5,000

Exclusions

Major medical policies clearly state that only the services specifically identified in the policy are covered. Nevertheless, policies also typically list exclusions, with the following being among the more common:

- services furnished by or on behalf of government agencies, unless there is a requirement for the patient or the patient's medical expense plan to pay
- cosmetic surgery, unless such surgery is to correct a condition resulting from illness, accidental injury, or a congenital defect of a newborn child covered under the policy since birth
- custodial or rest care services
- eye refraction (testing to determine the degree of vision acuity), or the purchase or fitting of eyeglasses or hearing aids (exclusion eliminated if coverage is provided as an additional benefit)
- expenses either paid or eligible for payment under Medicare or other federal, state, or local government medical expense programs
- unnecessary, ineffective, experimental, or investigational medical treatment
- expenses resulting from suicide or war, declared or undeclared
- any expense that the insured is not required to pay
- occupational injuries or diseases to the extent that benefits are provided by workers' compensation laws or similar legislation

As mentioned earlier, there are also exclusions for any benefits that are not purchased because they are optional. However, any exclusion for dental care typically does not apply to (1) treatment required because of injury to natural teeth and (2) hospital and surgical charges associated with hospital confinement for dental surgery.

preexisting condition

Most major medical plans also contain an exclusion for preexisting conditions. A *preexisting condition* is defined as any condition, including illness or injury, not fully disclosed on the application that occurred within a specified time period prior to the effective date of the policy, and either (1) for which symptoms existed that would cause an ordinarily prudent person to seek diagnostic care or treatment, or (2) for which medical advice, treatment, or service was recommended by or received from a physician. Thus, a preexisting condition may exist without actual diagnosis or treatment having occurred prior to the effective date of the policy. However, benefits for preexisting conditions usually become payable subsequent to a specific period after the effective date of the policy, such as 12 months. A preexisting condition does not include known conditions revealed in the application or otherwise identified. An insurer may specifically exclude or limit coverage for such known health conditions as discussed in the subsequent section on riders.

As explained in chapter 5, the preexisting-conditions exclusion may not apply or have full effect because of the provisions of the Health Insurance Portability and Accountability Act (HIPAA).

Additional Insurance

Some individual medical expense policies provide opportunities to purchase additional types of insurance, such as supplemental accident, term life, and accidental death and dismemberment (AD&D).

Supplemental Accident Insurance

Individual policies frequently offer supplemental accident insurance as a first-dollar accident benefit option. This type of insurance provides a maximum benefit (available from $300 to as high as $5,000) without copayments or deductibles for the charges of covered services incurred as a result of injuries received in an accident. Some policies require that initial treatment be received within 72 hours of an accident or injury with claim expenses filed with the insurer within 90 days of the event. Other policies allow initial expenses to be incurred within 6 months of the accident, with subsequent expenses incurred within 1 year of the accident.

Term Life Insurance and Accidental Death and Dismemberment (AD&D) Insurance

Term life insurance and accidental death and dismemberment (AD&D) insurance are sometimes offered in conjunction with a medical policy. Term life insurance is a form of life insurance in which the death proceeds are payable if the insured dies during a specified period. However, nothing is paid if the insured survives to the end of the period. A dependent term life option is frequently extended to a spouse, a child aged 14 days to 19 years, or an older child if he or she is a full-time student. Benefits available to dependents are substantially lower than those available to the insured policyowner, however.

Accidental death and dismemberment insurance is a policy or rider to a policy that designates a dollar benefit or *principal amount* payable at the insured's accidental death. The benefit under term life and AD&D insurance may be as high as $300,000. In the case of AD&D insurance, payment of all or part of the principal amount is also made in the event of the accidental loss of a hand, foot, and/or eye, or at a degree of complete and irreversible paralysis of the limbs.

High-Deductible Major Medical Insurance

high-deductible major medical insurance

As discussed earlier, individual major medical policies offer high-deductible options. Policies with deductibles of $1,000 and more constitute traditional *high-deductible major medical insurance*. Historically, these policies have been purchased alone. However, they are now the focus of attention as the high-deductible health plan (HDHP) component of consumer-directed medical expense plans when they satisfy certain criteria and are established in conjunction with a tax-preferred savings account. Consumer-directed health insurance medical expense plans are covered in chapter 4. Catastrophic policies constitute a variation of high-deductible major medical insurance.

Traditional High-Deductible Policies

Traditional high-deductible policies are major medical plans that have at least a $1,000 annual deductible per person, although as mentioned previously, deductible amounts may reach as high as $10,000. The assumption with these policies is that there is no other underlying insurance plan and the selected deductible level represents an insured's affordable out-of-pocket payment before benefits begin.

These programs are very popular. As stated previously, the average deductible for most medical expense policies that are purchased is $2,000. The majority of policies, then, are high-deductible policies. The reason for this popularity is most likely the lower premium compared to low-deductible/high-option programs. For example, depending on the geographic area and the specific benefit package, the premium for a 35-year-old male may decrease by more than 30 percent if he selects a $1,000 deductible instead of a $250 deductible. Indeed, with catastrophic-level deductibles discussed below, such as $20,000 or more, the premium reduction could exceed 80 percent.

Critics argue that high-deductible plans are attractive to those who are healthy and do not anticipate needing health care (sort of a reverse adverse selection), leaving less healthy persons in the remaining eligibility pool for non-high-deductible individual coverage. In addition, those with high-deductible coverage tend to postpone routine expenses for diagnosis and treatment because they must be paid out of pocket. This procrastination can sometimes worsen their condition and thus drive their expenses beyond the deductible.

Catastrophic High-Deductible Policies

catastrophic high-deductible policies

There is a more limited market for *catastrophic high-deductible policies*, with individual and family deductibles ranging from $20,000 to $1 million per year and aggregate maximums up to several million dollars per person. Some policies permit the deductible to be satisfied over a 2- or 3-year period. In general, catastrophic plans operate as umbrella or excess major medical plans to fill gaps after an underlying principal plan reaches its maximum. However, an insured is not required to have an underlying plan to obtain this type of coverage. Some insureds also use catastrophic insurance as supplementary coverage when their HMO or PPO plans exclude or limit nonnetwork benefits.

Like most major medical insurance, catastrophic plans often contain internal limits on benefits for specific services, such as private-duty nursing and extended, home, and hospice care. Once a deductible is satisfied, benefits may continue for as long as 3 years without the insured having to satisfy a new deductible. Depending on the policy terms, the high-deductible amount may be satisfied by covered expenses paid out of pocket as well as those paid by an existing underlying plan, including Medicare. After the deductible has been met, catastrophic plans usually pay 100 percent of reasonable and customary charges for covered services but do not duplicate benefits paid by an underlying plan.

Example: Ian and Rhoda, both in their early 60s, are covered under a retiree medical plan of her former employer. The plan has a $250,000 lifetime maximum and numerous internal limits. Because a friend of theirs recently incurred medical expenses of about $500,000 as a result of a stroke, Ian and Rhoda have decided to purchase a catastrophic high-deductible policy. They have found one that has a $50,000 per person deductible and a $2 million lifetime limit. The premium for each of them is $300 per year.

MANAGED CARE

The growth of managed care plans over the last two decades has had a profound effect on medical expense insurance. While this growth has mostly influenced group medical plans, it has significantly affected individual medical expense insurance as well. Policies with varying elements of managed care are offered by many organizations and entities, including insurance companies, HMOs, Blue Cross–Blue Shield plans, physician groups, hospitals, labor unions, consumer groups, and private investors.

Managed Care Characteristics

Regardless of sponsorship, effective managed care plans have five distinguishing characteristics: controlled access to providers, risk sharing, utilization and quality management, preventive care, and high-quality care.

Controlled Access to Providers

It is difficult to control costs if plan members (the term commonly used for persons with managed care coverage, particularly from HMOs) have unrestricted access to physicians and hospitals. Through either direct employment of or contract with health care professionals, a managed care plan creates a participating provider network for the delivery of institutional, professional, and related health care services. Managed care plans channel their members to designated participating providers in order to obtain the benefits for covered services. Because a major portion of medical expenses results from referrals to specialists, managed care plans may use primary care physicians as gatekeepers to determine the necessity and appropriateness of specialty care. By limiting the number of providers and validating the need for services, managed care plans are better able to control costs through reduced utilization and favorable provider prices.

Risk Sharing

Managed care plans are most successful if providers share in the financial consequences of medical decisions. As part of their plan participation agreements, providers are given financial incentives and penalties to eliminate unnecessary utilization and expense through various

capitation

types of payment mechanisms, such as *capitation* (payment per member per month without regard to services rendered) and other arrangements to encourage cost-effective care. For example, physicians who stay within budgeted diagnostic test and referral patterns may receive a bonus. Such arrangements intend to eliminate only unnecessary services, not medically appropriate care.

Utilization and Quality Management

Successful managed care plans perform utilization review at all levels and conduct quality assurance programs. This involves reviewing a patient's medical condition to determine the type of treatment necessary, monitoring ongoing care, and evaluating the appropriateness and success of treatment after it has been given.

Preventive Care

HMOs encourage preventive care through routine physicals, targeted age- and gender-specific diagnostic screenings, and immunizations as well as the attainment of healthy lifestyles.

High-Quality Care

A managed care plan is not well received by or selected by participants if it is known for inferior or inconvenient medical care. Managed care plans strive to select health care providers carefully throughout the plan's service area. In addition, they monitor quality on a continuing basis using practice parameters and guidelines for medical care processes and outcomes. The majority of the nation's managed care organizations voluntarily seek accreditation and performance rating by recognized external bodies, such as the National Committee for Quality Assurance (NCQA), URAC (formerly the Utilization Review Accreditation Commission), and the Joint Commission on Accreditation of Healthcare Organizations (JCAHO).

Managed Care Elements in Major Medical Expense Insurance

Managed care elements have permeated individual products to such an extent that it is difficult to find a major medical policy that does not incorporate these elements or offer them as an option. Managed care elements in current major medical insurance take the form of provisions for treatment authorization, designated outpatient surgeries, case and disease management, selected benefit management, centers of excellence, preventive care, and preferred-provider organization arrangements.

Treatment Authorization

Treatment authorization or certification requires that all nonemergency hospital admissions, including those for inpatient surgery, undergo a review process to determine their medical necessity. Authorization is frequently required for emergencies within 24 to 48 hours after admission to the hospital. A determination of the required length of the proposed hospital stay is also made, although a physician may request a reevaluation of the number of hospital days certified.

Failure to comply with the required certification procedure may result in a denial of benefits, but more often reduces benefits through an additional deductible and/or a reduction in the coinsurance payment. Outpatient surgeries and courses of treatment may also be subject to an authorization process.

Designated Outpatient Surgeries

Certain surgical procedures are designated for performance on an outpatient basis. If such surgery is performed on an inpatient basis, benefits are reduced. The outpatient requirement is waived if the physician provides satisfactory evidence that confinement is medically necessary or that appropriate outpatient facilities are unavailable in the insured's geographic area, usually defined as 50 miles. Selected examples of designated outpatient surgeries are

- carpal tunnel repair
- cataract removal
- dilation and curettage (D&C)
- certain endoscopic procedures
- certain excisions
- eye muscle surgery
- hernia repair
- hemorrhoidectomy
- tonsillectomy

Case and Disease Management

case management

Case management, usually called large or catastrophic case management, focuses on the provision of health care to disproportionately high-cost patients. These patients are identified when first hospitalized, as in the case of trauma, or prior to hospitalization, as in the case of high-risk pregnancy or end-stage renal disease. The goal is to coordinate the care to improve continuity, quality, and outcomes and lower expenses through cost-effective resource utilization.

disease management

A logical extension of case management is the related function of *disease management,* which is a continuous program of care conducted across a broad range of settings affecting the course of chronic illnesses, such as emphysema, asthma, diabetes, and heart disease. Disease management includes the use of care guidelines by physicians and self-care education of patients. Some companies offer participation in self-care programs involving proper diet and exercise to reduce the potential for illness, such as cholesterol control, and the need for more invasive treatment, as in the case of heart disease. The goal of disease management is to eliminate or reduce the frequency and severity of critical episodes associated with a chronic illness, thereby reducing costs as well.

Selected Benefit Management

In order to control costs, some insurers carve out selected services covered under the major medical plan. Benefits are then provided by a managed care plan that specializes in those services, such as prescription drugs, rehabilitation programs, and mental health and/or substance abuse programs. Managing services with these plans often allows for more generous benefits through coordinated care and cost controls that emphasize outpatient treatment. In addition, this approach to benefits management has been successful in encouraging people to begin prescribed treatment and to finish treatment once it has started.

Centers of Excellence

centers of excellence

Specialized facilities may be placed under contract as designated centers for transplant surgeries, for example. Such specialized facilities are known as *centers of excellence.* If the facility is outside the insured's geographic area (more than 50 miles, for instance), travel (including emergency transport), lodging, and meal expenses incurred by the transplant patient and an accompanying family member would be covered, usually up to a specified limit (such as $10,000). While the same services may be received at a nondesignated facility, they may be subject to limitations, such as $100,000 per benefit treatment period.

Preventive Care

Major medical policies frequently highlight prevention benefits by providing each covered person with a routine physical exam and associated laboratory services. Additional regular examinations prompted by the insured's age and gender and by physician recommendation are often covered. Among these examinations are prostate exams, mammograms, Pap smears, and associated office visits. The prevention benefit often extends to childhood immunizations as well. Benefits for these services may be subject to the plan deductible and coinsurance or sometimes a flat dollar maximum benefit. Policies featuring participating provider network arrangements usually cover these same benefits subject only to a copayment if members use network providers.

Preferred-Provider Organization (PPO) Arrangements

preferred-provider organization (PPO)

Preferred-provider organization (PPO) arrangements represent the most extensive application of managed care elements to traditional major medical policies. They can be defined in general as the features of health benefit plans that make available to insureds an identified network of participating providers to obtain cost-effective medical services. The network is considered risk based if provider compensation is adjusted for the utilization of plan services by members. A network in which providers may receive discounted payments but no adjustment for the utilization of services is a nonrisk-based network.

PPO arrangements involve well-structured negotiated agreements that establish a network of participating providers available to insureds for all or almost all covered services. The network includes primary care physicians, specialty physicians, and hospitals. Radiology, laboratory, and physical therapy services are also available through network providers.

These arrangements produce advantages for the insurers, insureds, and providers; the savings from negotiated provider rates and utilization and quality management should allow the policy to compete effectively in the marketplace based on price and service.

Major medical plans with preferred-provider features can create powerful incentives to purchase this type of coverage and obtain care from network providers. Policies that offer preferred-provider features as an option sometimes encourage the insured to select them by doubling the aggregate (lifetime) maximum without additional premium. The major advantage of these arrangements to the insured is greater flexibility in the choice of providers than is allowed under a more restrictive HMO program. Services received from nonparticipating providers are still covered, albeit at a lower benefit. The insured may obtain primary and specialty physician or hospital care within the network without being locked into the same choices for future services. Although some referral requirements for specialists may exist under these arrangements, they are uncommon.

Under PPO network arrangements, providers typically bill the insurer directly, knowing the payment amount in advance with no disallowed charges—thereby also relieving the insured of the sometimes complicated claim-filing process. Providers anticipate increased patient volumes because the arrangement directs insureds to the providers by notifying insureds of the participants in the network and encouraging the use of these participants through a higher benefit. In addition, the network may be limited in size because the number of participating physicians is tailored to the size of the covered population. As a result, ensured patient volume levels may be incorporated into the provider reimbursement agreement.

Like major medical plans, covered services and benefit incentives are available in a broad array of alternatives. PPO arrangement alternatives are illustrated by the standard and copay models in table 3-4, whose features are frequently interchangeable.

Under the copay model, there is a different benefit structure for network and nonnetwork services. As table 3-4 illustrates, the network benefits are provided using nominal copayments by the insured for many services. For radiology and pathology services, there is no copayment because 100 percent of the expense is paid by the plan. As in the standard model example, routine/preventive care is usually covered only when received from a network provider. For the network services presented, there are no other payments by the insured for deductibles, coinsurance balances, or disallowed amounts. The nonnetwork benefits, on the other hand, follow a typical major medical plan structure and are less generous. Instead of a modest copayment, the insured must pay a deductible and a 30 percent payment in most cases. In many cases, the coinsurance benefit for nonnetwork providers may be determined as a percentage of the charges paid to network providers and therefore would likely be even less generous than traditional reasonable and customary charge levels would allow. For example, if an insured's incurred charge of $1,000 for non-network services is fully allowable as a reasonable and customary benefit, the insured's payment at 30 percent would be $300. However, if the negotiated charge for the same services from a network provider is $800, then the nonnet-work benefit at 70 percent is $560, leaving the insured with a payment of $440.

Under the standard model, the typical major medical benefit structure is used for both network and nonnetwork services. The incentive to use network providers is created by making the insured's payment (after deductible and coinsurance benefit) appreciably lower for services received from network providers compared to the payment applicable to services received from nonnetwork providers. Table 3-4 illustrates a much larger payment by insureds if they use nonnetwork services. In addition, some services, such as routine/preventive care, are often covered only when rendered by network providers. Although the network provider services remain subject to the insured's payment of the deductible and coinsurance balance percentage, there are no disallowed charges because of the negotiated agreement on the price of services. However, some programs may eliminate the deductible for network services. This model also frequently

TABLE 3-4
Payments by Insureds for Selected Covered Services under Alternative Formal PPO Arrangement Models

Covered Services	Payment by Insureds under Copay Model		Payment by Insureds under Standard Model	
	Network[a]	Nonnetwork (after deductible and coinsurance)[b]	Network (after deductible and coinsurance)[c]	Nonnetwork (after deductible and coinsurance)[d]
Inpatient hospital and surgical facility	$500 copay	30%	10%	40%
Physicians' visits (office or hospital)	$20 copay	30%	10%	40%
Radiology and pathology services	$0	30%	10%	40%
Routine preventive care	$20 copay	Not covered	10%	Not covered
Emergency room[e]	$50 copay	40%	10%	40%
Prescription drugs	$10 copay (generic)	20% (generic)	10% (generic)	30% (generic)
	$25 copay (brand name, preferred)	30% (brand name, preferred)	20% (brand name, preferred)	40% (brand name, preferred)
	$40 copay (brand name, nonpreferred)	40% (brand name, nonpreferred)	30% (brand name, nonpreferred)	50% (brand name, preferred)

a. Insured's payments for network services are not subject to any deductible or disallowances above maximum allowable amounts. However, these payments do not contribute to the satisfaction of the separate nonnetwork deductible or out-of-pocket limit.
b. The coinsurance benefit percentage paid to nonnetwork providers is based on the rates negotiated with network providers. Insured is responsible for any amount above those levels in addition to the out-of-pocket percentage payment indicated.
c. Insured's payments for network services are not subject to disallowances above maximum allowable amounts. Indicated payments apply to a separate network out-of-pocket limit.
d. Insured is also responsible for any amounts disallowed as exceeding reasonable and customary limits. Indicated payments apply to a separate nonnetwork out-of-pocket limit.
e. Paid as an inpatient hospital expense if insured is admitted.

establishes a separate deductible and out-of-pocket limit for network services and nonnetwork services to encourage the insured to continue to use network providers after the network deductible and out-of-pocket limit is satisfied and the policy benefit increases to 100 percent. Otherwise, after expenses exceed a single deductible and out-of-pocket limit, the insured would have a 100 percent benefit for nonnetwork services as well.

three-tier copayment or deductible structure

More recently, a few managed health care plans have implemented a *three-tier copayment or deductible structure* for network services. Under such a structure, members pay one of three copayment or deductible amounts for services, especially hospital services, depending on their selection of a network provider and the cost to the plan for using that provider.

Health Maintenance Organizations

The most fully developed and integrated managed care structure is the health maintenance organization.

health maintenance organization (HMO)

Health maintenance organizations (HMOs) are generally regarded as organized systems of health care that provide a comprehensive array of medical services on a prepaid basis to voluntarily enrolled persons living within a specified geographic region. HMOs act like insurance companies and the Blues in that they finance health care. Unlike insurance companies and the Blues, however, they also deliver medical services. HMOs can be either for-profit or not-for-profit organizations. They may be sponsored or owned by insurance companies, the Blues, consumer groups, physicians, hospitals, labor unions, or private investors.

HMOs are unique among managed care plans in several ways. First, HMOs provide for the delivery of medical services, which in some cases are performed by salaried physicians and other personnel employed by the HMO. Although this approach is in contrast to the usual fee-for-service delivery system of medical care, HMOs frequently contract with providers on a fee-for-service basis. Unlike PPOs and traditional major medical plans, HMOs often have unlimited lifetime benefit maximums.

Second, members are required to obtain their care from providers of medical services who are affiliated with the HMO. Because HMOs may operate in a geographic region no larger than a single metropolitan area, this requirement may result in limited coverage for members if treatment is received elsewhere. Most HMOs do have out-of-area coverage but only in the case of medical emergencies.

Third, HMOs emphasize coordinated care through the use of primary care physicians and specialists. Primary care physicians fulfill a gatekeeper function and historically have controlled access to specialists. The traditional HMO covers benefits provided by a specialist only if the primary care physician recommends the specialist, who may be a fellow employee in a group-practice plan or a physician who has a contract with the HMO. The member may have little or no choice regarding the specialist selected, which has been one of the more controversial aspects of HMOs and one that has discouraged larger enrollment. In response to consumer concerns, many HMOs now make the process of seeing a specialist easier. Referrals can often be made by nurses in physicians' offices or by HMO staff members whom members can contact by telephone. Some HMOs, referred to as direct-access or self-referral HMOs, allow members to see network specialists without going through a gatekeeper. However, the specialist may have to contact the HMO for authorization before proceeding with tests or treatment.

The popularity of flexible preferred-provider arrangements has encouraged many HMOs to loosen strict exclusive-provider restrictions and specialist referral requirements to allow members to obtain covered services outside the network with additional out-of-pocket payments. This approach, known as a *point-of-service (POS) option*, would approximate the copay model for network and nonnetwork services in table 3-4.

point-of-service (POS) option

Table 3-5 shows an example of HMO benefits and required member copayments.

TABLE 3-5
Selected HMO Covered Services and Member Copayment

Covered Services	Member Copayment
Hospital inpatient services (includes all room and board and other inpatient services as well as physician and specialist services)	$500 per admission
Outpatient services (includes physician and specialist visits and consultations as well as routine examinations, tests, and immunizations)	$20 per visit; waived for covered children up to age 3
Diagnostic testing and X rays	$0
Outpatient surgical procedures (includes facility charges for services, tests, drugs, and supplies)	$50
Urgent care services outside the service area	$20 per visit limited to a $500 maximum per year for continuing/follow-up care
Extended care in a skilled-nursing facility	$0 for up to 100 days per year following hospitalization
Home health and hospice service	$25 per day
Mental health services Inpatient Outpatient	 $500 per admission $25 per individual visit after 3 visits; $45 per individual visit after 11 visits

A COMPARISON

Table 3-6 compares the major types of principal medical expense policies.

TABLE 3-6
Comparison of Health Insurance Plans

	Traditional Major Medical Insurance	PPOs	HMOs
Provider choice	Unlimited	Unlimited in network, but benefits are greater if network provider is used	Network of providers must be used; care from non-network providers covered only in emergencies
Required use of gatekeeper	None	None	Used for access to specialists
Out-of-pocket costs	Deductibles and percentage participation	Deductibles and percentage participation, which are lower if network providers are used; may have small copayment for network services	Small copayments for some services
Utilization review	Traditionally little, but several techniques are likely to be used now	More than traditional plans, but less than HMOs; network provider may be subject to some controls	Highest degree of review, including financial incentives and disincentives for providers
Preventive care	Little covered other than that required by law	Usually, more coverage than traditional major medical plan but less coverage than HMOs and POS plans	Covered
Responsibility for filing claims	Covered person	Plan provider for network services; the covered person for nonnetwork services	Plan providers

Determining which type of policy is best for a particular person involves a consideration of several factors:

- How comprehensive are benefits?
- To what degree is the person willing to accept limitations on the choice of providers?
- Are an adequate number of primary and specialty providers available?

- To what degree is the individual willing to have his or her medical care managed?
- How much is the person willing to spend on premiums?
- What is the cost of coverage? If all other factors are the same, premiums are lower with higher degrees of managed care.
- Has the person previously been covered by a managed care plan, and what has been his or her experience with managed care?
- How convenient is access to health care services?
- Can the person afford to pay the required deductibles and copayments in case of large medical expenses? High degrees of managed care are often accompanied by lower and fewer deductibles and copayments.
- How does the person feel about keeping receipts and filing claims?

NOTES

1. The policyowner is the buyer of the insurance and is often the insured, although he or she may purchase coverage for another person only, such as a child. Under family policies, the policyowner is the insured along with other covered family members, such as a spouse and/or a child or children.
2. *Individual Health Insurance: A Comprehensive Survey of Affordability, Access, and Benefits*, America's Health Insurance Plans, August 2005.
3. Ibid.
4. Ibid.
5. Ibid.

Consumer-Directed Health Insurance Plans for Older Clients

Chapter Outline

The last few years have seen considerable interest in the concept of consumer-directed health insurance. Consumer-directed health plans promise to restore personal financial incentives to restrain spending for health care services while maintaining broad benefits and freedom of choice. These plans attempt to restructure health care benefit programs in a way that gives plan members a strong reason to use health care services with the same prudence and economy they would use when paying any expense with their own money.

INTRODUCTION

**consumer-directed
health plan**

A *consumer-directed health plan* commonly features a high-deductible health (medical expense) plan (HDHP) and an annual deposit of funds to a tax-favored savings account for the payment of health care expenses unreimbursed by the plan. There are few limits on provider choice, although many HDHPs incorporate a PPO network.

Employers establish most consumer-directed health plans. Employees may benefit from these plans after retirement. In some cases, for example, with respect to a health savings account, persons without a relationship to employment, including early retirees, can establish a consumer-directed health plan.

When employers establish an HDHP, the employer and/or employee then also contributes to some type of savings account from which the employee can make withdrawals to pay medical expenses that are not covered because of the HDHP's deductible. These funds are often withdrawn with an electronic payment card (such as a debit card), which has a dollar limit equal to the available savings account balance. The employee can carry forward any unused amount in the account and add it to the next year's contribution. Such a plan gives the employee an immediate incentive to purchase medical care wisely because, if the amount in the account is exceeded, the employee will have to pay the full cost of medical expenses out of his or her own pocket until the plan's high deductible is satisfied. The plan often incorporates a preferred-provider network of health care professionals. As long as an employee receives medical treatment within the network, any charges that the employee must pay because of the deductible are limited to the amount negotiated with the preferred provider.

Employers might use this approach for all employees, but most employers make it available as an option to a more traditional medical expense plan. In addition, because of the newness of the approach to providing medical expense coverage, some employers have limited these plans to a select group of employees on a trial basis.

The rationale for using a high-deductible medical expense plan along with a savings account is that significant cost savings can occur for two primary reasons. First, the expense of administering and paying small claims is largely eliminated, as demonstrated by the fact that a major medical policy with a $2,500 deductible can often be purchased for about one-half the cost of a policy with a $250 deductible. Second, employees now have a direct financial incentive to avoid unnecessary care and to seek out the most cost-effective form of treatment.

A very small number of employers have used this approach for some time with positive results. Costs have been lowered or have risen less rapidly than would otherwise be expected. Reactions of employees have generally been favorable, but until federal legislation in 1996 there was one major drawback—employer contributions to most types of savings accounts constituted taxable income to employees.

As with almost any approach to cost containment, this type of medical expense plan has its critics. It is argued that employees will minimize treatment for minor medical expenses and preventive care that would have been covered under a plan without a high deductible. Critics contend that this avoidance of medical care may lead to major expenses that could have been averted or minimized with earlier treatment. However, some types of consumer-directed medical expense plans pay benefits for preventive care without regard to the deductible. Another criticism is that a high-deductible plan tends to favor healthy individuals and those in high income tax brackets. A final criticism is that this type of medical expense plan does not focus on the problem of the uninsured. In rebuttal to this criticism, proponents argue that any technique that lowers costs for employers will ultimately benefit everyone and encourage small employers to provide coverage that would have previously been unaffordable.

Consumer-directed medical expense plans using the savings-account approach may be designed so that employer decisions about specific benefit plans are eliminated, or at least minimized. Some employers view this as a way of minimizing their legal exposure for health care decisions because a certain level of responsibility is transferred back to employees and health care providers. Under such a plan, an employee can use an employer contribution (along with any additionally needed employee contribution) to shop at some type of "health care supermarket," where many different types of medical expense plans are available. These plans are often required to provide detailed information about their operations so that consumers can make more informed decisions in selecting a medical expense plan. An insurer or some type of Internet provider may offer these plans, and the employer may or may not be involved in the selection of the supermarket that an employee uses. Most consumer-directed medical expense plans that use the savings-account approach, however, only make a single medical expense plan available to employees.

There are still legal, regulatory, and tax issues that need to be addressed for some types of consumer-directed medical expense plans that use savings plans. Whether employers and individuals will embrace these newer types of plans on a large scale is still open to conjecture. So far there seems to be more interest in the approach than in its implementation, but that is often the way with new concepts. It took many years for managed care plans to be widely used, even with legislative encouragement. However, significant growth in health reimbursement arrangements and health savings accounts has taken place recently.

The remainder of this chapter is devoted to four tax-favored approaches that use savings accounts:

- health reimbursement arrangements
- flexible spending accounts
- health savings accounts
- Archer medical savings accounts

The first two approaches must be established by employers for their employees, and the benefits to retirees are relatively small and short-term. Health savings accounts are typically established by employers or individuals during their working years and may have significant benefits and use after retirement. However, health savings accounts may also be established after retirement by individuals who are not yet enrolled in Medicare. New Archer medical savings accounts can no longer be established, but some retiring employees may still have them.

HEALTH REIMBURSEMENT ARRANGEMENTS

health reimbursement arrangements (HRAs)

Some employers provide their employees with high-deductible medical expense plans and create a savings account for each covered employee under which he or she can obtain reimbursement for certain medical expenses that are not covered under a high-deductible plan. However, there was uncertainty about the tax treatment of such reimbursements, particularly if account balances were carried over to subsequent plan years. This uncertainty was settled in 2002 when the IRS issued a ruling that specifically allowed such tax-favored *health reimbursement arrangements (HRAs)* as long as specified criteria were satisfied. HRAs are the dominant form of consumer-directed health plans. By 2005, over 2 1/2 million people were covered by such plans, nearly five times the enrollment in 2003.[1]

Normally, a person anticipating retirement who has funds in an employer's HRA should anticipate the termination of that account when active employment ends. Under certain circumstances, however, these funds may play a role in a retiree's medical expense benefit planning. First, HRAs are treated as group health plans subject to COBRA. If a terminating employee elects this option, he or she has access to the unused balance in the HRA during the COBRA continuation period. Second, an employer can (but is not required to) allow a terminated employee to spend down an HRA balance for unreimbursed medical expenses incurred after termination of employment. Indeed, the employer may set up the HRA so that the funds are dedicated in whole or in part for use in an employee's retirement years.

Example:	Ned's employer provides each employee with a high-deductible health insurance plan that has a $2,500 annual deductible for each employee and covered dependent. The deductible does not apply to certain preventive services. There is no cost to Ned for his coverage, but he must pay 50 percent of the cost for his wife.
	In addition, Ned's employer contributes $2,000 at the beginning of each year to an HRA for unreimbursed medical expense incurred by either Ned or his wife.
	The unused balance in the HRA carries over from year to year. After retirement, the employer allows Ned to use these funds to pay any unreimbursed medical expense, which would include premiums for Medicare or Medicare supplement policies.

Requirements for Health Insurance Plans

Although HRAs are almost always used with high-deductible insurance plans, there is no requirement for the size of the deductible. In fact, a plan with any size deductible can be used. The deductible can also be waived for certain services, including prescription drugs and preventive services, such as physical exams, immunizations, and mammograms.

Eligibility

HRAs can be established by any size employer for its employees, but they cannot be established by or for self-employed persons.

Contributions

Contributions to an HRA must be made solely by the employer. However, employees may be required to pay part of the underlying medical expense coverage. Some employers make a single annual HRA contribution to each employee's account. Other employers make contributions that are spread throughout the year, such as each pay period.

There is no requirement that contributions be made to a trust or custodial account. In fact, HRAs are typically unfunded, and the employer contributions are merely credits to a savings account. Reimbursements are then paid from the employer's current revenue, at which time the employer receives an income tax deduction.

Contributions in an employee's account can be carried over to subsequent years to the extent they have not been withdrawn to reimburse eligible medical expenses.

Distributions

Under IRS rules, employees can take tax-free distributions from an HRA as reimbursement only for medical expenses that are not paid by any other medical expense plan. The medical expenses may be for the employee, his or her spouse, or any other persons who are dependents for tax purposes. The reimbursements may be for any medical expenses that would be deductible, ignoring the 7.5 percent of adjusted gross income limitation, if the employee itemized his or her income tax deductions. Tax-free withdrawals therefore are permitted for the purchase of COBRA continuation coverage, Medicare premiums, and Medicare supplement policies. They are also permitted for the purchase of long-term care insurance up to the deductible limits shown in table 13-1 of chapter 13. (Note that withdrawals for Medicare premiums are not used to directly pay such premiums. Rather they are reimbursement for Medicare premiums that are automatically deducted from an individual's Social Security checks.)

Despite the broadness of the IRS rules, an employer can design an HRA to reimburse only specific types of medical expenses. For example, an HRA might provide reimbursement for copayments, percentage participation, deductibles, and expenses that are not covered by the employer's medical expense plan. Reimbursements for required employee premiums for the medical expense coverage are generally not allowed.

HRAs that are unfunded (as is usually the case) are treated as self-funded medical reimbursement plans and are subject to the nondiscrimination rules applicable to such plans. Therefore, if HRAs are set up on a discriminatory basis, highly compensated employees may be taxed on all or a portion of any benefits they receive.

Effect of Retirement

At retirement or other termination of employment, an employee's HRA usually terminates, and the employee cannot receive any further taxable or nontaxable benefit from the account. However, the employer can (but is not required to) allow a terminated employee to spend down an HRA balance for unreimbursed medical expenses incurred after termination of employment.

HRAs are treated as group health plans and generally subject to COBRA requirements (see chapter 2). If any employee elects this option, he or she has access to unused balances in the HRA account during the COBRA continuation period. In addition, the employer must continue to make HRA contributions as long as the HRA remains in effect. The COBRA cost must be determined by actuarial calculations based on aggregate HRA experience. As a result, the COBRA charge to the employee will typically be less than the employer's contribution because some HRA balances are never used by employees and ultimately forfeited.

Example:

When Martha retired at age 63, she elected to continue her high-deductible health insurance plan under COBRA until she qualifies for Medicare in 18 months. She also had a balance of $2,692 in her HRA, which her employer had been funding at $100 per month. She can also elect to continue the HRA, which would have otherwise terminated, under COBRA. Her employer, using actuarial calculations, determined that the COBRA cost was $90 per month. Over the next 18 months, Martha will pay a total COBRA premium for the HRA coverage of 18 x $90, or $1,620. However, her employer must still contribute $100 per month, or $1,800, during this period. Together with her balance at termination of employment, Martha will have an HRA balance of $4,492 available to her during the next 18 months.

As long as Martha expects to have at least $1,620 in unreimbursed medical expenses over the next 18 months, the COBRA continuation for the HRA is a prudent financial decision.

FLEXIBLE SPENDING ACCOUNTS UNDER CAFETERIA PLANS

flexible spending account (FSA)

cafeteria plan

A discussion about consumer-directed health plans is not complete without a description of flexible spending accounts even though they are seldom available to individuals after retirement. A *flexible spending account (FSA)* allows employees to make annual elections to set aside funds for unreimbursed medical (including dental) expenses by electing a salary reduction. FSAs are a type of cafeteria plan that became popular in the 1980s and are commonly used today. In the broadest sense, a *cafeteria plan* permits employees to design their own benefit packages by purchasing benefits with a prescribed amount of employer dollars. Cafeteria plans are often referred to as *flexible benefit plans* or *Sec. 125 plans.* Sec. 125 of the Internal Revenue Code permits cafeteria plans to exist and grants them certain favorable tax treatment.

Cafeteria plans can take several forms; the following is an example of a very broad plan with significant employee choices.

Example:	Under the cafeteria plan of the Alpha Corporation, all employees receive a minimum level of benefits, called *basic benefits,* as follows:

- term life insurance equal to one-half of salary
- travel accident insurance (when on the employer's business)
- disability income insurance
- 2 to 4 weeks' vacation

Employees are also given *flexible credits,* equal to between 3 and 6 percent of salary (depending on length of service, with the maximum reached after 10 years), which can be used to purchase additional or "optional" benefits. There is a new election of benefits each year, and no carryover of any unused credits is allowed. The optional benefits are the following:

- an array of medical expense options. Although there is no charge for HMO coverage, a charge is made for coverage under a traditional PPO plan. However, additional flexible credits are given if a person elects no medical expense coverage or elects a high-deductible health plan.
- additional life insurance, up to 4 1/2 times salary, subject to a maximum of $500,000
- accidental death insurance when the basic travel accident insurance does not apply
- dental insurance for the employee and dependents
- up to 2 weeks' additional vacation time
- cash

If an employee does not have enough flexible credits to purchase the desired optional benefits, the employee may contribute additional amounts on a payroll-deduction basis for all the noncash options except more vacation time. In addition, a salary reduction may be elected for contributions to an FSA that provides benefits for unreimbursed medical expenses and/or dependent-care-assistance benefits. (The nature of these salary reductions is described below.)

Under some cafeteria plans, employees are allowed to allocate only a predetermined employer contribution for benefits. Other cafeteria plans are designed so that employees can obtain additional benefits by taking optional payroll deductions or salary reductions.

Many cafeteria plans that provide a wide array of benefits allow an employee to elect an after-tax payroll deduction to obtain additional benefits. For example, under a cafeteria plan an employee might be given $300 per month with which to select varying types and levels of benefits. If the benefits the employee chooses cost $340, the employee has two options—either to decrease the benefits selected or to authorize a $40 payroll deduction. Even though the payroll deduction is on an after-tax basis, the employee gains to the extent that the additional benefits are selected at a lower cost through a group arrangement than in the individual marketplace.

Sec. 125 also allows employees to purchase certain benefits on a before-tax basis through the use of a premium-conversion plan or an FSA. Premium-conversion plans or FSAs, both of which are technically cafeteria plans, can be used by themselves or incorporated into a more comprehensive cafeteria plan. They are frequently used alone by small employers who are unwilling to establish a broader plan, primarily for cost reasons. The cafeteria plans of most large employers contain one or both of these arrangements as an integral part of their benefit plan, similar to the plan shown in the previous example.

premium-conversion plan

A *premium-conversion plan* (also called a premium-only plan, or POP) allows an employee to elect a before-tax salary reduction to pay his or her premium contribution to any employer-sponsored medical expense plan. For example, an employer might provide medical expense coverage to employees at no cost but make a monthly charge for dependent coverage. Under a premium-conversion plan, the employee can pay for the dependent coverage with a before-tax salary reduction.

Nature of FSAs

An FSA allows an employee to fund certain benefits on a before-tax basis by electing to take a salary reduction, which can then be used to fund the cost of an FSA. However, FSAs in practice are used almost exclusively for medical expenses not covered by the employer's plan and for dependent-care expenses. Although the following discussion focuses on health FSAs, seniors may incur day care expenses for disabled adult children or parents. As long as these persons qualify as tax dependents of a senior who still is employed, a dependent care FSA may be a way to lower income taxes.

A health FSA under Sec. 125 includes benefits for both medical and dental expenses. The amount of any salary reduction is, in effect, credited to an employee's reimbursement account, and benefits are paid from this account when an employee properly files for such reimbursement. Reimbursements are typically made on a monthly basis. The amount of the salary reduction must be determined prior to the beginning of the plan year. Once the amount is set, changes are allowed only under certain specified circumstances. A separate election must be made for each benefit (i.e., health versus dependent care), and the funds are accounted for separately. Monies from a salary reduction for one type of expense (such as medical and dental bills) cannot be used as reimbursement for another type of expense (such as dependent care).

The next example is of a salary-reduction-only cafeteria plan, which consists solely of the two types of salary reductions that can be used in a cafeteria plan: a premium-conversion option and an FSA.

Example: Beta Foundation is a small nonprofit organization's plan. Employees are allowed to elect salary reductions for each of the following:

- the employee's share of the cost of medical and dental insurance premiums for dependents under a premium-conversion plan. (Under this plan, the employer pays the full cost of the employee's coverage for a high-deductible health plan.)

- qualifying medical care expenses under a health FSA. These are any medical and dental expenses normally deductible on an employee's federal income tax return (without regard to any gross income limitations). Note that these deductible expenses must not have been reimbursed by insurance.

- eligible dependent-care expenses under a dependent care FSA. These are expenses for the types of benefits that could be provided in a qualified dependent-care-assistance program.

Requirements for Health Insurance Plans

There is no requirement that an FSA be used with a high-deductible health plan. An FSA can be used with any type of health plan to fund unreimbursed medical expenses.

It is important to point out that FSAs have been used for a much longer time than high-deductible health plans have been in vogue. An FSA is merely a vehicle through which an employee can receive favorable tax treatment for medical expenses. Many employers establishing consumer-directed health plans today are likely to use HRAs and HSAs.

Eligibility

FSAs can only be established by employers for their employees. There are nondiscrimination rules that apply to cafeteria plans, and they must be properly designed to avoid adverse tax consequences for key employees and/or highly compensated employees. Generally, a plan must be designed so that neither contributions or benefits are discriminatory in favor of these classes of employees.

Contributions

Contributions to an FSA are typically made only by employees on a before-tax basis in the form of a salary reduction. However, an employer can also make contributions without increasing an employee's income. To satisfy nondiscrimination rules, the contribution is often limited to a maximum dollar amount, such as $4,000 or $5,000.

Note that the amount of salary reductions are actually funds of the employer. In effect, the employee is electing to have an insurance benefit rather than income. Most employers do not fund FSA balances. As with HRAs, FSA amounts are merely credits to an account that will pay benefits from an employer's general assets.

Distributions

Employees can take tax-free distributions from a health FSA for medical expenses that are not paid by any other medical expense plan. Like an HRA the medical expenses may be for an employee, his or her spouse, and any other persons who are dependents for tax purposes. Tax-free withdrawals, however, are not permitted to pay for health insurance premiums, including long-term care insurance.

If the monies in an FSA are not fully used during a plan year (or up to 2 1/2 months after the plan year if allowed by the employer), the remaining account balance is forfeited. Thus, there is no carryover to the following year's account. As a result, employees need to plan their FSA deduction wisely.

An employee must be allowed to withdraw the full annual balance of a health FSA even if that amount has not yet been funded.

Example:	Martina contributes $200 per month to an FSA. During the first 2 months of the plan year, her salary is reduced by $400. If she incurs $3,000 in unreimbursed medical expenses at that time, she can received the entire balance of $2,400 that would be credited to her account during the plan year. As long as she remains employed, she must, however, continue to pay $200 into the account for the remainder of the year but can receive no further distributions. Note that if she terminates employment during the plan year before these amounts are paid, she has no further obligations for funding the account or returning any of the $2,400.

Effect of Retirement

At termination of employment, including retirement, an FSA usually ceases to exist. If the employer is subject to COBRA, however, COBRA coverage needs to be offered for the remainder of the plan year if the maximum benefit available for that period exceeds the amount that could be charged for COBRA coverage during the remainder of the plan year.

Example:	Assume that an employee contributes $100 per month to a health FSA. If the employee terminates employment after 6 months, the potential FSA premium for the remainder of the plan year is $612 (that is, $100 per month for 6 months plus the 2 percent administrative fee). If the employee has incurred less than $588 (and therefore could still receive more than $612) in FSA benefits during the 6 months of employment in the plan year, COBRA continuation must be offered.

HEALTH SAVINGS ACCOUNTS

health savings accounts (HSAs)

In addition to providing prescription drug coverage for older Americans, the Medicare Prescription Drug, Improvement, and Modernization Act established *health savings accounts (HSAs)*. HSAs are designed to be successors to Archer

MSAs, which are discussed later, and the two have many features in common. However, they also have some notable differences that make HSAs more attractive than Archer MSAs and available to a much larger pool of consumers.

HSAs were allowed as early as 2004. While there is considerable interest in these products among health insurers, their development is proceeding cautiously. Employers, who are expected to take the lead in establishing these new arrangements, are evaluating how HSAs fit into their health benefit programs. Moreover, because employer plans are often on a calendar-year basis, 2005 was the earliest that many employers could establish medical expense plans that incorporate HSAs. Various estimates of the number of HSAs established by mid 2005 vary from 500,000 to 1,000,000.

HSAs raise a number of specific issues about their development and use. The Treasury Department continues to issue clarifications, known as "guidance," to address these issues. Because of this, readers should be aware of changing developments. Updated and detailed information from the Treasury Department is available from the government's Web site at www.treas.gov/offices/public-affairs/hsa.

General Nature

An HSA is a personal savings account from which unreimbursed medical expenses, including deductibles, percentage participation, and copayments, can be paid. The HSA must be in the form of a tax-exempt trust or custodial account established in conjunction with a high-deductible health (medical expense) plan. An HSA is established with a qualified trustee or custodian in much the same way that an IRA is established. Any insurance company or bank (as well as certain other financial institutions) can be a trustee or custodian, as can any other person or entity already approved by the IRS as a trustee or custodian for IRAs.

HSAs are individual trusts, which prohibits a husband and wife from having a joint HSA. But as long as both are eligible, each may have a separate HSA.

Some insurers that sell HDHPs for use with HSAs also market the HSA accounts; other insurers leave it to the purchasers of an HDHP to establish their HSAs with other institutions.

Even though employers can sponsor HSAs, these accounts are established for the benefit of individuals and are portable. If an employee changes employers or leaves the workforce, the HSA, including the balance in the account, remains with the individual.

Eligibility

HSAs can be established by employees, the self-employed, and anyone else who meets the following rules for qualification:

- The individual must be covered by a high-deductible health plan. That plan may be insured or self-insured if offered by an employer as long as it meets the criteria for a qualifying high-deductible plan.
- The individual is not eligible to be claimed as a dependent on another person's federal income tax return.
- With some exceptions, a person who is covered under an HDHP is denied eligibility for an HSA if he or she is covered under another health plan that does not meet the definition of a high-deductible plan but that provides any benefits that are covered under the HDHP. The exceptions include coverage for accident, disability, dental care, vision care, and long-term care as well as liability insurance, insurance for a specified disease or illness, and insurance paying a fixed amount per period of hospitalization.

Generally, an individual covered by Medicare (by attaining age 65 or disability) or receiving Veterans Administration benefits is considered as having another health plan and, therefore, may not establish an HSA or continue contributing to an existing HSA. Nevertheless, an individual who is (1) eligible for Medicare but not enrolled or (2) eligible to receive medical benefits through the Veterans Administration but not receiving them may contribute to an HSA. However, individuals covered by TRICARE (the insurance program for members of the uniformed services) are not eligible.

An employer can establish HSAs for its employees, or an individual (whether employed or not) may establish his or her own HSA.

High-Deductible Health Plan

For purposes of HSA participation, a high-deductible health plan is defined as having the following deductibles and annual out-of-pocket limitations for covered services. These figures are for 2006 and subject to annual inflation adjustments:

- In the case of individual coverage, the deductible must be at least $1,050, and annual out-of-pocket expenses cannot exceed $5,250.
- In the case of family coverage, the deductible must be at least $2,100, and annual out-of-pocket expenses cannot exceed $10,500.

If these high-deductible plans use preferred-provider networks, they can have higher out-of-pocket limits for services provided outside the network, and any deductibles for nonnetwork services are not taken into account when determining the out-of-pocket limits specified above.

One point should be emphasized about the deductible for family coverage. It is not a family deductible as was described in the discussion on major medical insurance. In that situation, there is an individual deductible that applies to each family member as well as a separate deductible for the family. This is sometimes referred to as a stacked deductible, and policy benefits are paid for any family member once his or her deductible is satisfied, even if the family deductible has not been met.

In the case of a high-deductible policy used with an HSA, there will usually not be an individual deductible if a policy is written for a family. Rather, there will be a single deductible—referred to as a common deductible—that must be satisfied before any benefits are payable, even if all claims are for one family member. It is permissible, however, to use a stacked deductible, but only if the individual deductible is equal to at least the required HSA family deductible of $2,100. For example, a policy with an individual deductible of $2,500 and a family deductible of $5,000 would be acceptable.

The following incurred expenses do not count toward the plan's required deductible and out-of-pocket limit:

- payments for services not covered by the high-deductible health plan
- payments for services received from nonnetwork health care providers, if the plan uses a preferred-provider network
- amounts above a plan's reasonable specific service or lifetime maximums
- amounts in excess of reasonable and customary fees
- penalties for failure to obtain a plan-required certification

Nevertheless, copayments count toward the out-of-pocket limit, even if the plan does not consider copayments as contributing toward the satisfaction of the deductible.

Preventive Care

Generally, an HDHP established in conjunction with an HSA cannot provide benefits before the deductible is satisfied, but there is an exception for benefits for preventive care. An HDHP may provide benefits for the following preventive care services before the insured satisfies the plan's required high deductible:

- annual physicals, immunizations, and screening services
- routine prenatal and well-child care
- tobacco cessation programs and obesity weight-loss programs
- employee assistance, disease management, or wellness programs
- treatment of a related condition that is incidental or ancillary to a preventive care service or screening, such as removal of polyps during a diagnostic colonoscopy

- drugs or medications taken by a person who has developed risk factors for a disease before the disease manifests itself or to prevent the reoccurrence of a disease from which the person has recovered. An example is the drug treatment of high cholesterol to prevent heart disease, or the treatment of recovered heart attack or stroke victims with medications to prevent a recurrence. Other prescription drugs that do not qualify under this exception remain subject to the plan's high deductible.

Preventive care generally does not include treatment of existing conditions.

Contributions

Contributions to an HSA for a self-employed or unemployed individual are made directly by that person. For an employed person, contributions can be made by the employer, the employee, or a combination of the two. Family members may also make contributions to an HSA on behalf of other family members. Contributions to the HSA can also be made under a cafeteria plan. Contributions must be in the form of cash.

Contributions by an individual are deductible for federal income tax purposes even if the individual does not itemize deductions. Contributions by an employer are tax deductible to the employer and are not included in an employee's gross income or subject to Social Security, Medicare, and other employment taxes.

An employer that makes contributions to HSAs is subject to a nondiscrimination rule that requires the employer to make comparable contributions for all employees who have HSAs. However, full-time employees and part-time employees (those working fewer than 30 hours per week) are treated separately. The comparability rule requires that the employer contribute either the same dollar amount for each employee or the same percentage of each employee's deductible under the health plan. Failure to comply with this rule subjects the employer to an excise tax equal to 35 percent of the aggregate amount contributed to HSAs during the period when the comparability rule was not satisfied.

Account balances from Archer MSAs can be rolled over to HSAs on a tax-free basis. Similarly, account balances from an existing HSA can be rolled over to a new HSA.

The maximum annual contribution to an HSA in 2006 is $2,700 if the account holder has individual coverage and $5,450 if the account holder has family coverage. These amounts are subject to annual indexing for inflation. The annual contribution, however, cannot exceed the deductible amount under the high-deductible health plan unless participants are eligible for a catch-up contribution. If both a husband and wife establish an

HSA and have family coverage (that is, a single policy covering both of them), they can allocate the maximum contribution in any way they determine. If they have separate individual policies, each is subject to the limits that apply to single coverage.

Individuals aged 55 or older are also permitted an additional annual catch-up contribution of up to $700 in 2006. This amount will increase by $100 per year until it reaches $1,000 in 2009. If both a husband and wife are aged 55 or older, the catch-up contribution is available to each of them only if they have separate HSAs.

Annual contributions can be made in a lump sum or spread out over time. However, the contributions for a specific tax year cannot be made before the tax year begins or after the taxpayer's original filing date (without extensions) for that tax year. For most individuals, this is the earlier of April 15 of the following year or the date a return is filed. This is similar to the rules for IRA contributions.

Example:	Jack and Eva, a married couple, retired last year when they each reached age 56. They purchased a family medical expense policy with a $5,000 deductible, and Jack established an HSA. The maximum contribution to the HSA for 2006 is $5,700, which consists of the $5,000 deductible amount and an addition catch-up amount of $700 for Jack.
	However, if they each established an HSA, they both would be eligible to make the $700 catch-up contribution to their own accounts. The $5,000 contribution could be allocated among the two accounts as they agreed upon. The net effect is that the total HSA contributions would increase to $6,400.
	These contributions can be made in one or more payments between January 1, 2006, and the date they file their 2006 tax return (but no later than April 15, 2007, if they obtain a filing extension).

The actual HSA contribution that can be deducted in a tax year is limited to 1/12 of the annual amount, as described previously, times the number of months that an individual is eligible for HSA participation.

Example:	Paul is eligible for an HSA. His individual health plan deductible is $2,500, and he is making an annual catch-up contribution of $700. Therefore, his

maximum annual contribution is $3,200. If Paul turns 65 on July 1 and obtains Medicare coverage, he is no longer eligible to contribute to an HSA. Therefore, his deductible contribution for the year is only 6/12 of $3,200, or $1,600. Note, however, that there are not requirements that contributions be made on a monthly basis or at any particular time. In this example, the full $3,200 could have been made early in the year. The amount over $1,600 would then be an excess contribution.

An excess contribution occurs to the extent that contributions to an HSA exceed the deductible limits or are made for an ineligible person. Any excess contribution made by the employer is included in the employee's gross income. Whether the excess contribution was made by an employer or an account holder, the account holder is subject to a 6 percent excise tax on excess contributions for each year these contributions are in an account. This excise tax can be avoided if the excess amount and any net income attributable to the excess amount are removed from the HSA prior to the last day prescribed by law, including extensions, for filing the account holder's income tax return. The net income attributable to the excess contributions is included in the account holder's gross income for the tax year in which the distribution is made.

Employer contributions belong to the employee and are nonforfeitable.

Account Growth and Investment Options

Unused amounts in an HSA accumulate on a tax-free basis and carry over to subsequent years without limit. The size of an HSA balance carried over from prior years has no effect on a current year's contribution.

Account holders can invest HSA funds in essentially the same manner as IRA funds. Allowable investments include bank accounts, annuities, certificates of deposit, stocks, mutual funds, and bonds. They cannot be invested in life insurance policies or most types of collectibles. In addition, an HSA trust or custodial agreement may limit the investment options available.

HSA funds are not guaranteed even if held by a bank and can decrease in value if the underlying investments also decrease in value. Therefore, an account holder must be prudent in how HSA funds are invested.

Distributions

An individual can take distributions from an HSA at any time. The amount of the distribution can be any part or all of the account balance.

Subject to some exceptions, distributions of both contributions and earnings are excludible from an account holder's gross income if used to pay medical expenses of the account holder and the account holder's legal spouse and tax dependents as long as these expenses are not paid by other sources of insurance. There is no requirement that these family members be covered by a high-deductible health insurance plan. If both a husband and wife have HSAs, the reimbursement for any family can come from either or both HSAs but together cannot exceed the amount of the unreimbursed expense.

For the most part, the eligible medical expenses are the same ones that would be deductible, ignoring the 7.5 percent of adjusted gross income limitation, if the account holder itemized his or her tax deductions. Tax-free withdrawals are permitted for the purchase of COBRA continuation coverage, or for the purchase of health coverage while an individual receives unemployment compensation. They are also permitted for the purchase of long-term care insurance up to the deductible limits shown in table 13-1 of chapter 13. However, tax-free withdrawals are not otherwise permitted for the purchase of health insurance by persons under age 65.

Even though contributions cannot be made after an individual reaches age 65 and becomes a Medicare beneficiary, tax-free distributions can still be used for any future qualified medical expenses, which include Medicare premiums, premiums for Medicare Advantage plans, and premiums for medical expense coverage under employer-sponsored plans. However, tax-free distributions cannot be used to pay premiums for Medicare supplement policies.

It should be pointed out that from a financial planning standpoint, account holders may want to wait until after retirement or age 65 to take HSA distributions as long as they have the resources to pay for unreimbursed medical expenses prior to that time. This will allow their HSA balances to grow on a tax-favored basis for use in their older years when unreimbursed medical expenses may be higher and/or income may be lower.

Distributions are permitted for other reasons, but they are subject to income taxation and possibly to a 10 percent penalty tax. However, the penalty tax does not apply in the case of distributions after an individual's death, disability, or the attainment of age 65.

Example:	Kirby has a balance of $7,000 in his HSA. At age 67, he rediscovered his childhood sweetheart and fell madly in love. She agreed to marry him if he gave her a big diamond ring. Because she told Kirby that she would take care of him for life, he decided to cash in his HSA and apply the proceeds to the purchase of the ring. His tax accountant informed Kirby that this arrangement would not be a qualified medical expense. He can withdraw the funds without

penalty because he is at least age 65, but the $7,000 must be included in his gross income for federal income tax purposes.

Effect of Retirement

Retirees can continue HSAs that were established prior to retirement, and the rules for contributions and distributions are as previously described.

Retirees who did not have an HSA prior to retirement can establish one at that time as long as all the proper rules are satisfied. Such an HSA may present an opportunity for a retiree to reduce income taxes. However, the requirement of having a high-deductible plan will probably negate this advantage if an individual has substantial medical expenses.

Example:	Kathleen, a widow, retired at age 60 from her job as an attorney. Her medical expense coverage had been under an Archer MSA and a high-deductible health plan. Her current account balance is $9,360. She enjoys excellent health and is in a high income tax bracket. She likes the concept of consumer-directed health plans and has decided to establish an HSA and to roll over her Archer MSA balance into this account. In order to be eligible for the HSA, she purchased a major medical policy with an annual deductible of $2,500. She plans on making the maximum allowable contribution to the HSA until she is eligible for Medicare. She will then use her HSA balance to pay her Medicare premiums.

There are fees involved in establishing an HSA. These fees may affect any potential tax advantages if an HSA is established near the time of Medicare enrollment.

Estate Tax Treatment

Upon death, the remaining balance in an HSA is includible in the account holder's gross estate for estate tax purposes. If the beneficiary of the account is a surviving spouse, the HSA belongs to the spouse and he or she can deduct the account balance in determining the account holder's taxable estate. The surviving spouse can then use the HSA for his or her medical expenses. If the beneficiary is someone other than the spouse, the HSA ceases to exist, and the beneficiary must include the fair market value of the account in his or her gross income for tax purposes. If no beneficiary is named, the tax is payable by the estate or the beneficiary of the estate.

ARCHER MEDICAL SAVINGS ACCOUNTS

Archer MSA

HSAs were designed to be successors to Archer MSAs. Like an HSA, an *Archer MSA* is a personal savings account from which medical expenses can be paid. In some respects, Archer MSAs are virtually identical to HSAs, but in several important circumstances, they are different and therefore less attractive to consumers.

HIPAA provided favorable tax treatment for medical savings accounts (MSAs) under a pilot project that began on January 1, 1997, and continued through 2005. In 2001, these MSAs were given the name Archer MSAs. During this period, the act allows for the establishment of up to 750,000 Archer MSAs. Fewer than 100,000 were actually established despite great initial enthusiasm about their potential success. No more Archer MSAs can be established after 2005, but those that were in existence at the end of 2005 can remain in effect, with future contributions still allowed for eligible participants. However, it is expected that most Archer MSAs will eventually be converted to HSAs through tax-free rollovers.

How Archer MSAs Differ from HSAs

Archer MSAs differ from HSAs primarily with respect to eligibility, the nature of the high-deductible health plan used, contributions, and distributions.

Eligibility

Two types of individuals were eligible to establish and now to continue making contributions to Archer MSAs:

- an employee (or spouse of an employee) of a small employer who obtains self-only or family coverage through a high-deductible health plan sponsored by that employer
- a self-employed person (or spouse of a self-employed person) maintaining an individual or family high-deductible health plan covering that individual

A small employer is defined as an employer who has an average of 50 or fewer employees (including employees of controlled-group members and predecessor employers) on business days during either of the two preceding calendar years. After the initial qualification as a small employer is satisfied, an employer can continue to make contributions to employees' Archer MSAs until the first year following the year in which the employer has more than 200 employees. At that time, participating employees may take over contributions to their accounts, but no employer contributions can be made. Alternatively, the employer could convert the plan to an HSA.

Nature of High-Deductible Health Plan

An HDHP, for purposes of Archer MSA participation, is a plan that has the following deductibles and annual out-of-pocket limitations. These amounts are for 2006 and subject to inflation adjustments.

- In the case of individual coverage, the deductible must be at least $1,800 and cannot exceed $2,700. The maximum annual out-of-pocket expenses cannot exceed $3,650.
- In the case of family coverage, the deductible must be at least $3,650 and cannot exceed $5,450. The maximum annual out-of-pocket expenses cannot exceed $6,650.

The deductible must apply to all medical expenses covered by the plan.

Contributions

Either the account holder of an Archer MSA or the account holder's employer, but not both, may make a contribution to an Archer MSA. If the employer makes a contribution, even one below the allowable limit, the account holder may not make a contribution.

The amount of the annual tax-deductible contribution to an employee's account is limited to 65 percent of the policy deductible for the health coverage if the Archer MSA is for an individual. The figure is 75 percent if the account holder of an Archer MSA has family coverage. If each spouse has an Archer MSA and if one or both of the spouses have an HDHP with family coverage, the aggregate contribution is equal to 75 percent of the deductible for the family coverage with the lowest deductible. The contribution is split equally between the two persons unless they agree to a different division.

Distributions

The rules for distributions from Archer MSAs are less liberal than those for HSAs. Tax-free distributions cannot be made for medical expenses of an "ineligible individual" in any year that contributions are made to an Archer MSA. An ineligible individual is a person who incurs medical expenses when the individual is not covered by a high-deductible health plan.

Example:	Derek has an Archer MSA. However, his wife is an ineligible individual because she is retired and covered by Medicare and therefore is not covered by a HDHP. As long as Derek or his employer contribute to the Archer MSA, he cannot take tax-free reimbursements for her unreimbursed medical expenses.
	Note that when he retires and Archer MSA contributions are not made in a tax year, such a tax-free distribution would be allowed.

How Archer MSAs Are Similar to HSAs

Archer MSAs are essentially identical to HSAs with respect to account growth and estate tax treatment.

Effect of Retirement

Individuals who retire retain ownership of balances in their Archer MSAs. Distributions can be taken under the tax rules as previously described for HSAs, but no additional contributions can be made unless they continue to meet the eligibility requirements.

Retirees under age 65 may still wish to participate in a consumer-directed health plan. They may maintain their Archer MSAs, and they are eligible to establish health savings accounts. They can also roll over Archer MSA balances to such a newly established account on a tax-free basis.

A COMPARISON CHART

Table 4-1 compares HRAs, FSAs, HSAs, and Archer MSAs.

TABLE 4-1
Savings Accounts Comparisons

	HRAs	FSAs	HSAs	Archer MSAs
Persons eligible	Employees only	Employees only	Anyone	Employees of employer with 50 or fewer employees and self-employed
Use of high-deductible health plan with account	Not required but usually used	Not required	Required	Required

TABLE 4-1 (continued)
Savings Accounts Comparisons

	HRAs	FSAs	HSAs	Archer MSAs
Waiver of deductible requirement for preventive care	Permitted	Permitted	Permitted	Not allowed
Contribution	By employer	Usually by employee through salary reduction, but employer can contribute	By employer, employee, or both	By employer or employee but not both
Qualified medical expenses	Any unreimbursed medical expenses allowed by the employer and Internal Revenue Code, including insurance premiums	Most unreimbursed medical expenses allowed by the employer and Internal Revenue Code, but not health insurance premiums or long-term care expenses	Most but not all unreimbursed medical expenses allowed by the Internal Revenue Code; some restrictions on insurance premiums	Most but not all unreimbursed medical expenses allowed by the Internal Revenue Code; some restrictions on insurance premiums
Taxation of distribution to participants	Tax free if for qualified medical expenses only	Tax free if for qualified medical expenses only	Tax free if for qualified medical expenses; other distributions subject to taxation and possibly penalty tax	Tax free if for qualified medical expenses; other distributions subject to taxation and possibly penalty tax
Portability	No—account usually terminates with employment	No—account usually terminates with employment	Yes—account owned by employee	Yes—account owned by employee
COBRA	Applies	Applies	Does not apply	Does not apply
Funding	Account usually unfunded and paid from employer's current revenue	Account usually unfunded and paid from employer's current revenue	Account must be funded	Account must be funded

NOTE

1. *Inside Consumer-Directed Care,* Atlantic Information Services, Inc., Volume 2, Number 24 (Dec. 17, 2004), p. 1.

5

Underwriting Medical Expense Insurance and Insuring the Unhealthy

Chapter Outline

underwriting

Underwriting is the process of evaluating an insurance applicant, making decisions about the applicant's acceptability for insurance coverage, and determining the appropriate basis on which to determine the price for the coverage.

The applicant for individual insurance must generally provide evidence of insurability. This means that the applicant must meet the standards that the insurance company has determined are necessary before it will issue a policy. An insurer may restrict the coverage and benefits that it offers and may refuse to offer coverage at all. Clearly, the underwriting process has important implications for the availability and cost of individual coverage for retirees because of their age and their greater likelihood of health problems.

In some cases, traditional underwriting leads to an applicant for individual medical expense insurance being rejected for coverage. However, insurance protection is often available because of federal or state laws that modify the underwriting process or establish high-risk plans.

UNDERWRITING

This section on underwriting looks at its key role, the agent and home office underwriter, classification factors, selection factors, sources of information, final underwriting actions, reunderwriting, and implications for retirees.

Key Role

An understanding of why an insurer rejects some applicants or restricts their coverage or benefits makes it clear that underwriting is one of an insurer's major functions. Underwriting enables an insurance company to provide its services to insureds—including the payment of claims—and to make a profit. Without underwriting, the company would be vulnerable to financial loss caused by adverse selection. *Adverse selection* means that those who are likely to have claims are also those who are most likely to seek insurance. It is the underwriter's responsibility to minimize adverse selection so that the insurance company can obtain the "average" group of insureds assumed in the rate structure.

Underwriting relates directly to the premiums paid by those covered by an individual policy. If the premium does not reflect the assumed average potential for health claims, then the insurance is a bargain for some and an overcharge for others, setting the stage for adverse selection. Those with likely medical expenses try to obtain insurance in much larger numbers than those who are less likely to have such expenses. As premiums rise, lower-risk individuals drop coverage. Moreover, many other potential applicants who found health insurance difficult to afford previously might now find its cost completely prohibitive.

It would seem that the best way to avoid adverse selection would be to accept only the best applicants for insurance. However, if underwriting is too restrictive, agents may direct their clients to other companies, making it difficult for an underwriter to meet the insurer's profit objectives. As a result, underwriting must balance adverse selection with selecting only the best applicants. It results in the selection of most applicants for insurance, but it also involves rejecting some applicants or accepting them with conditions attached.

The Agent and the Home Office Underwriter

Underwriting is accomplished by the insurer's home office (or regional office) underwriter and the field underwriter—the agent. Their roles are complementary and mutually supportive. Timely and effective communication between them is essential for a successful underwriting process. The insurer's underwriting department determines the underwriting rules to be carried out by its agents and its company personnel. Agents receive

(margin note) **adverse selection**

instruction on what types of applications are unacceptable and what kinds of business the company particularly desires.

Well-qualified agents choose clients who meet the insurer's underwriting rules. In the application process, insurers regularly stress to agents their responsibility to obtain a complete and accurate application, especially with respect to the applicant's medical condition. The agent must also communicate all known or even suspected relevant facts about the applicant. Insurers encourage agents to identify special circumstances or any other special issues, as well as to clarify questionable situations. Extra efforts in these areas bolster the home office underwriter's confidence in the agent and facilitate the approval of current and future applications.

This completeness and candor assist both the agent and the applicant to avoid the declination of a claim or rescission of a policy for misrepresentation. In turn, the underwriter owes the agent timely processing of applications and prompt communication about the pending and final status of applications. When an underwriter declines an application, the agent needs as much background information regarding that decision as the underwriter can legally divulge in order to communicate sensitively and effectively with the applicant. Helping the agent to deal effectively with a client is an essential aspect of maintaining good field force morale.

The home office underwriter, however, is not totally dependent on the agent as the sole source of applicant information. Without diminishing the importance of the agent's role as the field underwriter, the home office underwriter may access information from the applicant directly through a variety of sources, such as a follow-up telephone interview, a face-to-face assessment, or a review of medical records. The use of these sources of direct applicant information varies significantly among insurance companies.

Classification Factors

An underwriter must first identify the rate categories into which applicants may be classified. The rate categories and the premium for each category are ultimately determined by the company's actuaries, but with input from underwriters. However, there are federal and state laws that prohibit classification based on certain factors, such as race, ethnic origin, and religion. Rate categories for health insurance are frequently based on the following factors:

- number of insureds
- age
- gender
- geographic area
- tobacco use versus nonuse
- medical condition

Number of Insureds

Individual medical expense insurance policies usually extend coverage to the applicant and the applicant's immediate family. For older insureds, this will often include a spouse, and possibly dependent children under a certain age. The number of insureds under a single policy determines the premium. While insurance companies aggregate insureds differently to set premiums, a typical structure is as follows:

- applicant male or applicant female only
- applicant and spouse
- applicant and 1 child, 2 children, or 3+ children
- family with 1 child, 2 children, or 3+ children

Example: An insurer in Nevada offers a PPO plan with a $1,000 per person annual deductible. The plan is very comprehensive and includes prescription drug coverage. The monthly cost for this coverage for an applicant aged 60–64 is as follows:

Category	Monthly Premium
Single male	$383
Single female	334
Applicant and spouse	700
Applicant and 1 child	449
Applicant and 2 children	498
Applicant and 3 or more children	547
Applicant, spouse, and 1 child	761
Applicant, spouse, and 2 children	816
Applicant, spouse and 3 or more children	864

Note that these premiums would be about 17 percent lower if the deductible were raised to $2,000.

Age

Age is such a definitive predictor of the need for medical care that it also forms an explicit basis for establishing product premium rates. A level (no-age) rate in which the same premium is charged for all age classes is not generally found in medical expense insurance (except as required by law in some states), but it is sometimes used in accident and travel policies. The two common age-rating methods are *issue age* and *attained age,* with attained age being the more common.

issue-age rates

Issue-Age Rates. *Issue-age rates,* also known as *at-entry rates,* create an initial premium based on the insured's age when the policy is first purchased. Premiums are the same for anyone buying the policy initially at that same age. Future premium increases reflect the experience of those insureds who purchased policies at the same age. Thus, all 60–64 year olds purchasing a policy are rated in future years as part of the same cohort of 60–64-year-old initial purchasers. This method maintains *persistency*—the length of time a policy remains in force—because rate increases are more restrained than under attained-age rates.

persistency

attained-age rates

Attained-Age Rates. Under *attained-age rates*, premiums increase as the insured gets older, and the insured is charged whatever premium the company is charging insureds at that age who have that policy without regard to the insured's age at the time of initial purchase. The premium levels and their increases may be determined yearly or in 5- or 10-year-range bands. For example, at ages 55–59 an insured is charged a premium based on the anticipated experience of persons in this category, regardless of when they may have purchased their policies. This method is more typical in medical insurance because it generally produces lower—and therefore more attractive—initial rates than the issue-age method. However, declining persistency as rates increase with age is a drawback of the attained age method.

Example: One insurer has the following rates for single females who purchase its major medical policy:

Age	Monthly Premium
45–49	$242
50–54	302
55–59	318
60–64	334

Gender

Prior to middle age, women tend to incur greater medical expenses than men. As middle age approaches, the differences narrow as men become more likely to incur medical expenses in subsequent years. Separate gender-based rates are quite common in the individual market. However, antidiscrimination laws have encouraged the creation of unisex rates in some states that place both men and women in the same class for premium purposes.

Geographic Area

Differences in price and utilization of health care services cause medical claim expenses to vary significantly by area of the country. For example, the East and West Coasts are generally more expensive than the Midwest or South. Urban areas are more expensive than rural areas. These differences are due to many factors, including the cost of living, availability of medical facilities and services, physician practice patterns, individual attitudes, and socioeconomic status. Areas with similar medical expense levels are grouped into rate categories to reflect these differences. Depending on the type of insurance, these rate categories may be broad enough to include several states or narrow enough to reflect differences by zip code groupings.

Tobacco Use versus Nonuse

Because the use of tobacco, including smoking cigarettes, cigars, or pipes, as well as chewing, poses a significant health hazard, some companies offer separate tobacco nonuse rates to reflect the anticipated differences in claims and to encourage good health habits. For some insurers, this price differential may be 40 percent or more. Other insurers do not have separate rates but consider tobacco use when underwriting an application.

Medical Condition

Insurers often establish rate categories for some or all of their health insurance policies based on the insured's medical condition. For example, applicants in excellent health with no medical conditions may be insured in a preferred class with rates that are 85 percent of the insurer's standard rates. A standard rate class may apply to applicants of average health who may have minimal medical conditions. In addition, there may be one or more substandard rate classes for applicants who remain insurable but whose health is somewhat impaired by varying degrees of moderate medical conditions. Substandard rates may range from 125 to 200 percent of the standard rate. As the following discussion explains, medical condition is also the primary determinant in the underwriter's decision to issue a medical insurance policy to an applicant.

Selection Factors

The underwriter looks at numerous factors to determine whether insurance should be offered to the applicant within the company's established rate categories. These factors include:

- medical condition
- occupation
- avocation

- income
- duplicate coverage
- habits
- moral hazard

Each of these factors takes on a greater or lesser degree of importance, depending on the type and amount of coverage applied for.

Medical Condition

Medical condition is the most important single factor in individual medical insurance underwriting. As just discussed, insurers often establish their rate categories based on medical condition. Medical condition also determines the basis on which insurance is offered or refused. Medical history and current physical status, which constitute a person's medical condition, are basic indicators of the probability of future problems that may require hospitalization or other medical treatment. Underwriters evaluate an applicant's potential for incurring medical expenses primarily by estimating the probable influence of previous medical histories and current impairments on future claims.

From an underwriting viewpoint, applicants are considered impaired if they have a medical history or current condition that could either contribute to future injuries or sickness or create complications that prolong recovery. Underwriters classify applicants according to the extent that their medical condition differs from that of unimpaired applicants.

Medical condition can be evaluated by reviewing the applicant's medical history and current physical status.

Medical History. Underwriters review histories of previous conditions to determine

- the possibility of recurrence
- the effect on the applicant's general health
- complications that may develop at a later date
- the normal progression of any impairment
- the interaction of disease progression on future illnesses from an unrelated cause

Some prior diseases have a tendency to recur. An applicant with a history of digestive disorders is more likely to require hospitalization for those conditions in the future than someone who has never had them. Many previous acute disorders can be disregarded, however, if recovery has been prompt and complete and without evidence of any residual impairment. Examples include bone fractures and appendectomies.

Current Physical Status. In addition to medical history, current physical status also needs to be assessed. To do this, the underwriter evaluates

- evidence of current medical care and expense
- current medical conditions that need, or will shortly need, treatment
- physical conditions, such as high cholesterol level, that increase the likelihood of future illness

Sometimes a condition, such as diabetes, has current and future implications for medical expense and is likely to require ongoing medical care. Excess weight and elevated blood pressure, while normally not disabling themselves, are considered indicators of future cardiovascular impairment.

Family Information. Information about family members is also important when they are proposed for coverage and, in some cases, when they are not applicants.

If the application requests coverage for eligible family members, the underwriter must have medical history and current condition information on each family member. Some insurers also may require a statement verifying that coverage has been requested for eligible family members.

If family members are not part of the coverage being applied for, insurers may question the reasons for their omission because they may affect the risk of insuring the applicant. Thus, insurers may directly or implicitly seek to ascertain if family members have been diagnosed or are being tested or treated for a contagious disease, including acquired immunodeficiency syndrome (AIDS) or AIDS-related complex (ARC). However, the omission from proposed coverage may be accounted for by such reasons as other insurance or military service of a son or daughter.

morbidity statistics

Insurers only rarely include questions on family history for underwriting medical insurance policies. Historically, *morbidity statistics* (that is, the incidence of sickness and disability) have not shown family medical history to be important except in specific instances. Also, regulators and public policy makers may perceive the gathering of a family's medical history as an initial incursion into genetic information. However, family medical history is routinely the subject of life insurance applications. Diabetes or hemophilia, for example, may prompt additional tests or adverse action. To the extent that certain medical policies, such as critical illness and specified disease insurance, emulate life insurance by providing sizable lump-sum benefits, family history may be subject to underwriter inquiry. In addition, insurers are beginning to request family history information on applications for long-term care insurance.

Occupation

In general, occupation is a less important underwriting factor for individual medical expense coverages for those who are retiring. Nevertheless, these persons may continue or undertake income-producing activities in retirement. Moreover, occupation also serves as a proxy for such socioeconomic factors as education, income, and lifestyle that also affect the underwriting of individual medical expense insurance. Occupation is becoming more important as an underwriting factor with the increase in self-employed individuals who constitute a primary market for individual medical expense insurance. These individuals usually are not subject to workers' compensation, and the nature of their occupations may exhibit a wide spectrum of potential for medical expenses. Finally, identifying occupation permits the insurer to inquire about the existence or availability of employment-based coverage that may signal either possible adverse selection or a duplicate coverage situation.

Avocation

An avocation is a hobby or other personal activity pursued for enjoyment rather than financial gain. If most of the population participated in an activity of similar hazard, such as driving an automobile, the cost of the extra hazard would be covered by the regular premium structure. However, if only a small percentage of the population actually participates, the underwriter must determine the increased exposure to danger. Some insurers require completion of a special questionnaire when there is evidence that an applicant engages in a specific hazardous avocation, such as scuba diving, hang gliding, mountain climbing, or motorcycle racing. From this questionnaire, an underwriter can determine whether the exposure to danger is minimal and can be safely ignored or whether the exposure is excessive.

Where permitted by law, the underwriter may decline coverage, although the usual remedy is an exclusion rider eliminating coverage for injury resulting from certain types of activities. In some cases, an extra premium may be used.

Income

While the applicant's income is a prime consideration in underwriting some coverages, such as life and disability income insurance, it is less important for medical expense insurance. Nevertheless, in some instances it affects medical expense underwriting. For example, an insurer would be concerned about issuing a hospital indemnity policy with a daily benefit that could quickly exceed the insured's income and potential hospital expenses. Often coverage is geared to the average semiprivate room rate in the applicant's geographic area to ensure adequate coverage. In addition, an underwriter might be concerned about fraudulent claims and a policy remaining in force if the premium represents a disproportionate share of an applicant's individual or family income.

Duplicate Coverage

Information also is requested about similar forms of insurance presently in force or applied for on any person for whom coverage has been requested. Duplicate coverage—for example, two major medical policies covering the same individual—might result in insurance payments in excess of the medical expenses actually incurred by an insured. This concerns an underwriter because it provides an incentive to profit from the utilization of benefits.

In general, companies decline to issue principal policies for individuals and families if duplicate coverage remains in effect through any group or other individual insurance source without the applicant's stated intention to terminate that coverage. If subsequent information confirms that the previous group or individual policy continues, the insurer retains the right to rescind its policy within the contestable period (2 years in most states).

Habits

Habits—or, more properly, bad habits or vices—also concern underwriters. Drug addiction usually results in refusal to issue coverage, but there are degrees of alcohol abuse. An underwriter would likely decline coverage for a person who has a serious problem with alcohol. In less severe circumstances, the underwriter may take action ranging from standard issue to an extra premium rating.

Tobacco use may also be a selection factor when it has not been taken into consideration in determining rate classes.

Moral Hazard

moral hazard

Moral hazard is the dishonest tendency that may increase the frequency and/or severity of a loss because insurance is present. Persons who present moral hazards are those who might be dishonest in their dealings with the insurer. The underwriter must approach the subject with an objective viewpoint, considering the type of job an individual has and his or her living environment and lifestyle. Warning signs of moral hazard are unethical or questionable business practices, bankruptcies, criminal records, actual or attempted overinsurance, and excessive claims experience.

Sources of Information

The underwriter must select those applicants who are within the insurer's range of acceptability, as determined by the underwriting objectives of the insurer for types of policies issued and claims experience anticipated. In the process of determining insurability and classifying applicants, the underwriter relies on many sources of available information. These include

- the application
- telephone interviews
- paramedical examinations
- physician examinations
- medical provider statements
- inspection reports
- MIB Group, Inc.

The extent to which the underwriter uses these sources of information varies within companies by product and geographic area, the extent of the potential loss that the applicant presents, and company experience.

The spectrum of information sources accessed also depends on a company's satisfaction with the responses to routine questions contained in the application. Indeed, based on their experience with certain products and in certain areas of the country, some companies may rely exclusively on the information contained in the application.

Nevertheless, in addition to the application and the agent's statement that accompanies it, the telephone interview and paramedical examinations remain standard information sources for all applicants. Other sources, such as attending physicians' statements, hospital medical records, other investigative reports, and the use of MIB, Inc., may be enlisted selectively to resolve questions that arise from the standard information sources.

The Application

application

The *application* is the basis for the underwriter's decision to provide the requested coverage, to modify it, to try to obtain more information, or to reject the application entirely. The application format usually contains the following sections:

- applicant and insured identification
- other insurance determination
- coverage and benefit selection
- insurability declarations (medical history and health status)
- authorizations and notifications
- applicant's signature
- agent's statement (certifying completeness of the information)

Telephone Interviews

After the application is received in the home office, the proposed insured is often contacted for a telephone interview. Although some companies may contract with specialized agencies to conduct telephone interviews as their authorized agents, most companies use their own personnel, who are likely to be medically qualified. Telephone interviews provide an independent verification of information on the application, and they afford an opportunity to clarify responses. Increasingly, the telephone interview is integrated with the application; the application solicits a defined but general level of information, leaving required, specific inquiries to the telephone interview.

Paramedical Examinations

Paramedical examinations by trained personnel other than physicians are a routine source of information for insurers to determine an applicant's medical history and current health status. The basic advantages of paramedical examinations are the speed and ease with which they are arranged and conducted and the considerable volume of medical information they provide to the home-office underwriter at a modest cost.

Physician Examinations

In some instances, uncertain or unfavorable results of the paramedical examination prompt a request for a regular medical examination by a physician. Insurers may also require a physician examination because of the amount of coverage applied for, the applicant's age, and the need for more specific details of medical history.

Medical Provider Statements

attending physician's
statement (APS)

The application, paramedical exam, or physician exam may disclose a serious or questionable medical history. In that case, underwriters routinely request an *attending physician's statement (APS)* and often actual medical records from the applicant's primary care physician and other physicians who have treated the applicant for conditions that have a bearing on underwriting decisions. In addition to soliciting general medical information about the applicant, the attending physician's statement asks the physician to provide information about dates of treatment, length of treatment, tests ordered, medications prescribed, and the degree of recovery or control achieved for medical conditions. A similar statement may also be requested from other medical providers or hospitals. Medical provider statements are the best source of information for an accurate description of medical history.

Inspection Reports

inspection report

Although used infrequently for medical expense insurance, inspection reports can be an important source of underwriting information. An *inspection report* is completed by an independent agency that specializes in insurance investigations. These reports are valuable not just for gathering factual data but also for identifying a prospect's poor habits or risk of moral hazard through such sources as employers, neighbors, or associates. The report, which usually is written, covers such pertinent factors as occupation, financial status, and health history. Credit reports and driving records may also be obtained.

MIB Group, Inc.

MIB Group, Inc.

Some insurers also request information from *MIB Group, Inc.* (often referred to as MIB). MIB is a not-for-profit association of insurance companies that exchanges information among its members relevant to underwriting life, health, disability income, and long-term care insurance. Its purpose is the protection of insurers, and ultimately their policyowners, from losses by facilitating the detection and deterrence of fraud by those who may omit or try to conceal facts essential to proper classification and selection of insurance applicants.

Only MIB members are allowed to submit information to and obtain reports from the association's databases. A report from a search of an MIB database is only one step that an insurer might use in the underwriting process. The insurer who receives an MIB search report compares the results with information already received. If the report is not consistent, the insurer must seek further information about the applicant.

The MIB Underwriting Services database maintains a list of more than 200 medical conditions and/or test results that are of underwriting significance. Conditions commonly reported include height and weight, blood pressure, EKG readings, and X-ray results. Submitted information does not indicate what action a reporting member company took, nor does it indicate the type or amount of insurance applied for or issued. The MIB Underwriting Services database provides three basic reporting services: Checking Service, Follow-Up Service, and Insurance Activity Index. Checking Service allows members to compare the applicant's information against information in the MIB database. Follow-Up Service provides a company with any future information about an individual reported to MIB during the 2-year contestable period. This service alerts companies to nondisclosure of conditions that if known at the time of the original application would have caused the insurer to rate the original application differently or to decline it. The Insurance Activity Index alerts the company to applicants who might be applying for life, health, disability income, critical illness, and/or long-term care policies with multiple companies and informs the insurer of the purpose of earlier searches.

MIB as well as independent investigative companies must comply with federal legislation dealing with credit reporting and privacy. Insurers must also comply with federal privacy legislation as well as state privacy requirements based on the NAIC Insurance Information and Privacy Protection Model Act.

Final Underwriting Action

Underwriting information is collected until the underwriter determines that there is enough information to make a final decision. That decision may be standard issue (issue exactly as applied for), declined, or modified issue (issue on an other-than-applied-for basis). Sometimes no action is taken because insufficient or incomplete information is received. After a period of time, such files are closed.

Standard Issue

standard issue

Standard issue is the usual underwriting decision to approve as applied for. Most insurers approve 70 to 80 percent of their applications on this basis.

Declination of Issue

The most drastic and fortunately the rarest underwriting action is to decline any coverage. This choice is required only for serious medical or other reasons that cause the applicant to exceed a particular company's parameters for acceptance. On average, company declination rates are 10 to 11 percent.

Modified Issue

modified issue

Modified issue or modified underwriting approval is perhaps the most difficult aspect of health insurance underwriting. Approximately 20 percent of underwritten applications receive modified issue approval. The modification may be an exclusion rider, an extra premium, a change in benefits, a special policy for qualified conditions, or some combination of these approaches.

exclusion riders

Exclusion Riders. Health insurers have long used *exclusion riders* (also called waivers) as a means of issuing coverage to persons who would otherwise have to be declined. Such riders state that the insurer will not pay for a medical expense resulting from a particular medical problem (such as a back disorder) or an unusually hazardous occupation or avocation (such as automobile racing). The rider may be worded to exclude coverage for only a specific disorder, such as "hernia," or it may exclude an entire system or bodily area, such as "disease or disorder of the stomach or intestines." The actual wording is determined by the nature and severity of the applicant's medical history or impairment as well as by the insurer's underwriting philosophy. Although exclusion riders generally exclude all liability for the condition named in the rider, some insurers use a limited-period waiver that may be long or short depending on the condition.

Example: In his retirement, Rufus spends considerable time pursuing his favorite avocation of hang gliding. When he applied for individual medical insurance after his COBRA coverage ended, Rufus found that many insurers would issue a policy only with an exclusion of benefits for any injuries resulting from hang gliding. However, with the help of his insurance agent, he was able to find an insurer that wrote coverage without such an exclusion.

Extra Premiums. Some conditions, such as nervous disorders, are too broad in scope and too difficult to define to be covered adequately by an exclusion rider. Many other conditions, such as obesity, hypertension, or diabetes, have too many complications that would have to be excluded. For such conditions, the rider would be either too broad to protect the insured or too narrow to protect the insurer. One answer to this dilemma is to give the policyowner full protection through use of the extra-premium approach. Many insurers prefer use of the extra premiums rather than exclusion riders for modifying coverage. Payment of an additional premium that grants the insured full coverage usually is more acceptable to the applicant than an exclusion.

If an application was initially submitted for a preferred-risk rate class and the applicant's condition that concerns the underwriter is only mild, the premium increase may occur by simply reclassifying the applicant to a standard rate class. Generally, conditions that are insurable, but of concern to an underwriter, usually have more than a mild degree of severity. The underwriter typically places applicants with these conditions in a special rating or substandard class in which the extra premium is expressed as a percentage above the standard premium. The substandard class premium usually ranges from 25 to no more than 100 percent above the standard premium, although some insurers may allow even higher rates.

Change of Benefits. Another method of modification is to change the benefits to something other than what the applicant requested. Examples of such modifications are a larger deductible on a major medical expense policy or a smaller indemnity benefit on a hospital and medical-surgical policy. Benefits also may be reduced to counteract overutilization of medical expense policies. An insured who participates in the cost of medical treatment is less likely to prolong periods of hospitalization. Change-of-benefit modifications are often used when finances, business situations, or borderline medical problems indicate that standard coverage is available but some question exists regarding the applicant's overall suitability. Sometimes, these modifications occur in conjunction with extra premiums, a rate reclassification, or exclusion riders.

Example: Penelope, aged 63, has a history of hypertension and an irregular heartbeat. Her conditions are controlled by inexpensive generic medication, and she has had very few medical expenses related to her condition. She has had individual medical expense coverage for several years since her retirement. However, a change in residence has necessitated finding a new insurer. Because of her medical conditions, she is no longer insurable at standard rates. She has found an insurer that has a plan that meets her needs. However, this insurer will charge her a monthly premium that is 20 percent above the standard monthly premium. In addition, the insurer requires her to have an annual deductible of at least $1,000.

Special Policies for Qualified Conditions. To offer coverage to a greater number of applicants with modified premiums, some insurers have developed special policies that provide limited coverage for specified (qualified) conditions and full coverage for all other losses. This approach uses a separate insuring clause, worded to address preexisting-conditions limitations indicated on the application, as well as special rating of the qualified condition.

Reunderwriting

As a rule, medical expense policies are guaranteed renewable and not subject to underwriting at renewal. However, applicants may be reclassified because of changes in age or place of residence. An insured can request a reevaluation of previous underwriting decisions to limit coverage or charge a higher premium if, for example, he or she no longer uses tobacco or suffers from a particular medical condition. Finally, reunderwriting may be required to reinstate a lapsed policy or reissue an interim medical expense policy.

Implications for Retirees

Sound underwriting is indispensable to the broad availability of medical expense insurance in the individual market. Nevertheless, retirees, because they are in their 50s or early 60s, may face two challenges when they seek coverage in this market: availability and cost.

Retirees are more likely than younger persons to have health conditions that require an insurer to issue coverage on a modified (nonstandard) basis that would require exclusion riders, extra premiums, or reduced benefits as just discussed. For the same reasons, retirees also are more likely to experience denial of coverage. However, those who are unable to obtain underwritten coverage may be eligible to obtain coverage without underwriting under HIPAA's group to individual insurance portability provisions for those who leave employment prior to age 65 or through a high-risk insurance pool, which exists in most states. In either case, retirees should expect premiums to be high. Coverage that insurers must offer without underwriting under HIPAA's requirements has no restrictions on premiums. Although coverage purchased through high-risk pools is subsidized, it is nonetheless expensive—possibly more than double the standard rates. Both of these nonunderwritten alternatives are the subject of the following section on insuring the unhealthy.

Cost may also be a challenge for retirees, not only because of the potential for extra premiums for modified issue coverage, but also more importantly because health insurance policies are attained-age rated. As a result, the premium for older persons in relatively good health is substantially higher than the same coverage for younger persons.

Example:	Based on standard rates, healthy persons in their early 60s in Virginia may pay between $3,300 and $5,500 per year for self-only coverage depending on the comprehensiveness of coverage purchased, whereas persons in their early 30s would pay between $900 and $1,600 for comparable coverage. Similarly, the annual premium for that older applicant and a spouse (both in their early 60s) would range from approximately $6,000 to nearly $10,800, while the same coverage for a couple in their early 30s would range from approximately $1,800 to $3,200.

Retirees may obtain lower premiums by selecting less comprehensive health plans and/or plans with a high deductible. Nevertheless, initial premiums at every level will increase over time with the rise in health care costs and because they are attained-age rated.

Example:	A large insurer offers several deductible options with its medical expense plans. Depending on the plan chosen, the monthly premium is between 28 and 32 percent lower if a person aged 55 to 59 selects a $2,000 deductible rather than a $500 deductible.

INSURING THE UNHEALTHY

Historically, for the underwriting reasons just discussed, some persons may have difficulty obtaining individual medical expense coverage because of their medical condition. That difficulty is easy to summarize. If the medical condition were severe, insurers would often decline coverage. If the medical condition was less severe, insurers might write coverage on a non-standard basis by doing one or more of the following: charging an additional premium, excluding the condition, or imposing a waiting period before benefits would be payable for the condition.

Over time, the ability of the unhealthy to obtain coverage has improved significantly. If there is prior employer-provided coverage, federal legislation like COBRA and HIPAA eliminates the availability, but not necessarily the affordability, problem for many persons. States have also increasingly addressed the issue of access to individual medical expense coverage. Some of these state actions, such as the mandate of a conversion provision in group medical expense contracts, date back many years. In addition, some Blue Cross and Blue Shield plans, in return for preferential regulatory and tax status, offer periodic enrollment periods when normal medical underwriting requirements are reduced or waived.

In more recent years, more than 30 states have established some type of high-risk pool, whereby anyone turned down for medical expense coverage in the normal marketplace can obtain coverage through the pool. While these pools vary among the states, basic major medical coverage is usually available, but benefits for preexisting conditions are often subject to waiting periods. Premiums tend to be higher than regular medical expense insurance, but state subsidies keep premiums below the level needed to fully cover expenses and claims costs.

The best way to find out about the options for insuring an unhealthy person is to contact the insurance department of the state where that person resides.

The following sections describe coverage required under HIPAA and state high-risk health insurance plans as two ways to address the availability of coverage for those who cannot obtain underwritten coverage in the individual market. These alternatives may be an important option for retirees not yet eligible for Medicare.

HIPAA

A major purpose of HIPAA is to maintain health insurance coverage for workers and their families when they change, lose, or terminate their jobs. As long as they had prior employer-provided medical expense coverage, they are guaranteed access to and renewability of coverage provided by a new employer or coverage provided in the individual market. The name of the act (the Health Insurance Portability and Accountability Act) is somewhat misleading because workers and their families do not keep the same insurance program and are likely to have different benefits under the

portability

subsequent program. *Portability* means that preexisting-conditions limitations for medical insurance purposes are defined under the act and once satisfied may not serve to deny, limit, or delay a qualified person's coverage or the renewal of that coverage as required by the act. State laws apply to the extent that they contain provisions that are more favorable to consumers.

It is important to point out several things that HIPAA is not. First, it is not applicable if a person changes from one individually purchased medical expense policy to another individually purchased policy. Second, HIPAA does not guarantee that insurance protection will be available at a price everyone can afford; it only guarantees access to available coverage. Because of adverse selection, individual policies available under HIPAA often have a high cost. And third, HIPAA coverage is not necessarily the only available medical expense coverage. Too often it is viewed as the only alternative to someone with medical problems.

Example: Jack and his wife Charlotte, both aged 62, selected COBRA coverage when Jack retired 18 months ago. Now they must obtain individual coverage until they are eligible for Medicare. They have heard that they can obtain guaranteed coverage under HIPAA without any preexisting-conditions exclusions. However, in exploring the situation they have found that the HIPAA coverage is significantly more expensive than identical coverage that is individually underwritten. Even though they have minor medical problems, individually underwritten coverage is available to them at a price lower than HIPAA coverage.

General Insurance Provisions

Although HIPAA applies to group "health" plans maintained by an employer, a union, or both, the act does not apply to certain types of health benefits. These include

- coverage for accidents, including accidental death and dismemberment
- disability income insurance

In addition, certain other benefits are not subject to HIPAA under specified circumstances:

- limited vision or dental benefits, long-term care insurance, nursing home insurance, home health care insurance, and insurance for community-based care if these benefits are offered separately rather than as an integral part of a medical expense plan

- coverage for a specific disease or illness or for hospital or other fixed indemnity insurance if the benefits (1) are provided under a separate policy, certificate, or contract of insurance and (2) are not coordinated with other coverage under a medical expense plan

- Medicare supplement insurance or other similar supplemental coverage if the policy is offered as a separate insurance policy rather than as a continuation of coverage under a plan that also covers active employees

Group Insurance Provisions

Employers, whether large or small, cannot refuse coverage or renewal of coverage because of employee, spouse, or dependent health status. An employer may limit or delay coverage up to a maximum of 12 months (18 months for late entrants) for a preexisting condition that was treated or diagnosed in the 6-month period prior to group enrollment. The 12-month delay period must be reduced by the period the employee was continuously covered in another group or individual plan prior to his or her enrollment in the employer's plan.

With some exceptions, insurers serving the small group market (defined as groups of 2 to 50 employees) are required to accept both every small employer that applies for coverage and every employee of that employer who wishes to enroll.

Individual Insurance Provisions

The individual market is the market for health insurance coverage offered to individuals other than in connection with a group plan. HIPAA individual market provisions apply to major medical, HMO, and similar types of principal medical insurance benefit programs. These provisions establish requirements for the guaranteed issue and renewal of individual medical expense coverages for eligible individuals. To a great extent health insurers are only indirectly affected; 41 states satisfy the HIPAA individual insurance requirements by implementing a federally qualified alternative mechanism. Approximately 25 of these states have opted to use their high-risk pools (discussed in the following section) for the medically uninsurable as the alternative mechanism to guarantee coverage in the individual market under HIPAA. Modifications to some of these programs qualified them as an alternative mechanism under the federal requirements. The alternative mechanism in other states may be the use of the state's existing guaranteed issue and renewal mandates in the individual market or reliance on a single insurer of last resort.

In the remaining 9 states and the District of Columbia, which have no alternative mechanism, insurers providing individual coverage in these markets are subject to HIPAA's federal fallback standards for guaranteed issue and renewal. However, these standards do not apply to insurers offering coverage only in conjunction with group health plans, including one-life group and group conversion policies. In addition, there are special rules for association plans.

Guaranteed Issue Requirements. To be eligible for guaranteed issue of medical coverage under HIPAA, a person must have

- 18 months of "creditable qualifying coverage," the most recent of which was under an employer, government, or church group health plan
- no gaps in coverage of 62 or more full days within or after the 18 months of creditable coverage
- exhausted any other coverage, if eligible under COBRA or similar state programs
- no eligibility for another group plan, Medicare, or Medicaid
- no other health coverage
- no cancellation of prior coverage for fraud or nonpayment of premium

creditable qualifying coverage

Creditable qualifying coverage is prior coverage under a medical expense plan or policy. HIPAA does not require that individuals without prior coverage be insured. Nor does it provide guaranteed issue for individuals moving from one individual medical insurance policy to another. Furthermore, it leaves to the states the decision regarding limitations to be imposed on premiums charged for individual health insurance coverage required by HIPAA.

In the absence of a federally qualified state mechanism, a carrier offering coverage in the individual market may not refuse coverage or enrollment to an eligible individual under at least two of its health insurance policies and may not impose any preexisting-conditions exclusions with respect to such coverage. There are standard exceptions to this requirement for insurers that have insufficient financial capacity or whose provider network (in the case of managed care plans) does not encompass the location where an eligible individual lives, resides, or works.

Although individual insurers may elect to offer coverage to eligible individuals under all of their current policy forms, HIPAA allows insurers two other elections, which may be more appealing. Under these elections, insurers may limit the policy forms available to eligible individuals to either (1) their two most popular policies, as measured by the largest and second-largest premium volume; or (2) two representative individual health insurance policies typically offered by the insurer in the state. These two representative policy forms must include a lower and higher level of coverage, each of which is substantially similar to other levels of coverage offered by the insurer in the state as determined by specified actuarial value tests. Blocks of business closed under applicable state laws may be excluded from calculating premium volume. Policies under these two elections must be made generally available and actively marketed to both HIPAA-eligible and other individuals. Whatever election an insurer makes must remain effective for not less than 2 years and must apply uniformly to all HIPAA-eligible individuals in the state.

Guaranteed Renewability Requirements. HIPAA requires health insurers offering individual medical insurance coverage to renew such coverage at the individual's option. Exceptions to these requirements include: (1) nonpayment or untimely payment of premiums, (2) fraud, (3) termination of coverage in the market in accordance with applicable state law, (4) the individual no longer living, residing, or working in the plan's service area, and (5) discontinuance of membership in a bona fide association.

The guaranteed renewal provisions also apply to individuals with existing individual coverage, regardless of whether or not they were originally offered coverage as "eligible individuals" under the HIPAA provisions. In addition, similar to group plan requirements, all insurers in the individual market must provide certifications of prior creditable coverage automatically to beneficiaries when their individual coverage ceases and forward the same information upon request to new plans in which the beneficiaries may enroll. These certificates of individual coverage help persons in reducing or eliminating preexisting-conditions limits or delays in benefits when obtaining coverage under a group plan.

Eligibility for Medicare is not a basis for an insurer to decline to renew or terminate an individual's health insurance coverage in the individual market. If permitted by state law, however, policies that are sold to individuals before they attain Medicare eligibility may contain provisions that exclude payment under the policy to the extent that Medicare provides benefits. As a practical matter, many persons terminate principal policies of medical expense insurance at age 65 and may purchase Medicare supplement policies.

Association Plans under HIPAA. Association plans are a significant source of health insurance for persons seeking individual coverage, including some retirees. Typically, insurers market association plans to individuals through literature or direct-mail solicitation, or an agent may underwrite (that **association plan** is, accept or deny and rate) each applicant individually. An *association plan* may be established through professional or other affiliation groups or as a construct by insurers (known as discretionary plans) to provide coverage to individuals who are not affiliated with each other (other than to obtain insurance). An association plan may also provide group coverage to employers, through an automobile dealers association, for example.

HIPAA, however, considers only those association plans that cover individuals and qualified dependents as individual insurance. Therefore, all of HIPAA's individual insurance provisions relate to such association plans, but carriers insuring these plans are not required to otherwise offer coverage more broadly in the individual market. HIPAA defines a bona fide association as one that (1) has actively existed for 5 or more years; (2) is formed and maintained for purposes other than obtaining insurance; (3) does not condition membership on health status; (4) makes insurance available only in connection with membership in the association; and (5) otherwise meets requirements of state law. HIPAA establishes somewhat different rules governing guaranteed issue for plans of bona fide associations versus non–bona fide associations, but its guaranteed renewal rules are the same for both.

- *guaranteed issue.* An insurer that writes coverage only for one or more bona fide associations must issue coverage to any member of that association and his or her qualified dependents. Otherwise, these insurers are not subject to HIPAA's individual insurance rules. Insurers in all other situations (they write non–bona fide association business and/or nonassociation individual business) must heed HIPAA's individual insurance rules, which vary depending on whether the state has accepted the federal fall-back standard or an acceptable alternative under HIPAA. Insurers in either situation may deny association coverage to any applicant (HIPAA eligible or otherwise) who is not a member of the association.
- *guaranteed renewal.* Insurers may decline to renew individual insurance certificates in an association plan if the insured individual leaves the association. However, HIPAA does require insurers to renew an association master contract or, if the plan is canceled, offer the association all other products that it sells in the individual market.
- *rating factors.* HIPAA prohibits insurers from using health status to establish insurance rates within group plans, but it is silent with respect to the factors that insurers may use to set rates for individual health insurance products. Thus, insurers may continue to consider health status to set rates for individual association plans, subject to state law.

State High-Risk Health Insurance Plans[1]

State high-risk health insurance plans were initiated under state legislation over the last two decades, beginning with Connecticut and Minnesota.

high-risk pool

The main feature of these plans is a mechanism to broadly share the risk of above-standard financial losses for the benefit payments of comprehensive medical insurance offered to individuals whose preexisting health conditions denied them standard coverage in the private market. This mechanism, operated as a not-for-profit association, is known as a *high-risk pool*. Thirty-four states now have a health insurance high-risk pool or a similar program that provides coverage for uninsurable persons. Pools in a few of these states may not be fully operational, and some may limit access. As stated previously, approximately 25 states have opted to use their high-risk pools to guarantee coverage in the individual market required by HIPAA for people who leave their employer or other source of group coverage.

On an annual basis, the total number of enrollees for all states exceeds 180,000, with each state's participation level ranging from a few hundred (Iowa) to approximately 33,000 (Minnesota). Risk pool insurance typically costs more than standard coverage in the private market but by law maintains a cap on premiums. Most state premium limits range from 125 to 150 percent of average for a comparable plan in the private market, although some states may allow up to 200 percent of average. Total claims from operational programs is approaching $1.4 billion annually.

Each pool loses money because it is not feasible to pool a group of individuals with known major health problems and expect their premiums to cover the entire cost. Consequently, each pool requires a subsidy of roughly 40 percent on average that states generate from various sources. The sources for funding the subsidy may include the following:

- an assessment of all insurers, including HMOs and other health plans
- shared funding of the subsidy whereby the assessment of insurers is offset by a state tax credit
- an appropriation from state general tax revenue
- a designated revenue source, such as a tobacco tax, or a hospital or health care provider surcharge

Risk pools are not created expressly to serve the indigent or poor who cannot afford health insurance; they are designed to serve people who are unable to purchase health insurance because it is simply unavailable or because they are uninsurable. Thus, these pools largely serve the same market as that served by standard insurance products: small business owners, employees of small businesses that do not offer insurance, the self-employed, and other individuals. However, some state risk pools do have a subsidy for lower-income, medically uninsurable people.

An appointed board of directors governs the programs with day-to-day administration by a private third party, typically with supervision by the state's insurance department.

NOTE

1. The material in this section is taken in part from "Comprehensive Health Insurance for High-Risk Individuals," 16th edition, 2002/2003, Communicating for Agriculture and the Self-Employed (CA) and updated by a conversation with Bruce Abbe, CA vice president of public affairs, 9/23/2005, with the results of the yet to be published 18th edition (2005/2006) of the aforementioned report. Tennessee is the only state that has provided a program for uninsurables without a high-risk pool. The Tenncare program, which has offered coverage for the medically uninsurable as well as Medicaid eligibles and other low-income persons who are uninsured, is financed by pooling federal, state, and local funds. Severe financial restrictions have caused Tenncare to limit the availability of coverage.

Interim, Supplemental, and Ancillary Medical Expense Insurance

Chapter Outline

Older individuals may want to purchase one or more of several specialized types of medical expense insurance. Some of these policies can be used to cover needs that are temporary because of a gap in permanent medical expense protection or that sometimes arise but are not addressed by principal medical expense insurance. Other types of policies are of a more permanent nature and supplement principal policies or provide protection that principal policies exclude. This specialized medical expense insurance can be classified as interim, supplemental, and ancillary.

INTERIM MEDICAL EXPENSE INSURANCE

interim medical expense insurance

While most policyowners purchase medical expense insurance without an explicitly predetermined period of coverage in mind, many do purchase coverage to meet a need for only a specifically identified period. This type of policy is called *interim medical expense insurance* and includes temporary and international travel policies. These policies may supplement existing coverage or be a principal insurance policy if they represent the insured's underlying or fundamental program of benefits.

Interim medical expense policies may be relevant to retirees and those planning for retirement. If a person is within a year or two of Medicare eligibility at age 65, a temporary policy may function as a bridge for that person and provide coverage for that person's spouse and dependents, if any. The less comprehensive nature of this protection and its temporary nature keep the premiums relatively low.

Students who are frequently covered under their parents' benefit plan at work may turn to a separate policy of student insurance if their parents retire.

Finally, international travel medical insurance is virtually a required coverage for retirees age 65 and over who travel abroad. In general, Medicare excludes treatment outside of the United States from coverage. Nevertheless, before traveling abroad younger retirees with private medical coverage should review their policies carefully for any exclusions or restrictions on treatment in foreign countries. International travel insurance includes coverage and benefits that may be excluded or limited under Medicare or private medical expense insurance.

Temporary Medical Policies

temporary medical policies

Temporary medical policies provide individuals and families with medical expense insurance for limited periods of time. They are generally marketed to those who lack coverage because they are

- losing employer-provided coverage but will not be eligible for Medicare for a year or two
- between jobs
- self-employed
- part-time and temporary employees
- newly divorced
- dependents who are no longer eligible under their parents' benefit plan
- employees during temporary interruptions of employment
- foreigners temporarily residing in the United States

Eligibility

Eligibility under temporary policies usually includes:

- individuals under age 65
- spouses under family coverage
- dependent children through age 20 (age 24 if full-time students) under family coverage or as individuals through identified ages, such as 2 through 17

These situations typically create ineligibility for temporary coverage:

- the existence of any hospital, major medical, group medical, or other medical insurance currently in force
- pregnancy, or in family coverage, a family member who is pregnant
- denial of insurance due to health reasons or the presence of health conditions that would make a person ineligible for individually underwritten insurance
- coverage by Medicare or Medicaid, or attainment of age 65 during the term of coverage
- permanent residency in the United States for less than a specified number of years
- the need for coverage while traveling abroad

Coverages and Benefits

Temporary medical expense policies are almost always major medical insurance that provides coverage for the core services listed in chapter 3. Additional coverage may include prescription drugs, private-duty nursing, skilled-nursing facility care, home care, and ambulance services with identified limits.

Temporary policies offer a broad spectrum of benefit choices. Deductibles, which may apply to the policy term or on a per cause basis, are usually available in a range from $250 to $2,500. Once the deductible is satisfied, a coinsurance benefit (usually 80 percent, although it may be lower) applies to the next $5,000 or $10,000 of covered expenses. Thereafter, the policy often pays 100 percent of covered expenses up to the policy's maximum benefit. An aggregate policy maximum benefit may be $1 million to $2 million. Usual, customary, and reasonable limits apply to benefits for covered services. Lower out-of-pocket costs encourage the use of network participating providers and precertification of hospital admissions and surgeries.

Coverage Period

Most policies require the purchase of a minimum coverage period of 30 days. Some companies allow longer periods in daily or monthly increments up to the maximum coverage period of 6 or 12 months. Alternatives for premium payment include a single payment option if the exact number of days of desired coverage is known, or monthly billing allowing the insured to pay for protection as needed on an ongoing basis up to the maximum coverage period.

Because a temporary policy is designed to fill a specific need during a defined policy period and is not intended to be permanent, it is usually not renewable but may be rewritten for a subsequent period. The subsequent policy is usually not a continuation of coverage from the first policy. Therefore, the insured must reapply and satisfy eligibility requirements, including underwriting, that normally exclude conditions or symptoms that may have occurred during a previous policy period. Indeed, if a claim has been filed or the health of the individual has significantly changed since taking out the initial policy, the reapplication for a subsequent policy period is likely to be denied.

Insurer practices regarding the rewriting of temporary policies for additional periods vary widely. Some companies offer no additional coverage periods; others limit the periods to two or three; and still others rewrite additional periods indefinitely. In addition, some companies continue benefits for covered conditions that occurred during a previous coverage period.

Exclusions and Limitations

Exclusions and limitations are also typical of those listed previously for major medical policies. However, preexisting conditions are excluded from coverage, with a look-back period of 3 to 5 years from the policy's effective date. In addition, limits apply to the benefits for the following conditions or services, if covered:

- transplants
- AIDS
- mental or nervous disorders
- substance abuse
- childhood immunizations

Even when these policies do not include other managed care restrictions, they frequently require completion of a treatment authorization for selected services (usually elective surgery and hospitalization) to receive maximum benefits (that is, to avoid a coinsurance benefit reduction) or any benefits in some cases, such as for organ transplantation.

Extension of Coverage

Because of the policy's interim nature, the extension of coverage for treatment that is in progress upon the expiration of the policy is an important issue. Temporary medical policies may include two provisions that extend coverage beyond this date. First, if a covered person becomes totally disabled and is being treated for the disabling condition during the benefit period, the policy extends benefits to the earliest of (1) 12 months following the termination date, (2) the end of total disability, or (3) the date on which treatment is no longer required. Other policies may simply specify that even if the insured is receiving benefits for services on the date the policy terminates, coverage does not continue beyond 90 days from the otherwise regular termination date. Second, a benefit of up to $1,000 may be provided for follow-up care for any injury or sickness that occurred during the policy period. To qualify, the insured must have met the policy deductible and the expense must be incurred within 60 days of policy expiration.

International Travel Medical Policies

International travel medical policies may also provide a principal program of benefits for international travelers. Not all medical expense programs—for example, Medicare—cover medical services received by Americans in foreign countries. Many private medical policies limit coverage to emergency medical care subject to defined maximums, such as up to 30 days of treatment within the first 180 days of travel. In addition, international travelers from other countries with national health service programs are not likely to receive benefits for medical care services received outside their home countries. Thus, people traveling abroad for any reason may seek interim medical expense insurance.

Fortunately, medical insurance programs are available for people, regardless of age, who are traveling, working, or living away from their home countries or countries of residence. U.S. citizens and foreign nationals with international destinations, as well as foreign nationals visiting the United States, may purchase some form of this coverage for themselves, their spouses, and their dependent unmarried children within identified age brackets, such as over 14 days but under age 19. Child-only coverage is also available.

International travel policies feature medical expense benefits but also cover emergency medical evacuation and repatriation of mortal remains; they may include additional types of insurance and provide nonhealth-related benefits. Premiums are usually based on either the duration of the trip or the duration of the coverage, although in some cases, such as vacation travel, the premium may vary based on the value of the trip.

Medical Coverages and Benefits

Covered medical services are quite similar to those identified under the core services of a major medical policy and generally include

- hospital services
- physicians' services
- prescription medicines
- laboratory and X-ray services
- outpatient services
- local ambulance

Available maximum benefit amounts for these services range from $10,000 to as much as $2 million or more. Maximums may apply as an aggregate amount for the coverage period or to covered services for each distinct unrelated condition. Within these limits, the policy benefits are similar to major medical insurance. A single deductible during the period of coverage, such as $100 to $2,500, may be featured. After the deductible has been met, the policy's coinsurance benefit could be 80 percent of the next $5,000 or $10,000 of covered expenses. Thereafter, the policy may pay 100 percent of covered expenses up to the selected maximum benefit. Some policies pay 100 percent of covered expenses immediately after satisfying the deductible. Reasonable and customary charge limits may also be stipulated.

An international travel policy may also include a hospital indemnity benefit (such as $100 per night), a supplemental accident benefit (such as $300 per injury), and an emergency dental benefit (such as $100 per tooth). Stand-alone dental policies for international travelers provide broader coverage for emergency dental care.

Available Coverage Periods

Available coverage periods vary widely as well, depending on the type of trip being taken. Policies are tailored to meet individual market needs of short-term or long-term travel. Minimums may be a few days, 2 weeks, or even 6 months for some policies. Additional periods may be added beyond the minimum in daily, weekly, or monthly increments, depending on the policy. Representative maximum coverage periods are 90 days, 180 days, and 12 months.

Coverage usually ceases when the insured returns home, but policies written for periods of 3 or more months frequently cover all trips taken during the specified coverage period. Many policies allow single or multiple renewals; thus a 12-month initial period may extend to 3 or even 5 years. Some policies are designed specifically for persons spending extensive periods away from home, such as retired couples living full-time or for several months of the year in a foreign country. These policies have the characteristics of permanent medical insurance; the policy requires an annual premium and is annually renewable, the coverage is continuous when renewed, and the lifetime benefits may be $5 million or more. Note, however, that retirees who qualify as permanent residents of a foreign country are also eligible for government or private health plans in that country.

Exclusions

Exclusions are similar to those listed under major medical policies, with preexisting-conditions exclusions having a look-back period that may range from 180 days to 3 or as long as 5 years, depending on the policy. In addition, treatment paid for or furnished under any other policy or health plan, whether private sector or government sponsored, is a common travel policy exclusion.

Because of the interim nature of the insurance, the dates of treatment received after the trip for an illness or injury that occurred during the trip may become an issue. A policy typically limits coverage only to expenses incurred within 6 months of the occurrence of an injury. Initial treatment of an injury must occur within 60 days of an accident, and sickness must first manifest itself during the period of coverage.

Other Medical Benefits

Separate benefit limits are usually set for other medically related coverages. For example, emergency medical evacuation covers transportation associated with medical emergencies or in situations where relocation is necessary in order to receive appropriate medical care. Available benefits range from $10,000 to $100,000. In addition, if a physician decrees that a family member should accompany the insured during the medical evacuation, that family member's travel and lodging expenses are covered up to a set maximum (for example, $10,000). If the insured is traveling with a minor child when hospitalized, the additional expense associated with returning the child to his or her home country is also covered up to a set maximum, such as $2,500. Emergency dental treatment, usually as a result of an accident during a trip, may be covered up to $1,000. Repatriation of an insured's mortal remains to his or her home country may be limited to $20,000.

Additional Coverages

Travel policies frequently include accidental death and accidental death and dismemberment coverage. The benefit amount is usually available at various optional levels that may range from $25,000 to $250,000 or more. The insured's spouse is usually covered at the same benefit amount, with dependent children covered at a lower level, such as 20 or 25 percent of the parents' amount. Policies written for periods of 3 or more months may also include an offer of term life insurance.

Optional riders may provide coverage for a range of hazardous activities that includes motorcycling, skydiving, and surfing; specified athletic activities; and continued benefits at a reduced level for a limited period during an incidental home country trip.

In addition, nonhealth-related coverage often provides benefits for baggage delay and baggage loss or damage. These may be set, for example, at $300 and $2,500, respectively. Travel policies may also provide a formal assistance program that includes the following:

- 24-hour medical care location
- provider payment guarantees

- medical case monitoring and arrangement of communication between patient, family, physicians, consulate, etc.
- medical transportation arrangements
- emergency message service for medical situations

When purchasing coverage through a travel agent, protection is usually available for the value of the travel arrangements themselves. For example, coverage in the event of trip cancellation and interruption may be provided in amounts to $10,000, with delayed arrival and missed connection benefits up to $1,000.

SUPPLEMENTAL MEDICAL EXPENSE POLICIES

There are three types of medical expense insurance designed to supplement the benefits that are available under principal policies of medical expense insurance, such as major medical insurance. These policies— hospital indemnity insurance, specified disease insurance, and critical illness insurance—share certain characteristics. The insured is assisted with the significant additional financial consequences of a serious episode of illness or injury by receiving direct cash payments, usually made in addition to any benefits received from other coverages. These payments may be used for

- out-of-pocket expenses of medical treatment left uncovered by even principal medical expense insurance
- associated nonmedical expenses, such as travel, lodging, meals, dependent care, and loss of income

Hospital indemnity insurance, specified disease insurance, and critical illness insurance are described below. However, they are no substitute for adequate medical expense and disability income insurance.

Hospital Confinement Indemnity Insurance

hospital confinement indemnity insurance

Hospital confinement indemnity insurance provides covered individuals with a fixed daily cash benefit during a hospitalization. A spouse or dependent child is usually eligible for coverage, although benefits may be reduced.

The policy provides daily benefits in the event of hospital confinement at a specified dollar amount (such as $250 per day) for a defined period (such as 180 days). These additional benefits are available as a standard feature or as a rider:

- a lump-sum payment on the first day of hospital confinement
- an intensive care benefit, such as $400 for a specified number of days, in addition to the standard daily payment

- surgical and anesthesia benefit for surgery performed by and anesthesia administered by a physician, with scheduled limits and a yearly maximum
- payment for emergency room and related physician services due to an illness or accident, with limitations on duration or expense per event or per year
- outpatient sickness benefit, with limits per treatment and per year
- daily payment for recovery after a qualified hospital stay
- an accidental death and dismemberment benefit

Exclusions are those typically listed in principal medical insurance policies, which are found in chapter 3. However, the preexisting-conditions exclusions period may be limited to a 12-month delay in benefits for any condition that occurred 12 months prior to the effective date of the policy. As discussed previously, benefits for fully disclosed conditions may also be limited or excluded. Table 6-1 is an example of a schedule of benefits under a hospital confinement indemnity policy.

accident-only policy

Accident-only policies are a variation of hospital confinement indemnity policies and constitute another category of supplemental insurance. They

---

TABLE 6-1
Hospital Confinement Indemnity Insurance
Schedule of Benefits

Benefits	Covered Persons	
	Policyowner	Spouse/ Dependent
Inpatient Hospital		
Daily payment[a]	$ 250	$175
First day of confinement	$1,000	$500
Intensive care/coronary care[b]	$ 400	$200
Outpatient Sickness[c]		
Emergency room	$100	$100
Outpatient physician treatment	$ 50	$ 50
Emergency Accident [d]		
Emergency room	$300	$100
Physician services	$300	$100

a. Maximum benefit period per confinement is 180 days. Two or more confinements for the same or related causes in one or more hospitals and separated by less than 30 days are considered the same confinement.
b. Benefit is paid for a 30-day maximum in addition to the daily hospital benefit.
c. Indicated benefits are per sickness, with a family maximum of $500 per calendar year.
d. Benefits are provided per accident.

provide cash payments in the event of injury or death resulting from a covered accident within a specified period but not for hospitalization resulting from illness.

Specified (Dread) Disease Insurance

Specified (dread) disease insurance provides benefits to insured individuals and covered family members upon the occurrence of medical events or diagnoses related to the treatment of a disease named in the policy. It does not cover accidents or injuries. Specified disease insurance for cancer only has been the most prevalent form of this insurance. Today, however, policies frequently cover cancer in addition to other listed diseases that might include many or all of the following:

- Addison's disease
- amyotrophic lateral sclerosis
- botulism
- Budd-Chiari syndrome
- cystic fibrosis
- diphtheria
- encephalitis
- histoplasmosis
- Legionnaires' disease
- lupus erythematosus
- malaria
- sickle-cell anemia
- Tay-Sachs disease
- tetanus
- toxic shock syndrome
- trichinosis
- meningitis
- multiple sclerosis
- muscular dystrophy
- myasthenia gravis
- osteomyelitis
- poliomyelitis
- Q fever
- rabies
- Reye's syndrome
- rheumatic fever
- Rocky Mountain spotted fever
- tuberculosis
- tularemia
- typhoid fever
- undulant fever
- whooping cough

Specified disease policy benefits vary widely. Benefit provisions may utilize a combination of three payment structures: per-day or per-service, expense-incurred, or a lump-sum payment. Benefits are contingent on a diagnosis of the specified disease, but payments will cover the first day of care or confinement even though the diagnosis is made at some later date. This retroactive application of benefits usually applies to relevant services received within 90 days prior to the diagnosis. Table 6-2 presents a summary of illustrative benefits.

Specified disease policies frequently offer a first-occurrence benefit that pays a one-time amount for each covered person who receives a diagnosis of internal cancer. The amount may range from $1,000 to as high as $50,000 or more.

TABLE 6-2
Specified Disease Insurance
Example of Benefits

Service	Benefit
Hospital confinement	$300 daily for up to 90 days; $600 daily in coronary or intensive care unit up to 30 days
Surgery	Up to $7,500 per fee schedule
Anesthesia	Up to 25 percent of the surgical benefit
Physician's attendance	Actual charges up to $35 per day for in-hospital visits
Chemotherapy, radiation, immunotherapy, or radioactive isotopes therapy	50 percent of the first $50,000 of charges and 100 percent of the next $100,000, limited to $125,000 per calendar year
Experimental treatment	Up to $25,000 for experimental bone marrow transplant and $2,500 for donor-related expenses plus transportation
Transportation and lodging	Up to $50 per day for lodging, mileage, or coach airfare for travel for insured and companion (each)
Ambulance	Actual charges for an ambulance to the hospital and up to $5,000 for air ambulance
Artificial limbs and prostheses	Actual charges with lifetime maximum of $2,000 per insured person
Equipment	Up to $1,000 per calendar year for rental or purchase

Critical Illness Insurance

critical illness insurance

Critical illness insurance (sometimes referred to as serious illness insurance) is a relatively new form of supplemental medical insurance that provides a substantial one-time lump-sum cash benefit for a listed critical illness. Some of these conditions result from injury as well as disease and include specified major surgeries.

The applicant selects a maximum benefit amount, which can range from $10,000 to several hundred thousand dollars. The maximum benefit is payable only once—upon the first diagnosis of a listed condition or in combination with a specified surgical treatment or condition that is also covered. Each covered condition and surgical treatment is explicitly defined in the policy. Typically, the maximum benefit is payable for the following medical conditions or major surgery:

- Alzheimer's disease
- blindness
- deafness
- life-threatening cancer
- heart attack
- major organ transplant
- multiple sclerosis
- paralysis
- renal failure
- stroke

The policy may also provide a lesser benefit, such as 25 percent of the maximum benefit, for each of the following:

- initial coronary angioplasty (surgical treatment)
- initial coronary artery bypass (surgical treatment)
- initial diagnosis of cancer in its original site (other than skin cancer)

The percentage payment of the maximum benefits for the above surgeries or conditions is payable only once; the maximum benefit is reduced by the amount paid, and the premium is also reduced accordingly. The policyowner is notified of the new maximum amount and the new premium. Coverage terminates on the date the maximum benefit amount is paid under the terms of the policy. Optional coverage may provide a disability income benefit and/or an accidental death and dismemberment benefit.

SELECTED ANCILLARY MEDICAL EXPENSE POLICIES

Dental and vision coverage are two forms of ancillary or limited benefit insurance that are available in the individual market. Because the need for dental and vision services typically increases with age, these policies may be valuable to persons entering retirement to encourage them to maintain their dental health and vision acuity.

Retirees familiar with dental and vision plans in a former employer group setting will find that individual policies are more likely to include a lower maximum benefit, lower internal benefit limits, higher out-of-pocket payments, and longer waiting periods. The cost of these coverages is much less than the cost of principal policies but relatively expensive in relation to the benefits available.

Insurers frequently include discount cards for the purchase of dental, vision, and other ancillary services as a value-added feature with their policies. Persons with coverage simply present the card when purchasing services from providers identified as honoring the card. Discounts, which reduce the retail or objectively determined price, usually range up to 30 percent but can be higher. The discount card supplements or extends the purchasing power of an insured ancillary benefit policy when services are obtained from providers participating in the discount program. For example, the insured benefit may apply to dental or vision services subject to the discount, thereby reducing the insured's out-of-pocket costs. Alternatively, an insured benefit may apply to specified services, such as a routine dental or vision exam, with noncovered services and materials available at a discounted price.

Some card program sponsors also market their discount card programs directly to consumers who may or may not have any type of medical expense insurance.

Dental Insurance

Dental insurance is fairly common, but it is usually provided through employer-sponsored programs. However, dental coverage is also purchased in the individual market. In some cases, dental coverage is offered as an optional benefit or rider to a comprehensive medical policy for an additional premium. In other cases, dental coverage is purchased as a stand-alone policy.

The subsequent discussion considers dental insurance under the headings of unique benefit features, benefit payment methods, and managed care plans.

Unique Benefit Features

Dental insurance usually contains features that are unique to the management of dental claims expenses. These features include service-level groupings, least expensive treatment alternatives, prior authorization, benefit maximums, frequency limitations, program phase-in, and other limitations and exclusions.

Service-Level Groupings. Dental insurance typically aggregates professional treatment categories into four service-level groups for plan design purposes:

- service level I—routine preventive and related diagnostic services, including cleanings, oral exams, X-rays, and applications of topical fluoride
- service level II—basic services, including minor restorative procedures (fillings) as well as endodontic, periodontic, and oral surgery services
- service level III—major services, including major restorations (crowns, inlays, onlays, veneers) and prosthodontic procedures (dentures, bridges)

- service level IV—orthodontic services. Benefits for this level service, if provided in an individual policy, are limited to dependent children under age 19 (or older if a student).

A typical dental policy provides its most complete payment for level I services, somewhat less complete payment for level II services, and the least complete benefit for level III and level IV services (if covered). Benefits for these service levels give insureds financial incentives to seek routine services for prevention of future expenses and have a greater stake in decisions for more costly major services. The objective is to reduce spending on optional care and promote cost-effective dental practices.

Least Expensive Professionally Acceptable Treatment. Because dental problems can often be successfully treated in more than one way, insurers usually focus their benefits on the least expensive professionally acceptable treatment. For example, a policy pays for an amalgam filling that effectively repairs a tooth but not for a gold inlay or crown, which would also be effective but much more expensive. If the more expensive option is used, then the insured pays the difference between the amalgam filling and the gold inlay or crown. Thus the insured has a substantial incentive to obtain the least expensive, but acceptable, treatment.

Nevertheless, if the more expensive treatment is used, patient cost sharing encourages the insured to protect his or her investment by practicing good oral hygiene and taking advantage of routine diagnostic and preventive services, usually provided at little or no out-of-pocket cost.

Prior Authorization. An insurer frequently requests the insured's dentist to complete a preauthorization-of-benefits form for major services and orthodontia that describes the dental diagnosis, the proposed treatment, and the charges. This process is called prior authorization (also commonly referred to as predetermination, precertification, or pretreatment estimate) and consists of filing a claim form in advance of treatment when anticipated charges exceed a stated amount, such as $300. The insured or the dentist sends the completed form to the insurer's claim office. Frequently, X rays, photographs, and models for orthodontia are also submitted to substantiate the required treatment and to avoid delaying benefit payment pending a subsequent request.

Prior authorization promotes better quality dental care and reduces costs by identifying unnecessary expenses, treatments that cannot be expected to last, and charges that exceed policy allowances. Prior authorization also gives the insurer some control over the performance of procedures; before extensive and expensive work begins, both the dentist and the insured understand that benefits will be limited to the least costly alternative or even denied.

Benefit Maximums. Virtually all individual dental policies feature a calendar-year maximum benefit amount, usually in the range of $750 to $1,500, that applies in the aggregate to all dental expenses except orthodontia. Calendar-year maximums encourage insureds to seek less costly care, and they may help to spread out dental expenses over several years. Most policies have a separate lifetime maximum for orthodontia benefits.

Frequency Limitations. Dental policies include limitations on the frequency of covered services. Typical frequency limitations are as follows:

- bitewing X rays—one set every 12 consecutive months
- prophylaxis (cleaning)—one in any 6 consecutive months
- filling replacements—after 24 months from initial filling
- crown replacements—after 84 months from initial restoration
- bridges and denture replacements—after 84 months from initial delivery

Program Phase-in. Program phase-in, as table 6-3 displays, can occur in a number of ways, including the following:

- waiting periods
- incremental benefit levels
- incremental annual maximums

Waiting Periods. Dental policies frequently impose a waiting period before certain types of expenses are covered. For example, there may be no coverage for major dental services (level III) until the second policy year. Orthodontic benefits (level IV), if included, would be payable after the beginning of the third year.

Incremental Benefit Levels. Dental policies may also phase in the benefit level for covered services starting at a lower coinsurance benefit level; increasing percentages in each subsequent year encourage insureds to spread out claims. For example, the preventive and maintenance benefit may be initiated at 100 percent to encourage routine care, but benefits for major services (level III) could be 60 percent of expenses in the first year, increasing to 70 percent in the second, and finally to 80 percent thereafter.

Incremental Annual Maximums. An annual maximum can be introduced at a lower level and incremented annually, limiting the claims expense in the policies' early years while still encouraging diagnostic and preventive services.

Other Limitations and Exclusions. Dental policies exclude coverage for all cosmetic services. In addition, they frequently limit or exclude coverage for medical services, temporomandibular joint (TMJ) dysfunction, and orthodontia. Orthodontic benefits, if covered, are limited to persons under age 19.

TABLE 6-3
Individual Dental Major Medical Benefit Summary
(Stand-Alone Product)

	First Year	Second Year	Thereafter
Level I—preventive and diagnostic services (exams, X rays, cleanings)	75%	80%	85%
Level II—basic services (fillings, extractions, oral surgery)	50%[a]	60%	70%
Level III—major services (crowns, bridges, dentures, root canals, periodontal surgery)	Not covered	50%[b]	50%
Level IV—orthodontic services (straightening teeth)	Not covered	Not covered	50%[c]
Deductibles	$25 lifetime and $75 per calendar year per insured except for level I services, which have a $35 one-time deductible		
Maximums	$1,000 per calendar year for all Level I to Level III services per insured $400 per calendar year for Level IV services and $1,000 lifetime per insured		

a. 3-month waiting period
b. 18-month waiting period
c. 24-month waiting period

Note: All benefit percentages apply to allowable amounts based on reasonable and customary dental fees.

Termination. Benefits for a dental service received after termination may still be covered as long as (1) the charge for the service was incurred prior to the termination date, and (2) treatment is completed within 60 or 90 days after termination.

Benefit Payment Methods

The two common benefit payment methods under individual dental insurance are dental major medical and scheduled maximum payments.

Dental Major Medical Benefits. Dental major medical is a common method of benefit payment and utilizes the same provisions discussed in chapter 3 under major medical insurance—namely, deductibles and coinsurance benefits. However, this benefit payment method uses an annual maximum benefit and has no overall out-of-pocket limit. Table 6-3 presents a benefit summary of this method based on an individual stand-alone dental product.

Individual stand-alone dental products tend to have lower benefits than dental coverage purchased in conjunction with or as a rider to a principal medical expense policy. Such products, because of their greater potential for adverse selection, use more stringent benefit design to control the cost of coverage. More generous benefit designs are evident in subsequent tables.

Dental deductibles usually are written on a calendar-year or lifetime basis, with the calendar-year approach the more common. Annual deductibles for an individual range from $50 to $100 per person. Dental deductibles usually differ by service level with a lower or one-time deductible applicable to preventive services. Lifetime deductibles in individual dental policies are usually low; they function somewhat like an initiation fee and are only paid once.

The coinsurance benefit level, as under major medical insurance, leaves the insured to pay a portion of the allowable charges. However, in most dental policies, the coinsurance benefit is uniquely structured to reduce spending on optional care while promoting cost-effective practices by varying the benefits for the different service levels.

- level I—Preventive and diagnostic expenses (for example, cleanings, examinations, and X rays) generally are reimbursed between 80 and 100 percent of allowable fees.
- level II—The reimbursement level for restorative, replacement, and surgical procedures generally is lower than for preventive and diagnostic procedures, typically 70 to 85 percent. In some cases, reimbursements for replacements and major surgery may be lower. Some policies categorize X-rays as level II services.
- level III and level IV—Major replacements (crowns and prostheses) and orthodontics have the lowest reimbursement levels; in most instances, reimbursement is no more than 50 to 60 percent of the reasonable and customary fees for these procedures.

Scheduled Maximum Payment Benefits. The scheduled maximum payment (SMP) method, frequently used in individual dental products, is similar to that found in basic medical-surgical expense policies. Benefits are paid up to the amount specified in the dental fee schedule for an all-inclusive list of services. For example, the benefit may be $40 for a cleaning and $300 for root canal therapy. If a service is not on the list, it is generally covered, but only at the listed rate for a suitable substitute. The SMP method provides benefits on a first-dollar basis and usually contain no deductibles or specified coinsurance percentages, although there may be exceptions. In order to encourage diagnostic and preventive services, dental schedules are designed so that the fees for these services are more completely covered, while benefits for other dental services are paid at a lower level. Table 6-4 presents a benefit summary using a scheduled maximum payment method.

TABLE 6-4
Individual Dental Scheduled Maximum Benefit Summary

Covered Services	Benefit	Waiting Period
Level I—preventive and diagnostic services	Fee schedule ($40 for a cleaning)	None
Level II—basic services	Fee schedule ($80 for a filling)	6 months
Level III—major services	Fee schedule ($250 for a crown)	18 months for crowns and dentures 12 months for all others
Level IV—orthodontic services	50% of reasonable and customary charges	18 months
Maximums	$750 per calendar year for level I and II services per insured $1,000 per calendar year for levels I, II, and III services per insured $750 lifetime maximum for level IV services per insured (benefit limited to insureds under age 19)	

Dental Managed Care Programs

Managed care is becoming more common in individual dental insurance with the use of dental PPO products. They are similar in concept to PPO arrangements for medical benefits discussed earlier. Individual dental HMO products are also available, but are less common. Managed care arrangements are a more likely feature of dental coverage offered in conjunction with medical benefits than when dental coverage is offered as a stand-alone product. Insureds are rarely required to fill out claim forms or other paperwork when they receive services from dentists in managed care arrangements.

Dental PPOs. A dental PPO is an arrangement between an insurer and a network of dentists whereby the dentists agree to accept a negotiated payment (usually less than their customary fees) in anticipation of a higher volume of patients. Typically, the agreement requires the participating dentists to take part in utilization review and quality assurance programs. However, these programs are usually not as extensive as those found in dental HMOs.

The higher volume of patients results from a benefit structure that gives the insured financial incentives to use dentists in the network. These incentives typically take the form of reduced cost sharing or greater benefits.

Preferred-provider dental products frequently use the dental major medical benefit method. As with medical expense insurance, insureds are not required to use participating dentists, but they receive more liberal benefits if they do. Insureds who go outside the network are responsible for additional out-of-pocket expenses for charges that exceed either what a network dentist would have been reimbursed or a determined reasonable and customary amount.

Some PPO products create an even greater incentive to use the network by increasing the indicated deductible and/or patient payment participation levels as indicated in table 6-5, which compares benefits when using a typical dental preferred-provider network with those that would be provided outside the network.

TABLE 6-5
Dental PPO Benefit Summary

Covered Services	Network Benefits	Nonnetwork Benefits
Level I—preventive and diagnostic services	100% of negotiated charge[a]	100% of R&C[b]
Level II—basic services	85% of negotiated charge	75% of R&C
Level III—major services	50% of negotiated charge	50% of R&C
Level IV—orthodontic services	50% of negotiated charge	50% of R&C
Deductible[c]	$50 (individual) $100 (family)	$75 (individual) $100 (family)
Orthodontia Lifetime Maximum	$1,000	$1,000
Annual Maximum for Other Benefits	$1,000	$1,000

a. Negotiated charge—fee that the dentists participating in the network accept as payment in full
b. Reasonable and customary—charge based on prevailing fees charged by dentists in the area, although an insurer may determine an allowed amount on another basis, such as a negotiated payment rate
c. Not applicable to level I

Other PPO dental products may use a combination of benefit payment methods. For example, the benefit may pay 100 percent for preventive and diagnostic services received from a network dentist and have a scheduled maximum benefit if such services are received outside the dental PPO network. Services in all other categories may be paid at a scheduled maximum amount regardless of whether or not they are received from dentists participating in the network. However, the insured pays less out of pocket if services are received from participating dentists because the insurer has negotiated favorable rates with them.

Dental HMOs. A dental HMO (DHMO) is a prepaid health plan that provides dental care services to insureds in a defined geographic area. It accepts responsibility for delivery of services (not just the payment); pays participating dentists either a fixed periodic amount based on the number of insureds, called a per capita rate, or a negotiated charge per service; and is organized under state law as a dental HMO. Per capita payments are common in DHMOs and are usually made on a monthly basis for each individual or family regardless of the number or types of services rendered or the number of insureds seen. Thus the dentist or dental group is at financial risk for the insureds' utilization and has every incentive to encourage dental health and avoid unnecessary procedures.

Because DHMOs provide service benefits, in contrast to nonmanaged and PPO products, they typically have no deductibles and no maximum benefit level. Flat copayment amounts are associated with benefits for basic services (such as $20 for a filling), major restorative services (such as $300 for a crown), and orthodontic services (such as $2,500 for braces). However, some DHMOs use coinsurance benefits for the payment of major restorative and orthodontia services. Prior authorization is usually not used in DHMO programs. Typically, the member is limited to the dentists participating in the DHMO network unless the plan has a point-of-service option that allows the insured to seek treatment outside the DHMO at a reduced benefit level.

Vision Benefit Products

In the individual market, products that cover routine services to correct vision are uncommon. Most principal medical insurance policies cover diagnosis and treatment of eye diseases and injuries. Procedures to improve vision in the absence of disease or trauma are explicitly excluded. Even the most comprehensive medical policies, when they cover routine eye care, limit services to examinations and glaucoma and vision acuity testing and do not cover corrective eyewear. Discounts for vision products and services are offered with medical policies, however. Under these arrangements, the insured is eligible for discounts for exams and eyewear, including frames, lenses, and contact lenses, at designated retail optical locations. Discounts may range from 15 percent to 50 percent depending on the service or product selected. Sometimes an initial eye exam may be provided at no charge.

Nevertheless, there are limited stand-alone insured products that provide benefits for routine vision care, as the example in table 6-6 presents. This product is discussed under the headings of benefits, eligibility, and exclusions.

Benefits

Benefits may be offered in conjunction with other ancillary coverages, such as dental coverage, or with principal policies of medical expense insurance.

TABLE 6-6 Individual Vision Benefit Summary				
	First 12 months	**Second 12 months**	**Thereafter**	**Frequency Limits**
Eye exam	75%	80%	85%	1 per year
Eyewear (lenses, frames, and contact lenses)	Not covered	50%	50%	1 pair every 2 years
Deductibles	$25 lifetime and $75 per calendar year per insured			
Maximum	$200 per calendar year per insured			

The major medical–type benefit structure illustrated in table 6-6 features a calendar-year deductible and coinsurance benefits using reasonable and customary charges with a limited annual maximum. Similar to stand-alone dental products, there is no out-of-pocket limit, and a minimal one-time or lifetime deductible is used. The product design phases in the benefits and covered services over a 2-year period. The frequency limits for exams and eyewear are also identified.

Eligibility

The program is offered to individuals who are under age 65 as well as their eligible dependents, including a spouse and unmarried children from birth to age 19 (extended to age 24 or some other specified age if a full-time student). In some cases, retirees are not eligible for coverage because there is a requirement that the applicant be employed and working at least 20 hours per week.

Exclusions

The cost of a lens in excess of the cost of a standard lens is not covered. (A standard lens fits a frame with an eye size less than 56 millimeters in diameter.) Charges for replacement lenses are not covered unless there is a change in prescription.

The cost of a frame in excess of the cost of a standard frame is also not covered. A standard frame is defined by a specific retail value, such as $80 or less. The cost of replacement frames is not covered unless the existing frame is not compatible with the replacement lenses.

In addition to excluding any services or materials not listed as an eligible expense, the following expenses are not covered:

- any procedure, service, or supply that is covered under other medical expense insurance

- special procedures, such as orthoptics (treatment of eye movement disorders), vision training, and subnormal vision aids
- prescription and nonprescription sunglasses
- medical or surgical treatment of the eyes, including hospital expenses
- replacement of lost or broken lenses and/or frames

Medicare

Chapter Outline

Most Americans aged 65 or older are eligible for medical expense coverage under Medicare. Except for those who are still working and are covered under employer-provided plans, this is their principal medical expense insurance.

Because Medicare does not cover all medical expenses, many persons have additional coverage through private insurance. Slightly more than one-quarter of Medicare beneficiaries now have some type of Medicare carve-out or supplement as a result of prior employment (although, as explained in chapter 2, the number of employers providing postretirement medical expense coverage is decreasing). A similar number purchase individual Medicare supplement policies, commonly referred to as medigap policies. These policies are described in chapter 8. The remaining one-third to one-half has no private supplemental coverage and includes a wide spectrum of persons. In some cases, these persons are financially well off and can easily assume any additional medical expenses. In other cases, they are relatively poor and rely on public assistance (usually Medicaid) when Medicare is inadequate. And in other cases, they fall between these two extremes and may find their retirement savings depleted if certain types of medical expenses arise.

This chapter focuses on Medicare by first looking at its historical development and nature as a social insurance program. This is followed by a discussion of eligibility requirements, the benefits under the various parts of Medicare, and issues regarding Medicare financing. The chapter ends by addressing some of the mechanics of dealing with Medicare, from enrollments to handling treatment disputes.

HISTORICAL DEVELOPMENT

The Great Depression made it obvious that economic security was lacking for many Americans. Arguably, the most significant result of this situation was the passage of the Social Security Act in 1935. This act established several programs aimed at proving financial security for certain segments of society. These included the unemployed, children, the blind, and the aged. The focus of these programs, however, was largely on providing cash assistance, not medical care.

Over the years, the Social Security Act has been expanded and amended numerous times to provide benefits to an even larger number of Americans. The most significant expansion occurred in the mid-1960s with the establishment of Medicare and Medicaid. For the first time, the federal government became a major player in providing medical expense protection by creating national health insurance programs for two specific segments of society—the elderly and low-income persons. Despite criticisms of these programs, there is little doubt that both Medicare and Medicaid provide benefits to a large numbers of persons who would otherwise be unable to receive adequate medical care.

Medicaid

Medicaid is a public assistance, or welfare, program for certain classes of low-income individuals and families and is discussed in chapter 9.

Medicare

Medicare is a social insurance program primarily for people aged 65 and older. Today, there are four major parts to the Medicare program, and their financing comes from three sources: government revenue, premiums from Medicare beneficiaries, and Medicare taxes paid by most working persons and employers.

Before continuing, one point should be made about terminology. In the broadest sense, Medicare and Medicaid are "social security." However, as commonly used, the term Social Security refers to the certain programs enacted by the Social Security Act to provide cash benefits to the aged, survivors, and the disabled. Technically, these benefits are paid under the old-age, survivors, and disability insurance program (OASDI). But almost everyone calls it Social Security, and that is how the term is used in this book.

Nature of Social Insurance

social insurance

Social insurance programs exist to solve major social problems that affect a large portion of society. Often these problems result from the difficulty of privately insuring against certain types of losses. In the case of medical expense insurance, difficulties arise because many persons who are not in the labor force have insufficient resources to pay for broad medical expense coverage.

Even though there are variations in social insurance programs, and exceptions to the rule always exist, social insurance programs tend to have the following distinguishing characteristics:

- compulsory employment-related coverage
- partial or total employer financing
- benefits prescribed by law
- benefits as a matter of right
- emphasis on social adequacy

Compulsory Employment-Related Coverage

Most social insurance programs are compulsory and require that the persons covered be attached—either presently or by past service—to the labor force. If a social insurance program is to meet a social need through the redistribution of income, it must have widespread participation.

Partial or Total Employer Financing

While significant variations exist in social insurance programs, most require that the cost of the program be borne fully or at least partially by the employers of the covered persons. The remaining cost of most social insurance programs is paid primarily by the persons covered under the programs. However, in the case of Medicare, the general revenue of the federal government also pays a major portion.

Benefits Prescribed by Law

Benefit amounts and the eligibility requirements for social insurance benefits are prescribed by law. In the case of Medicare, benefits are uniform for everyone.

Benefits as a Matter of Right

Social insurance benefits are paid as a matter of right under the presumption that a need for the benefits exists. This feature distinguishes social insurance programs from public assistance or welfare programs under which applicants, in order to qualify for benefits, must meet a needs test by demonstrating that their income or assets are below some specified level.

Emphasis on Social Adequacy

social adequacy

Benefits under social insurance programs are based more on social adequacy that on individual equity. Under the principle of *social adequacy*, benefits are designed to provide a minimum floor of security to all beneficiaries under the program regardless of their economic status. Above this floor of benefits, persons are expected to provide additional resources from their own savings, employment, or private insurance programs. This emphasis on social adequacy also results in disproportionately large benefits in relation to contributions for some groups of beneficiaries. For example, under Part A of Medicare, high-income persons, single persons or small families, and the young are subsidizing low-income persons, large families, and the retired.

If social insurance programs were based solely on individual equity, benefits would be actuarially related to contributions just as they are under private insurance programs.

The Current Medicare Program

The Medicare program continually evolves. Hardly a year goes by without some changes. In some years, these changes are minor. In other years, the changes have a major effect on Medicare beneficiaries (the term used to describe persons who are covered under Medicare) and the providers of medical services. Major changes were made to Medicare in late 2003 by the passage of the Medicare Prescription Drug, Improvement, and Modernization

Act. The act, the most significant change to Medicare since its enactment, affects all parts of Medicare, and its provisions are being phased in over a period of time.

The current Medicare program consists of four parts:

- Part A—Hospital Insurance
- Part B—Medical Expense Insurance
- Part C—Medicare Advantage
- Part D—Prescription Drug Coverage

original Medicare program

Part A and Part B are often referred to as the *original Medicare program*. Part C is a series of options that beneficiaries can elect in lieu of the original program. Most of the available options are forms of managed care. However, most beneficiaries remain in the original program. In 2006, Part D became effective for all Medicare beneficiaries.

More detailed information than is contained in this chapter can be found on the Medicare Web site, www.medicare.gov. The site contains many excellent brochures on various aspects of the program that can be easily downloaded. This chapter includes many dollar figures that are indicated as being for 2006. These amounts are subject to annual indexing, and the amounts for a given year are posted on the Web site in October or November of the previous year.

ELIGIBILITY FOR ORIGINAL MEDICARE

Different eligibility requirements apply to the two parts of the original Medicare program.

Part A

Part A, the hospital portion of Medicare, is available at no monthly cost to any person aged 65 or older as long as the person is entitled to monthly retirement benefits from Social Security or the Railroad Retirement Board. It is not necessary for these workers to actually be receiving retirement benefits, but they must be fully insured for purposes of retirement benefits. This means that have met all the requirements to receive retirement benefits. Some persons do not elect retirement benefits on or before age 65 because they are still working or because they are living off other resources. By deferring retirement benefits, future benefits will be actuarially increased when benefits do commence.

It is estimated that about 98 percent of Americans will be eligible for Part A benefits at no cost. Those who will not include the following:

- ministers who elected out of Social Security and Medicare coverage because of conscience or religious principles
- some former state and local government employees. Historically, employees covered under state and local retirement plans were covered under Social Security and Medicare only if a state entered into a voluntary agreement with the Social Security Administration. Under such an agreement, the state may require that employees of local governments be covered or allow local governments to decide whether to include their employees. It is estimated that over 80 percent of state and local employees are covered under such agreements. The remaining state and local employees are usually covered under a state retirement program, but those employees hired after March 1986 are required to be covered under Medicare.
- Americans working abroad for foreign employers
- Americans working abroad for foreign affiliates of U.S. companies, unless the U.S. employer owns at least a 10 percent interest in the foreign affiliate and made arrangements with the Secretary of the Treasury for the payment of Social Security and Medicare taxes

The following persons are also eligible for Part A of Medicare at no monthly cost:

- persons aged 65 or older who are dependents of fully insured workers aged 62 or older
- survivors aged 65 or older who are eligible for Social Security survivors benefits. The largest group in the category is widows who spent their married lives as homemakers and did not have wages from which to earn their own Social Security benefits.
- disabled persons at any age who have been eligible to receive Social Security benefits for 2 years because of their disability. This includes workers under age 65, disabled widows and widowers aged 50 or over, and children 18 or older who were disabled prior to age 22.
- most workers at any age and their spouses and dependent children with end-stage renal (kidney) disease who require renal dialysis or kidney transplants. Coverage begins either the first day of the third month after dialysis begins or earlier for admission to a hospital for kidney-transplant surgery.

Even though the persons mentioned previously are eligible for Medicare Part A without paying a monthly premium after enrollment, they have been paying for their benefits over their working years. Part A of Medicare and all the benefits of the Social Security program are financed through a system of payroll and self-employment taxes paid by all persons covered under the programs. In addition, employers of covered persons are also taxed. These taxes are often referred to as FICA taxes because they are imposed under the Federal Insurance Contributions Act.

In 2006, an employee and his or her employer each pay a tax of 7.65 percent on the first $94,200 of the employee's wages. Of this tax rate, 6.2 percent is for Social Security and 1.45 percent is for the hospital insurance portion of Medicare. The Medicare tax rate of 1.45 percent is also levied on all wages in excess of $94,200. The tax rates are currently scheduled to remain the same after 2006. However, the wage bases are adjusted annually for changes in the national level of wages. Therefore, if wage levels increase by 4 percent in a particular year, the wage base for the following year will also increase by 4 percent. The tax rate for the self-employed is 15.3 percent on the first $94,200 of self-employment income and 2.9 percent on the balance of any self-employment income. This is equal to the combined employee and employer rates.

Over the years, both tax rates and wage bases have risen dramatically to finance increased benefit levels under Social Security and Medicare as well as new benefits that have been added to the program. The adequacy of the current funding structure to pay for Social Security and Medicare benefits continues to be a source of public concern and political debate. The issue is addressed in more detail for Medicare after the program is described.

Most persons aged 65 or over who do not meet the previously discussed eligibility requirements, as well as resident aliens who have lived in the United States continuously for at least 5 years immediately prior to enrollment, may voluntarily enroll in Medicare. However, they must pay a monthly Part A premium and also enroll in Part B. The monthly Part A premium in 2006 is $393 for individuals with fewer than 30 quarters of Medicare-covered employment and $216 for individuals with 30 to 39 quarters. The premium is adjusted annually, and the $393 amount reflects the full cost of the benefits provided.

Part B

Any person eligible for Part A of Medicare is also eligible for Part B. However, a monthly premium must be paid for Part B. This premium ($88.50 in 2006) is adjusted annually to equal 25 percent of the cost of the benefits provided. The remaining cost of the program is financed from the general revenues of the federal government. As a result of the Medicare Prescription Drug, Improvement, and Modernization Act, the Part B premium will continue to equal 25 percent of Part B benefit costs, but only for beneficiaries with modified adjusted gross income under $80,000 for a single person and $160,000 for a couple. Beginning in 2006, higher-income persons will pay a larger premium that increases with income. These increases will be phased in over 5 years, until persons with incomes above $200,000 ($400,000 for a couple) will have a Part B premium equal to 80 percent of the benefits provided. Starting in 2007, these income figures will also be indexed.

If an individual fails to enroll in Part B at age 65, the premium is increased by 10 percent for each full 12 months during which the person could have been enrolled. However, if a person declines to enroll at a time when Medicare is secondary to an employer-provided medical expense plan, the months of coverage under that plan do not apply in determining the amount of the late-enrollment penalty.

Medicare Secondary Rules

Medicare secondary rules

Because most employees and their dependents are eligible for Medicare on reaching age 65 (and possibly under other circumstances), a provision that eliminates any possible duplication of coverage is necessary. The simplest solution is to exclude any person eligible for Medicare from eligibility under a group plan. However, in most cases this approach conflicts with the Age Discrimination in Employment Act, which prohibits discrimination in welfare benefit plans for active employees. This and certain other situations of duplicate coverage are handled by the *Medicare secondary rules*. When Medicare is secondary to another source of medical expense benefits, Medicare payments are made for any expenses covered by Medicare that are not paid by the other plan.

Under the Medicare secondary rules, employers with 20 or more employees must make coverage available under their medical expense plans to active employees aged 65 or older and to active employees' spouses who are eligible for Medicare. Unless an employee elects otherwise (by rejecting the employer's coverage), the employer's plan is primary and Medicare is secondary. Except in plans that require large employee contributions, it is doubtful that employees will elect Medicare to be primary because employers are prohibited from offering active employees or their spouses a Medicare carve-out, a Medicare supplement, or some other incentive not to enroll in the employer's plan.

Medicare is the secondary payer of benefits in certain other situations. One involves persons who are eligible for Medicare benefits to treat end-stage renal disease with dialysis or kidney transplants. Medicare provides these benefits to any insured workers (either active or retired) and their spouses and dependent children, but the employer's plan is primary only during the first 30 months of treatment; after that, Medicare is primary and the employer's plan is secondary. It should be noted that the employer's plan could totally exclude dialysis and/or kidney transplants, in which case Medicare would pay. However, federal regulations prevent the employer from excluding these benefits for the first 30 months if they are covered thereafter. This rule for renal disease applies to medical expense plans of all employers, not just those with 20 or more employees.

Medicare is also the secondary payer of benefits to disabled employees (or the disabled dependents of employees) under age 65 who are eligible for Medicare and who are covered under the medical expense plan of large employers (defined as plans with 100 or more employees). Medicare, however, does not pay anything until a person has been eligible for Social Security disability income benefits for 2 years. The rule applies only if an employer continues medical expense coverage for disabled persons; such continuation is not required.

Other situations in which Medicare is secondary include (1) when medical expenses are paid under no-fault insurance or liability insurance and (2) when an individual is entitled to veterans' benefits, black lung benefits, or workers' compensation benefits.

MEDICARE PART A: HOSPITAL INSURANCE

Medicare Part A

Medicare Part A is referred to as the hospital insurance portion of Medicare. However, it also provides benefits for care in skilled-nursing facilities, home health care, and hospice care. For benefits to be paid, the facility or agency providing benefits must participate in the Medicare program. Virtually all hospitals are participants, as are most other facilities or agencies that meet the requirements of Medicare.

Part A of Medicare, along with Part B, provides a high level of benefits. However, as described in the next few pages, deductibles and copayments may be higher than in prior employer-provided or individual coverage. In addition, certain benefits that were previously provided may be excluded or limited. For this reason, persons without supplemental retiree coverage from prior employment may wish to consider the purchase of a Medicare supplement (medigap) policy in the individual marketplace.

Hospital Benefits

Part A pays for inpatient hospital services for up to 90 days in each benefit period (also referred to as a *spell of illness*). A benefit period begins the first time a Medicare recipient is hospitalized and ends only after the recipient has been out of a hospital or skilled-nursing facility for 60 consecutive days. A subsequent hospitalization then begins a new benefit period.

In each benefit period, covered hospital expenses are paid in full for 60 days, subject to an initial deductible of $952 in 2006. This deductible is adjusted annually to reflect increasing hospital costs. Benefits for an additional 30 days of hospitalization are also provided in each benefit period, but the patient must pay a daily copayment ($238 in 2006) equal to 25 percent of the initial deductible amount. Each recipient also has a lifetime reserve of 60 additional days that may be used if the regular 90 days of benefits have been exhausted. However, once a reserve day is used, it cannot be restored for use in future benefit periods. When using reserve days, patients must pay a daily copayment ($476 in 2006) equal to 50 percent of the initial deductible amount.

There is no limit on the number of benefit periods a person may have during his or her lifetime. However, there is a lifetime limit of 190 days of benefits for treatment in psychiatric hospitals.

Covered inpatient expenses include the following:

- room and board in semiprivate accommodations. The extra cost of private rooms is covered only if required for medical reasons.
- nursing services (except private-duty nurses)
- use of regular hospital equipment, such as oxygen tents or wheelchairs
- drugs and biologicals ordinarily furnished by the hospital
- diagnostic or therapeutic items or services
- operating room costs
- blood transfusions after the first three pints of blood. Patients must pay for the first three pints unless they get donors to replace the blood.

There is no coverage under Part A for the services of physicians or surgeons.

Skilled-Nursing Facility Benefits

In many cases, a patient may no longer require continuous hospital care but may not be well enough to go home. Consequently, Part A provides benefits for care in a skilled-nursing facility if a physician certifies that skilled-nursing care or rehabilitative services are needed for a condition that was treated in a hospital within the past 30 days. In addition, the prior hospitalization must have lasted at least 3 days. Benefits are paid in full for 20 days in each benefit period and for an additional 80 days with a daily copayment ($119 in 2006) that is equal to 12.5 percent of the initial hospital deductible. Covered expenses are the same as those described for hospital benefits.

skilled-nursing facility

A *skilled-nursing facility* may be a separate facility for providing such care or a separate section of a hospital or nursing home. The facility must have at least one full-time registered nurse, and nursing services must be provided at all times. Every patient must be under the supervision of a physician, and a physician must always be available for emergency care.

One very important point should be made about skilled-nursing facility benefits. Custodial care is not provided under any part of the Medicare program unless skilled-nursing or rehabilitative services are also needed. Older individuals often need custodial care to help them with such personal needs as walking, bathing, dressing, or taking medication. This care may be short-term in nature, but often it is long-term and a major health care expense. Long-term care insurance and other sources for obtaining long-term care are discussed in later chapters.

Home Health Care Benefits

If a patient can be treated at home for a medical condition, Medicare pays the full cost for home health care in the form of an unlimited number of home visits by a home health agency. Such agencies specialize in providing nursing services and other therapeutic services. To receive these benefits, a person must be confined at home and be treated under a home health plan set up by a physician. No prior hospitalization is required. The care needed must include skilled-nursing services, physical therapy, or speech therapy. In addition to these services, Medicare also pays for the cost of part-time home health aides, medical social services, occupational therapy, and medical supplies and equipment provided by the home health agency. There is no charge for these services other than a required 20 percent copayment for the cost of such durable medical equipment as iron lungs, oxygen tanks, and hospital beds. Medicare does not cover home services furnished primarily to assist people in activities of daily living, such as housecleaning, preparing meals, shopping, dressing, or bathing.

If a person has only Part A of Medicare, all home health care services are covered under Part A. If a person has both Parts A and B, the first 100 visits that commence within 14 days of a hospital stay of at least 3 days are covered under Part A. All other home health visits are covered under Part B.

Hospice Benefits

Hospice benefits are available under Part A of Medicare for beneficiaries who are certified as being terminally ill persons with a life expectancy of 6 months or less. While a hospice is thought of as a facility for treating the terminally ill, Medicare benefits are available primarily for services provided by a Medicare-approved hospice to patients in their own homes. However, inpatient care can be provided if needed by the patient. In addition to the types of benefits described for home health care, hospice benefits also include drugs, bereavement counseling, and inpatient respite care when family members need a break from caring for the ill person.

To qualify for hospice benefits, a Medicare recipient must elect such coverage in lieu of other Medicare benefits, except for the services of the attending physician or services and benefits that do not pertain to the terminal condition. There are modest copayments for some services.

The benefit period consists of two 90-day periods followed by an unlimited number of 60-day periods. These periods can be used consecutively or at intervals. A beneficiary may cancel the hospice coverage at any time (for example, to pursue chemotherapy treatments) and return to regular Medicare coverage. Any remaining days of the current hospice benefit period are lost forever, but the beneficiary can elect hospice benefits again. However, the beneficiary must be recertified as terminally ill at the beginning of each new benefit period.

The concept of hospice care is covered in more detail in chapter 11.

Exclusions

There are some circumstances under which Part A of Medicare does not pay benefits. These include

- services outside the United States and its territories or possessions. However, there are a few exceptions to this rule for qualified Mexican and Canadian hospitals. Benefits are paid if an emergency occurs in the United States and the closest hospital is in one of these countries. In addition, persons living closer to a hospital in one of these countries than to a hospital in the United States may use the foreign hospital even if an emergency does not exist. Finally, there is coverage for Canadian hospitals if a person needs hospitalization while traveling the most direct route between Alaska and another state in the United States. However, this latter provision does not apply to persons vacationing in Canada.
- elective luxury services, such as private rooms or televisions
- hospitalization for services not necessary for the treatment of an illness or injury, such as custodial care or elective cosmetic surgery

MEDICARE PART B: MEDICAL INSURANCE

Benefits

Medicare Part B

Medicare Part B provides benefits for most medical expenses not covered under Part A. These include

- physicians' and surgeons' fees. These fees may result from house calls, office visits, or services provided in a hospital or other institution. Under certain circumstances, benefits are also provided for the services of chiropractors, podiatrists, and optometrists.
- diagnostic tests in a hospital or in a physician's office
- X rays
- physical therapy in a physician's office, or as an outpatient of a hospital, skilled-nursing facility, or other approved clinic, rehabilitative agency, or public-health agency
- blood transfusions
- drugs and biologicals that cannot be self-administered
- radiation therapy
- medical supplies, such as surgical dressings, splints, and casts
- rental of medical equipment, such as oxygen tents, hospital beds, and wheelchairs

- prosthetic devices, such as artificial heart valves or lenses after a cataract operation
- ambulance service if a patient's condition does not permit the use of other methods of transportation
- mammograms and Pap smears
- diabetes glucose monitoring and education
- diabetic screening for persons at risk of diabetes
- screening blood test for early detection of heart disease
- colorectal cancer screening
- bone mass measurement
- prostate cancer screening
- pneumococcal vaccinations and flu shots
- dilated eye examinations for beneficiaries at high risk for glaucoma
- home health care services as described for Part A when a person does not have Part A coverage or Part A benefits are not applicable

Exclusions

Although the preceding list may appear to be comprehensive, there are numerous medical products and services not covered by Part B, some of which represent significant expenses for the elderly. They include the following:

- most drugs and biologicals that can be self-administered, except drugs for osteoporosis, oral cancer treatment, and immunosuppressive therapy under specified circumstances. However, benefits are now available under Part D, which is discussed later.
- routine physical, eye, and hearing examinations, except those previously mentioned. However, as part of the Medicare Prescription Drug, Improvement, and Modernization Act, all Medicare beneficiaries are now eligible for a one-time physical examination within 6 months of enrolling in Part B.
- routine foot care
- immunizations, except pneumococcal vaccinations, flu shots, or immunization required because of an injury or immediate risk of infection
- cosmetic surgery, unless it is needed because of an accidental injury or to improve the function of a malformed part of the body
- dental care, unless it involves jaw or facial bone surgery or the setting of fractures
- custodial care
- eyeglasses, hearing aids, or orthopedic shoes

In addition, benefits are not provided to persons eligible for workers' compensation or to those treated in government hospitals. Benefits are provided only for services received in the United States, except for physicians' services and ambulance services rendered for a hospitalization that is covered in Mexico or Canada under Part A.

Amount of Benefits

The benefits available under Part B are subject to a number of different payment rules. A few charges are paid in full without any cost sharing. These include (1) home health services, (2) pneumococcal vaccinations and flu shots, (3) certain surgical procedures that are performed on an outpatient basis in lieu of hospitalization, (4) diagnostic preadmission tests performed on an outpatient basis within 7 days prior to hospitalization, (5) mammograms, and (6) Pap smears.

For other charges, there is a $124 calendar-year deductible in 2006. (As a result of the Medicare Prescription Drug, Improvement, and Modernization Act, the deductible is now indexed for medical inflation.) When the deductible is satisfied, Part B pays 80 percent of approved charges for most covered medical expenses other than professional charges for mental health care and outpatient services of hospitals and mental health centers. Medicare pays only 50 percent of approved charges for the mental health services of physicians and other mental health professionals. There is a separate payment system under which Medicare determines a set payment for each type of service for outpatient services of hospitals and mental health centers. However, this amount varies across the country to reflect such factors as the level of hospital wages. For some services, Medicare patients are required to pay an amount equal to 20 percent of the set payment amount, with Part B paying 80 percent. For other services, there is a fixed copayment that may be more or less than 20 percent of the set payment amount. In no case can the amount paid by a Medicare patient for a single service exceed a dollar figure equal to the Part A hospital deductible.

The approved charge for doctor's services covered by Medicare is based on a fee schedule issued by the Centers for Medicare & Medicaid Services, which administers Medicare. A patient is reimbursed for only 80 percent of the approved charges above the deductible—regardless of the doctor's actual charge. Most doctors and other suppliers of medical services accept an assignment of Medicare benefits and therefore are prohibited from charging a patient in excess of the fee schedule. They can, however, bill the patient for any portion of the approved charges that were not paid by Medicare because of the annual deductible and/or coinsurance. They can also bill for any services that are not covered by Medicare.

Doctors who do not accept assignment of Medicare benefits cannot charge a Medicare patient more than 115 percent of the approved fee for nonparticipating doctors. Because the approved fee for nonparticipating doctors is set at 95 percent of the fee paid for participating doctors, a doctor who does not accept an assignment of Medicare benefits can charge a fee that is only 9.25 percent greater than if an assignment had been accepted (115 percent x 95 percent = 109.25 percent). As a result, some doctors either do not see Medicare beneficiaries, or limit the number of such patients that they treat.

The previous limitation on charges does not apply to providers of medical services other than doctors. Although a provider who does not accept assignment can charge any fee, Medicare pays only what it would have paid if the provider had accepted assignment. For example, assume the approved charge for medical equipment is $100 and the actual charge is $190. Medicare reimburses $80 (.80 x $100), and the balance is borne by the Medicare beneficiary.

MEDICARE PART C: MEDICARE ADVANTAGE

In 1985, Congress amended the Medicare program to allow a beneficiary to elect coverage under a health maintenance organization (HMO) as an alternative to the original Medicare program. At first, the number of persons electing this option was relatively small. Many of the elderly had not had HMO coverage during their working years and viewed such coverage with some skepticism. In addition, many HMOs continued to focus on expanding their traditional market of younger, healthier lives rather than entering a new and demographically different market. Moreover, there were complex federal rules that had to be satisfied to enter the Medicare market.

The situation slowly changed as more HMOs got into the Medicare market and the public became more familiar with HMO coverage. In addition, as medical costs continued to rise, the election of an HMO option made more sense from a cost standpoint. As a result, HMO coverage for Medicare beneficiaries grew rapidly in the mid to late 1990s, and approximately one out of six beneficiaries had such coverage.

Under the 1985 rules, an HMO was basically given 95 percent of what Medicare would expect to pay to provide benefits if a beneficiary electing HMO coverage had stayed in the original Medicare program. In turn, the HMO was expected to provide at least the same benefits as those that are available under Medicare. While an HMO could provide additional benefits and charge an extra premium, many HMOs provided additional benefits, such as prescription drugs, without charging an additional premium. Such zero-premium plans were very popular among Medicare beneficiaries. While they had to continue paying the Part B Medicare premium, these beneficiaries were able to receive coverage that was broader than the original Medicare and thus had no reason to purchase a Medicare supplement policy. Since 2003, such plans can be set up so that the Part B premium can be reduced rather than having benefits increased above what is available under Parts A and B.

In 1999, Part C of Medicare (originally called Medicare+Choice) went into effect. It expands the choices available to most Medicare beneficiaries by allowing them to elect medical expense benefits through one of several alternatives to Parts A and B as long as the providers of these alternatives enter into contracts with the Centers for Medicare & Medicaid Services. However, beneficiaries must still pay any Part B premium.

The plans include

- HMOs. (Most of the HMOs previously in the Medicare market became part of the Medicare+Choice program.) These plans are frequently referred to as *Medicare managed care plans* even though other alternatives usually have elements of managed care.
- point-of-service (POS) plans called *Medicare cost plans*. They provide HMO benefits inside a plan network. They also pay for out-of-network services if there is a plan referral or in certain emergency situations. Other out-of-network services are covered by original Medicare.
- preferred-provider organizations (PPOs)
- other specialty plans, such as private contracts with physicians and provider-sponsored organizations (PSOs). PSOs are similar to HMOs but established by doctors and hospitals that have formed their own health plans.
- private fee-for-service plans

These plans must provide all benefits available under Parts A and B of Medicare. They may include additional benefits as part of the basic plan or for an additional fee.

Unfortunately, the initial reaction to Medicare+Choice was less than overwhelming. Few new providers of alternative coverage entered the marketplace, and the enrollment in alternatives to the original Medicare program had decreased after several years of growth. One reason for this is that the Medicare+Choice rules were extremely complex, and it is questionable if many of the potential providers could have entered the market in a viable way. As a result, there was a decrease in the number of HMOs offering coverage. While some HMOs, PPOs, and other types of plans continued to enter the Medicare market or expand their service areas for Medicare beneficiaries, a large number of plans either ceased providing Medicare coverage or reduced their service areas. While many of those who lost Medicare coverage had other plans available, a change to another plan often required the use of different physicians and hospitals. Other HMO participants had no choice but to return to the original Medicare program. Finally, some HMOs increased premiums, reduced benefits, and/or no longer offered zero-premium plans. These changes stemmed from two factors. First, managed care costs had increased significantly in recent years, partially because of major increases in the cost of prescription drugs (which many

Medicare+Choice plans covered to some degree), which are a major source of medical expenses for the elderly. Second, the rate of growth of Medicare payments to Medicare+Choice plans had been reduced so that many plans received increases that failed to match their increases in expenses.

Medicare Advantage

The situation, however, changed as a result of provisions in the Medicare Prescription Drug, Improvement, and Modernization Act. The act changed the name of Medicare+Choice to *Medicare Advantage*, and as of January 1, 2006, all materials for such plans must use this terminology. The act makes numerous administrative changes to the program aimed at increasing participation. The method for calculating reimbursement to participating plans has been changed, and many plans are receiving larger reimbursements. This has already resulted in some plans increasing benefits and/or lowering premiums, and participation has begun to increase. Today, about one out of every seven Medicare beneficiaries is enrolled in a Medicare Advantage plan. About 85 percent of these enrollees are in HMO plans; the remainder are scattered among the other types of Medicare Advantage plans. The participation rate varies significantly among states, with some states having almost no participants and other states having participation rates over 20 percent. To some extent these statistics have been influenced by the fact that most Medicare Advantage plans are HMOs, and some parts of the country are either served by a single Medicare Advantage plans or have no such plans. In other parts of the country, there is a very competitive Medicare Advantage market.

Beginning in 2006, PPOs can begin offering Medicare Advantage plans on a regional basis that is broader than the typical service areas used for non–Medicare Advantage participants. These regions are determined by the Secretary of Health and Human Services. This gives PPOs a broader base from which to solicit members and should also increase competition. These regional plans must use a single deductible and out-of-pocket limit for Part A and Part B benefits.

In 2006, beneficiaries are able to enroll in a Medicare Advantage plan or switch plans (including reenrollment in Parts A and B) once during the first 6 months of the year. In 2007, an annual change will be allowed only during the first 3 months of the year.

Medicare Advantage plans are required to submit proposals to participate in the program. Such proposals are subject to negotiation, and the Secretary of Health and Human Services will determine whether a plan can participate in the program based on statutory criteria. This is similar to the procedure used to select the medical expense plans available to employees of the federal government under the Federal Employees Health Benefits Program.

Is a Medicare Advantage Plan an Appropriate Option?

It is clear from the earlier part of this chapter that the original Medicare program provides less than complete protection for medical expenses. As a result, many retirees have some type of medical expense coverage to provide additional benefits. Some retirees have this coverage under employer-provided postretirement medical expense plans; other retirees purchase a Medicare supplement (medigap) policy. These alternatives are described in other chapters.

The selection of a Medicare Advantage plan is also a viable option that may provide broad coverage at a relatively modest cost. However, Medicare Advantage plans are not available in all parts of the country, and the number of plans in a given area may be very limited. In addition, most of the plans that are currently in existence are structured as HMOs. For a retiree who was covered by an HMO plan while working, the nature of the coverage will be familiar, and the HMO plan may even be with the same insurer that provided coverage previously. For other retirees, the inherent nature of such plans may be less than desirable. For example, HMOs control the selection of physicians that a member can use. The selection of a Medicare Advantage plan may require a retiree to stop seeing a long-time trusted physician and select a physician who participates in the HMO network. On the other hand, the retiree's physician may already be in the HMO network, and no change would be necessary. HMOs also have limited coverage when a member receives medical care outside the plan's relatively small geographic service area. Retirees who plan to spend winter or summer months at another location may have limited coverage except in emergency situations unless they return home for treatment.

MEDICARE PART D: PRESCRIPTION DRUG COVERAGE

Medicare Part D

Along with numerous other changes to Medicare and the establishment of health saving accounts, the Medicare Prescription Drug, Improvement, and Modernization Act adds a prescription drug program to Medicare—*Medicare Part D*. Until Part D became effective in 2006, the act also provided for Medicare-approved drug discount cards. Medicare no longer approves such cards, but some are still issued, often by retail pharmacies and pharmaceutical companies. Some Medicare prescription drug plans also issue them so subscribers to the plan can receive discounts. The act also gives employers a financial incentive to provide or continue to provide drug coverage to retirees as an alternative to enrollment in Part D.

Part D has been a subject of considerable controversy. Some members of Congress argue that it does not go far enough in meeting the needs of seniors; other members of Congress contend that its cost will saddle the government with another major entitlement. Part D is also viewed by some as a boon to the pharmaceutical industry that will cost $400 to $700 billion over the next 10 years. In addition, the rules for this program are very complex.

As with any new program of this magnitude, there will undoubtedly be situations that come to light during its infancy. As a result, changes will undoubtedly take place. Whether they be major or minor, readers need to keep themselves abreast of current developments. One source of such information is the Medicare Web site, www.medicare.gov.

Eligibility

Part D is a voluntary prescription drug benefit that is available to all Medicare beneficiaries enrolled in either Part A and/or Part B (original Medicare) or enrolled in any of the various Medicare Advantage plans. Each enrollee must pay a monthly premium. No one can be denied coverage because of income level or for health reasons. Hereafter, Part D benefits are referred to as *Medicare prescription drug plans*.

Medicare prescription drug plans

Types of Plans

Medicare prescription drug plans are private plans offered by insurance companies, managed care plans, and other organizations. These sponsors typically contract with pharmacy benefit managers to design plan formularies. The plans must meet certain standards and be approved by the Secretary of Health and Human Services.

There are two basic types of Medicare prescription drug plans. One type of plan is for persons enrolled in most Medicare Advantage plans. Typically, members will receive their prescription drug coverage through the drug programs of these plans. The other type of plan, referred to as a *stand-alone plan,* is available to persons enrolled in original Medicare or in certain Medicare Advantage plans. The main differences between these two types of plans are in the process of enrollment and premium payment. This topic is expanded upon later in the section on enrollment.

The Standard Benefit Structure

The act provides for a standard prescription drug plan but also allows for alternative plans to be approved if certain requirements are met and the plans are at least as generous as the standard plan. Most plans that are now available do provide broader coverage than the standard plan, as explained later.

The standard prescription drug program has an initial annual deductible of $250 in 2006. This amount and other dollar figures mentioned below will increase in later years if the expenditures for prescription drugs by Medicare beneficiaries increase.

After the deductible has been satisfied, the plan will pay 75 percent of the next $2,000 of prescription drug costs covered by the plan. Benefits then cease until a beneficiary's total drug costs (including the deductible) reach $5,100. This range where no benefits are paid is often referred to as the *coverage gap* or *doughnut hole*. Once the $5,100 amount is reached, the beneficiary will have had out-of-pocket costs of $3,600 (often referred to as

coverage gap

TROOP or true out-of-pocket costs) in addition to the $420 annual premium. For covered drug costs in excess of $5,100, the beneficiary will then pay for each prescription the greater of (1) 5 percent of the cost of the prescription or (2) a modest copay of $2 for a generic or $5 for a brand name drug. For all but inexpensive drugs, this means that the plan will pay 95 percent of the cost to fill a prescription.

It is important to point out all of the above limits apply to drug costs covered by the plan. If a beneficiary purchases a drug that is not covered by the plan, the beneficiary must pay the full cost for the drug and cannot apply this amount toward the initial deductible or use it to satisfy the previously mentioned limits. In addition, certain other drug costs do not count towards the limits. These include the cost for drugs purchased outside the United States, the cost of drugs specifically excluded by Medicare, and any payments made by most other private or government drug programs. However, drug costs paid by family members and certain state assistance programs do count toward these limits.

The following example shows that beneficiaries with $810 or less in annual prescription drug expenditures will receive no net benefit from the Medicare prescription drug plan, assuming the prescription drug premium is $35 per month. Approximately half of Medicare beneficiaries fall into this category and will need to decide whether they should purchase coverage. The negative side of not signing up when initially eligible, as discussed later, is that there will be a financial penalty for enrollment at a later date when a beneficiary might have significantly higher drug costs.

Example: Roger incurs $810 in covered drug costs during the year.

Payment by drug plan [.75 x ($810 – $250)]	$420
Less premium ($35/month)	–420
	0
Percentage of drug cost paid by Roger	100

The next example shows that Medicare beneficiaries with $5,100 or less in annual prescription drug expenditures will also pay a significant percentage of their drug costs.

Example: Wendy and her husband Keith have annual prescription drug costs of $2,318 and $5,100 respectively. (Wendy's costs are equal to the average prescription drug costs for Medicare recipients.)

Wendy and Keith will each receive $1,500 under their Medicare prescription drug plans. This amount is equal to 75 percent of this first $2,000 in drug costs in excess of the deductible. In Wendy's case, she will have out-of-pocket costs equal to $1,238, or 53 percent of her expenditures. This $1,238 figure is calculated as follows:

Premium	$ 420
Deductible	250
25% of first $2,000 above deductible	500
100% of expenses in excess of $2,250	68
	$1,238

In Keith's case, his expenses in excess of $2,250 are $2,850, and his total out-of-pocket costs and premium are $4,020, or about 79 percent of his drug expenditures.

The percentage of drug costs will drop as costs exceed $5,100 because Part D plans pay 95 percent of this excess amount.

Example: Todd takes several expensive drugs for an assortment of ailments. This year, he expects drug costs to be $20,000. As in the previous example for Keith, Todd will have out-of-pocket costs of $4,020 for the first $5,100 of his drug expenditures. Of the remaining $14,900 in expenditures, he will be responsible for only 5 percent, or $745. Thus his total out-of-pocket costs are $4,765, or about 24 percent of his expenditures.

Medicare prescription drug plans are permitted to incorporate certain cost savings features that are found in many other types of prescription drug plans. These include prior approval for certain drugs, quantity limits, and the use of step therapy.

Covered Drugs

Each Medicare prescription drug plan has a formulary, which is a list of approved drugs that the plan will cover. Formularies do not need to cover every prescription drug. By law, they must include at least two drugs in every therapeutic class. (There are 146 therapeutic classes.) Most plans cover more than the minimum required number of drugs. Medicare drug plans, however, are required to cover a majority of drugs in certain classes. These classes include antidepressant, antipsychotic, anticonvulsant, antiretroviral, anticancer, and immunosuppressant drugs.

There are also some drugs that are excluded from Medicare coverage by law. These include nonprescription drugs, prescription vitamins and minerals, certain barbiturates and benzodiazepines, and drugs for anorexia, weight loss or weight gain, fertility, cosmetic purposes, hair growth, and relief of such symptoms of cold as cough and stuffy nose. It should be pointed out that plans may provide enhanced benefits and cover some of these excluded drugs. However, charges for the drugs will not count towards meeting out-of-pocket limits.

There are two other important points that need to be mentioned about covered drugs: formulary changes and the coverage of nonformulary drugs.

Formulary Changes

A prescription drug plan is allowed to make formulary changes at any time. Such changes must be posted on the plan's Web site at least 60 days prior to the change, and the plan must notify beneficiaries taking the drug of the change. This notification must include (1) the reasons for the formulary change; (2) alternative drugs that are covered and their cost; and (3) information about filing an appeal for an exception (see below). This notification should also be at least 60 days before the change. If later, the beneficiary must be allowed to obtain an additional 60-day supply of the drug.

Nonformulary Drugs

If a prescription drug is not on a plan's formulary, a beneficiary has the right to request that the plan cover a medically necessary drug. Such an "exception" to the formulary is allowed under two circumstances:

- The drug is currently being used and is removed from the plan's formulary for reasons other than safety.
- The beneficiary's doctor prescribes a nonformulary drug because the doctor believes a formulary drug will not work for the beneficiary.

If the plan turns down the exception, there is an appeals process that has several levels. The first level is to ask the plan to reconsider its denial. If the plan still denies the exception, the beneficiary can appeal to an independent review entity, then to an administrative law judge, and finally to the Medicare Appeals Council. There are time frames in which these appeals must be made and in which the body to whom an appeal is made must make its decision. If all appeals fail, a judicial review can be requested in federal court as long as the annual cost of the drug exceeds a specified amount ($1,050 in 2006, subject to indexing thereafter).

Other Qualifications for Drug Plans

In addition to standards for covered drugs and benefits, Medicare prescription drug plans must satisfy several criteria that are designed to protect beneficiaries. Some of these include the following:

- Plans must provide beneficiaries with information on access to covered drugs, how the plan formulary works, copayment and deductible requirements, and any medication therapy management program.
- Plans must provide a mechanism for responses to beneficiary questions, including toll-free telephone access.
- Plans must provide meaningful procedures for hearing and resolving grievances.
- Plans must allow any willing pharmacy to participate as long as it complies with the terms and conditions of the plan.
- Each pharmacy dispensing drugs must inform the beneficiary of any differential between the price of a drug and the price of the lowest-priced generic that is therapeutically equivalent.
- Plans must include in their provider network a sufficient number of pharmacies that dispense drugs other than by mail order to ensure convenient access. Plans do not have to offer drugs by mail order, but almost all do.
- Plans must provide methods for quality-assurance measures and systems to reduce medication errors and adverse drug interaction.
- Plans must provide for medication management programs for beneficiaries who have multiple chronic diseases, who are taking multiple medications, and/or who have high drug expenses.

Plan Variations

Very few Medicare prescription drug plans can be classified as the standard benefit plan. There are several major ways in which most plans might provide more comprehensive benefits, but there are significant variations in how they do this.

Formulary Drugs

Most, if not all, plans have more drugs on their formularies than they are required to include by law. In some cases, the additional drugs are mostly generics; in other cases, there are both generic drugs and brand name drugs.

Reduced Deductibles

Although many drug plans have an annual calendar-year deductible of $250, the majority of drug plans have no initial deductible. There are also a small number of plans that have a deductible under $250, often $100.

Tiered Copayments

In lieu of paying 75 percent of the cost of each drug after the deductible is met, most plans have a tiered copayment structure. This is acceptable as long as the average amount paid by the plan for the initial level of benefits is at least 75 percent.

The following examples show some of these variations.

Example 1:	The plan has a three-tiered copayment structure. Tier I consists of generic drugs and has no copay. Tier II is preferred brand name drugs and has a $15 per prescription copay. The copay is $50 for other brand name drugs, which make up tier III
Example 2:	The plan has a four-tiered copayment structure. It is similar to the plan in example 1, except there is a fourth tier for certain unique and expensive specialty drugs. The copays for the first three tiers are $7, $30, and $60, respectively. The beneficiary must pay 25 percent of the cost of drugs in tier IV.
Example 3:	The plan has a three-tiered copayment structure, but copays also vary by the length of the prescription and whether a network or out-of-network pharmacy is used. Within the network, the copay for tier I generic drugs is $5 for a 30-day supply and $15 for a 90-day supply. For tier II preferred brand drugs, the copays are $30 and $90; for tier III, they are $50 and $150. The beneficiary must pay 40 percent of the cost of formulary drugs purchased from an out-of-network pharmacy.

Benefits in the Coverage Gap

A small number of plans provide benefits in the coverage gap, when drug costs exceed $2,250 but are less than $5,100. In some cases, there is coverage for generic drugs only; in other cases, both generic and brand name drugs are covered.

When there is coverage in this gap, the full cost of the drugs is used to calculate whether the $5,100 threshold has been met.

Where Prescription Can Be Filled

Prescription drug plans use a network of providers to dispense drugs. Some plans operate on a national basis; others operate within defined regions. In some case, the network may include many local pharmacies; in other cases, it may consist of a single large retail chain.

Beneficiaries are allowed to use out-of-network pharmacies only if they cannot be reasonably expected to use a network pharmacy, and they do not get their drugs from the out-of-network pharmacy on a regular basis.

All plans must use walk-in pharmacies. They can, and most plans do, also fill prescriptions through mail-order pharmacies that can be accessed by mail, telephone, fax, or Internet. Unlike other types of prescription plans, Medicare plans do not allow prescriptions to be filled for longer periods of time if a mail-order pharmacy is used. For example, if a 90-day supply can be obtained by mail order, a 90-day supply must be available at local pharmacies. However, some plans have a financial incentive—such as lower copayments—to use mail order.

Cost

The federal government pays a significant subsidy out of general tax revenue to each Medicare prescription drug plan. On the average, this subsidy is about 75 percent of the plan cost for a plan with the standard benefit structure. There are, however, significant variations in the premiums that a beneficiary must pay. Nationally, the premiums average about $32 per month for 2006, but some stand-alone plans cost as little as $10 in many states and may be as high as $70. (For example, the range in Pennsylvania for 2006 runs from $10.14 per month to $68.61.) Premiums for drug coverage under Medicare Advantage drug plans are generally somewhat lower, and a few plans even offer the benefit at no cost. (Again, using Pennsylvania as an example, the premiums range from $0 to $57.41.)

These variations are a function of several factors, including the drugs covered, deductibles, copays, the pharmacies used, and the ability of the plan to negotiate with manufacturers of drugs. Some lower-cost plans are also attempting to buy market share.

Help for Low-Income Beneficiaries

Low-income beneficiaries pay very little for prescription drug plans as a result of additional government subsidies. Persons who receive Supplemental Security Income (SSI) or who are covered by Medicaid or certain other government programs are automatically eligible for the subsidy and pay no premiums. They also have no deductibles or coverage gaps. The only cost is a per prescription copayment of $1 or $2 for generic drugs, depending on income, and $3 to $5 for brand name drugs. And this copayment drops to $0 for persons on Medicaid who reside in nursing homes or certain other institutions and for other low-income persons after prescription drug cost paid by the beneficiary and the drug plan exceed $3,600.

Beneficiaries who are not automatically eligible for the subsidy may apply for it as long as their annual income is below 150 percent of the federal poverty level (for purposes of prescription drug plan elections through early 2006, the federal poverty level is $9,570 for an individual and $12,830 for a married couple living together) and their assets are less than $11,500 ($23,000 if married). The assets included in these amounts are calculated in the same manner as for Medicaid (see chapter 9) and exclude a home and its furnishings, a car, and certain other items. As shown in table 7-1, low-income persons are divided into three categories for purposes of assistance with prescription drug costs.

One important point needs to be mentioned about the premiums for low-income individuals. The previous discussion assumes that their coverage is under a plan that has the average premium for such a plan. If they select a more expensive plan, they will have to pay the incremental premium cost.

TABLE 7-1
Prescription Drug Plan Costs for Low-Income Individuals

	Monthly Premium	Deductible	Drug Costs
Income less than or equal to 135 percent of the federal poverty level and assets below $7,500 ($12,000 if married)	$0	$0	$2 for generic drugs and $5 for other covered drugs; drops to $0 after total annual drug costs exceed $3,600
Income less than or equal to 135 percent of the federal poverty level and assets between $7,500 and $11,500 ($12,000 and $23,000 if married)	$0	$50	15 percent per prescription; drops to $2 and $5 copayments after total annual drug costs exceed $3,600
Income above 135 percent of the federal poverty level but less than or equal to 150 percent of the federal poverty level and assets not more than $11,500 ($23,000 if married)	Varies by income level but discounted	$50	15 percent per prescription; drops to $2 and $5 copayments after total annual drug costs exceed $3,600

Enrollment

In discussing enrollment in Medicare prescription drug plans, it is necessary to look at the initial enrollment period, the penalty for late enrollment, and switching plans. There are also differences in the enrollment process by type of Medicare beneficiary.

Initial Enrollment Period

The initial enrollment period for Medicare prescription drug coverage began November 15, 2005, and extends through May 15, 2006. After that time, the initial enrollment period for a person who becomes eligible for Medicare is the 7-month period that includes the month of eligibility and 3 months before and after that date. This is the same as the enrollment period for Part B. If an individual enrolls during the first 3 months of this period, coverage begins on the first day of the month of Medicare eligibility. If the individual enrolls later, coverage begins the first day of the month after the plan receives the application.

Penalty for Late Enrollment

creditable prescription drug coverage

If an individual fails to enroll in a Medicare prescription drug plan at the time of initial eligibility, there is a penalty unless the person had prior *creditable prescription drug coverage*. Creditable coverage includes prescription drug coverage under other plans that is at least as good as Medicare. These other plans, such as an employer or union plan, must certify the actuarial equivalency of their plan benefits with Medicare. It is not necessary that these plans meet the Medicare prescription drug plan rules; they only must be at least as good. For example, an employer plan might have higher copays than permitted for Medicare plans when prescription costs exceed a specified amount, but this might be offset by no coverage gap. By law, health plans that provide prescription drug coverage must notify persons aged 65 or older whether their prescription drug coverage is creditable or not.

If an individual fails to enroll in a prescription drug plan and has not had creditable coverage, there is a penalty added to the premium. The penalty is equal to 1 percent of the average national Medicare prescription drug plan premium for each month of late enrollment. The percentage does not change after an individual enrolls, but the size of the penalty changes each year as the average premium changes.

Example: Ruth decided not to purchase Medicare prescription drug coverage when she was first eligible because she took no medications. Twenty-four months later, she was taking several medications and decided that drug coverage made sense. If the average monthly Medicare prescription drug plan premium was then $40, her monthly penalty would be 24 percent of the amount, or $9.60. This would be added to the regular premium of the plan she selected. Next year, if the average monthly premium increased 10 percent to $44, her penalty would be $10.56 per month.

The penalty does not apply as long as an individual had prior creditable coverage and does not have a gap in coverage of more than 63 days if prior coverage ceased.

Switching Plans

Beneficiaries of Medicare prescription drug plans can switch to other plans during annual election periods and special election periods.

Annual Election Period. An individual may change prescription drug plans, without evidence of insurability, during an annual election period that runs from November 15 until December 31 of each year. The new plan is effective on the following January 1.

Special Election Period. There are also special enrollment periods when certain events take place. These include

- moving out of the plan's service area
- losing creditable prescription drug coverage by retirement or any other reason that is not the fault of the beneficiary
- returning to original Medicare from a Medicare Advantage plan
- entering or leaving a long-term care facility
- losing coverage because a Medicare prescription drug plan stops offering coverage, fails to provide benefits on a timely basis, or misled the beneficiary about benefits
- enrolling in certain government programs, such as a program of all-inclusive care for the elderly (PACE). PACE is discussed in chapter 18.

Differences by Category of Beneficiary

Different categories of Medicare beneficiaries follow different procedures to enroll in Medicare prescription drug plans. The following sections look at Medicaid recipients, enrollees in original Medicare, and enrollees in Medicare Advantage plans.

Medicaid Recipients. Medicaid recipients receive prescription drug coverage from Medicare rather than their state Medicaid program, starting in 2006. Medicare will tell each recipient the plan they will be enrolled in. A recipient can elect to join a different plan but may be responsible for part of the premium if it is above a specified amount.

Enrollees in Original Medicare. Enrollees in original Medicare may enroll in any stand-alone plan that is available to them. Each enrollee has the option of paying the monthly premium directly to the plan or having it deducted from his or her monthly Social Security benefit.

Enrollees in Medicare Advantage Plans. Most Medicare Advantage plans that operate as HMOs or PPOs offer prescription drug coverage. Members can only obtain their coverage through the plan. If the Medicare Advantage plan does not offer prescription drug coverage, a member may switch to a Medicare Advantage plan that does offer this coverage, or return to original Medicare and purchase stand-alone prescription drug coverage.

Medicare Advantage plans that operate under private fee-for-service arrangements do not have to make prescription drug coverage available. Their enrollees will need to enroll in a stand-alone drug plan.

Making Choices

It is obvious from the prior discussion that the Medicare prescription drug plan is very complex. Seniors will need to make decisions on whether to obtain coverage and, if so, what plan to purchase. Some seniors will need the help of others to help them make their decisions. Information is available on the Web site of Medicare (www.medicare.gov) and such consumer groups as AARP (www.aarp.org) as well as from financial services professionals.

Many factors that should enter into these decisions have previously been addressed. In this final section on Medicare prescription drug plans, these factors are summarized and sometimes discussed in additional detail.

Necessity of Coverage

Seniors fall into three categories with respect to the necessity for coverage: those with creditable coverage, those with less-than-creditable coverage, and those with no drug coverage.

Those with Creditable Coverage. Some seniors are eligible for prescription drug coverage from an employer or union health plan. If this coverage is creditable, there is probably little reason to join a Medicare prescription drug plan. There may be some circumstances when a senior may find the Medicare plan to have features that make it more attractive than the existing coverage. However, extreme caution must be exercised in deciding to drop existing coverage because the individual may not be able to rejoin the plan at a later date. The individual may also be unable to drop the drug coverage without also dropping the entire medical expense coverage under the employer or union plan.

Example: Wilma is retired. She has prescription drug coverage from her previous employer. Her previous employer notifies her that her current coverage, on average, is at least as good as Medicare prescription drug coverage. She reviews the information provided by her previous employer, and she decides to keep the coverage. Because her current coverage is at least as good as Medicare prescription drug coverage, if she later decides to get Medicare prescription drug coverage, she won't have to pay a penalty. If her employer later stops offering prescription drug coverage, she can join a Medicare drug plan within 63 days after her current coverage ends and avoid paying the penalty.

One concern of Congress is that employers or unions that provide prescription drug coverage to retirees will drop this coverage and, possibly, other retiree medical expense coverage because Medicare prescription drug coverage is available. To minimize this from occurring, Medicare provides a subsidy to employers or unions that continue drug coverage as long as it is at least actuarially equivalent to the coverage under a standard prescription drug program.

The annual subsidy is equal to 28 percent of the cost of providing a retiree with up to $5,000 in prescription drugs, subject to a $250 deductible. After 2006, these dollar amounts will be indexed.

Those with Less-Than-Creditable Coverage. Some seniors have employer or union drug coverage that is not creditable. In this case the individual has several choices:

- keep the current plan and join a Medicare drug plan to obtain more complete protection. If an employer is subject to the Medicare secondary rules, the employee's plan pays its drug benefit first and Medicare is secondary.
- drop the current plan and purchase a stand-alone plan along with original Medicare or join a Medicare Advantage plan that has prescription drug coverage. The same caveats previously mentioned for dropping coverage apply in this situation as well.

- do nothing. Unfortunately, the penalty premium will be charged if a Medicare prescription drug plan is later needed and purchased.

As the following example shows, some retiree plans with less-than-creditable coverage are helping seniors with the cost of obtaining adequate coverage.

Example:	Jake is retired. He is in the original Medicare plan. He has prescription drug coverage from his former employer under a Medicare supplement plan. His former employer notifies him that his current prescription drug coverage, on average, is not at least as good as standard Medicare prescription drug coverage. He reviews the information on his options provided by his former employer. He learns that his former employer now has a contract with a certain Medicare prescription drug plan. He also learns that if he joins that plan, his employer will pay part of his Medicare prescription drug coverage monthly premium. Jake joins that Medicare prescription drug plan.

Those with No Coverage. Some seniors without prescription drug coverage prior to enrollment in Medicare will easily realize the importance of prescription drug coverage—particularly if they are already incurring significant drug expenses. Other seniors may question the need for coverage if they are currently incurring few or no prescription drug expenses. They need to be made aware that the use of medications increases with age and the failure to purchase coverage when initially eligible will result in increased premiums if coverage is purchased in the future. Some advisors to seniors suggest that these persons be encouraged to buy the least expensive plan available; they can always change to a different plan if their circumstances change.

Cost

As previously mentioned, the premiums and cost sharing for Medicare prescription drug plans vary considerably. In comparing costs, however, it is important to keep in mind that a lower-cost plan may not be the best choice if it does not cover all the drugs an enrollee is taking, has higher copayments, or requires prescriptions to be filled at inconvenient locations.

Covered Drugs

Not all formularies are alike. Before purchasing a Medicare prescription drug plan, an individual needs to evaluate whether the drugs he or she is taking are covered included on the drug plan's formulary. Plans have Web sites where this can be determined. If the drugs are not available, perhaps a different plan is better. Alternatively, the individual might consult his or her physician to see if there is a formulary drug that is an acceptable substitute.

Example:	Ian takes a relatively expensive drug for his arthritis. He is considering the purchase of a Medicare prescription drug plan that does not include this drug on its formulary. Ian's physician says he should not take the drugs that are on the plan's formulary because of possible side effects. The physician says he can request an exception but feels Ian should try to find a plan that includes the current drug on its formulary. Ian finds another plan, but it is slightly more expensive.

Convenience. Convenience is important to many seniors. They, for example, need to be able to obtain prescription drugs easily and in the way they prefer.

Example:	Claire, a widow, has been in frail health for the last few years. When she became eligible for Medicare, her sister who lives in another state suggested a prescription drug plan that she liked very much and felt provided excellent benefits at a reasonable cost. Unfortunately, the plan uses the pharmacies of a large discount chain, and the nearest such store to Claire is 18 miles away. She also is reluctant to use mail order. Claire checks with her local pharmacy that is only a block's walk away and finds that it participates in two plans that cover the drugs she takes. She has a modest fixed income and selects the lower-cost plan.

ADEQUACY OF FINANCING

partial advance funding

    Part A of Medicare (and Social Security) is based on a system of funding that the Social Security Administration refers to as *partial advance funding.* Under this system, taxes are more than sufficient to pay current benefits and also provide some accumulation of assets for the payment of future benefits. Partial advance funding falls somewhere between *pay-as-you-go financing,* which was once the way Part A was financed, and *full advance funding* as used by private insurance and retirement plans. Under pay-as-you-go financing, taxes are set at a level to produce just enough income to pay current benefits;

under full advance funding, taxes are set at a level to prefund all promised future benefits for those making current contributions.

All payroll taxes and other sources of funds for Parts A and B of Medicare are deposited into two Medicare trust funds. Benefits and administrative expenses are paid out of the appropriate trust fund from contributions to that fund and any interest earnings on accumulated assets. The trust funds have limited reserves to serve as emergency funds in periods when benefits exceed contributions, such as in times of high unemployment. However, current reserves are relatively small and could pay benefits for only a limited time if contributions to a fund ceased. In addition, the reserves consist primarily of IOUs from the Treasury because the contributions have been "borrowed" to finance the government's deficit.

In the early 1980s, considerable concern arose over the potential inability of payroll taxes to pay promised benefits under both Part A of Medicare and Social Security in the future. Through a series of changes, the most significant being the 1983 amendments to the Social Security Act, these problems appeared to have been solved—at least in the short run. The changes approached the problem from two directions. On one hand, payroll tax rates were increased; on the other hand, some benefits were eliminated and future increases in other benefits were scaled back. However, the solutions of 1983 have not worked in the long run. Without further adjustments, the trust funds for the programs have inadequate resources to pay claims in the foreseeable future.

Because of an increasing number of persons aged 65 or older and medical costs that continue to grow at an alarming rate, estimates are that the Medicare trust funds will be depleted by about 2020. The seriousness of this problem was made clear by one of the earliest actions of the second Clinton administration. That action was the passage of legislation to help maintain the solvency of the Medicare trust funds for a few additional years, primarily through encouraging additional enrollment in managed care plans and trimming projected payments to HMOs, hospitals, and doctors. Even though there have been changes to Medicare since that time—most notably the Medicare Prescription Drug, Improvement, and Modernization Act—these changes seem to focus more on expanding benefits rather than addressing how future costs will be met.

It is obvious that changes must be made—either now or later—in the Medicare program. Probably the most important step in finding a solution is to convince the public that changes in this very popular entitlement program must be made. Changes, of course, have significant political implications. While most members of Congress realize the need for reform, neither political party has been willing to risk losing public support by compromising and thus taking the necessary initiative.

In the broadest sense, the solution lies in doing one or both of the following: increasing revenue into the trust funds or decreasing benefit costs. Changes that would increase revenue include the following:

- increasing the Medicare tax rate
- increasing the Medicare Part B premium for everyone beyond its projected levels
- using more general tax revenue to fund the programs

Suggested changes that have been made for decreasing benefit costs include

- increasing the Medicare eligibility age beyond 65
- increasing Medicare deductibles and copayments
- lowering or slowing the growth of payments to Medicare providers
- encouraging or requiring Medicare beneficiaries to enroll in managed care plans

Any single change to the program will offend one important group of voters or another. As a result, the ultimate solution will probably involve a combination of several of the previously mentioned suggestions for change so that everyone will bear a little of the pain.

DEALING WITH MEDICARE

With private insurance, the provisions pertaining to the coverage are spelled out in the policy itself or in a plan document if a person still has employer-provided coverage. Although this is the case with Medicare Advantage plans and Medicare prescription drug plans, it is not the case with original Medicare. Its provisions are contained in the relevant laws, rules, and regulations that pertain to the program. Seniors, their families, and professionals who deal with older clients need to be aware of the mechanics of dealing with Medicare. In this final section of the chapter, some of these details are addressed. They include enrollment, Medicare rights, claims processing, and discharging planning.

Before proceeding, two important resources for seniors should be mentioned. First, the best place to find detailed information about Medicare is to go to its official Web site, www.medicare.gov. On this site are numerous excellent booklets, brochures, and fact sheets. Unfortunately, they are not always that easy to find if a visitor is unfamiliar with the site. The suggestion of the authors of this book is to do a search for the "Medicare Publications Catalog." Once it is located, it lists all the documents that are available. With the name or the publication number, the document can then be accessed. All publications are online and can also be ordered for delivery by mail. Many publications are in Spanish, braille, and/or large print. A small sample of the publications includes the following:

- Medicare and You
- Enrolling in Medicare
- Medicare Coverage of Durable Medical Equipment
- Medicare Hospice Benefits
- Medicare and Home Health Care
- Medicare and Your Mental Health Benefits
- Guide to Medicare's Preventive Services
- Medicare Coverage of Diabetes Supplies and Services
- Your Medicare Rights and Protections

State Health Insurance Assistance Plan (SHIP)

Second, each state has a *State Health Insurance Assistance Plan (SHIP)*. These plans are state programs that get money from the federal government to give free health insurance counseling and assistance to people with Medicare. SHIP counselors can answer questions about Medicare that pertain to such topics as Medicare benefits, dealing with denials and appeals, Medicare rights and protections, sending complaints about care or treatment, and selecting the appropriate Medicare and prescription drug plan. A SHIP also should be able to give guidance about enrolling in Medicaid, selecting a Medicare supplement policy, and buying long-term care insurance. Phone numbers for each state's SHIP can be found on the Medicare Web site.

Enrollment

Enrollment in Medicare Advantage plans and Medicare prescription drug plans is with the private insurers that offer these coverages. The process of enrolling in original Medicare is relatively simple and may be automatic. In other situations, enrollment requires action on the part of a senior.

Individuals who are already receiving retirement benefits from Social Security or the Railroad Retirement Board prior to age 65 are automatically enrolled in both Parts A and B. The Part B premium is then deducted from their retirement benefit. In some cases, individuals may not want Part B. This usually occurs when they are still working and covered under an employer-provided medical expense plan that is primary to Medicare. These individuals must notify Medicare and reject the coverage. Automatic coverage begins the first day of the month an individual turns age 65.

If an individual is nearing age 65 and applies for retirement benefits to begin at that time, Part A is automatic and he or she can elect whether or not to have Part B. Anyone else must contact the Social Security Administration to enroll.

Example 1:   Flora retired this year at age 65. She will not be eligible for full Social Security retirement benefits until she is age 65 and 4 months and has decided not to take a reduced benefit by starting benefits earlier. However, she needs to apply so that her Medicare benefits begin at age 65.

Example 2:   Bob is still working at age 65 and plans on continuing to work for several more years. His employer-provided medical expense coverage costs him $170 per month and has high deductibles and copayments. Bob is convinced that he will have better coverage at a lower cost under Medicare. Even though he does not plan on applying for Social Security retirement benefits, Bob can drop his employer-provided coverage and elect Medicare. However, he must apply. Bob also needs to be aware that he will need a Medicare supplement policy to fill in the gaps of Medicare. The cost of this policy may cause him to change his mind.

If an individual needs to take action to enroll in Part B, there is a 7-month initial enrollment period that begins 3 months before the month a person turns 65. As long as an individual signs up during the first 3 months of this period, coverage begins at the beginning of the month the person turns 65. Application during the last 4 months of the period will delay the effective date of Part B coverage beyond age 65.

If an individual does not elect Part B coverage during the initial enrollment period and is not covered under an employer-provided plan, there is a general enrollment period during the first 3 months of each calendar year. Coverage begins on July 1, and the Part B premium is increased by 10 percent for each full 12-month period of late enrollment.

Example: Gus retired at age 64 and had significant financial resources. Therefore, he decided not to apply for Social Security until age 70 when he would receive much higher benefits because of the delayed retirement credit. Unfortunately, he procrastinated about applying for Medicare when his retiree coverage terminated at age 65 because he was in excellent health and rarely saw a doctor. At age 66, Gus was hospitalized and found himself without medical expense protection. When he did apply, he found out that coverage was not retroactive and that his future Part B premium would be 10 percent higher than normal.

Individuals who do not elect Part B because they are still working and covered under an employer-provided medical expense plan can enroll in Part B without any increase in cost as long as they apply within 8 months of losing the employer-provided coverage. However, they should apply as soon as possible so as to have no gap in their medical expense protection.

Medicare Rights

The Medicare program's laws, rules, and regulations spell out many rights and protections that Medicare beneficiaries have. However, many individuals and their families are often unaware that such rights and protections exist. In some cases, beneficiaries are made aware of their existence but are not in the physical or mental condition to be able to understand them. Perhaps the best way for a Medicare beneficiary or his or her family to understand these rights is to download "Your Medicare Rights and Protections" from the Medicare Web site. This 38-page booklet spells out the Medicare rights and protections and lets readers know where to file complaints and grievances.

The publication lists the following rights that all Medicare beneficiaries have:

Advance Beneficiary Notice (ABN)

- to be treated with dignity and respect at all times
- to be protected from discrimination. This includes the right to have someone help a beneficiary overcome language, physical, or communication barriers.
- to get information about Medicare that can be understood to make health care decisions. For example, a physician, other medical provider, or supplier is required to give beneficiaries an *Advance Beneficiary Notice (ABN)* if they think Medicare will not pay for an item or service. The ABN lists the items or services and explains why Medicare will not pay. This gives a beneficiary the opportunity to make an informed decision about whether he or she still wants the item or service. In some cases, coverage may be available through other insurance that the beneficiary has.
- to have questions about the Medicare program answered
- to get emergency care when needed
- to learn about treatment choices in clear language that can be understood
- to file a complaint about payment, services received, other concerns or problems in getting health care, and the quality of care received. For example, there is an appeals process if a beneficiary feels he or she is being discharged from a hospital too soon. The discharge cannot take place until the appeal is resolved.

- to have personal information that Medicare collects kept private
- to talk with health care providers in private and have health care information kept private by them

There are other specific rights and protections that apply if a Medicare beneficiary elects coverage through a Medicare Advantage plan.

Claims Processing

Most Medicare beneficiaries are under the original Medicare program, and they get their covered treatment and supplies from a wide variety of providers, such as physicians, hospitals, skilled-nursing facilities, home health agencies, and suppliers of medical products and equipment. In most cases, these providers accept assignment of Medicare benefits and are required by law to file claims with Medicare. Medicare then pays the provider directly for any covered benefits or services minus any copayments, percentage participation, or deductibles that are a beneficiary's responsibility. The provider can then bill a beneficiary for these amounts only. The payment from a beneficiary, along with the payment from Medicare, is considered payment in full.

Example:	Following Egnar's first visit of the year to his physician, a bill for $340 was submitted to Medicare. The Medicare-approved charge turned out to be $300, and this is the amount the physician can collect. Medicare paid the physician $160. The remaining $140 represents Egnar's annual Part B deductible of $100 and 20 percent of the remaining $200 of approved charges. The physician can bill Egnar for this amount.

If providers or suppliers do not accept assignment, they are still required to submit bills to Medicare. If they fail to do so, there are provisions for Medicare beneficiaries to file their own claims. In any case, Medicare payments, which Medicare pays directly to a beneficiary, are based on its approved charge, and any balance of a bill is the beneficiary's responsibility. Remember, however, that there is a limit on what physicians who do not accept assignment can charge.

In addition to paying more to a provider or supplier when assignment is not accepted, a beneficiary is often required to pay the full bill at the time of service.

Medicare Summary Notice (MSN)

Medicare beneficiaries get a *Medicare Summary Notice (MSN)* that explains the services and supplies that are billed to Medicare within a 30-day period. The MSN, which is provided by a Medicare carrier or fiscal intermediary that contracts with Medicare, shows billed charges, Medicare-approved charges, and the amount for which a beneficiary can be billed. There are provisions for appealing any Medicare decisions about coverage or the amount of benefits.

Medicare beneficiaries (or someone on their behalf) should read the notice carefully to determine that all the services and supplies that were billed have actually been received. If not, they should contact the provider or supplier for an explanation. If it is unsatisfactory, beneficiaries should contact the Medicare carrier or fiscal intermediary that sent the notice. Their name, address, and phone number are printed on the front page of the notice. A thorough analysis of the MSN may also show that a Medicare beneficiary has not gotten treatment that he or she should be receiving.

Medicare beneficiaries who have elected a Medicare Advantage plan or a Medicare prescription drug plan are subject to the claims processing of that particular plan rather than the provisions previously described. However, these plans must follow rules that are prescribed by Medicare.

Discharge Planning

discharge planning

Medicare was the pioneer in the concept of hospital *discharge planning*, which is a process used to decide what a patient needs for a smooth move from hospital care to another level of care. This process, long required for Medicare beneficiaries, is now the norm for all hospital discharges. It should be pointed out that a discharge from a hospital does not mean that a patient is fully recovered and able to care for himself or herself. It only means that hospital-level care is no longer required. Further care of a medical or custodial nature is still often needed.

A hospital's discharge planner is usually a nurse, social worker, or other appropriately trained person who works with the physician, patient, and family members to determine safe and adequate follow-up care after release from the hospital. But the final authorization for discharge must come from the physician. As mentioned earlier, discharge decisions can be appealed if an individual or family member feels the discharge is premature.

A discharge planner should seek out family members to discuss future care, particularly if it appears that they may have to either provide or arrange for it. If the planner does not, family members should seek out the discharge planner. A good discharge planner will be aware of facilities and agencies that provide care and will often arrange, for example, for home health care or admission to a skilled-nursing facility. He or she should also be aware of the benefits that Medicare provides and that might be available from Medicaid, community agencies, or private insurance polices that an individual may have.

Medicare Supplements

Chapter Outline

Although Medicare provides significant medical expense benefits to its beneficiaries, not all health insurance expenses of older clients are covered. This chapter identifies these gaps and describes the ways in which they might be filled.

GAPS IN THE ORIGINAL MEDICARE PROGRAM

As mentioned in chapter 7, the original Medicare program has many limitations. These limitations create out-of-pocket costs for beneficiaries, known as gaps in benefits, that fall into three categories: fully covered, partially covered, and uncovered services.

Benefit Gaps for Fully Covered Services

Benefit gaps for fully covered services include

- the Part A deductible for each hospital benefit period
- the Part B annual deductible
- the 20 percent participation share of charges for most covered services under Part B

Benefit Gaps for Partially Covered Services

Gaps in benefits for services that are only partially covered include

- home health care that does not meet the program's required conditions
- the first three pints of blood
- all costs for skilled-nursing facility care after day 100 in a benefit period

The only nursing home care that Medicare covers is skilled-nursing care that is provided in a Medicare-certified skilled-nursing facility and is typically needed after a serious illness or hospitalization.

Benefit Gaps for Services That Are Not Covered

Gaps due to services that are not covered include

- vision or dental care
- hearing aids
- private duty nursing
- preventive services other than those mentioned in chapter 7
- emergency care while traveling outside the United States (except in limited cases)
- custodial/long-term care
- outpatient prescription drugs. However, an individual may have coverage under a Medicare prescription drug plan.

FILLING THE GAPS

Estimates indicate 50 to 60 percent of Medicare beneficiaries have some type of coverage to supplement Medicare; these beneficiaries are split among those with coverage provided by a former employer, those who purchase coverage in the individual marketplace, and those who elect Medicare Advantage plans. In addition, Medicaid can be a supplement to Medicare for certain persons with limited assets and income.

Employer-Provided Coverage

Some employers still provide retirees with medical expense benefits to supplement Medicare. These may take the form of Medicare carve-outs or supplements. As mentioned in chapter 2, these benefits are not always secure. Employers may eliminate benefits for future retirees or raise contributions for coverage paid by retired employees. In addition, some retirees may find these benefits eliminated entirely. These retired employees, however, can still obtain additional coverage through Medicare supplement policies or Medicare Advantage plans.

Medicare Supplement (Medigap) Insurance

After the passage of the initial Medicare legislation in 1965, Medicare supplement policies became as diverse as the companies that sold them. This led to some confusion in the marketplace, especially among the older members of the population—the primary market for these products. It also led to some questionable sales practices and duplications of coverage. As a result, in 1990, the Medicare supplement market became directly subject to federal regulation. However, this legislation does not apply to employer-provided Medicare carve-out or Medicare supplement insurance.

Congress directed the NAIC to develop a standardized array of individual policies, all of which would include at least a common core of basic benefits. The technical name of these plans is *Medicare supplement insurance,* but they are often referred to as medigap policies.

In addition to standardizing Medicare supplement policies, Congress mandated several other features, including a 6-month open enrollment period, limited preexisting-conditions exclusions, prohibition of the sale of duplicate coverage, increased individual loss ratios (defined as claims divided by premiums), and guaranteed renewability. Indeed, when describing the benefits of each of the Medicare supplement policies, insurance companies must use the same format, language, and definitions. They also are required to use a uniform chart and outline of coverage to summarize the benefits in each plan. These requirements are intended to make it easier for beneficiaries to compare policies and to select between them based on service, reliability, and price.

Federal laws have also generated several restrictions on the markets to which Medicare supplement policies may be sold. Under these restrictions, known as antiduplication provisions, it is generally illegal for an insurance company to sell a Medicare supplement policy to

- a current Medicare supplement policyowner, unless that person states in writing that the first policy will be cancelled
- a Medicaid recipient
- an enrollee in a Medicare Advantage plan

An insurance company that violates these provisions is subject to criminal and/or civil penalties under federal law.

Medicare supplement insurance

Standardization of Plans

The NAIC initially adopted ten standardized plans of benefits called A through J to fill the gaps in original Medicare. Plan A is the basic benefit package. Each of the other nine original plans includes the basic plan A package and a varying combination of additional benefits, with plan J providing the most comprehensive coverage of all the plans. There are now two additional standard plans (called K and L) that contain consumer-directed health plan features. (Note that plans A through L are often referred to as policies A through L.)

States may approve, and insurers may offer, fewer than the 12 standard plans, but all states must permit the basic benefit plan to be sold. Insurers must sell plan A if they wish to sell any other plan. Most states now permit the sale of all 12 plans, but a few states limit the types sold, and three states (Massachusetts, Minnesota, and Wisconsin) maintain somewhat different standardized plans that were already in place prior to the federal legislation. Despite their differences, the standardized plans in these three states are required to contain the basic Medicare supplement (plan A) benefits available in all other states.

The Basic Benefit Plan. The basic benefits contained in plan A, and that must be included in all the other nine original plans, consist of the following:

- hospitalization—payment of the beneficiary's percentage participation share of Medicare Part A expenses for the 61st through the 90th day of hospitalization and the 60 lifetime reserve days. In addition, full coverage is extended for 365 additional days after Medicare benefits end.
- medical expenses—payment of the beneficiary's percentage participation share (generally 20 percent) for Medicare-approved Part B charges for physicians' and medical services
- blood—payment for the first three pints of blood each year

Table 8-1 compares benefit payments by original Medicare and Medicare supplement plan A with remaining beneficiary payment amounts. These are the amounts for 2006; many of the dollar amounts are subject to annual inflation adjustment.

Additional Medicare Supplement Plan Benefits. The other nine original Medicare supplement plans include, in addition to the basic benefits, an array of coverage and benefits that are not included in original Medicare. These additions encompass the following:

- paying the hospital inpatient Part A deductible for each benefit period
- paying the Part A percentage participation share for the 21st through the 100th day of skilled-nursing facility care

TABLE 8-1
Comparison of Payment Responsibility (for 2006) by Original Medicare, Basic Medicare Supplement (Plan A), and the Beneficiary

	Medicare Pays	Medicare Supplement (Plan A) Pays	Beneficiary Pays
Medicare Part A			
Deductible[a]	0	0	$952
First 60 days	100%	0	0
61 to 90 days	All but $238 a day	$238 a day	0
91 to 150 days (lifetime reserve)[b]	All but $476 a day	$476 a day	0
Up to an additional 365 days (lifetime)	0	100% of Medicare-eligible expenses	0
Blood[c]	All but 3 pints	3 pints	0
Hospice care	Most expenses	0	Balance
Skilled-nursing facility			
First 20 days	100%	0	0
21 to 100 days	All but $119 a day	0	Up to $119 a day
Medicare Part B			
Deductible[d]	0	0	$124
Coinsurance benefit[e]	80% (generally)	20% (generally)	0
Blood[f]	80% after 3 pints	3 pints and then 20%	0
Clinical laboratory services	100%	0	0
Home health care (includes Part A benefits)			
Skilled services and supplies	100%	0	0
Durable medical equipment	80%	20%	0

a. The hospital inpatient deductible, applicable once per benefit period
b. Sixty days of care after the first 90 days of a hospital stay, available for payment by Medicare, which the beneficiary may use only once during a lifetime
c. Received in a hospital or skilled-nursing facility during a covered stay
d. Deductible satisfied once per calendar year when the beneficiary is billed the first $124 in approved amounts for all Part B services in that year
e. Beneficiary responsible for all Part B excess charges (above Medicare-approved amounts) for approved services because such charges are unpaid by Medicare and not covered by plan A
f. Received as an outpatient or as part of Part B covered services

- paying the annual Part B deductible
- paying charges for physicians' and medical services that exceed the Medicare-approved amount (either 80 or 100 percent of these charges up to the charge limitation set by Medicare or the state)
- paying 80 percent of the charges after a $250 deductible for emergency care in a foreign hospital (with several limitations) and a $50,000 lifetime maximum
- paying (up to $1,600 per year) for a care provider to give assistance with activities of daily living (at-home recovery) while a beneficiary qualifies for Medicare home health care benefits (with certain limitations)
- certain preventive care that is not covered by Medicare, such as an annual physical

Plans H, I, and J were originally designed to pay 50 percent of outpatient prescription drug charges after a $250 deductible up to an annual $1,250 or $3,000 calendar limit. Beginning in 2006, insurance companies may no longer issue these policies to new insureds with a drug benefit included. Persons already insured under these policies have several options. They may continue to renew them with drug benefits included as long as they do not enroll in the new Medicare prescription drug program. However, they will then probably be subject to the penalty for late enrollment if they later enroll in the program because the benefits under the Medicare supplement policy will likely not qualify as creditable coverage. If they enroll in the Medicare prescription drug program, they may keep in force their existing Medicare supplement policies but with the drug benefit eliminated and the premium adjusted accordingly. Alternatively, they can switch to another available Medicare supplement policy that has no drug benefit. Such a switch is allowed without evidence of insurability or a penalty for preexisting conditions as long as it occurs during the initial Part D enrollment period.

Table 8-2 indicates which of these other benefits plans B through J provide.

Consumer-Directed Plans. Plans K and L provide the basic Medicare supplement benefits previously described plus the Part A hospital deductible and skilled-nursing facility care for days 21 through 100. They also pay a portion of any cost sharing for hospice care and respite care covered by Medicare Part A. Compared to the ten original Medicare supplement plans, plans K and L require cost sharing by the insured for certain covered services, subject to an out-of-pocket limit.

Plan K requires the insured to pay 50 percent of the following:

- the Part A deductible
- the daily copayment for days 21 through 100 of skilled-nursing facility care

TABLE 8-2
Benefits Under Medicare Supplement Policies

	A	B	C	D	E	F	G	H	I	J
Basic benefits	X	X	X	X	X	X	X	X	X	X
Skilled-nursing facility (days 21–100)			X	X	X	X	X	X	X	X
Part A deductible		X	X	X	X	X	X	X	X	X
Part B deductible			X			X				X
Part B excess charges						100%	80%		100%	100%
Foreign travel emergency			X	X	X	X	X	X	X	X
At-home recovery				X			X		X	X
Preventive medical care					X					X
Prescription drugs								$1,250*	$1,250*	$3,000*

* Not available with the new plans; can be eliminated by persons who enroll in a Medicare prescription drug plan

- the first three pints of blood
- the percentage participation for Part B services except preventive services, which are covered at 100 percent
- hospice and respite care cost sharing

When the insured's out-of-pocket payments for these services plus the Part B deductible equal $4,000, plan K will pay 100 percent of the self-responsible amounts (any required copayments and percentage participation) for Medicare services for the rest of the calendar year. However, provider charges that exceed Medicare-approved amounts (excess charges) do not count toward the annual out-of-pocket limit.

Plan L is identical to plan K except that the percentage the insured must pay is 25 percent rather than 50 percent. In addition, the out-of-pocket limit is $2,000.

Medicare Supplement Variations. Except for conformance with the alternative standards in Massachusetts, Minnesota, and Wisconsin, insurance companies cannot offer Medicare supplement policies that differ from these standardized options and cannot change the combination of benefits or the letter names of any of the policies. However, there are two allowable variations: high-deductible policies and Medicare SELECT policies.

High-Deductible Policies. Companies can offer two high-deductible Medicare supplement standard policies. These policies are identical to plans F and J except that they have a high-deductible amount ($1,790 for 2006, subject to annual adjustment) before the plan pays any benefit. Separate annual deductibles for prescription drugs ($250) in plan J and foreign travel emergencies ($250) in plans F and J also apply. The monthly premium for plans F and J under the high-deductible option is generally less than the monthly premium for plans F and J without a high-deductible option. However, the savings may be offset by the out-of-pocket payments for services required before satisfying the deductible. Perhaps reflecting their lack of popularity, few insurers offer high-deductible Medicare supplement policies.

Medicare SELECT

Medicare SELECT. Medicare SELECT may be any one of the 12 standardized Medicare supplement insurance policies (although plans C, D, and F are most popular) in which the beneficiary must use the insurance plan's designated hospitals and doctors for nonemergency services to be eligible for full supplemental insurance benefits. Medicare SELECT policies are issued by insurance companies as PPO products and by some HMOs.

When a beneficiary goes to the Medicare SELECT preferred provider, Medicare pays its share of the approved charges and the insurance company is responsible for all supplemental benefits in the Medicare SELECT policy. In general, Medicare SELECT policies are required to pay full benefits only if a preferred provider is used for nonemergency services. However, Medicare pays its share of approved charges in any case. As an inducement to increase beneficiary and provider participation, physicians and suppliers under contract with Medicare SELECT insurers may waive Part B service cost-sharing amounts for beneficiaries under Medicare SELECT policies. Medicare SELECT policy premiums are generally 15 to 25 percent less than the monthly premium for the same plan without the required use of a preferred-provider network.

A beneficiary who has had a Medicare SELECT policy for at least 6 months has the right to switch to a regular Medicare supplement policy sold by the same company, as long as the new policy has equal or less coverage than the Medicare SELECT policy. This right is in addition to the other enrollment options discussed in the following section on eligibility.

Plan Popularity. The most widely available Medicare supplement plans are A, C, D, and F. Plan A generally represents less than 5 percent of Medicare supplement sales, however. Plan F represents more than half, while plans C and D make up approximately a third of total sales. Medicare

SELECT policies, which are generally less available, represent no more than 10 percent of total Medicare supplement sales.

The popularity of plan F is presumed to result from seniors' desire to obtain its coverage of easily identified and likely to be incurred out-of-pocket amounts for deductibles, percentage participation shares, and excess physician charges. In addition, plan F premiums may be more attractive because they are unburdened by desirable but costly benefits for prescription drugs, preventive medical care, and/or at-home recovery featured in other plans.

Eligibility

In the absence of any Medicare supplement regulation to the contrary, insurers are free to conduct normal underwriting, including premium rating, preexisting-conditions exclusions, and waiting periods. However, federal regulation creates a broad area of protected enrollment circumstances for beneficiaries who purchase Medicare supplement policies. These protected circumstances are categorized as either normal open enrollment or specified coverage changes. However, even outside of these circumstances, when a beneficiary replaces a Medicare supplement policy, federal requirements may apply.

Open Enrollment. There is an open enrollment period for the purchase of a Medicare supplement policy during the 6-month period that starts on the first day of the month in which a beneficiary is both age 65 or older *and* enrolled in Medicare Part B. During this 6-month period, a beneficiary may buy any Medicare supplement policy sold by a company doing Medicare supplement business in the beneficiary's state. The insurance company cannot deny insurance coverage, place conditions on a policy (like delaying the start of coverage), or change the price of a policy because of past or present health problems. The company can use preexisting-conditions restrictions or exclusion periods for up to 6 months after the effective date of the policy for medical treatments or advice the beneficiary received within 6 months before the date that the policy goes into effect. However, such restrictions are limited, as the company must reduce even this exclusion period for any period of creditable coverage. Thus, if the beneficiary had at least 6 months of creditable coverage, any health problem would be covered immediately. In general, creditable coverage includes medical coverage under a group, individual, or government-sponsored health plan, including the time already spent under Medicare Part A or enrolled in Part B. In order to receive credit toward preexisting-conditions restrictions, breaks in health coverage must last no longer than 63 calendar days.

Specified Coverage Changes. Three specific situations involving health care coverage changes permit the beneficiary to buy a Medicare supplement policy under protected enrollment circumstances (also known as Medicare supplement protection rights) after the normal Medicare supplement open enrollment period has ended. These circumstances, which are subject to very specific conditions, can be summarized as (1) when existing coverage ends involuntarily, (2) after Medicare supplement coverage is dropped to enter a Medicare Advantage plan for the first time, and (3) when an initially selected Medicare Advantage alternative to the original Medicare program is dropped. In each case, the beneficiary receives the same enrollment protection provided under normal open enrollment with immediate coverage for all preexisting conditions. However, the beneficiary must apply for the new Medicare supplement policy within 63 days after the end of the previous coverage.

When Existing Coverage Ends Involuntarily. A protected Medicare supplement enrollment period exists if the beneficiary's current health coverage that pays for Medicare services—including a Medicare Advantage alternative plan, employer group health plan, Medicare supplement policy, or Medicare SELECT policy—ends involuntarily because

- an alternative plan no longer provides Medicare services to beneficiaries in the enrollee's area
- the beneficiary moves outside the alternative plan's service area
- the alternative health plan fails to meet its contract obligations
- a Medicare supplement insurance company discontinues a Medicare supplement or Medicare SELECT policy (must cancel all policies of the same type in a state)

Under these circumstances, the beneficiary has the right to buy Medicare supplement plan A, B, C, or F (whichever is available in the beneficiary's state). However, the beneficiary must remain with the existing health plan until its coverage ends.

After Medicare Supplement Coverage Is Dropped to Enter an Alternative Medicare Plan for the First Time. A protected Medicare supplement enrollment period exists if a beneficiary drops coverage under a Medicare supplement policy to join a Medicare Advantage alternative plan or purchase a Medicare SELECT policy for the first time and then leaves that plan or policy within one year to return to original Medicare. The beneficiary is allowed to return to his or her former Medicare supplement plan from the same insurance company, if it is available. If the same policy is unavailable, the beneficiary may choose among Medicare supplement plans A, B, C, and F, whichever are available in his or her state. In either case, the beneficiary must apply for Medicare supplement coverage within 63 calendar days after the previous health plan coverage ends. Again, all the open enrollment protections apply, as well as immediate coverage of all preexisting conditions.

When an Initially Selected Medicare Advantage Plan Is Dropped to Return to Original Medicare. A protected Medicare supplement enrollment period exists when a beneficiary joins a Medicare Advantage plan after first becoming eligible for Medicare at age 65 and voluntarily leaves that plan within 1 year to enroll in original Medicare. The beneficiary must be allowed to buy any Medicare supplement policy sold in his or her state.

Other Voluntary Replacements. Finally, a beneficiary may wish to replace an existing Medicare supplement policy with a new one from the same insurer or another company to obtain better benefits, more extensive services, or a more affordable premium. If the existing plan is a standardized Medicare supplement plan issued subject to federal regulations, the insurer must give credit for the time the policy was in effect toward the 6-month preexisting-conditions restrictions in the new policy. However, if a benefit is included in the new policy that was not in the old one, a waiting period of up to 6 months may be applied to that particular benefit. As noted earlier, the insurer must obtain a statement that the beneficiary intends to cancel the existing policy.

The federal Medicare supplement requirements do not apply to Medicare supplement policies sold before such policies were standardized. Consequently, some beneficiaries may be required to switch if an older policy was not guaranteed renewable and the company discontinues that type of Medicare supplement coverage. Others with guaranteed renewable policies may wish to switch to a standardized Medicare supplement policy for better rates and/or service. In both cases, the beneficiaries may face medical underwriting and are not allowed to go back to the previous nonstandardized Medicare supplement policy.

Medicare Supplement Policy Premiums

While health status is prohibited from being used as a factor, insurers, subject to state law, set their own premium rates for the Medicare supplement policies that they offer. Thus, Medicare supplement premiums differ depending on the company issuing the policy and the geographic location and age of the enrollee.

Insurance companies have three different ways of pricing policies based on age. No-age-rated, or community-rated, policies charge everyone the same rate no matter his or her age. Issue-age-rated policies charge a premium based on enrollee age when the policy is first purchased. The cost does not automatically increase as the enrollee gets older, and it is the same for anyone buying the policy for the first time at the same age. Attained-age-rated policies are based on the enrollee's age each year. So while attained-age policies cost less at age 65, their costs go up automatically as the enrollee gets older. Regardless of the method used, premiums can and do increase because of inflation and rising health care costs.

A few states require companies to sell only community-rated policies, and several allow only issue-age rates. Insurers generally favor attained-age rates because the resulting lower initial premiums can be more attractive to price-sensitive shoppers comparing standardized products. However, some companies may offer their customers a choice of attained-age or issue-age rates. Insurers may vary Medicare supplement premium rates or offer discounts based on gender, health habits (such as tobacco use), and marital status.

Under-Age-65 Enrollment Issues

In addition to covering persons aged 65 or older, Medicare also covers the disabled and those with end-stage renal disease under age 65. These beneficiaries may also purchase any available Medicare supplement policy during the 6-month period that begins on the first day of the month in which they become 65 and are also enrolled in Part B, even if the Part B enrollment occurred prior to age 65.

More than a third of the states go beyond federal law and require insurance companies in the Medicare supplement market to offer at least one kind of Medicare supplement policy during an open enrollment period for Part B beneficiaries under age 65. These beneficiaries will also receive the normal Medicare supplement open enrollment opportunity when they become 65. Some companies voluntarily sell Medicare supplement policies to people with Medicare under age 65.

Medicare supplement policies sold to Medicare eligibles under age 65, whether by state mandate or voluntarily, must conform to the same standardized requirements as programs sold to beneficiaries who are age 65 and older.

Ease of Claims Filing

Under most circumstances, the beneficiary obtains services that are covered by both Medicare and Medicare supplement insurance without having to file a separate claim with the Medicare supplement insurer. By law, the Medicare carrier that processes Medicare Part B claims must send the claim to the Medicare supplement insurer. The Medicare supplement insurance company makes payments directly to the doctor or other provider when the following conditions are met:

- the doctor or supplier has signed a participation agreement with Medicare to accept assignment of Medicare claims for all patients who are Medicare beneficiaries
- the beneficiary has a Medicare supplement policy
- the beneficiary indicates on the Medicare claim form that payment of the Medicare supplement benefit is to be made to the participating provider

In most cases, Medicare supplement insurance companies have special agreements with Medicare under which claims are sent directly to the insurance company, even if the doctor does not accept assignment.

Medicare Advantage Plans

Medicare Advantage plans, discussed in chapter 7, typically provide comprehensive benefits that fill many gaps in the original Medicare program. Indeed, beneficiaries enroll in these alternatives to obtain benefits for the otherwise self-responsible amounts unpaid by Medicare for covered services and to expand coverage—for prescription drugs and additional hospital days, for example. As stated previously, Medicare Advantage plans may and often do charge an additional premium for these benefits.

Consequently, Medicare Advantage plans affect Medicare supplement policies directly because they render the benefits of these policies inapplicable or redundant. Indeed, that is the intention of the framers of the Medicare Advantage legislation. By law, Medicare supplement policies must be written exclusively in conjunction with the original Medicare program that continues to cover about 85 percent of beneficiaries. In addition, beneficiary enrollment and disenrollment in alternative plans requires the guaranteed issue of Medicare supplement policies under certain circumstances.

Medicaid

Medicare beneficiaries who have low incomes and limited resources may also receive help from the Medicaid program. For such persons who are eligible for *full* Medicaid coverage, Medicaid pays the Medicare premium and cost-sharing amounts. It also supplements Medicare coverage with services that are available under their state's Medicaid program. These additional services may include, for example, nursing facility care beyond the 100-day limit covered by Medicare, prescription drugs, eyeglasses, and hearing aids. For person enrolled in both programs, any services that are covered by Medicare are paid for by the Medicare program before any payments are made by the Medicaid program (since Medicaid is always the "payer of last resort").

For certain other low-income persons who are ineligible for full Medicaid coverage, Medicaid provides assistance with the payment of Medicare premium and cost-sharing amounts only.

Medicaid is discussed in detail in chapter 9.

PUTTING IT ALL TOGETHER

In the last two chapters, the discussion focuses primarily on ways that persons aged 65 and older can meet their insurance needs for medical expenses. The possibilities are many—original Medicare, Medicare Advantage plans, Medicare prescription drug plans, and Medicare supplements. Most, but not all, seniors will have to make choices among available alternatives when they turn 65. It should be pointed out that, unlike the situations in earlier years when coverage may have been under a family policy that covered both a husband and wife, the plans available to persons aged 65 and older are provided to each individual separately. A husband and wife will need to make separate decisions and are not required to make the same choices.

Several factors influence seniors when they make these decisions. For many, the most important factor is cost. Not every mix of alternatives is priced the same. And the lowest-priced alternative might have unacceptable drawbacks to some seniors. Another factor is plan availability. For example, not every senior lives in a geographic region served by a Medicare Advantage plan. Personal preferences and lifestyle may also enter into these decisions.

The following examples show some of the ways that needs and preferences of seniors may differ when confronted with decisions that need to be made at age 65.

Example 1:	José is still employed and is covered under a very good medical expense plan, for which he pays a modest monthly premium. For José, the situation is easy. He needs to do nothing now. His decisions are deferred until he retires.
Example 2:	Marjorie has been widowed for several years and has extremely meager financial resources. She has no alternative but to rely on public assistance in the form of Medicaid (discussed in chapter 9). Her decisions are largely made by her state's Medicaid program.
Example 3:	Julia is very fortunate in that her employer provides excellent retiree coverage, including prescription drug benefits. The retiree coverage is coordinated with original Medicare, so all she needs to do is enroll in Medicare.
Example 4:	Felix is in good health and was previously covered under an HMO plan with which he was satisfied. Original Medicare, a Medicare prescription drug plan, and a Medicare supplement policy will cost him $250 per month. However, the HMO under which Felix has been covered also has a Medicare Advantage plan for seniors (including drug coverage) for a monthly premium of $137. Felix sees no reason not to select the Medicare Advantage plan even though he could afford the $250.

Example 5:   Geri has been covered by an employer-provided PPO plan at the same place Felix works. Unlike Felix, her resources in retirement are more limited. For this reasons, she seriously considered the Medicare Advantage plan to save $113 per month. Unfortunately, this would have required her to change her long-time primary care physician, which she is unwilling to do as long as she can afford the higher cost of original Medicare and purchasing the other policies.

Example 6:   Tara was covered by an employer-provided PPO plan prior to retirement but has no retiree coverage. She lives in a region that is not served by any Medicare Advantage plans. Therefore, Tara will need to sign up for original Medicare and select both a Medicare prescription drug plan and Medicare supplement policy. After analyzing the available drug plans, Tara picked a plan that covers two medications that she takes on a regular basis and which uses the local pharmacy that she has used for many years. Tara intends to travel during her retirement and selected a Medicare supplement plan that includes benefits for foreign travel emergencies.

Example 7:   Peter will work until age 67 so that he can have employer-provided coverage for his wife, Janet, until she reaches age 65. Janet has severe health problems and sees several specialists. They have ruled out a Medicare Advantage plan for Janet at age 65 because of restrictions on her ability to see the specialists of her choice and the necessity for referrals. Janet will enroll in original Medicare. She will select a Medicare prescription drug plan that covers the many medications that she takes. She will also purchase a Medicare supplement plan F because it covers 100 percent of Medicare Part B excess charges. Peter, who is in excellent health, is still undecided which options he will select.

Example 8:   When Christopher retired at age 65, he elected original Medicare because he planned to spend winters in Key West and summers in Provincetown. Even though he had been used to managed care when he was employed, the Medicare Advantage plan available in his home town of Philadelphia had limited benefits for care received outside its Pennsylvania service area. In addition to a Medicare supplement policy, Christopher purchased a Medicare prescription drug plan that used pharmacies throughout the country.

Example 9:   Prior to her retirement, Mabel worked for an employer who only offered managed care plans. She was never happy with any of the plans that the employer provided. After retirement, she was more than happy to sign up for original Medicare rather than a Medicare Advantage plan. She views this and the purchase of a prescription drug plan and a Medicare supplement policy to be worth the cost to free her from unwanted managed care restrictions.

9

Medicaid and Veterans' Benefits

Chapter Outline

Chapter 7 introduced Medicare as an important government program that pays for medical care and some limited long-term care services that retirees may need. This chapter discusses two other public programs to meet medical and long-term care needs: Medicaid and veterans' benefits.

Medicaid, like Medicare, came into existence in the mid-1960s through amendments to the Social Security Act. Medicaid is a public assistance or welfare program; it provides medical and long-term care benefits to low-income persons, but bases those benefits on categories of eligibility and levels of financial need. Each state has its own rules, which must meet federal guidelines. In return, the federal government finances the major portion of each state's program. At the federal level, the Centers for Medicare & Medicaid Services (CMS) administers Medicaid.

The federal Department of Veterans Affairs provides various health care benefits to military veterans. For certain veterans, this includes not only medical care, but also some types of long-term care.

This chapter begins with Medicaid and discusses the program in detail. After Medicare, Medicaid is the public program that is most likely to be relevant to retirees, although few of them initially would consider it so. The chapter concludes with a summary of the health care services available through veterans' benefits.

MEDICAID

Medicaid is a federal/state program that is the largest source of payments for the medical care of eligible individuals and families with low incomes and assets. Medicaid has more than 40 million beneficiaries, with annual expenditures comprising state funds and matching federal funds in excess of $275 billion. The Medicaid program is also the largest payer of long-term care services in institutional settings and will continue to be so in the years ahead. In the upcoming decades, Medicaid is projected to be second only to Medicare in payment for home health services.

As a condition of participation, the federal government mandates that states cover certain groups of individuals under Medicaid and provide certain mandatory benefits. At the same time, states have a great deal of flexibility to broaden coverage to additional populations and offer additional benefits. This flexibility allows states to use federal matching funds under Medicaid to adapt the program to meet their own specific needs. Indeed, optional services provided and optional populations served by Medicaid account for over 60 percent of all Medicaid spending. Significantly, approximately 85 percent of the optional spending is for the elderly and persons with disabilities.[1]

Moreover, within broad federal requirements, each state also (1) establishes its own eligibility standards, (2) determines the type, amount, duration, and scope of services, (3) sets the rate of payment for services, and (4) administers its own program. Not surprisingly, Medicaid is a complex program that varies considerably among states, even those of similar size or geographic proximity.

In general, persons must be American citizens to be eligible for Medicaid. Illegal aliens who are otherwise eligible for Medicaid cannot qualify except for emergency care. Legal immigrants can qualify under certain circumstances, depending on their date of entry into the United States. A person must also be a resident of the state offering Medicaid coverage for which the person is applying. In general, a person is a resident of a state if he or she is living there with the intention of remaining indefinitely, regardless of the brevity of that residency prior to application for Medicaid.

This section of the chapter continues with a discussion of retirees and the need for Medicaid, qualifying as a Medicaid beneficiary, and the benefits that Medicaid provides.[2] It then reviews the Medicaid program safeguards. The section concludes with a description of Medicaid shortcomings and a discussion about Medicaid planning. Throughout this section, the discussion also points out several effects on Medicaid from the Deficit Reduction Act of 2005 (DRA) enacted on February 8, 2006.

Retirees and the Need for Medicaid

Most persons who plan for retirement usually do not anticipate a need for Medicaid. Medicaid is a welfare or "safety net" program that is normally unneeded by persons of means. Nevertheless, unanticipated circumstances may cause persons of means to need such a safety net to pay for medical and long-term care services. For example, a calamitous personal financial loss can wipe out substantial financial resources accumulated over a lifetime. Similarly, the protracted cost of treatment and care as well as a loss of income arising from an illness, accident, or disability can have the same outcome for persons usually considered well off.

Many other persons who may be financially independent but have modest personal incomes and assets may be more likely to need a safety net. These persons enjoy retirement by relying largely on a combination of Social Security income and Medicare, which they supplement with their own resources. They, too, may need the Medicaid program if faced with major adverse events.

Still other persons of means who need health care, in particular long-term care, spend down resources to pay for the care and then qualify for Medicaid. Adopting this strategy is a personal decision. Some persons will make every attempt to avoid public assistance and will apply for Medicaid only as a payer of last resort. Other persons have no qualms about accepting Medicaid and view it as their right.

Qualifying as a Medicaid Beneficiary

In general, to qualify as a Medicaid beneficiary, a person must be in an eligible category and satisfy income and resource criteria. Medicaid covers three main groups of low-income Americans: the elderly (persons aged 65 and over), the disabled (including the blind), and parents and children. Of the more than 47 million Americans who are Medicaid beneficiaries, about 11 percent are elderly, 12 percent are disabled, 53 percent are children, and 24 percent are parents, mostly women, in families with children.[3] For each eligible category, Medicaid qualification also requires the satisfaction of financial criteria. These criteria specify income and resource requirements that each state determines within federal guidelines.

Subsequent sections of this chapter review the eligible categories under which retirees may be eligible for Medicaid. Two likely categories of Medicaid eligibility in which a retiree may qualify for Medicaid is as a low-income person aged 65 or older or a disabled person if younger.

Ongoing legislative and regulatory changes continue to increase a state's ability to obtain federal matching funds for a broad spectrum of services and eligibility alternatives that go beyond federally mandated requirements. Generally, these changes broaden the low-income populations that can qualify for Medicaid. Consequently, retirees of any age with modest resources whose future is challenged by a lack of resources to pay for medical care and their advisors should carefully examine the Medicaid eligibility requirements in their state. The best place to begin the search for detailed information on Medicaid is at the federal government's Web site, www.cms.hhs.gov/medicaid. This site contains consumer information on Medicaid with access to specific state Medicaid program information. In addition, some local governments (cities and counties) provide health care programs for residents that a state's Medicaid program may not provide.

Upon qualification, a Medicaid beneficiary may receive reimbursement of out-of-pocket costs for covered services during the 3-month period prior to application for Medicaid as long as the program's qualification requirements were satisfied as of that date. Qualification for Medicaid, once established, is subject to redetermination as to both category and financial criteria at least once every 12 months.

Beneficiaries who, due to a change in income or resources, no longer satisfy the financial criteria in their state under their eligibility category lose their entitlement to Medicaid coverage. Disabled persons on Medicaid are also subject to periodic review as to whether they remain disabled for purposes of Medicaid. However, before terminating Medicaid coverage, the state Medicaid agency must determine that the beneficiary does not qualify under any other applicable financial criteria or eligibility category.

Medicaid Benefits

State Medicaid programs must cover a minimum set of benefits, known as mandatory benefits. States may cover additional types of services, known as optional benefits, and receive federal matching funds for their costs. Because states have flexibility to design their own benefit packages, subject to federal minimum requirements, these vary significantly from state to state.

States have discretion to vary the amount, duration, or scope of mandatory or optional services that they cover, but in all cases, the services must be reasonably sufficient to achieve their purpose. For example, a state may not limit coverage for inpatient hospital stays to 1 day of care. With amendments to their plans, states may also impose premiums and/or cost sharing on most nonemergency services, including prescription drugs. DRA expands this authority. However, states may not impose such payment requirements upon children, pregnant women, the terminally ill, and certain nursing home residents.

States may not vary the amount, duration, or scope of mandated or optional services based on the individual's residence or solely based on an individual's diagnosis, types of illness, or condition. For example, when providing benefits, a state may not provide them only in urban areas or exclude cancer patients from treatment with drugs. Nevertheless, through waivers authorized by the Secretary of Health and Human Services (HHS), states can target services to certain regions of a state, populations, and categories of illness.

The following paragraphs present Medicaid benefits under the headings of mandatory benefits, optional benefits, waiver services, and assistance with Medicare premiums and cost-share payments.

Mandatory Benefits

States must provide most Medicaid beneficiaries with coverage for a broad array of basic acute and long-term care services if the services are medically necessary. Table 9-1 lists these mandatory items and services.

TABLE 9-1
Medicaid Benefits Categories

Mandatory Items and Services	Optional Items and Services
Acute Care	
Physicians' services Laboratory and X-ray services Inpatient hospital services Outpatient hospital services Early and periodic screening, diagnostic, and treatment services for individuals under 21 Family planning services and supplies Federally qualified health center services Rural health clinic services Nurse midwife services Certified nurse practitioner services	Medical care or remedial care furnished by licensed practitioners under state law Prescribed drugs Diagnostic, screening, preventive, and rehabilitative services Clinic services Primary care case management services Dental services; dentures Physical therapy and related services Prosthetic devices; eyeglasses Tuberculosis-related services Other specified medical and remedial care
Institutional Services for Long-Term Care	
Nursing facility services for individuals 21 and over	Inpatient hospital and nursing facility services for individuals aged 65 and over in an institution for mental diseases Intermediate care facility for individuals with mental retardation Inpatient psychiatric hospital services for individuals under age 21
Home and Community-Based Services for Long-Term Care	
Home health care services (for individuals entitled to nursing facility care)	Home health care services Case management services Respiratory care services for ventilator-dependent individuals Personal care services Private duty nursing services Hospice care Home and community-based services (under waivers subject to budget-neutrality requirements)

Source: *Medicaid Enrollment and Spending by "Mandatory" and "Optional" Eligibility and Benefit Categories,* The Kaiser Commission on Medicaid and the Uninsured, Washington, DC, February 2005, p. 3.

Optional Benefits

States have the option of covering additional services and receiving federal matching funds for them. Table 9-1 also identifies these optional services. All states cover several, if not most, of the optional service categories. In some states, Medicaid expenditures for optional services are greater than expenditures on mandatory services.

Waiver Services

As stated previously, a state can implement waiver services that allow greater flexibility than Medicaid statutes otherwise permit for the implementation of mandatory and optional services. Generally, there are two categories of waivers distinguished by the section of the Social Security Act that authorizes them: section 1915(c) waivers and section 1115 waivers.

Section 1915(c) Waivers. To obtain a section 1915(c) waiver, a state must show that the services provided under the waiver are budget neutral to the federal program. Generally, this means that the average per capita expenditure for persons covered by the waiver will not increase because of the waiver. For example, every state that uses a 1915(c) waiver to provide home and community-based services (HCBSs) specifically for frail elderly or disabled individuals must show that HCBSs avoid more costly institutional care for which these persons are at risk. Waivers enable states to target services to certain populations, such as the frail elderly or disabled individuals without offering them broadly to other Medicaid-eligible populations.

HCBSs include homemaker/home health aide services, adult day health services, habilitation services, and respite care. Habilitation services are defined as services designed to assist individuals in acquiring, retaining, and improving the self-help, socialization, and adaptive skills necessary to reside successfully in home and community-based settings. These include prevocational, educational, and supported employment services beyond those otherwise available. For individuals with chronic mental illness, HCBSs include day treatment or other partial hospitalization services, psychosocial rehabilitation services, and clinic services. Some HCBSs, notably case management services and personal care services, overlap with existing optional service categories.

Effective January 1, 2007, DRA allows states to implement HCBSs as optional benefits without waivers and their cost justification requirements. States may continue targeting HCBSs to specific populations, however.

Section 1115 Waivers. Section 1115 waivers enable states to engage in demonstration, pilot, or experimental projects that the secretary believes promote Medicaid objectives and obtain federal matching funds without the budget-neutral cost justification required under a section 1915(c) waiver.

Assistance with Medicare Premiums and Cost-Share Payments

Medicaid beneficiaries who qualify for the mandatory and/or optional benefits identified in table 9-1 or the waiver services that their states may provide are considered full Medicaid beneficiaries. Full Medicaid beneficiaries are also entitled to assistance with their Medicare premiums and cost-sharing amounts. In addition, this assistance extends to certain other categories of low-income and low-resource persons who do not qualify for any other Medicaid benefit. The following sections on retirees qualifying for Medicaid explain this assistance.

dual eligibles

Medicaid uses the term *dual eligibles* to describe persons who are eligible for Medicare and any level of Medicaid assistance. As chapter 7 explains, the Medicare prescription drug program has particular significance for dual eligibles. For those who receive full Medicaid benefits, coverage for prescription drugs shifts from Medicaid to Medicare on January 1, 2006. All dual eligibles, including those who do not qualify for full Medicaid benefits, receive assistance with the premium for the prescription drug coverage and other drug cost sharing amounts.

Retirees Qualifying for Medicaid

Retirees of all ages who seek or anticipate the need for public assistance must keep in mind the previous discussion on Medicaid's eligible category requirements. There is no Medicaid eligibility category for childless adults under 65. Adults who are not disabled, pregnant, or elderly and have no minor children generally cannot qualify for Medicaid regardless of their degree of impoverishment. States can and do obtain federal Medicaid matching funds for childless adults as a group through a waiver. However, such programs are limited: relatively few uninsured low-income nonelderly adults without children qualify for Medicaid. Some of these programs are highlighted in a following section on other Medicaid coverages.

The following section reviews three categories under which a retiree may be eligible for Medicaid and the financial criteria of those categories that must be satisfied to qualify for Medicaid. Specifically the discussion proceeds under the headings of retirees who reach age 65, disabled retirees younger than age 65, and retirees with children.

Retirees Who Reach Age 65

Retirees who reach age 65 are by that occurrence in a category that makes them eligible for Medicaid if they satisfy the financial criteria as low-income elderly. Although almost all elderly Medicaid beneficiaries are also eligible for Medicare, Medicaid broadens their Medicare coverage to services not covered by Medicare, including long-term care services. While many persons with higher incomes have private supplemental insurance to cover Medicare's gaps, the low-income elderly who qualify for Medicaid are less likely to have such coverage. As a result, they may rely on Medicaid to fill this role.

This following section reviews the financial criteria to qualify for full Medicaid benefits available to the low-income elderly and for assistance with the payment of Medicare premiums and cost sharing.

Financial Criteria to Qualify for Full Coverage. Low-income elderly persons may gain access to full Medicaid coverage by satisfying one of several available levels of criteria for financial need.

SSI-Related Criteria. Most states satisfy their obligation to this eligible population by providing coverage to the elderly persons who receive *Supplemental Security Income (SSI)*. SSI is a federal entitlement program that provides cash assistance to low-income persons who are aged, blind, and disabled. In 2006, to qualify for SSI, an elderly person must have an income of less than $603 per month ($904 per month for a couple) and countable resources of less than $2,000 ($3,000 for a couple). Countable resources include most assets with specified exclusions, such as a home. A following section on Medicaid safeguards identifies these exclusions.

Supplemental Security Income (SSI)

At the same time, states have the option to be more generous in their qualifying criteria for Medicaid. Under SSI law, states may provide cash payment, known as a state supplementation payment (SSP), even if the elderly person's income exceeds the SSI standards. Under the SSP-only eligibility option, a state may make Medicaid available to elderly individuals receiving these payments. About half the states make Medicaid coverage available to elderly persons living independently and receiving state supplementation payments but not SSI benefits.

In some cases, cost-of-living increases in the Social Security benefit may cause persons to lose their SSI or SSP benefits. Nevertheless, they remain eligible for Medicaid in those states that cover elderly individuals receiving SSI or SSP benefits. These states are required to disregard the Social Security cost-of-living increases received by the individual for Medicaid purposes.

However, approximately a dozen states have chosen to satisfy their mandatory coverage obligation to the elderly population by applying a more restrictive method for determining Medicaid eligibility than the SSI or SSP criteria, because their previous use of such a method has grandfathered status. If a state uses the more restrictive method for determining income and resources, it must also allow Medicaid applicants to "spend down" into Medicaid eligibility by deducting incurred medical expenses from income.

Medically Needy Criteria. Many low-income elderly individuals and couples with Medicare coverage have incomes that exceed the SSI eligibility level and also incur medical expenses that Medicare does not cover. States that want to offer Medicaid coverage to assist these persons or couples with their medical expenses have the option of covering them with federal matching funds using "medically needy" criteria. More than 30 states elect to offer coverage using this approach. These criteria often apply to elderly persons residing in nursing facilities or to persons living in the community who have high prescription drug or medical equipment expenses.

Under the medically needy option, a state establishes an income standard as well as a resource standard. In counting income or resources for the elderly, a state must apply methodologies no more restrictive than those under the SSI program. In determining eligibility based on income, but not resources, the state deducts the medical expenses an individual has incurred from the individual's countable income. If the individual's income, minus incurred medical expenses, is less than the state's medically needy income standard, and if the individual's countable resources are less than the state's medically needy resource standard, then the individual is eligible for Medicaid coverage. If this is the case, Medicaid simply makes up the difference between the individual's income that must be devoted to paying for care and what Medicaid would pay in the absence of this income.

Example:	Marjorie, a recent retiree, has her only medical expense coverage from Medicare. She suffers from renal failure that requires outpatient dialysis three times a week. The 20 percent participation share of the dialysis cost and her other medical expenses average $2,000 per month. With her Social Security check of $1,100 per month as her only income, she applies for Medicaid and meets her state's medically needy criteria. Her income minus her medical expenses is less than her state's income standard based on SSI requirements.
	Marjorie's defined-contribution retirement plan was invested in her employer's stock and is now almost worthless. She rents her apartment. Her automobile and other personal assets are excludible as countable assets. Because she is also within the resource standard of $2,000 in countable assets, Marjorie qualifies for Medicaid.

Nursing Facility Criteria. Special financial criteria apply to the coverage of nursing facility services received under Medicaid by the elderly and the disabled.

Under the medically needy criteria, there is no upper limit on the amount of monthly income a person can receive and still qualify for Medicaid coverage. As long as the individual's incurred medical expenses are sufficiently high to reduce the individual's income to the state medically needy income standard, the individual will qualify for Medicaid. Many individuals in nursing homes qualify this way. However, states that wish to provide Medicaid coverage for the elderly in nursing facilities but want to set an upper limit on the beneficiary's income have another option: the so-called "special income rule" for persons in nursing facilities and other institutions.

Under the special income rule, a state may set an income standard at up to 300 percent of the SSI benefit for individuals in nursing facilities and other institutions. This income standard is $1,809 per month for 2006. Institutionalized individuals with Social Security, pension, and other income of more than this amount may not qualify for Medicaid, even if their monthly costs of care in the nursing facility exceed their income. If their countable income is under the state-established limit, these individuals must also meet the SSI resource test to qualify for Medicaid. Individuals who satisfy the special income rule must apply all of their income, except for a small personal needs allowance, towards the cost of nursing home care.

Example: In a continuation of the previous example, Marjorie's health continues to decline. She now requires nursing facility care and relocates to be near her family. Her new state uses the special income rule for such care under the Medicaid program. However, she continues to qualify for Medicaid because her income is less than 300 percent of the SSI benefit level. She must now contribute her income except for a personal allowance toward the cost of her care.

As mentioned previously, more than 30 states have a medically needy program under which long-term care services are provided. The remaining states utilize the special income rule.

Federal Poverty-Level Criteria. In counting income or resources, states may use the SSI methodology described above or they may use any methodology that is "less restrictive" than the SSI methodology. However, under the latter option, elderly individuals are not permitted to spend down into Medicaid eligibility by incurring large medical expenses, as they are able to do through the medically needy criteria. Approximately 20 states have expanded income eligibility standards for the elderly to at least 100 percent of the federal poverty level, which in 2006 is $817 per month for an individual and $1,100 for a couple. Federal poverty level amounts change in the spring of each year.

Financial Criteria for Assistance with Medicare Premiums and Cost Sharing. The financial criteria for Medicaid eligibility discussed in the previous sections leads to coverage for the full Medicaid benefits package of acute and long-term care services that a state may offer. Elderly persons eligible for Medicaid are usually dual eligibles because they are Medicare beneficiaries as well. For these dual eligibles, the benefits package extends to assistance with Medicare premiums and cost-sharing obligations. This assistance includes payment of the Part A hospital deductible and copayments and the Part B monthly premium, deductible, and percentage participation.

For all full-benefit dual eligibles, the federal government pays their prescription drug premiums for the standard plan. Their deductibles are also paid, and they have no coverage gaps. Beneficiaries who reside in institutions, such as a nursing home, also have no copayments. In 2006, other full-benefit dual eligibles pay a per prescription copayment of $1 or $2 for generic drugs, depending on income, and $3 to $5 for brand-name drugs. Their copayment drops to $0 after total annual drug costs exceed $3,600.

While Medicare covers basic health services, including physician and hospital care, dual eligibles rely on Medicaid to provide benefits that Medicare does not cover, such as dental and vision care, and long-term care. The majority of Medicaid expenditures for dual eligibles are for long-term care services; nearly one-quarter of dual eligibles are in nursing homes. Medicare pays first for services that both programs cover and Medicaid pays the difference up to the state's coverage and payment limit. Medicaid as the payer of last resort seeks to maintain dual eligibility with Medicare whenever possible.

Under Medicaid, states are also required to offer assistance by way of payment for Medicare premiums and cost sharing (but not any other Medicaid benefits) to certain other categories of low-income Medicare beneficiaries. The federal government matches the costs of this assistance at the same rate that it matches the costs of the full benefits package.

Example:	Doris and Andrew have not planned well for their retirement. When they worked, their income was far less than the maximum subject to Social Security taxes. Consequently, their retirement income barely exceeds the federal poverty level. As they struggle to meet day-to-day expenses, friends recommend that they seek public assistance. Medicaid determines that their income level and resources are too high to qualify for full Medicaid benefits. However, their income level, which is at 115 percent of the federal poverty levels, results in Medicaid paying their full Part B premiums.

Table 9-2 presents the categories under which persons can qualify for this type of Medicare assistance based on low income and resources. The two required categories are qualified Medicare beneficiaries (QMBs) and specified low-income Medicare beneficiaries (SLMBs). In addition, states may obtain funding for a third category, known as qualified individual beneficiaries (QIs). The availability of benefits to persons in this category is subject to an annual funding cap and is not guaranteed. Although the resource test for the three categories is the same, the categories differ with respect to qualifying income level and the extent of benefits. Qualifying income levels range from below the federal poverty level for QMBs to as high as 135 percent of that level for QIs.

Medicaid pays Medicare Part A premiums, if any, and Part B premiums and cost shares for QMBs, but limits such assistance to payment of the Medicare Part B premium in the two higher income categories. In addition, persons in all three categories qualify as low-income beneficiaries if they enroll in the Medicare prescription drug program. Similar to the levels just described for full-benefit dual eligibles, persons in these categories can receive federal assistance with premiums for prescription drug coverage and other drug cost-sharing amounts.

TABLE 9-2
Eligibility Criteria for Elderly Persons Qualified for Medicaid Assistance with Medicare Premiums and Cost Sharing

Category	Income	Resource Test	Medicaid Payment
Qualified Medicare Beneficiaries (QMBs)	≤100% FPL*[a]	≤200% of SSI limit ($4,000 for individuals, $6,000 for couples)[a]	Medicare Part A premiums, if any; Part B premiums; and all cost-sharing charges[b]
Specified Low-Income Medicare Beneficiaries (SLMBs)	>100% but ≤120% FPL*[a]	≤200% of SSI limit ($4,000 for individuals, $6,000 for couples)[a]	Medicare Part B monthly premium
Qualified Income Medicare Beneficiaries (QIs)	>120% but ≤135% FPL*[a]	≤200% of SSI limit ($4,000 for individuals, $6,000 for couples)[a]	Medicare Part B monthly premium

*Through early 2006, 100 percent of the federal poverty level is $779.50 for individuals and $1,069.17 for couples per month.

[a] States may use income and resource methodologies that are less restrictive than those that would otherwise apply.

[b] States are not required to pay for Medicare cost sharing if the Medicaid payment rates for a given service are sufficiently lower than the Medicare payment rates.

Disabled Retirees under Age 65

Retirees under age 65, if they meet Medicaid's disability requirements, would be in a Medicaid eligible category as a disabled adult. Disabled adults aged 65 and older do not have to meet disability eligibility requirements because they are already in an eligible category by virtue of their age. To qualify for Medicaid, disabled retirees under age 65 must also satisfy the financial criteria relating to income and resources.

Medicaid beneficiaries with disabilities are also likely to qualify for Medicare if they have received Social Security disability benefits for 2 years. Approximately a quarter of all Medicaid disabled beneficiaries fall into this category. Just as it does for dual-eligible beneficiaries who have reached age 65, Medicaid supplements the basic Medicare coverage of Medicaid beneficiaries with disabilities under age 65 and provides additional benefits and services, such as long-term care, that are left uncovered by Medicare. Medicaid also pays the Medicare premium and cost-sharing amounts for these beneficiaries and for other disabled persons who are unqualified for full Medicaid benefits. Federal assistance with premiums for prescription drug coverage and other drug cost-sharing amounts is available to these beneficiaries just as it is for dual eligibles over age 65.

Determination of Disability. In general, states are required to use the definition of disability that is used for SSI purposes. Approximately a dozen states also have the option to use a more restrictive definition of disability because of a grandfathering provision in the law. Under the SSI definition of disability, a person must have a severe medically determinable physical or mental impairment. Blindness is a separate eligible category under Medicaid that generally is treated as a disability.

The impairment must also cause the person to be unable to engage in any substantial gainful activity. The person is assumed to be able to engage in substantial gainful activity if he or she earns above a specified monthly income level that adjusts annually for inflation (in 2006, $860 per month for the nonblind and $1,450 per month for the blind). Therefore, earnings may not exceed that level if a person seeks to qualify based on inability to engage in any substantial gainful activity. Most states make their own determination of a person's disability for purposes of categorical Medicaid eligibility. However, they may enter into an agreement to have the Social Security Administration make the determination, which is then binding on the state.

Financial Criteria to Qualify for Full Coverage. The Medicaid qualification for full Medicaid coverage for nonelderly adults with disabilities is summarized in the following categories: the working disabled, disabled persons at risk of institutional care, and institutionalized disabled adults.

The Working Disabled. The working disabled category could apply to some retirees. Many retirees, especially those under age 65, continue to earn some level of income in retirement. Other persons may be on the verge of retirement but still working. These persons could be stricken with a disability that places them in a Medicaid-eligible category.

The working disabled may qualify for Medicaid based on their status in the following groups. Although the first group is mandatory, the other two are optional groups that states may establish.

- *Qualified Severely Impaired.* States continue to provide Medicaid coverage to persons classified as "qualified severely impaired." These persons (1) are under 65 and eligible for both SSI payments and Medicaid coverage, (2) continue to have the disabling physical or mental impairment on which they were found to be disabled, (3) need continued Medicaid coverage to enable them to continue working, and (4) would lose categorical eligibility for Medicaid because their earnings push them over the substantial gainful activity limits.

  These persons are entitled to continue to receive Medicaid coverage, even after they have lost their SSI benefits due to earnings, until they have earned income sufficient to enable them to purchase a reasonable equivalent of SSI, Medicaid, and other publicly funded care services that they are receiving. The SSA publishes state-specific thresholds for annual gross income to be used as the basis for this reasonable equivalent determination.

- *Other Working Disabled.* States also have a broad spectrum of optional income criteria that they may apply to persons who meet the SSI definition of disability but have earnings that exceed the maximum amount allowed for qualified severely impaired persons as discussed above. In effect, the states have the flexibility to use less restrictive methodologies to raise the income and resource requirements to whatever level they choose in relation to the federal poverty level. If states use such optional methodologies, they may impose a monthly premium or other cost-sharing amounts that may be set on a sliding scale according to income. This approach is known as a buy in.

- *Working with a Medically Improved Disability.* Some persons continue to have a severe medically determinable impairment, but they lose their eligibility for SSI or Social Security disability income benefits because of a determination that there has been medical improvement. In such cases, states also have optional criteria they may apply to continue Medicaid benefits. States may implement a buy-in program for these beneficiaries as well.

Disabled Persons at Risk of Institutional Care. Some disabled persons are unable to work and have impairments that are sufficiently severe to warrant institutional placement but want to remain in the community. This category of eligible individuals may also qualify for Medicaid. The bases for qualification are the same mandatory or optional income qualifications discussed previously that states may employ for the low-income elderly under the headings of SSI-related criteria, medically needy criteria, and home and community-based service criteria.

Institutionalized Disabled Adults. Some nonelderly adults with disabilities are unable to remain in the community. For various reasons, they require institutional care. Medicaid eligibility policy contains three basic criteria for financing these services that were also discussed previously for the low-income elderly: SSI-related criteria, medically needy criteria, and special income rule criteria.

Financial Criteria for Assistance with Medicare Premiums and Cost Sharing. Just as they do for the low-income elderly, states pay the Medicare premiums and cost-sharing amounts for disabled Medicaid beneficiaries who are entitled to full Medicaid benefits (if Medicare benefits are available to them). Many Medicare beneficiaries under age 65 may have disabilities that meet Medicaid's eligibility requirements, but they have incomes that are too high to qualify for full Medicaid benefits. Medicaid also requires states to offer assistance for Medicare premiums and cost sharing to certain categories of low-income disabled persons who are not entitled to the full Medicare benefit package. These categories, identified in table 9-2 for the low-income elderly, also apply to the low-income disabled. Such low-income disabled persons are also eligible for the federal subsidies of the Medicare prescription drug program described previously.

However, there is one category of Medicare premium assistance that is specific to Medicare beneficiaries with disabilities—assistance for qualified disabled working individuals (QDWIs). Those eligible under the QDWI criteria are individuals with disabilities who are not otherwise eligible for Medicaid but who meet the following criteria: (1) they are eligible for Medicare Part A benefits on the basis of disability; (2) their income is 200 percent of the federal poverty level or less; and (3) their resources do not exceed twice the SSI standard ($4,000 for an individual, $6,000 for a couple). Both income and resources must be determined using SSI or no less restrictive methodologies.

Persons who qualify as QDWIs are entitled to payment of their Part A premiums if they have not worked enough quarters to qualify for Medicare without paying a premium. However, QDWIs are not entitled to assistance with Medicare Part A or Part B deductibles or Part B premiums. In addition, for QDWIs with an income level between 150 and 200 percent of the federal poverty level, states may impose a sliding payment scale using a percentage of the Medicare premium. QDWIs with incomes above 150 percent of the federal poverty level are generally ineligible for a low-income subsidy of the Medicare prescription drug program.

Retirees with Children

Children under age 19 and parents (regardless of their ages) with children under age 19 constitute additional categories of eligibility for Medicaid benefits. Although retirees of any age usually do not qualify in these categories, such a situation may occur.

The financial criteria required for Medicaid qualification of children in low-income families are based on a relationship of family income to the federal poverty income level that may be more restrictive at increased child ages. For example, a child under age 5 may qualify if his or her family income is 133 percent of the federal poverty level, but for a child aged 10, family income may have to be 100 percent or less of the federal poverty level to qualify. States may, but are not required to, impose resource tests that can be as low as $1,000 in countable resources, but they are most often less restrictive.

States have generally extended benefits to children at family income levels beyond Medicaid minimums and have largely reduced differences in qualification by age. In addition, the State Children's Health Insurance Program (SCHIP) has expanded coverage for children significantly by raising the child's qualifying family income standard up to and even beyond 200 percent of the federal poverty level.

Although children may qualify for Medicaid because of their families' low income, their parents may not qualify because the family income level threshold for parents may be more stringent (higher). Increasingly, however, states are expanding coverage to low-income parents by aligning their criteria with those applicable to low-income children. Parents are more likely to enroll their children if they themselves are qualified for Medicaid.

Children or parents who become ineligible for Medicaid due to increased family earnings are entitled to receive Medicaid benefits for an additional 6 to 12 months under a program known as Transitional Medical Assistance.

Other Medicaid Coverage

This section discusses three federal eligibility categories that give states the option to extend limited Medicaid coverage to three populations of uninsured or potentially uninsured low-income individuals, including childless individuals under 65 who are not disabled: (1) newly unemployed workers and others entitled to COBRA continuation coverage, (2) individuals infected with tuberculosis, and (3) women diagnosed with breast or cervical cancer.

COBRA Continuation Beneficiaries

The federal Medicaid statute allows states to pay COBRA premiums on behalf of low-income unemployed workers and to receive federal Medicaid matching funds for these costs. In order to qualify for a premium subsidy, the individual must have an income that does not exceed 100 percent of the federal poverty level and resources that do not exceed twice the allowable amount for SSI benefits. Eligible individuals are entitled only to a premium subsidy, not to the full Medicaid benefits package.

Individuals Infected with Tuberculosis

Federal Medicaid law gives states the option of extending limited Medicaid coverage to low-income individuals who are infected with tuberculosis (TB), regardless of whether they would otherwise qualify for Medicaid. To qualify, an individual must be infected with TB and have an income and resources no greater than the amounts allowed an individual with disabilities to qualify for Medicaid in the state. Eligible individuals are not entitled to the full Medicaid benefits package; they are covered only for physician and clinic services, diagnostic tests, prescription drugs, case management, and directly observed therapy relating to treatment of the TB.

Women with Breast or Cervical Cancer

An optional Medicaid eligibility category now exists for women under age 65 in need of treatment for breast and cervical cancer. Women who qualify are entitled to coverage for the basic Medicaid benefits package. However, eligibility is not determined using an income or resource test. Instead, women qualify if they (1) are not already covered as a mandatorily eligible Medicaid beneficiary, (2) are under age 65, (3) have been screened at the early detection program funded by the Centers for Disease Control and Prevention (CDC) and need treatment for breast or cervical cancer, and (4) do not have private health insurance or other health care coverage. Most states have elected to implement this option.

Medicaid Program Safeguards

Medicaid has become the primary source of long-term care for the elderly and individuals with disabilities, including middle-income individuals who spend down their financial resources. As a result, expenditures for home health and nursing facility services have strained state and federal budgets.

To protect Medicaid's financial stability, Congress continues to enact legislation that reaffirms the exclusive purpose of the program as a safety net for the health care of the poor and those impoverished by their health care needs. Specifically, the legislation accomplishes this purpose through constraints on the Medicaid program that can be summarized under the headings of spousal impoverishment methodologies, transfers of wealth, estate recovery, and the need for care. In the absence of such safeguards, virtually anyone in an eligible category, regardless of income or wealth, could potentially seek qualifications for Medicaid.

DRA significantly strengthens safeguards in all these areas. In fact, the new restrictions are so substantive, especially due to the increased look-back period for asset transfers at less than fair market value and the new penalty period start date, that states must establish specific criteria for hardship waivers and notify Medicaid applicants about them. Indeed, nursing homes are now eligible for limited payments while their patients' hardship waiver applications are pending.

Spousal Impoverishment Methodologies

community spouse

Federal Medicaid law requires states to apply a special set of income and resource methodologies in determining eligibility when one spouse is in a nursing facility and the other spouse, known as a *community spouse*, remains in the community. States may, but are not required to, use them when one member of a couple receives home and community-based services under Medicaid. The purpose of these methodologies is to enable the institutionalized spouse to receive Medicaid coverage for nursing facility care while leaving the community spouse with sufficient resources and monthly income to avoid hardship. These rules in effect determine how much the Medicaid beneficiary must contribute to the cost of care and how much of the beneficiary's income and resources are protected for use by the community spouse. These methodologies apply to any eligibility criteria that a state uses under its Medicaid program in determining Medicaid eligibility for nursing facility residents, including the medically needy and special income rule options. Once Medicaid eligibility has been established, these methodologies also govern the calculation of the amount of the couple's monthly income that must be applied toward the cost of nursing facility care for the institutionalized spouse.

The spousal impoverishment methodologies on income and resources are triggered when one spouse enters a nursing facility (or hospital) and is likely to be there for at least 30 days, whether the spouse applies for Medicaid at the time of institutionalization or after.

Income. Income is all the money that a person receives from any source, such as Social Security benefits, pension, trusts, annuities, investments, or any payments received on a one-time or continuing basis. In every state, the community spouse's income is not considered available to the applicant, and the two individuals are not considered a couple for income eligibility purposes.

The state uses the income eligibility standard for one person rather than two, and the Medicaid income test applicable in the state is used.

In addition, there is a separate process for the treatment of income after Medicaid eligibility is determined that also affects a community spouse's income. This posteligibility process ascertains how much the Medicaid recipient must contribute toward the cost of care and also determines how much of the recipient's income is protected for use by the community spouse. The calculation begins with the recipient's total income from which the following items are deducted:

- a personal needs allowance of at least $30 per month
- a community spouse's monthly income allowance (between $1,604 and $2,489 for 2006) to the extent that payment is actually made to him or her
- a family monthly income allowance if there are other family members living in the household
- an amount for medical expenses incurred by the recipient

If the community spouse has his or her own income, the amount of that income reduces the community spouse's monthly income allowance. Similarly, any income of family members, such as dependent children, reduces the family monthly income allowance. Once the above items are deducted from the Medicaid recipient's income, any remaining income is contributed toward the cost of care.

Example 1:   Shortly after Chuck and Ann's 50th wedding anniversary, Chuck's growing dementia and physical frailties cause him to enter a nursing home. Their household income is based on Social Security payments of $1,500 per month to Chuck and $1,200 per month to Ann. In addition, Chuck has monthly income of $1,000 from a trust fund. Chuck applies for Medicaid and meets his state's medically needy income test: His total income of $2,500 per month is less than the $3,300 per month that Medicaid pays for nursing home care in his state.

The community spouse income allowance in Chuck's state is $2,266.50 per month. However, Ann will receive only $1,066.50 of this amount from this income because she has $1,200 of her own income. This leaves $1,433.50 of Chuck's $2,500 income that must be applied to the cost of Chuck's care, minus personal and medical expenses.

Example 2:   Margaret and Arthur are just beginning retirement when tragedy strikes. A cycling accident leaves Margaret paralyzed and with severe cognitive impairment. After discharge from the hospital, she needs nursing home care on a long-term basis and applies for Medicaid. Her only income now is $1,500 per month from Social Security. She meets her state's income cap test of $1,809 per month because only her income is considered. When she becomes eligible for Medicaid, Arthur receives no community spouse allowance because his Social Security benefits and pension income exceed the state-approved amount.

Assets. Medicaid applicants in every state must also pass an asset-limitation test. To make this determination, the state Medicaid agency first classifies assets as exempt or countable. Medicaid recipients, including those residing in nursing homes, may retain the following exempt assets without affecting Medicaid eligibility:

- the cash surrender value of life insurance policies with an aggregate face value of $1,500 or less
- personal property (such as clothing and jewelry) up to reasonable limits
- prepaid burial insurance
- a burial space
- an automobile, within certain limits
- a home and its furnishings. A home is exempt, provided it is the Medicaid recipient's principal place of residence and the recipient's home equity is within the threshold amount mentioned below. The home remains exempt after the recipient enters a nursing home, as long as a community spouse or a minor, blind, or disabled child continues to live there. Technically, a home could become a countable asset that would have to be spent for care if the recipient has no family in these categories. However, as a matter of practice, nursing home residents may continue to claim a home as their principal residence by making a declaration of their "intent to return," regardless of their actual likelihood of eventual discharge from the nursing home back to the community. Nevertheless, DRA declares that any person with home equity above $500,000 (up to $750,000 at a state's option) who has no spouse or a minor, blind, or disabled child is ineligible for Medicaid.

Virtually any asset that is not exempt is considered countable. Examples include

- cash and checking and savings accounts
- investments of all kinds, such as stocks, bonds, money market funds, certificates of deposit, and Treasury obligations
- retirement accounts, such as pensions, individual retirement accounts, and annuities
- second homes and vehicles

DRA significantly increases the scope of countable assets. Countable assets include the purchase price of an exclusive right to live in a home limited to one's lifetime (known as a life estate) with the remaining interest going to another party. This requirement is inapplicable, however, if the purchaser resides at the property for 1 year or the transferee is a family member. Entrance fees paid upon admission to a continuing care retirement community or life-care facility also may be considered countable assets. Loans of any type (including promissory notes and mortgages) are included as countable assets unless the repayment terms are actuarially sound, provide for equal payment, and prohibit the cancellation of the balance upon the death of the lender. New rules explicitly include as countable certain previously excludable annuities and require the state to be named as the remainder beneficiary.

The countable assets of the applicant and the community spouse, regardless of ownership, are combined. If the applicant is in or is entering a nursing home, the total marital assets are calculated, not on the date of the Medicaid application, but as of the date the applicant enters the nursing home. To determine whether an applicant with a community spouse meets the state's resource standard for Medicaid, the following procedure is used. From the couple's combined countable resources, a protected resource amount (PRA) for the community spouse is subtracted. The PRA is the greatest of the following:

- the spousal share, which is equal to one-half of the couple's combined resources but subject to a maximum of $99,540 in 2006. (This amount is adjusted annually.)
- the spousal resource standard amount adopted by the state at any amount between $19,908 and $99,540 in 2006 and adjusted annually
- an amount of resources transferred to the community spouse for support as directed by a court order
- an amount of resources designated by a state hearing officer as necessary to generate income for the community spouse up to the minimum maintenance needs standard. (This standard can vary from $1,604 to $2,489 per month for 2006.)

After the PRA is calculated and subtracted from the couple's combined countable resources, the remainder is considered available to the applicant as countable resources. If the amount of countable resources is above the state's resource standard amount (usually $2,000), the individual is ineligible for Medicaid and must spend down those resources to the standard amount to qualify under the test. If the amount of countable resources is below the state's resource standard, the individual meets the test. Once Medicaid eligibility is determined, any resources belonging to the community spouse are no longer considered available to the spouse on Medicaid.

In the case of both the income and resource protections, the law allows for exceptions to the general formulas in individual cases through both administrative and judicial procedures. DRA, however, mandates the use of a calculation method that requires a couple to deplete a larger share of their assets than under previous law.

Transfers of Wealth

Federal Medicaid law attempts to discourage individuals from transferring savings and other countable resources to adult children, siblings, or others in order to satisfy the Medicaid resource test and qualify for nursing facility coverage. It does so by imposing, for a specified period of time, an exclusion of nursing facility coverage upon those individuals who engage in such transfers.

Asset Transfers. Under the transfer-of-assets provisions, states must withhold or delay payment for various long-term care services for individuals who dispose of assets for less than fair market value. The term "assets" in this case includes both assets and income. These provisions apply when assets are transferred by individuals who are in long-term care facilities or receiving home and community-based services. They also apply to transfers by their spouses or someone else acting on their behalf. Now states can "look back" to find transfers of assets for 60 months prior to the date the individual is institutionalized or, if later, the date he or she applies for Medicaid. The look-back period for asset transfers taking place prior to the enactment of DRA (February 8, 2006) is only 36 months, however. For certain trusts, this look-back period continues to be 60 months, as explained later.

If a transfer of assets for less than fair market value is found, the state must withhold payment for nursing facility care (and certain other long-term care services) for a period of time referred to as the penalty period. The length of the penalty period is determined by dividing the value of the transferred asset by the average monthly private-pay rate for nursing facility care in the state. There is no limit to the length of the penalty period. If there is more than one transfer, all penalty periods are added and expire consecutively (not concurrently).

Formerly, the penalty period began with the date the asset transfer at less than market value occurred. DRA, in effect, now requires that penalty period begin on the date that an applicant would have been Medicaid eligible except for the penalty amounts.

Once one spouse qualifies for Medicaid, the community spouse is able to transfer his or her own assets without having the transfer affect the other spouse's Medicaid eligibility.

Example:	After DRA became effective, Roberta gave each of her six grandchildren a gift of $10,000.

Assume the following:

- Two years later, she suffers a severe stroke and requires ongoing nursing home care.

- After 2 years in a nursing home, she is unable to pay for her care and applies for Medicaid.

Under these circumstances, the state delays her Medicaid eligibility by imposing a 10-month penalty. The period is calculated by dividing the $60,000 in total gifts to her grandchildren by the state-determined $6,000 monthly private-pay rate for nursing home care. The penalty period begins as of the date her lack of resources would have made her eligible for Medicaid except for the penalty. Roberta now applies for a hardship waiver of the penalty based on health or life-threatening circumstances. Meanwhile, Medicaid will pay her nursing home care for up to 30 days while her hardship waiver application is pending.

Note that prior to DRA, Roberta's Medicaid eligibility wouldn't be delayed for two reasons. First, the shorter look-back period (36 months) would exclude consideration of gifts made 4 years ago. Second, the 10-month penalty period would have begun as of the date of the initial gift and would already have been satisfied by the date Roberta applied for Medicaid.

A transfer of a home to a close family member, however, may be made without penalty. The permitted transferees are

- a spouse
- a minor, blind, or disabled child
- one or more siblings who already have partial ownership of the home and who have lived there for at least a year before the transferor needed nursing home care
- a caregiver child, who for a period of at least 2 years provided hands-on care that delayed the need for nursing home care

Treatment of Trusts. When an individual, his or her spouse, or anyone acting on the individual's behalf establishes a trust using at least some of the individual's funds, that trust may be considered available to the individual for purposes of determining Medicaid eligibility.

As a general rule, payments actually made to or for the benefit of the individual are treated as income to the individual. Amounts that could be paid to or for the benefit of the individual, even if not paid, are also treated as available resources. Amounts that could be paid to or for the benefit of the individual but are paid to someone else are treated as asset transfers.

If a trust is revocable by the Medicaid applicant, the principal of the trust is always considered a countable asset for purposes of Medicaid eligibility. If a trust is irrevocable, any amount of the principal that could be removed by the trustee on a discretionary basis for the individual's care is also treated as a countable asset. In situations in which the Medicaid applicant cannot receive invasions of principal for any reason, monies put into an irrevocable trust are treated as asset transfers and subject to a 60-month look-back period.

There are a few exceptions to the trust rules previously described. For example, a trust is not counted as an asset available to an individual if the state determines that counting the trust would present an undue hardship. In addition, three specific types of trusts are not counted as being available to the individual:

- trusts established by a parent, grandparent, guardian, or court for the benefit of an individual who is disabled and under the age of 65, using the individual's own funds
- trusts established by a disabled individual, parent, grandparent, guardian, or court for the disabled individual, using the individual's own funds, where the trusts are made up of pooled funds and managed by a nonprofit organization for the sole benefit of each individual included in the trusts
- trusts composed only of pension, Social Security, and other income of the individual in states that make individuals eligible for institutional care under a special income level (income cap states) but do not cover institutional care for the medically needy

In these three situations, the trust must provide that the state receive any funds remaining in the trust when the individual dies, up to the amount of Medicaid benefits paid on the individual's behalf.

Estate Recovery

estate recovery

States must try to recover the cost of Medicaid benefits from the estates of certain nursing home residents and older persons who received home and community-based services. This law, referred to as *estate recovery*, applies to individuals who were aged 55 or older when they received Medicaid. At a minimum, states are required to file claims in probate court against the estates of certain deceased Medicaid beneficiaries.

Under probate laws, an estate is usually defined as all real estate and personal property that pass from a deceased person to an heir through a will or by rules of intestate succession. Property that passes directly to joint owners or to beneficiaries under a trust is normally not considered part of the probate estate. However, federal legislation gives states the option to expand the definition of estate to include these types of interests and any other property that the individual has any title or interest in at the time of death.

There are limits on a state's right to recover Medicaid benefits. Recovery cannot be made in the following circumstances:

- before the death of a surviving spouse. During a surviving spouse's lifetime, the state Medicaid agency cannot require repayment of the cost of Medicaid benefits provided to the deceased spouse. After the surviving spouse dies, however, the state may file a claim for repayment. Heirs receive their inheritance only after Medicaid's claim is paid.
- if the individual has a surviving child who is under age 21 or who is blind or permanently disabled
- against one's home on which the state placed a lien unless additional protections for siblings and adult children are satisfied

Need for Care Criteria

Often overlooked in the discussion of Medicaid qualification are the need-for-care criteria. These criteria, also called the level-of-care criteria, determine whether an individual is considered an appropriate recipient of long-term care and whether that individual should receive care in a nursing home, at home, or in the community. Need-for-care criteria vary by state and the type of service provided. States may also impose controls on utilization of services.

For federally mandated benefits, the need-for-care criteria must be based on medical necessity. States generally interpret medical necessity as an authorization of services by a medical professional, although the services authorized do not have to be strictly of a medical nature. Medical necessity encompasses severe functional limitations, both physical and mental, that if left unattended would ultimately lead to the need for medical care. Nevertheless, states maintain considerable leeway in setting their level-of-need criteria; some are strict, and others are more liberal. States with liberal standards may also look at the spectrum of alternative settings in which care may be safely and effectively provided and take into account such factors as the availability of informal caregivers or adequacy of housing in the community.

The stringency of the need-for-care criteria applied to federally mandated benefits must also apply to the additional home and community-based services that a state offers. Other optional benefits carry no federal statutory or regulatory provision regarding the type or level of impairment a person should have to receive them, other than being equally available to all recipients who qualify. For these optional benefits, states may establish their own measures of need and the particular level and/or combinations of needs a person must have.

Shortcomings of Medicaid

Medicaid has several related shortcomings from the recipient's perspective.

First, a Medicaid recipient is on public assistance and loses significant authority to direct his or her own care. The state, as the payer for care, largely determines when, where, and how care is provided.

A second and related drawback is the diminished availability of provider services. The Medicaid recipient may not use any available provider but must select one approved by Medicaid. A person on Medicaid, depending on where he or she lives, may find that many physicians don't see Medicaid patients. This is especially true in states with low Medicaid reimbursement. This situation is reflected in many categories of provider services, but especially evident with regard to nursing home care.

As the largest payer for nursing home services, Medicaid negotiates rates that are substantially below those paid by private patients and Medicare. Payment and budgetary tensions between long-term care providers and Medicaid agencies are chronic; providers believe they are paid far too little as state agencies face ever-growing expenses and tighter budget constraints. This situation, which limits providers' availability to serve Medicaid patients, is evident in several ways.

Nursing homes become highly selective in their admissions as they attempt to attract and maintain patients that are profitable, or at least more profitable than Medicaid patients. Most nursing homes allocate a certain number of beds for Medicaid, Medicare, and private-pay residents. Some of these nursing homes, if they become greatly dissatisfied with Medicaid payments, may reduce the beds available to Medicaid patients, preferring instead to admit higher-paying private-pay or Medicare patients. Other nursing homes admit private-pay or private-pay and Medicare patients only. These homes take the position that Medicaid patients require an unfair subsidy of the true cost of care by their private patients and would compromise the high level of service they provide. State agencies, on the other hand, may decertify the number of available beds or decline to approve new beds to control utilization and maintain their budgets. The net result for the Medicaid recipient is a limited choice of nursing homes and a possible wait for placement. An available provider may be at a location inconvenient to the recipient or the recipient's family. This problem becomes more acute as nursing home occupancy rises.

The policies of Medicaid-approved nursing homes with regard to patient transfer or discharge must be identical for all individuals, regardless of source of payment. It is illegal to evict a Medicaid recipient from a nursing home that accepts Medicaid residents. Nevertheless, if a Medicaid nursing home patient enters a hospital because of illness or injury, Medicaid will pay the nursing home to hold the bed for only a week or two. After that time, the bed may be given to another patient, and the recovering Medicaid patient once again may have to look for a facility.

Despite Medicaid's standards, a third drawback is frequently a lower level of service compared to that received by private patients. The likelihood of lower service levels is usually directly related to the proportion of Medicaid patients that a provider cares for.

For example, nursing homes with large Medicaid patient populations have difficulty maintaining profitability. A lower level of service may affect the quality of patient care if programs and staff are reduced to cut costs. Certainly, reduced service levels are reflected in the amenities that are far fewer than those provided to and paid for by private-pay patients. Medicaid patients may have spartan accommodations and sometimes share a four-bed room. Common areas can be austere. The patient or the patient's family must often supply TV, telephone, and other personal services and items for the Medicaid recipient's convenience, comfort, or enjoyment.

Medicaid Planning

Medicaid planning

Medicaid planning is the process of rearranging a person's financial resources to make that person eligible for Medicaid while sheltering his or her financial resources for use by a spouse, children, or others. Unlike someone who exhausts financial resources as a private-pay patient and turns to Medicaid to pay for care as a last resort, a person who uses Medicaid planning turns to Medicaid as the first resort. Medicaid planning is usually associated with qualification for Medicaid benefits for nursing home care. However, a person may plan to divest himself or herself of resources to obtain Medicaid coverage for a significant medical event, such as an organ transplant, which is often accompanied by continuing and expensive follow-up care.

Despite the restrictions on asset transfers and the use of trusts and estate recovery, strategies to qualify for Medicaid while shielding financial resources remain available. A discussion of the specifics of these extensive and quite complicated arrangements is beyond the scope of this textbook. Medicaid planning usually requires legal and tax advice. Congress tried to safeguard Medicaid as a program for the poor by imposing criminal penalties on those who use Medicaid planning or advise someone to make such arrangements. However, subsequent legislative amendments or injunctions against enforcement have nullified these enactments.

Even if Medicaid planning is successful in achieving eligibility while shielding assets, there are major drawbacks. These include the following:

- The individual is placed on public assistance and becomes subject to the shortcomings of the Medicaid program discussed previously.
- If done in advance of the need for long-term care, Medicaid planning may turn out to be a bad choice for a person who never requires long-term or medical care.
- The federal and state Medicaid requirements in effect at the time long-term care may be required could eliminate the effectiveness of the prior planning strategies used to shelter resources.
- The sale or transfer of assets or the creation of a trust to satisfy Medicaid planning may disrupt normal estate planning and could create losses or additional tax liabilities.
- The loss of legal control of one's financial resources creates dependence on the decisions of others for routine needs and when unanticipated circumstances arise.
- The individual may at some future date no longer need long-term care and find that there are insufficient assets to provide support outside a nursing home.

These serious drawbacks to Medicaid planning are more than sufficient to encourage anyone with even modest financial resources to at least consider other alternatives for financing his or her health care needs, particularly long-term care. One alternative is the use of available resources to purchase long-term care insurance tailored to meet an individual's financial objectives. Indeed, a number of states, recognizing the value of an individual's financial independence and avoidance of the need for Medicaid, have programs that actively encourage the purchase of long-term care insurance. These programs, known as partnerships, allow those who purchase approved policies to maintain significant assets should they exhaust their insurance benefits and have to turn to Medicaid as a last resort. Chapter 18 explains partnership programs.

VETERANS' BENEFITS

Another potential government source of medical and long-term care benefits for eligible seniors is the health care program of the Department of

Veterans Affairs, often referred to as the VA. The VA determines benefits and the eligibility for benefits on the basis of congressional appropriations to the department. Eligibility and benefits can change from year to year.

Currently, about 6 million veterans are enrolled in the program. Some of these veterans, although unlikely to be retirees, must rely entirely on their veterans' benefits for their medical care because of their disabilities and unemployability. Many others, including retirees, may also have medical coverage through employer-sponsored programs, private medical expense insurance, and/or Medicare.

Retirees who are eligible for veterans' benefits, even if they have other medical coverage, may seek care in a VA facility. Such care may be more accessible and more importantly may provide a special type and quality of service for their personal health needs, especially if that care is for a service-connected medical condition. In addition, there is little or no out-of-pocket expense for most categories of eligible veterans. For these persons, then, care in a VA facility could be less expensive than paying the self-responsible amounts of their medical benefit plans for services received outside the VA system.

However, the VA is authorized to recover reasonable charges from private medical expense plans for medical care for non-service-connected medical conditions. Indeed, all veterans applying for care are asked to provide information on their available medical expense coverage, including the coverage available under a spouse's plan. Generally, the VA cannot bill Medicare for medical services provided to veterans. Nevertheless, the VA can bill for the services that are covered by a Medicare supplement policy but not covered by Medicare.

Although veterans in most priority groups are not responsible for paying any balance of the VA's charges that remains unpaid by their private medical plan, some veterans whose income is above an applicable means level are responsible for VA copayments. Income-related copayments apply to services received by veterans in the last priority groups mentioned below.

Current information on veterans' health care programs is available at the Web site of the Department of Veterans Affairs, www.va.gov.

Eligibility

As a general rule, veterans can enroll in the health care program to the extent Congressional appropriations allow. If appropriations are limited, enrollment will occur based on the following priorities:

1. veterans with service-connected disabilities who are rated 50 percent or more disabled and veterans determined to be unemployable due to service-related conditions
2. veterans with service-connected disabilities who are rated 30 or 40 percent disabled

3. veterans who are former POWs or were awarded a Purple Heart, veterans with service-connected disabilities rated 10 and 20 percent, veterans whose discharge was for disabilities incurred or aggravated in the line of duty, and veterans awarded special eligibility classification as individuals disabled by treatment or vocational rehabilitation

4. veterans who are receiving an increased VA pension because of their need for aid and attendance or by reason of being permanently housebound, and veterans the VA has determined to be catastrophically disabled

5. veterans who are receiving VA pension benefits or are eligible for Medicaid, and non-service-connected veterans and non-compensated-service-connected veterans with 0 percent service-connected disabilities whose annual income and net worth are below the VA means test threshold

6. all other veterans who are not required to make copayments for their treatment. This includes veterans of the Mexican border period or of World War I; veterans seeking care solely for a disorder associated with exposure to a toxic substance or radiation, for a disorder associated with service in the Southwest Asia theater of operations during the Gulf War, or for any illness associated with service in combat in a war after the Gulf War or during a period of hostility after November 11, 1998; and veterans with 0 percent service-connected disabilities who are nevertheless compensated, including veterans receiving compensation for inactive tuberculosis

7. all other veterans who agree to pay copayments

The means test applicable to certain veterans in priority 5 looks at all sources of income and assets of a veteran and his or her household. A veteran who fails the means test can enroll under priority 7.

A veteran who enrolls under priority 7 is subject to certain copayments if his or her resources are above the means test threshold. These copayments apply to most health care services other than those of a preventive nature.

It should be noted that these categories are used for determining enrollment only. Once a veteran is enrolled, most of the services and treatments available are the same for all enrollees. However, a few of the services and treatments, such as nursing home care, are limited to more narrowly defined categories. Enrollment status is reviewed each year and is subject to change.

Benefits

Care is generally provided in VA facilities, but the VA may also contract with private providers for care. Currently, there are about 1,300 VA facilities, including 163 hospitals, 850 ambulatory care and community-based outpatient clinics, 206 counseling centers, 137 nursing homes, and 43 domiciliary facilities.[4] Although the available services are comprehensive, all services are not available at all VA locations.[5]

The VA health insurance program has a package of basic benefits for all enrollees. There are certain other benefits for which veterans may apply on a case-by-case basis.

Basic Benefits

The basic health benefits of the VA include the following:

- preventive services, including immunizations, screening tests, and health education and training classes
- primary health care
- diagnosis and treatment
- surgery, including outpatient surgery as well as mental health and substance abuse treatment
- urgent and limited emergency care
- drugs and pharmaceuticals. (There are copayments for veterans who do not have service-related disabilities.)

The basic benefits also include home health care and hospice/palliative care.

Seventy-five VA facilities provide in-home primary medical care to housebound veterans with chronic diseases as well as to veterans with terminal illnesses. The veteran's family provides the necessary personal care under the supervision of an interdisciplinary team based at the VA facility. The team plans for any needed medical, nursing, social, rehabilitative, and dietetic regimens and trains the veteran and family members in supportive care. The VA may also arrange for skilled nursing from community-based home health agencies in a manner similar to what is provided by Medicare. Annually, approximately 11,000 veterans receive home health care provided or financed by the VA.[6]

Some VA centers also have hospice/palliative care consultation teams that plan, develop, and arrange for the local provision of hospice care, either directly through the VA or through community-based programs. This care offers pain management, symptom control, and other medical services to terminally ill veterans or veterans in the late stages of chronic diseases as well as bereavement counseling and respite care to their families. About 40 percent of VA facilities have inpatient facilities if they are needed for this type of care, while 60 percent provide the consultative services.[7]

Other Benefits

Among the benefits that may be available to certain veterans in addition to the basic benefits are nursing home care, domiciliary care, adult day health care, and outpatient geriatric evaluation and management. The VA also supports state programs for elderly veterans.

Nursing Home Care. The VA will provide nursing home care to veterans who need skilled-nursing care and related medical services because of a service-related disability and to veterans with a service-connected disability rated at 70 percent or more who need the care for any reason. Other veterans may also receive care to the extent that resources are available. The VA annually serves over 40,000 veterans in its own facilities. Nearly 30,000 veterans are also treated in community nursing homes at VA expense.[8] Care in the latter facilities is designed to allow a veteran to make the transition from a hospital to the community.

Domiciliary Care. The VA also provides care to nearly 25,000 low-income veterans in its own domiciliary facilities or similar state-owned facilities.[9] These facilities are designed to provide rehabilitative and long-term care for veterans who need minimal medical care but not the level of skilled-nursing care provided by VA nursing homes.

Adult Day Health Care. There are a few VA programs that provide adult day health care programs for veterans. These programs are therapeutically oriented and offer maintenance and rehabilitative services to veterans in a congregate, outpatient setting.

Geriatric Evaluation and Management. The majority of VA centers have programs to provide care and services to the frail elderly. This care can be given to persons who are already in VA facilities or on an outpatient basis to prevent unnecessary institutionalization.

Support of State Programs. Several states have veterans' homes to provide long-term care for frail elderly veterans. The VA supports these homes through construction grants as well as per diem payments for certain veterans.

NOTES

1. *Medicaid Enrollment and Spending by "Mandatory" and "Optional" Eligibility and Benefit Categories,* Kaiser Commission on Medicaid and the Uninsured, February 2005.
2. Much of the discussion on eligibility and benefits is based in part on material in *The Medicaid Resource Book,* The Kaiser Commission on Medicaid and the Uninsured, Washington, DC, July 2002.
3. *Medicaid Enrollment and Spending by "Mandatory" and "Optional" Eligibility and Benefit Categories,* Kaiser Commission on Medicaid and the Uninsured, February 2005.
4. *Fact Sheet,* Department of Veterans Affairs, July 2002.
5. Testimony of Robert H. Roswell, MD, Undersecretary for Health, Department of Veterans Affairs, before Committee on Veterans Affairs, United States Senate, April 25, 2002.
6. Ibid.
7. Ibid.
8. Ibid.
9. Ibid.

10

The Need for Financing Long-Term Care

Chapter Outline

Long-term care often describes the help a person receives for an extended period of time due to physical or mental limitations. Although long-term care fitting this description has existed since the beginning of the human family, heightened concern about meeting its financial need is more recent. Over the last few decades, demographic, economic, and social factors have combined with advances in medical treatment and technology to raise the awareness of that concern among most Americans.

As individuals and as a society, we are getting older. Americans are living longer, and as a result, the elderly population is increasing. Yet at the very time we are more likely to need someone to take care of us (and our parents), we are less likely to look to our families to meet that need fully or even to a great extent. Whether at home or in a nursing home, professionals and institutions provide a rapidly increasing portion of long-term care—care that is costly and must be paid for. Nevertheless, Americans often pay little attention to how they will deal with long-term care financing.

This chapter and the next several chapters are about long-term care and the ways to meet the financial need associated with it. Whether the reader is a financial services professional or a consumer, the underlying goal of these chapters remains the same: a better understanding of long-term care, the options to provide and pay for it, and the importance of planning to meet its financial need. Indeed, the financial burden associated with an extended, sometimes indefinite, period of long-term care argues persuasively that a person's financial plan is not complete or even adequate unless the resources required to alleviate this burden are identified. These resources may include personal resources, government programs, and traditional health insurance. The limitations of these options, however, make a strong case that, for many people, a properly designed financial plan, especially relating to a secure retirement, should include long-term-care insurance.

This chapter sets the stage for the subsequent chapters by defining long-term care and its components, explaining its growing need and cost, and providing a brief summary of available financial resources to pay for it. Each of these resources is covered in much greater depth in later chapters.

Long-term care involves many types of services, settings, and caregivers. Chapter 11 describes them. Chapter 12 identifies the personal resources that might be available to meet the financial need of long-term care. The limitations of these programs and resources are also discussed.

Chapter 13 introduces long-term care insurance as an important resource to meet the financial needs of long-term care. It reviews the development and evolution of policy features and the effect that legislation and regulation has had on them. Chapter 14 presents insurance policy characteristics common in the market today. Chapter 15 looks at the underwriting of long-term care insurance policies.

Chapter 16 discusses the key role of consumers in the continued development of this new insurance product and the purchase patterns of available policies that indicate how consumers value specific benefit features. The chapter also addresses several of the decisions that consumers face in selecting the most appropriate policy. In addition, the chapter includes checklists or guidelines that aid consumer evaluation and comparison of long-term care policies and the companies that offer them. Chapter 17 describes the unique features of group and hybrid policies.

Chapter 18, the final chapter, explains government's important role in the success of long-term care insurance. Government is both a regulator and a force that creates an environment in which long-term care policies can flourish through partnerships between insurers and state Medicaid programs, favorable tax policy, and promotion of private insurance as an important resource to meet the financial needs of long-term care.

LONG-TERM CARE DEFINED

long-term care

Long-term care is the broad range of medical, custodial, social, and other care services that assist people who have an impaired ability to live independently for an extended period. This period can range from a few weeks to the remainder of a person's life. As explained in more detail in chapter 11, people often need more than one type of long-term care service at a given point in time. Needs may also change over time. Long-term care

acute care

excludes *acute care* services in which a patient receives medical care for a relatively brief period of time for a severe episode of illness (such as pneumonia), accident or other trauma, or recovery from surgery. Hospitals usually provide acute care.

Long-term care is provided in a wide variety of settings, including the home, community, and alternate living arrangements and institutions, such as nursing homes, assisted-living facilities, and Alzheimer's facilities. The benefits available to meet long-term care needs from both government and private sources depend on the type of long-term care needed as well as its setting.

The types of long-term care services—medical care, custodial care, social care, and other support services—require some further explanation.

Medical Care

Medical care services for long-term care recipients are professional services prescribed by and under the supervision of a physician. They are usually classi-

skilled care
intermediate care

fied as *skilled care* (often referred to as skilled-nursing care) or *intermediate care* (often referred to as intermediate-nursing care). In general, the major difference between skilled care and intermediate care is the frequency with which each is delivered: Skilled care may be available 24 hours a day or on a daily basis, whereas intermediate care is provided perhaps 2 to 4 days per week. The most common setting for skilled care is in a nursing home that is classified as a skilled-nursing facility. Intermediate care may also be provided in a nursing home, an intermediate-care unit of a nursing home, or at home.

Skilled and licensed health professionals, such as nurses, licensed practical nurses, and therapists, provide both forms of care. Procedures and treatments include injections, administration of medications, changing of dressings, and observation and monitoring of a patient's condition, including his or her temperature, pulse, respiration, and blood pressure. Specific forms of therapy are physical, speech, respiratory, infusion, and occupational.

The services of a medical social worker may also be required to deal with the social, emotional, and other problems associated with an illness or disability. Although both skilled and intermediate care usually anticipate rehabilitation or recovery from an accident or illness, the duration of care is often unspecified.

Example:	Charlene was recently discharged from a hospital and is recovering from a serious automobile accident. Her lack of mobility requires extensive physical therapy and other medical services. Although her period of long-term care is uncertain, she is expected to make a complete recovery and return to a fully independent life. Charlene's long-term care consists primarily of medical care, which is covered by her medical expense insurance.

Custodial Care

custodial care

Custodial care, often called personal care, assists a person who has a limited ability to conduct his or her routine daily activities because of deficiencies in physical and/or cognitive functions. Someone can usually provide custodial care without professional medical skills or training. Family members often give custodial care at home, and it is the most common type of care in nursing homes, where unlicensed professionals (such as nurse's aides and volunteers) usually provide it.

Physical Functions

activities of daily living (ADLs)

Physical functions are basic and necessary tasks of everyday life and are often called the *activities of daily living (ADLs)*. They include

- bathing
- dressing
- grooming/personal hygiene
- using the toilet
- maintaining continence
- eating
- walking/ambulating
- mobility inside the home
- transferring in and out of a bed, chair, or wheelchair

Example:	David, a patient with crippling arthritis, needs care in the form of assistance with ADLs. His period of long-term care has no foreseeable conclusion because he shows little progress toward recovery or self-sufficiency. David's long-term care need is primarily for custodial care.

Cognitive Functions

cognitive functions

Cognitive functions pertain to the mental processes of comprehension, judgment, memory, and reasoning. Recognizable symptoms and standardized tests identify and measure deficiencies in cognitive functions. Deficiencies in intellectual capacity are reflected in the necessary activities of life that require a greater degree of skill, judgment, and independence than ADLs. These activities include *instrumental activities of daily living (IADLs)*, such as the following:

instrumental
activities of daily
living (IADLs)

- shopping for personal items
- managing money
- using the telephone
- preparing meals
- managing medication
- doing housework

In addition to assistance with performing the above activities, individuals with diminished cognitive abilities often need substantial supervision to maintain their safety. Without this supervision, these persons may, for example, become lost, neglect to turn off stoves and other appliances, or fail to maintain proper hygiene. In the earliest stages of cognitive impairment, there may be the need only for some simple reminders. Cognitive impairments usually become worse over time, however, and continuous supervision may eventually be needed.

Social Care

social care

Social care consists of those services that help maintain an individual's personal interactions and identity as a member of a community. Obviously, a family—the basic social unit—maintains a primary responsibility to assist its cognitively impaired or physically disabled members to avoid the loneliness and isolation that can often accompany long-term care. If the care recipient resides in a nursing home or other institutional setting, the place of residence has a major responsibility to create and maintain a sense of community. Volunteer organizations established by churches, charities, and the government may have formal programs of visitation to long-term care recipients, as well as daily telephone communication.

Other Support Services

Other support services encompass any nonpersonal, nonmedical service that enhances the care recipient's security and well-being. These services include providing durable medical equipment and such services as home modification and home management. The following are examples of modifications that adapt the home environment to the care recipient's needs:

- ramps to allow wheelchairs and walkers to bypass stairs where possible
- medical response systems
- medication monitoring/dispensing systems
- stairway elevator seats
- bathroom balance bars
- enlarged shower stalls
- widened doorways
- improved lighting
- easier access to and operation of switches and controls
- nonslip flooring
- phones with amplification capability and larger, more legible dial pad buttons

Home management services maintain and repair a home as the care recipient becomes less able to perform such tasks.

THE GROWING NEED FOR LONG-TERM CARE

The need for long-term care is most often associated with the elderly, but it has no age barrier. Many younger persons are unable to care for themselves because of handicaps resulting from birth defects, mental conditions, illnesses, or accidents. For example, victims of accidents with severe head trauma and such illnesses as a stroke or multiple sclerosis may be any age. Indeed, almost 45 percent of individuals who receive help with everyday activities are working-age adults.[1] Most of this care is provided at home or through community services, and approximately 10 percent of nursing home patients are younger than 65.[2]

Nevertheless, the growing need for long-term care is related to age and increasing longevity.

Age

The greatest single predictor of the need for long-term care is advancing age and the gradual, inevitable decline in physical and mental abilities that usually accompanies it. The effect of age on the need for long-term care is obvious enough, but a few often-quoted statistics easily confirm this reality:

- Age-related disabling conditions, although not initially life threatening but causing a deterioration of health (for example, arthritis, senile dementia, and Alzheimer's disease), affect 20 percent of those over age 65. This figure jumps to about one in two for those older than 85.[3]

- Those who attain age 85 are nearly four times as likely to need long-term care as those who have attained age 65 (50 percent versus 14 percent).[4]

Not surprisingly, the older we become, the more vulnerable we are to the conditions that require long-term care. A healthy and long life brings many rewards but increases the chances of dependence on someone else. Simply put: Getting older is dangerous to your independent living!

Hidden in the average numbers above is an important gender difference with respect to the need for long-term care. Women generally live longer than men do. They usually outlive their husbands. They are more likely to live alone, and they are more likely to need institutional care. Indeed, women are twice as likely as men to need nursing home care after age 65.[5]

Increasing Longevity

As sobering as the previous statistics may be for anyone of advancing years, they become even more compelling with the realization that they are not static. Thanks to continuing giant strides over the last century in living conditions, nutrition, public hygiene and sanitation, maternity and infant care, inoculations, and other medical advances to treat infectious and acute illnesses, we are living longer. In 1900, life expectancy at birth was 47 years. By 1960, life expectancy had increased to 70 years; in 2002, life expectancy at birth was 79.9 years for women and 74.5 years for men. Perhaps more significantly, people who survive to age 65 can expect to live an average of 18.2 more years.[6]

Thus, there are more people entering the age categories discussed previously in which dependency on others is more prevalent. The baby-boom generation[7] that will reach age 65 between 2011 and 2029 will swell these numbers significantly. A few statistics using the population projections in figure 10-1 make the case:

- In mid-2004, there were approximately 38 million people aged 65 and over, constituting 13 percent of the country's population of 294 million; by 2029, after the last of the baby-boom generation reaches age 65, there will be 70 million seniors, constituting 20 percent of the population (351.1 million).
- Individuals aged 85 and older are the fastest-growing segment of the senior population. This segment is expected to increase from 4.3 million, or 1.6 percent of the population, in 2000 to almost 9 million by 2030, when it will represent over 2.5 percent of the population.
- By 2050, when the full effect of the baby-boom retirees is felt, the age-85-and-over category will exceed 19 million and constitute almost 5 percent of the population (403.7 million).

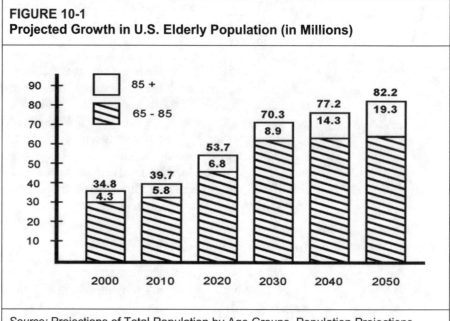

FIGURE 10-1
Projected Growth in U.S. Elderly Population (in Millions)

Source: Projections of Total Population by Age Groups, Population Projections Program, Population Division, U.S. Census Bureau, Washington DC, December 1999–January 2000, NP-T3A-F.

In other words, individuals are not only aging; they are getting even older and growing in number. A society of aging individuals presents new challenges. The increasing need for long-term care is a significant one. In the past, many persons needed long-term care because they suffered from such acute conditions as heart disease and stroke—ailments with formerly high mortality rates. But the age-adjusted death rate for heart disease and stroke has declined by one-third since 1981.[8] In the future, a larger portion of the elderly will be incapacitated by chronic conditions, such as Alzheimer's disease, arthritis, and osteoporosis—conditions that are more likely to require continuing assistance with day-to-day needs. Despite any declines in their rates of disabilities, the disabled elderly will increase in total with the rise in the number of the elderly population, especially those at more advanced ages. As a result, the aggregate need across the entire population will demand a growing share of national resources to pay for health facilities and professionals.

LIMITS ON THE ABILITY OF FAMILIES TO PROVIDE THE COMPLETE RANGE OF CARE

Family members (often at considerable personal sacrifice) provide a great deal of long-term care for their older relatives. More than 20 million families, almost one-fourth of all American households, provide informal and unpaid care for an older relative or friend who is ill or disabled. Cumulatively, such care represents approximately 70 percent of the long-term care rendered in the home. This care would cost over $200 billion per year if furnished by paid caregivers and would constitute the main source of seniors' long-term care financing.[9] Moreover, these caregivers spend additional billions of dollars of their own money in the process of providing that care; total out-of-pocket payments for long-term care made by care recipients and their families exceed $44 billion per year.[10]

Studies show that the principal caregivers are daughters (26.6 percent), spouses (23.4 percent), other female relatives (17.5 percent) and sons (14.7 percent). Almost 20 percent of caregivers for the elderly live with the person for whom they are caring. Cumulatively, women, including nonrelatives, make up over 63 percent of informal caregivers. The average age of family caregivers for someone aged 50 and older is estimated to be 46; many of these caregivers are over age 65.[11]

Because most families prefer to care for their older relatives at home, informal caregivers will continue as a principal source of long-term care. However, it is becoming more difficult for families to provide that care at the very time that the need for long-term care is increasing. Limits arise from demographic, economic, and social factors that can be categorized under the headings of availability and capacity.

Availability

Compared to previous generations, family members today are simply less available to meet the needs of their elderly parents because of a higher percentage of women in the paid workforce, lower birth rates, and geographic dispersion of families.

Higher Percentage of Women in the Paid Workforce

Women have been and continue to be the major providers of long-term care. However, their availability has become restricted because of their increased participation in the paid workforce. Due to economic necessity, the desire for a higher standard of living, and/or the pursuit of their own careers, a majority of women have joined their male counterparts in the workplace. Regardless of the motivation, the hours they spend at work are unavailable for caregiving and often exclude assistance to a parent who needs continuous care, thereby precipitating the need for professional care at home or in a nursing home. Still, many women (and also men) with jobs provide care to elderly parents. Indeed, about 64 percent of family caregivers are employed, most (52 percent) full-time.[12]

Lower Birth Rates

Unlike the baby-boom generation, today's average family is smaller, and there are fewer larger families. Because of the cost of living, standard-of-living concerns, and marriages later in life, families are having fewer children. In addition, there are more childless families, and more people are remaining single. As a result, today's aging parents have fewer children to look to for their care than in previous generations.

Geographic Dispersion of Families

Family members are dispersed geographically to a greater extent than in previous generations. Sons and daughters and brothers and sisters often leave the area in which they grew up when they marry or simply to take advantage of employment and career opportunities. To the extent they are dispersed geographically, family members are unavailable to care for elderly parents or other relatives.

Capacity

The capacity of family members to provide long-term care may be limited by an individual's capabilities, a family's situation, and the condition of the family member being cared for. These capacity limitations frequently arise from multiple priorities, increased longevity, divorce, and the need to use medical technology.

Multiple Priorities

sandwich generation

Even when family members are available to care for an aging parent or relative, they often face multiple priorities that restrict their ability to provide care. The caregiver may still be taking care of dependent children, or he or she may have a spouse who also needs care. Such people who provide care to children or spouses as well as older relatives are referred to as the *sandwich generation*. Financial priorities may also conflict if the family caregiver must pay a portion of a parent's long-term care expenses while meeting his or her own financial obligations for retirement and education of children.

Increased Longevity

Longevity makes it difficult to predict the availability of family support. An extended life span leaves a greater proportion of older people who require support from a younger but aging generation. Thus, family members are increasingly at an advanced age when they find themselves responsible for their spouse or their 80- or 90-year-old parents. At this period in their lives, their own declining capabilities could make them unable to provide the extent of care required by the age and condition of their loved one. A retiree's limited financial and other resources could easily be insufficient to support both the caregiver and a disabled spouse or parent, especially if medical care or other expensive services are needed.

High Divorce Rates

Divorce has the effect of restricting the capacity to provide informal care in several ways. Not surprisingly, a person is more likely to care for the parents of a spouse than for the parents of an ex-spouse. Aged divorced persons, especially fathers, are less likely to receive care from their adult children. Stepparents are only half as likely to receive care from their stepchildren as parents of natural children are. Single-parent families, often created by divorce, have lower incomes on average than two-parent families and are often below the poverty level. They are, therefore, less able to assume the burdens of or contribute to the care of a parent or other relative.

The Need to Use Medical Technology

The level of assistance a family gives an elderly relative at the initial stages of a chronic condition may be nothing more than occasional visits to check on or observe routine activities and offer help when needed. Inevitably, the initial level of assistance almost always escalates to continuous care with the caregiver assuming a major responsibility for meeting a broad range of needs. At some point thereafter, available medical technology to improve nutrition, provide therapy, and prevent infection may be necessary, even if the care setting is maintained in the caregiver's or recipient's home. Such technology continues to evolve and increase in cost. While the family member may continue to provide custodial care, the use of the medical technology may require professional assistance 1 or more days a week.

THE COST OF LONG-TERM CARE

The Congressional Budget Office (CBO) estimated the year 2004 national expenditures for care for the elderly in institutional settings at over $92 billion, with home health care exceeding $42 billion.[13] These expenditures, about 11 percent of national health care expenditures, are increasing faster than inflation because of the growing demand for nursing home beds and the shortage of skilled medical personnel. By 2020, these annual amounts are expected to rise to approximately $139 billion for nursing home care and $69 billion for home care.[14]

The out-of-pocket payments for long-term care by individuals who must use personal resources can be astronomical. Currently, average annual nursing home costs for a semiprivate room are approximately $64,000 and can be much higher. The average nursing home stay of current residents is approximately 2.5 years, but some stays exceed the average by many years.[15] Two visits a day by a home health aid to help with bathing and dressing and household chores can cost more than $2,500 a month. By 2030, the annual cost of nursing home care is expected to approximate $241,000 with comparable increases in home care charges.[16]

SOURCES OF PAYMENT FOR LONG-TERM CARE

Table 10-1 shows projections for the long-term care expenditures of the elderly in 2010 and 2020 by payer category.

Although the statistics in table 10-1 illustrate total overall payments by source, any individual might rely solely on government programs, solely on personal resources, or on a combination of the two. Other chapters cover these alternative sources in detail. However, they are briefly presented here to summarize their limits and provide the basis for introducing long-term care insurance covered in depth in chapters 13 through 18.

Government Programs

Medicare, Medicaid, and veterans' benefits are frequently cited government sources of payment for long-term care services.

TABLE 10-1
Projections of National Long-Term Care Expenditures for the Elderly (in Billions of Inflation-Adjusted Dollars)

Services Provided in Institutional Settings			
	2000	2010	2020
Medicare	$12.3	$ 16.0	$ 19.5
Medicaid	36.2	52.0	57.7
Private long-term care insurance	*	11.2	25.9
Out of pocket	34.3	29.3	35.6
Other	*	*	*
	$85.8	$108.5	$138.7

Services Provided in the Home			
	2000	2010	2020
Medicare	$17.1	$23.8	$31.0
Medicaid	7.1	14.9	17.1
Private long-term care insurance	*	5.5	10.2
Out of pocket	8.5	6.3	7.3
Other	*	*	*
	$37.2	$52.2	$68.6

* Less than $5 billion.
Source: Congressional Budget Office.

Medicare

Medicare is a medical expense insurance program for people aged 65 or older, people under age 65 with disabilities, and people with end-stage renal disease (permanent kidney failure requiring dialysis or a transplant). Medicare provides coverage for acute hospital, surgical, and physician's care but pays only limited benefits for long-term care expenses. These benefits do not extend to custodial care unless this care is needed along with medical or rehabilitative treatment (post-acute-skilled care) in nursing facilities or at home. Unfortunately, Medicare's limited coverage of post-acute services in a skilled-nursing facility and payment of certain home health care services often gives the mistaken impression that Medicare provides payment for custodial long-term care services required by the elderly with chronic conditions.

Medicaid

Medicaid (discussed in detail in chapter 9) is a federal/state-funded entitlement program that provides medical assistance for individuals and families with low incomes and resources. Medicaid is also the largest source of payment for long-term care services. To qualify for benefits, one must essentially be impoverished. In fact, many people do spend down their assets to meet the means test their state of residence requires. Others transfer ownership of their resources to qualify. However, there are a number of significant shortcomings to considering Medicaid eligibility as an appropriate source for financing a personal program of long-term care.

Veterans Administration Benefits

The Department of Veterans Affairs (VA) may provide limited nursing home benefits (discussed in chapter 9) for veterans in one of its own facilities or in private nursing homes. Service-connected disabilities and illnesses or low income are eligibility requirements for admission to VA nursing homes. This care is always further conditioned on available space. Use of private nursing homes is possible upon discharge from a VA facility, but it is normally not provided in excess of 6 months unless service-related care is required. Direct admission to a private nursing home is almost always limited to care for a service-related condition.

Personal Resources

Personal resources (covered in chapter 12) include income, savings, and assets that comprise one's personal or family wealth. The single question most relevant to personal resources is their sufficiency in total to pay long-term care expenses often incurred at unanticipated times and for extended or indefinite periods at the levels mentioned previously. Statistics indicate that 50 to 75 percent of all couples are impoverished within 1 year after one of them enters a nursing home, and only 15 percent of Americans can afford to pay for more than a 3-year nursing home stay at today's rates.[17] Even if personal wealth is sufficient to meet expenses for a specific episode of long-term care, the adequacy of the remaining resources to maintain a spouse's or a family's desired standard of living and an estate to pass to heirs must also be considered.

An often overlooked—but very real—personal resource in discussions of long-term care is the support of family members. This support can be in the form of caregiving or monetary contributions.

Benefits from traditional forms of life and health insurance may also be used under some circumstances to meet long-term care needs. However, these benefits are limited in both the amount and the situations in which they are available.

Long-Term Care Insurance

Finally, there is long-term care insurance, which is covered in detail in several later chapters. It is a form of health insurance that usually provides coverage for personal or custodial care, intermediate care, and skilled care in various settings. These settings may include nursing homes and at-home care, as well as adult day care and assisted-living facilities. Benefits often vary by setting and the kind of care received. These benefits may be in the form of either reimbursement of expenses incurred (usually up to a maximum) or payment of a defined amount. Approximately 6.2 million people have long-term care insurance, which is now offered by nearly 100 companies. While increases have been lower most recently, the average annual increases in policy sales exceeded 11 percent in the 5-year period ending in 2004.[18]

NOTES

1. The Henry J. Kaiser Foundation, *Long-Term Care: Medicaid's Role and Challenges,* publication #2172, November 1999, Washington, DC.
2. Centers for Disease Control and Prevention (CDC)/National Center for Health Statistics (NCHS), *1999 National Nursing Home Survey*, Table 3.
3. Congressional Budget Office, *Financing Long-Term Care for the Elderly,* April 2004, Section 3, p. 1.
4. *Who Needs Long-Term Care?,* Georgetown University Long-Term Care Financing Project Fact Sheet, May 2003.
5. Centers for Disease Control and Prevention (CDC)/National Center for Health Statistics (NCHS), *1999 National Nursing Home Survey*, Table 3.
6. *National Vital Statistics Reports,* vol. 53, no. 6, November 10, 2004, Table II.
7. During the World War (WW) II years from 1941 to 1945 and to some extent during the depression years that preceded them, many Americans put their plans for having families on

hold. At the conclusion of WW II, the birth rate increased significantly. This period of increased birth rates beginning in 1946 and generally accepted as ending in 1964 is known as the "baby boom." Currently, this population cohort is between the ages of 42 and 60 and will reach the traditional retirement age of 65 in 2011 to 2029. At that time, the combination of the elderly's increasing life spans and the surge of baby-boom retirees will cause those aged 65 and over to constitute 20 percent of the total population (compared to the current level of 13 percent).

8. *Older Americans 2004: Key Indicators of Well-Being,* Federal Interagency Forum on Aging-Related Statistics, from its Web site at www.agingstats.gov/chartbook2004.

9. *Long-Term Care: Aging Baby Boom Generation Will Increase Demand and Burden on Federal and State Budgets,* statement of David M. Walker, Comptroller General of the United States before The Special Committee on Aging, U.S. Senate, March 21, 2002, pp. 11–12.

10. *The Economic Value of Informal Caregiving,* Arno, P.C. Levine, and M. Memmot, 1999, Health Affairs 18(2), pp. 182–188.

11. Family Caregiver Alliance: Selected Caregiver Statistics, accessed at www.caregivers.org, January 14, 2005.

12. *Long-Term Care,* 3d ed., 1999, Dearborn Financial Institute, Inc., p. 20.

13. Congressional Budget Office, *Financing Long-Term Care for the Elderly,* April 2004, Section 3, p. 1.

14. *Projection of Expenditures for Long-Term Care Services for the Elderly,* The Congressional Budget Office, March 1999, pp. 3 and 4.

15. *The MetLife Market Survey of Nursing Home and Home Care Costs,* September 2005, The Mature Market Institute, pp. 3 and 8.

16. *Long-Term Care Insurance: What Long-Term Care Insurance Can Do for You,* American Council of Life Insurance, from its Web site at www.acli.org, accessed on January 17, 2005.

17. *The John Hancock/National Council on Aging 1997 Long-Term Care Survey,* prepared by Matthew Greenwald and Associates, Washington, DC, Report of Findings, p. 15.

18. *Long-Term Care and Medicare Supplement, Executive Summary, Annual 2004,* LIMRA International, Inc., 2005, p. 2, and *U.S. Group Long-Term Care Insurance, Executive Summary, Annual 2004,* LIMRA International, Inc., 2005, p. 2.

11

Caregivers and Settings for Long-Term Care

Chapter Outline

Long-term care is provided by caregivers and delivered in specific settings. Among the caregivers and the settings, there is a progression of care from less intensive to more intensive as the care delivered moves from family members to professionals and from the home setting to supportive-living arrangements. As mentioned in chapter 1, this progression is often called a care continuum. A care recipient's level of independence and the care options that satisfy his or her needs and match a family caregiver's availability and capacity determine the care recipient's place in the care continuum. Thus, although the home is usually the best care setting in which to maintain independence, it may not be the option selected. A supportive-living arrangement may better correspond with a family's caregiving limits and more completely satisfy the care recipient's need for social interaction.

CAREGIVERS

Formal and informal caregivers are the two main types of caregivers. In addition, respite caregivers, care coordinators, and even daily money managers provide long-term care services.

255

Informal Caregivers

informal caregiver

An *informal caregiver* is an individual who voluntarily cares for a long-term care recipient without pay and without formal education and training in long-term care. Informal caregivers include immediate family members such as spouses, children, brothers, and sisters, and others related to the care recipient by blood or marriage, such as aunts, uncles, cousins, and in-laws. Friends, neighbors, and volunteers from churches, charities, and community groups may also be informal caregivers. The informal caregiver with overall responsibility for a person's long-term care (usually a family member) is called a *primary caregiver*. All other informal caregivers are *secondary caregivers*.

primary caregiver
secondary caregiver

Formal Caregivers

formal caregiver

A *formal caregiver* in a long-term care setting is an individual who provides care as a profession or occupation and earns a living by rendering services to long-term care recipients. Formal caregivers include physicians, nurse caregivers, other licensed medical personnel, and nonlicensed personnel. Families may retain formal caregivers on an individual professional basis. However, formal caregiver services other than those furnished by physicians and other doctors are often obtained through home care agencies that assist informal caregivers in the home care setting.

Physicians

Physicians are formal long-term caregivers because they usually authorize and direct the medical care and other necessary services provided to long-term care recipients. Physicians may treat long-term care recipients directly for acute illness, such as pneumonia or medically manage a chronic condition, such as Parkinson's disease. A *geriatric physician* specializes in the treatment of the aged. Chapter 14 explains physician certification of an insured as eligible for long-term care insurance benefits.

geriatric physician

Nurse Caregivers

nurse caregiver

A *nurse caregiver* is a registered nurse, licensed practical or vocational nurse, or nurse assistant (aide) who is responsible for the medical treatment of actual or potential health problems with the goal of rehabilitating a care recipient or stabilizing his or her medical condition. A registered nurse supervises the conduct of nursing services that may include custodial services in conjunction with medical care. Thus, nurse caregivers also direct the services provided by nonlicensed personnel. Nurse assistants in the home care setting are called home health aides. Nurse caregivers are principal providers of skilled and intermediate care (discussed in chapter 10 and mentioned later in this chapter).

Other Licensed Medical Personnel

Other licensed medical personnel are those with special health care skills obtained through training and experience, such as therapists, speech-language pathologists, social workers, and dietitians. These professionals often work together, sometimes in teams, to care for their patients and advise nurse caregivers and physicians on important aspects of patient care.

therapist

Therapists. A *therapist* is a trained medical specialist who commonly performs one or more of the following services:

- physical therapy—treatment of physical impairments through the use of special exercise, application of heat or cold, and other physical modalities
- respiratory therapy—treatment that maintains or improves the breathing function through the administration of medications and oxygen and/or the use of ventilator equipment
- infusion therapy—introduction of fluids, electrolytes, or drugs directly into a vein, tissue, or organ
- occupational therapy—functional enhancement of persons who have physical, social, and emotional deficits arising from physical injury, illness, emotional disturbance, congenital or developmental disability, or aging

speech-language pathologist

Speech-Language Pathologists. A *speech-language pathologist* is a professional with advanced training and education in human communications, its development, and its disorders. Individuals with these skills measure and evaluate language abilities, auditory processes, and speech production and treat those with speech and language disorders. Speech-language pathologists often work with stroke victims.

social worker

Social Workers. A *social worker* is an individual with advanced education in dealing with social, emotional, and living environment problems associated with physical or cognitive impairments.

dietitian

Dietitians. A *dietitian* is a professional trained in the application of the principles of nutrition to the planning, preparation, and serving of foods to promote health and treat disease. For example, proper nutrition can be used to control high blood pressure and diabetes—two conditions that increase with age and affect many seniors. Monitoring weight gains and losses and planning special diets for people on tube feedings are also a dietitian's responsibility.

Nonlicensed Personnel

nonlicensed personnel

Nonlicensed personnel are employed to assist long-term care recipients with nonmedical tasks that usually relate to activities of daily living (ADLs), such as bathing and feeding, and instrumental activities of daily living (IADLs), such as cleaning, laundry, meal preparation, shopping, paying bills, and completing other chores. In the home setting, these nonlicensed personnel are called homemakers, companions, and chore workers. Although these caregivers are usually unlicensed, some states require that certain categories of personnel be certified. Personnel at this level may receive training in geriatric care, including helping persons with cognitive impairments.

Respite Caregivers

respite caregiver

A *respite caregiver* is an alternate caregiver who provides long-term care services to relieve a primary caregiver from the physical and emotional stress of rendering care over a long period of time and/or to allow the primary caregiver to have some period of personal time. This service is called *respite care*. Res-

respite care

pite care may occur in a number of settings and can be provided by informal and formal caregivers. Respite care can be relatively brief. For example, a neighbor who relieves a caregiver for an hour a day several days a week provides respite care by giving the primary caregiver the opportunity to take a break or pursue personal interests. Respite care can also have an extended duration. Usually, the longer the period of respite care, the more likely it is to be provided by formal caregivers. For example, a care recipient living at home could receive services from a home care agency or be placed in an assisted-living facility or a nursing home for a week or two when the caregiving family takes a vacation.

Care Coordinators

care coordinator

A *care coordinator*, also known as a care manager, geriatric care manager, or care planner, assesses an elderly patient who exhibits some degree of physical or cognitive impairment to determine the care needs and to develop a care plan to meet those needs. The plan also identifies and assesses the care resources available from the family (including financial resources) and resources available in the community. The plan effectively places the care recipient in the care continuum by recommending the proper care setting and the appropriate caregivers (or combinations of caregivers) in a manner that respects the care recipient's independence and needs and the informal caregivers' availability and capacity. A social worker typically functions as the care coordinator and develops the care plan. The charge for this service is usually on a fee-for-service basis and costs about $100 per hour.

A family caregiver or physician may request a care coordinator's services, or the care coordinator may be part of the certification process to determine eligibility for benefits under a long-term care insurance policy (discussed in chapter 14). The primary family caregiver or the coordinator can manage the plan by monitoring the quality and effectiveness of care and making changes as the care recipient's and caregiver's needs change.

Daily Money Managers

daily money manager (DMM)

A *daily money manager (DMM)* assists clients who, for any reason, may have difficulty conducting their routine personal financial affairs. Services that DMMs provide relate to budgeting, paying routine bills, and keeping track of financial matters. In addition, DMMs may balance checkbooks, make bank deposits, organize tax records and other paperwork, and confer with creditors. Many persons retain these professionals because they may simply have little time for or interest in managing their routine daily money matters. However, DMMs in effect serve as long-term caregivers when they assist a person with physical and/or cognitive disabilities, usually precipitated by aging, that inhibit the ability to manage one's own finances. These disabilities include limited vision, arthritis or other conditions that hamper writing ability, and cognitive impairments that reduce the ability to complete tasks. The goal is to help persons with such limitations continue living independently. An adult child of an older person may seek the assistance of a DMM if the child does not have the time or ability to manage a parent's financial affairs.

Most DMMs charge for their services on an hourly basis. Some local government agencies, church groups, and other not-for-profit organizations provide referrals to DMMs and may offer reduced fees or free services for low-income clients.

CARE SETTINGS

care setting

A *care setting* is an environment in which health care services may be given to care recipients. Long-term care settings also occur along a care continuum that begins with home care provided by informal caregivers. They advance to supportive-living arrangements outside the home with the use of formal caregivers. As the care recipient's needs become more intensive and complex, informal caregivers often need support to maintain the home as the care setting. Although supportive-living arrangements outside the home may indicate that the care continuum requirements exceed the home environment's capabilities, these care settings are often an alternative to the home environment when they involve independent living and assisted-living facilities. As supportive-living settings progress from independent living through assisted living and to nursing home care or Alzheimer's facility care, they also represent a care continuum. Because the nursing home or Alzheimer's facility setting provides the most intensive and complex form of long-term care using formal caregivers, these facilities often constitute an end point on the care continuum. Hospice care, which can be offered in many settings, and hospital care also mark the end of the care continuum for some long-term care recipients.

The key to the appropriate placement of a care recipient within the continuum of care is to select the setting and level of services that best meet the care recipient's needs. At the same time, the care recipient should maintain a maximum degree of independence and as normal a living situation as disability or declining health permits. In other words, the assistance should meet, but not exceed, the care recipient's needs and should allow as independent a life as possible. Because there are alternative settings that might be suitable, individuals and their families should discuss the settings for future care in advance of its need.

aging in place

Aging in place is a term that is frequently used to summarize this approach to placement in the care continuum; care recipients avoid nursing home care by receiving care where they live, usually at home and in the community, through a combination of formal and informal caregiver services.

Home Health Care

home health care

Home health care, as the name implies, takes place where the care recipient resides and encompasses virtually any home environment outside of a nursing home. Home may be the familiar family residence of many years or a new residence acquired by spouses for their retirement. The proximity of family members and reduced home maintenance and repair burdens are often the reasons seniors relocate, especially as they become less independent or after the death of a spouse. The care recipient's home may also be in a family member's residence, an independent living facility, or assisted-living facility.

The spectrum of long-term-care services available in the home setting is quite broad, encompassing medical and custodial services that use both informal and formal caregivers. These services are provided to the extent and in the combination necessary to meet the recipient's changing needs and the family caregivers' availability and capacity. Nationwide, an estimated 22.4 million families are providing physical and emotional assistance to older loved ones. Caregivers spend about $2 billion each month out of pocket on groceries, medicine, and support services.[1] More than 10 million Americans over age 65 live alone, and many have no one to turn to if they need help.[2]

Most care recipients and their families view the home as the ideal care setting, at least at the beginning of the care continuum when care needs are more easily managed. With familiar surroundings, possessions accumulated over a lifetime, and proximity to established neighbors and friends, the care recipient can flourish and function at a high level of independence despite a disability or chronic condition. To the extent recovery is possible after an illness or injury, it is often quicker when care is delivered in a preferred setting, such as at home. In the home setting, family members, to the extent they are available and have the capacity to do so, may provide the needed custodial services by assisting with activities of daily living, instrumental activities of daily living, and home maintenance. Assistance may be hands-on or in the form of supervision to make sure these tasks are properly and safely completed.

Many elderly with some disabilities live by themselves and need only minor assistance at the beginning and end of the day. Although the ideal location is the care recipient's own residence, the care recipient may move into a family member's home to make it easier for the family caregiver to provide assistance.

Example: Jane's mother, Dorothy, recently widowed at age 78, remains in reasonably good health, but she is becoming increasingly frail and suffers from macular degeneration that restricts her vision. Jane visits her mother two or more times a week to pay bills and to handle financial matters that are now beyond Dorothy's current abilities. When she visits, Jane brings her mother groceries and other necessary purchases. Jane also closely monitors her mother's routine daily activities, such as dressing and bathing, to make sure that she is completing them without major difficulty. Jane's husband cuts the grass, shovels snow, and keeps Dorothy's house in repair.

Jane, as the primary caregiver, and her husband are able to take care of Dorothy's current needs quite well as her informal caregivers in Dorothy's home where, despite some limitations, she maintains significant independence. They are giving Dorothy long-term care at a relatively low level in the care continuum by assisting with the IADLs and the ADLs, frequently on a stand-by basis, and performing home maintenance.

As care needs change with increased dependency, a family caregiver may have to seek additional assistance to maintain the care recipient at home. This assistance can include a range of support through home health care agencies, adult day care centers, and community services. The services that these groups provide allow a family member to maintain a relative in the home care setting when the relative's increasing needs exceed the informal caregiver's availability and/or capacity. In the absence of these services, the family caregiver would have little choice than to turn to supportive-living arrangements.

Home Health Care Agencies

home health care
agency

A *home health care agency* is a private company that specializes in care to the elderly and disabled. Many of these agencies employ a range of formal caregivers that frequently includes those previously listed under the headings of nurse caregivers, other licensed medical personnel, and nonlicensed personnel. These agencies can provide medical and custodial services. Specifically, they may provide intermediate nursing services; help the care recipient with bathing, dressing, and meals; and offer socialization and housekeeping. Some agencies, however, provide little medical care and specialize in home health aides (nursing assistants) and nonlicensed personnel (such as homemakers, companions, and chore workers) who may maintain and repair a home. These agencies are more appropriately referred to as home care agencies.

Example: To continue the previous example, Dorothy falls and breaks her hip. After release from the hospital and a less-than-30-day stay in a nursing home, she returns home to complete her recovery. A home health care agency now provides medical services in the form of nursing care services and physical therapy three times a week. A home health aide visits every weekday to help Dorothy with dressing, bathing, and transferring in and out of bed and chairs.

Jane has just received a letter from Medicare informing her that Dorothy's recovery is now complete to the extent that she no longer requires nursing care. The services of the home health aide who assisted Dorothy with her ADLs are also no longer covered because Medicare does not pay for custodial care in the absence of a need for intermediate nursing care.

Because Dorothy is left with limited agility after her surgery and is becoming more frail, Jane and Dorothy agree to retain the home health care agency's services for a few hours every weekday to assist with dressing, bathing, and personal hygiene while Jane and her husband are at work. On the weekend and sometimes during weekday evenings, Jane and her husband continue to care for Dorothy as they did before her accident. However, her needs now include hands-on assistance with ADLs that the home health aide provides during the week.

> Dorothy has returned to a lower level of care than when she required nursing care during her recovery from surgery. Nevertheless, although Dorothy remains at home, her increased dependency and the continuing services of a formal custodial caregiver have clearly advanced her along the care continuum beyond the point at which Jane and her husband began to care for her.

Home health care agencies are usually state licensed, but regulation varies widely among states and by the type of services provided. However, only about one-half of licensed home health care agencies meet the standards to receive the federal certification required for payment of services under the Medicare and Medicaid programs. The National Home Care Council, the Joint Commission on Accreditation of Healthcare Organizations, and the Community Health Accreditation Program are three prominent standard-setting organizations that accredit home health care agencies. State licensure, federal certification, and accreditation are important indicators of the home health care agency's staff qualifications and, therefore, of the quality of its services.

Adult Day Care Centers

adult day care center

The *adult day care center* is a relatively new care setting that provides social, medical, and rehabilitative services to people with physical and mental limitations. These centers are designed for the elderly, who may be severely impaired but live at home and whose family caregiver is unavailable to stay at home during the day because he or she is working. Without the services these centers provide, many people could not remain at home.

Adult day care centers are usually open 5 days a week from 6 to 12 hours per day and typically offer a full range of long-term care services. Custodial care is provided. Indeed, most of those receiving care at adult day care centers are frail and need help with the activities of daily living. Many have cognitive impairments, including the early stages of Alzheimer's disease. The centers also provide meals under the direction of a dietitian and meet social needs through recreational and educational activities. Many programs offer transportation between home and the center. Medical services include nursing care, as well as physical, speech, and occupational therapy. Not all centers provide medical services, however. Daily charges range from around $50 to over $100 if medical services are provided. These centers are frequently sponsored by community service agencies.

Insurance industry representatives often use the terms "adult day center" and "adult day services" to describe this form of long-term care, thereby avoiding the words "day care," which seniors may find offensive.

Community Services

Community services include community-sponsored programs and services funded by the Administration on Aging.

Community-Sponsored Programs. Almost every community, through volunteers, community groups, charities, churches, and the government, provides various arrays of services that support family caregivers and enhance a care recipient's ability to remain at home. Indeed, the development of adult day care centers discussed above demonstrates the important role community services can play in long-term care. Many communities offer organized classes ranging from art to exercise. Other social services include group sightseeing, scheduled transportation to local shopping facilities, and regularly scheduled movies. These services keep seniors not only physically active, but also mentally engaged. The significant variations in specific services that communities sponsor are beyond the scope of this text. However, a review of the categories of services funded by the Administration on Aging identifies the services that are common across communities.

Services Funded by the Administration on Aging. The federal Older Americans Act established the Administration on Aging (AOA), which supports local area agencies on aging (AAAs) through funds provided to each state. Nationwide, over 650 area agencies on aging receive funding from their respective states. The AAAs contract with public and private groups to offer services, or they may provide services directly to support in-home and community services for individuals aged 60 or older. There are several categories of these services[3]:

- in-home services—meals-on-wheels, housekeeping, chore services, telephone reassurance, friendly visiting, energy assistance and weatherization, emergency response systems, home health services, personal care services, and respite care
- information and access services—information and referral/ assistance, health insurance counseling, client assessment, care management (coordination), transportation, caregiver support, and retirement planning and education
- community-based services—employment services, senior centers, congregate meals, adult day care services, and volunteer opportunities
- housing—senior housing and alternative community-based living facilities
- elder rights—legal assistance, elder abuse prevention programs, and ombudsmen services for complaint resolution

Each community determines its own priorities for the services it offers within these categories and the extent to which they are offered. Consequently, services may differ markedly among adjacent communities. Eligibility requirements may relate both to income levels and care priorities, such as the homebound elderly with no family caregiver. Community services, even those with federal funding, do not constitute an entitlement program like Medicare or Medicaid. Budgets are limited; often, there are waiting lists for those who are otherwise eligible. In an effort to expand the reach of their services, agencies are accepting payments that vary and extending income eligibility requirements above their traditional thresholds.

Families are encouraged to contact local agencies to determine the specific services offered in their communities, as well as eligibility and payment requirements. AAAs are listed in telephone directories, usually under city or county government headings. With funding provided by the AOA, the state and area agencies on aging have established an Eldercare Locator administered in cooperation with the National Association of State Units on Aging. The Eldercare Locator helps elderly adults and their caregivers to find local services for seniors through a toll-free service at 800-677-1116; some locator features are available through the Internet at www.eldercare.gov. Many churches also have volunteers who are valuable resources for finding local caregivers.

Supportive-Living Arrangements

With advancing age, many seniors—although they continue to be in generally good health or have only minor limitations—become less willing to maintain a traditional home, especially if they live alone. They may need some degree of assistance from time to time or at least want the security of knowing that it is available. In addition, they may feel isolated living at home and miss the companionship of others, often after the death of a spouse. At the same time, they wish to remain as independent as possible for as long as possible before entering a nursing home. Supportive-living arrangements for these individuals are available in settings across a care continuum that ranges from independent housing to an assisted-living facility and eventually to a nursing home. Which setting individuals or couples may enter is directly related to their level of independence. Because these living arrangements are often available through unrelated facilities on a stand-alone basis, they are described separately. However, in many other cases, a combined facility may offer two or more types of supportive-living arrangements. This discussion excludes adult retirement communities that are typically designed for younger retirees in good health who must provide entirely for their own medical and long-term care needs.

Independent Housing

independent housing

Independent housing is a collective term for the array of supportive living arrangements for seniors in a domestic or homelike environment. Residents are free to come and go as they please and do not require facility-based care (described in the following sections). The support these arrangements afford may range from companionship when desired to special meal and recreation programs. Local transportation to shopping and community events may also be available. Limited assistance with daily activities, if offered under these arrangements, is provided on a scheduled basis, not on demand.

Examples of independent housing are shared residences, senior apartments, home sharing, and accessory apartments. In a shared residence, a number of seniors live in the same house as a family, usually with each resident having the privacy of a separate bedroom. A senior apartment is a unit in a "seniors only" complex that provides a sense of community and security. Shared housing is an arrangement in which a person, known as the host and usually elderly, agrees to share space in his or her own home with one or more elderly guests. The housemates can provide companionship and assistance to each other and the host may receive additional income from the guest(s). An accessory apartment is a separate living unit that is constructed, often for a family member, in a single-family home. Such a unit is called an elder cottage if it is built as a separate structure on the property of the single-family home.

Frequently, community, religious, and other charitable and not-for-profit organizations facilitate and/or operate independent housing programs. Although many of these living arrangements are licensed, the regulations governing their operations vary widely, as does the quality of the housing and services provided. Zoning requirements also regulate the construction of accessory apartments and elder cottages.

Assisted-Living Facilities

assisted-living facility

An *assisted-living facility* provides supportive-living arrangements for older residents who, despite some degree of impairment, remain independent to a significant degree but require continuing supervision and the availability of assistance on an unscheduled basis. There may be separate sections of assisted-living facilities devoted to caring for individuals with such cognitive impairments as Alzheimer's disease.

Residents may have single rooms or their own apartments with kitchens, or they may live in separate units. Services usually include meals, laundry, housekeeping, personal services (such as a hairdresser or a barber), and transportation outside the facility. Services also include assistance with one or more activities of daily living, and medication monitoring is routine. A nurse may be called for an assisted-living resident who needs limited amounts of nursing care. If constant nursing and/or custodial care is required, the resident may no longer qualify as a candidate for assisted living. Facilities, however, may use an aging-in-place approach in the assisted-living-care setting and avoid relocation of a resident to a nursing home or to another unit by allowing a higher than normal level of care in certain situations, such as when hospice care is needed.

Assisted-living facilities may serve as many as several hundred residents, but most are smaller. Although costs also vary widely, average annual costs are approximately $30,000, or about half the cost of a nursing home. Board-and-care homes and adult foster care are much smaller in scale than assisted-living facilities, yet provide similar supportive services.

Example:	To continue the previous example further, Dorothy's deteriorating condition impairs her independence to the point where the home care agency visits that assist her with bathing and dressing are insufficient to meet her changing needs. Dorothy can no longer be left home alone.

After performing an assessment, the care coordinator Jane hired agrees that Dorothy needs a higher level of care that includes continual supervision and hands-on assistance with bathing, dressing, and transferring in and out of bed and chairs. The coordinator recommends either an assisted-living facility or an adult day care center in the community if Jane is able to take care of Dorothy's needs after work and on weekends. Both options require Dorothy to give up her home of many years. Because Dorothy prefers the independence of a home-like setting, she decides to move to Jane's home, rather than an assisted-living facility, to allow her daughter to care for her on a daily basis. Jane is willing to meet the additional care needs, and having her mother live with her makes it possible. Dorothy applies and is accepted at the adult day care center. Jane and her husband adjust their work schedules to accommodate the center's hours. They are pleased that Dorothy receives care and supervision throughout the day, makes new friends, and is more active than she was previously.

This arrangement continues successfully for quite some time until Dorothy's needs at home increase to the point that they are more than Jane and her husband can handle. Somewhat reluctantly, Dorothy moves to an assisted-living facility where she receives supervision and the availability of support services on a continuing basis.

Dorothy continues to advance along the care continuum. Initially, a higher level of care at the adult day care center met her increased needs; the home remained the care setting, and informal caregivers provided more care. With the move to the assisted-living facility, both the setting and the dominant involvement of formal caregivers indicate that Dorothy is now at an even higher level on the care continuum.

Nursing Homes

nursing home

A *nursing home* is a state-licensed facility that provides skilled, intermediate, and custodial care services; the care recipient's condition determines the combination and extent of services provided. Nursing homes typically have separate sections or units for each level of service. Nursing homes are classified as approved skilled-nursing facilities when they meet the accreditation criteria required for reimbursement of services provided to Medicare and/or Medicaid patients. Not all nursing homes that offer skilled-nursing care services seek Medicare or Medicaid approval.

Hospitals usually discharge patients to nursing homes to complete their recovery from an acute illness or injury. Indeed, approximately two-thirds of people discharged from nursing homes were admitted from a hospital and stayed for 3 or fewer months.[4] Those who stay longer are often chronic long-term care recipients who enter a nursing home when they need more care than a home care setting or assisted-living setting can provide. These care recipients need around-the-clock care at least for custodial care and possibly nursing care. Other factors that affect the decision to enter a nursing home are

- the absence of a willing or available family caregiver
- limitations on an available family caregiver's capacity to provide home care even with the support of community and professional home care services
- the determination that the cost of home care needed to meet the recipient's needs makes the nursing home a more economical option

Nursing homes frequently represent the highest level of care and an end point on the long-term care continuum. They provide the most intensive long-term care services because of their setting and the array of formal caregivers available on a 24-hour basis.

Alzheimer's Facilities

Individuals with Alzheimer's disease and other serious forms of dementia often need specialized or unique forms of care that are not given to all patients

Alzheimer's facility

in most nursing homes. This care requires a high level of staffing to provide the social interaction, close monitoring, and significant personal assistance that these generally mobile patients need throughout the day. As a result, the *Alzheimer's facility* has been developed to furnish care to Alzheimer's patients and other persons with similar needs. These may be stand-alone facilities, but most Alzheimer's facilities are separate units of nursing homes or assisted-living facilities that are devoted to this type of care.

An Alzheimer's facility has a staff that is specially trained to deal with persons who have dementia. Such facilities are physically designed to alleviate the stress of disoriented patients. For example, the facilities may have few doors and a traffic flow to minimize dead-end corridors. There are numerous activities for patients and high levels of security—other than medication and restraints—to keep patients from harming themselves or wandering away.

Combined Facilities

continuing care retirement community (CCRC)

A combined facility offers two or more supportive-living arrangements that offer the same housing and services described previously under separate facility settings. Some combined facilities provide independent and assisted living, while others provide assisted living and nursing home care. In both of these situations, the combined facility usually gives no assurance or guarantee to the resident regarding access to or the cost of the next level of care, should it be required. By contrast, a *continuing care retirement community (CCRC)*, also known as a life-care facility, offers the full continuum of supportive-living arrangements and is obligated to provide access to housing and defined long-term care services at each level of care for the life of the resident.

Typically, CCRC residents must be capable of fully independent living upon entry, but they are assured of assisted living and nursing home levels of care as their future needs change. In some facilities, the residents may receive occasional home care services when they reside in their independent living accommodations. When a resident needs continuing supervision, he or she is usually required to move to the assisted-living unit of the CCRC. If, however, care needs escalate to the point where skilled care or custodial care is required on a continuing basis, the resident then moves to the CCRC's nursing home facility. Return to assisted living or independent living remains a possibility if the resident's/patient's condition improves. A resident spouse capable of independent living remains in the independent accommodations where the couple initially resided. Religious and other not-for-profit organizations sponsor CCRCs. Large corporations also develop them.

The financial arrangements under which the CCRC obligates itself to house and care for residents for life vary widely and are discussed in chapter 12 because they constitute a use of personal assets to meet long-term care needs.

Hospice Care

hospice care

Hospice care is a system of treatment designed to relieve the discomfort of a terminally ill individual and to maintain quality of life to the extent possible throughout the phases of dying. When hospice care is available, the cost of treating terminally ill patients is usually much less than the cost of traditional hospitalization. It is not designed to produce a cure. Hospice care, only recently considered a long-term care component, has a number of unique patient care features.

First, as the definition suggests, the care emphasizes comfort and palliative treatments to manage pain rather than the performance of heroic medical treatment and surgical procedures.

Second, in addition to the array of formal caregivers described previously, the hospice care team includes psychologists, spiritual advisors, and bereavement counselors. Counseling for the patient and family members from these professionals is a standard component of hospice care.

Third, hospice care can be provided in multiple settings, depending on the needs and circumstances of the care recipient. The home is the typical setting because of familiar surroundings and the likely presence of family members who are often caregivers. Individuals without family caregivers may enter a freestanding hospice facility, which provides a home-like setting, professional staff, and continuous access by family members. Nursing homes and hospitals may also serve as hospice care settings.

Finally, because hospice care is provided at the very end of an individual's continuum of care, its duration is usually measured in weeks or months, not years.

NOTES

1. *PCA Aging Advocacy*, Philadelphia Corporation for Aging (PCA), from its Web site at www.pcaphl.org/advocacy.html, accessed on January 19, 2005.

2. *A Profile of Older Americans: 2003,* The Administration on Aging, available at www.aoa.gov/prof/statistics/profile/2003/6.asp, accessed on January 19, 2005.

3. *Area Agencies on Aging: A Link to Services of Older Adults and their Caregivers*, National Association of Area Agencies on Aging, from its Web site at www.n4a.org/aboutaaas.cfm, accessed on January 19, 2005.

4. *The National Nursing Home Survey: 1999 Summary*, Centers for Disease Control and Prevention (CDC)/National Center for Health Statistics (NCHS), June 2002.

12

Personal Resources to Meet Long-Term Care Needs

Chapter Outline

Many individuals have personal resources—other than long-term care insurance—that they can use to help finance long-term care if the need arises. These resources may take numerous forms. Many individuals may have current or retirement income. Private medical expense insurance may provide limited benefits. A newer product—noninsurance service plans—may also be of help. An often overlooked but frequently used resource is the services and financial support of family members and friends. Finally, most Americans have assets in the form of savings and investments.

This chapter looks at these resources, including their limitations, for meeting long-term care needs. It also discusses the ways in which assets can be reconfigured to better finance long-term care expenses while meeting an individual's other financial objectives. This reconfiguration may take many forms; these forms include the purchase of annuities, the use of accelerated benefits or viatical settlements, the establishment of charitable remainder trusts, and home equity conversions.

Before continuing, however, two important points need to be made. First, the personal resources discussed in this chapter are often adequate to finance long-term care needs only for limited periods and/or up to limited amounts. In many cases, personal resources will be inadequate to fully finance long-term care expenses, and an individual may need to rely on Medicaid unless he or she has purchased long-term care insurance. Chapters 13 through 18 of this book are devoted to the use and characteristics of long-term care insurance.

Second, as has happened to many individuals in recent years, personal resources may diminish significantly in value. Potential economic changes need to be considered when planning for future contingencies.

INCOME

The majority of individuals who need long-term care will have some sources of personal income available to them. However, the amount of the income and the degree to which it can be used to finance long-term care expenses vary significantly. The following discussion examines these sources of personal income, the extent to which this income might be available to finance long-term care needs, and the factors that might cause the adequacy of the income to change.

Sources

In analyzing sources of income, it is appropriate to look at the income of a household unit in which each member of the household is committed to supporting any other member of the household. In most cases, this household unit is a husband and wife, but it might also consist, for example, of a mother and daughter or two or more siblings.

Possible sources of income include the following:

- income of a spouse or other household member
- Social Security retirement benefits
- private pension benefits
- Social Security disability income benefits
- private disability income benefits
- investment income
- annuity income
- trust fund income

Availability for Long-Term Care Needs

Even though an individual with the need for long-term care may have financial resources in the form of periodic income, much or all of this income may be necessary for other purposes. As the following examples illustrate, the amount of the income and the specific circumstances determine the income's availability to finance long-term care.

Example 1:	June and Rich, both aged 55, have annual incomes of $40,000 and $60,000, respectively. Both have employer-provided disability income insurance that, along with Social Security benefits, will replace 60 percent of their incomes until age 65 if they became disabled and need long-term care. They have a daughter who is still in high school, and they recently purchased a new home that has a higher monthly loan payment than their older home did. They estimate that a family income of $80,000 is necessary to maintain their current lifestyle and to pay for their daughter's education. If Rich needs long-term care, June's income and Rich's disability benefit of $36,000 will provide no resources to pay long-term care costs. If June needs long-term care, Rich's income and June's disability benefits of $24,000, will provide only $4,000 per year toward long-term care expenses.
Example 2:	April and Glenn, aged 64 and 67, respectively, live very comfortably on his annual retirement income of $100,000 per year. Their home is paid for, and they have annual investment income of $40,000. April and Glenn want to remain in their home as long as possible if either or both need long-term care. They estimate that they could continue to live well, excluding any long-term care expenses, on an annual income of $75,000. Therefore, they have $65,000 of annual income that could be used to finance long-term care.
Example 3:	Macy, a 68-year old widow, has retirement income of $20,000. After paying $800 per month for her subsidized apartment, Macy has no additional income that could be devoted to long-term care expenses provided at home. However, if she went into a nursing home, most of her income could be devoted to its cost.

Example 4:   Kirk, aged 78, has annual retirement and investment income of $45,000. His home is paid for, and his personal expenses do not exceed $30,000. He uses the remaining $15,000 of his income to help finance the care of a developmentally disabled granddaughter. Kirk feels he has no income resources that could be used to finance his own home health care, because he has no intention of ceasing payments for his granddaughter's care. However, most of the $30,000 on which he lives could be devoted to facility care.

Example 5:   Bruce, a 58-year-old bachelor, has an annual income of $150,000 and no financial debts or personal obligations. He expects to have an income of $90,000 if he retires at age 65 or is disabled prior to that time. He feels that $60,000 of this income could be devoted to home health care or $75,000 to facility care.

Future Adequacy of Income

Individuals who plan to rely on income to finance all or a portion of any future long-term care must be aware that all sources of income do not continue indefinitely. For example, a spouse's income may cease because of the spouse's retirement or own need for long-term care. Disability income payments often cease at age 65. Social Security disability income payments are replaced with comparable retirement benefits. This may not be the case, however, with individual or employer-provided disability income benefits. Income from an annuity or liquidation of an investment may also have a finite duration.

Consideration must also be given to the effects of inflation and other economic conditions. As the following example illustrates, what appears to be adequate income today may not keep up with the inflationary increases in the general cost of living or in long-term care costs.

Example: When Lou and Fran retired several years ago, they felt they would be able to devote at least $20,000 of their annual retirement incomes to home health care expenses. Since that time, their mostly fixed retirement income has failed to keep up with inflation, and they have had to lower this figure to $15,000. At the same time, home health care costs have increased at a much faster rate of inflation, thus further diminishing the percentage of these costs that their retirement incomes can finance.

Similarly, changes in other economic conditions can also play havoc with plans to finance long-term care needs.

Example 1:	Mark and Helen, both aged 58, retired 4 years ago when their 401(k) plans were worth $3 million. They felt that these plans would generate sufficient income to meet their living needs as well as finance any necessary long-term care expenses. However, the plans were invested in employer stock and have diminished greatly in value. Now Mark and Helen must reenter the workforce just to finance current living expenses.
Example 2:	Cal and Rhoda have always been conservative investors. By the time they retired 13 years ago at age 62, they had substantial income from certificates of deposit. As these certificates are maturing, however, the interest rates for new certificates are significantly lower. Cal and Rhoda had expected that they would be able to finance a sizable portion of any long-term care costs with their investment income. Now they will have to liquidate other assets that they had intended to leave to their children.

MEDICAL EXPENSE INSURANCE

Individuals may have some limited coverage for certain long-term care expenses from private medical expense insurance, through either individually purchased policies or employer-provided coverage. The situation is slightly different, depending on whether or not the individual is covered under Medicare.

Individuals Covered by Medicare

About two-thirds of individuals covered by Medicare have additional medical expense insurance to reimburse them for some health care expenses that Medicare does not cover. This coverage may be in the form of an individually purchased Medicare supplement policy or a continuation of coverage under a former employer's plan. However, in no case is this coverage a substitute for long-term care insurance or other resources to meet long-term care needs.

Medicare Supplement Insurance

Medicare supplement insurance (covered in chapter 8) is primarily designed to fill the deductible, coinsurance, and copayment gaps in Medicare's benefits for covered services that would otherwise result in out-of-pocket expenses for beneficiaries. However, in a few situations, additional benefits are provided.

Some of the standard Medicare supplement policies in the marketplace provide benefits for services that could be described as long-term care. Most policies provide reimbursement for the copayment required during days 21 through 100 for care in a skilled-nursing facility. Some of the Medicare supplement policies also provide benefits of up to $1,600 per year of at-home assistance with activities of daily living for persons who are recovering from illness, injury, or surgery at home or at any other location other than a hospital or skilled-nursing facility. However, this care must be received concurrently with the person receiving home health care under Medicare or within 8 weeks after the termination of the Medicare home health care. In addition to the $1,600 annual benefit limit, policies with these benefits will not pay for more than seven 4-hour visits in any week and no more than $40 of reimbursement for any visit.

Continued Employer-Provided Coverage

Somewhat over one-quarter of currently retired employees have some type of employer-provided coverage to supplement Medicare.

Some employers furnish coverage to supplement Medicare in a manner similar to what is provided by one of the standard Medicare supplement policies. Other employers use a Medicare carve-out under which the employer's medical expense plan reduces benefits to the extent that a retired employee has coverage under Medicare. The long-term care benefits under a Medicare carve-out are similar to those discussed below for individuals not covered by Medicare.

Individuals Not Covered by Medicare

Individuals not covered by Medicare usually have medical expense coverage through employer-provided plans or individually purchased policies. Some persons may also have a critical illness policy or specified disease insurance. As with the other types of medical expense coverage already discussed, there is limited coverage for long-term care expenses.

Medical Expense Coverage

Group and individual medical expense insurance primarily covers acute medical care for illness or injury. However, coverage often includes some benefits for services that may be received over an extended period of time in a variety of long-term care settings, such as a home, nursing home, or hospice. Coverage in these settings, as under Medicare, is limited to medical services rendered by licensed medical practitioners (such as physicians, nurses, and therapists) and to the cost of medical supplies and equipment (such as hospital beds and wheelchairs). Benefits are also subject to limitations. For example, nursing home benefits may be limited to 60 days for each episode of care, home health care may be limited to 100 visits per year, and hospice care may be capped at $5,000.

Medical expense policies also frequently contain a specific exclusion for custodial care, the most common form of care required by the elderly and others with chronic physical and cognitive impairments. The custodial care exclusion is defined broadly to eliminate coverage for the following:

- assistance with activities of daily living
- services that do not seek to cure or are provided during periods when the patient's medical condition is not changing
- services that do not require continued administration by trained medical personnel

Coverage of domiciliary care, which would include homemaker and chore services, as well as respite care is also typically excluded.

It should also be noted that insurers will sometimes pay for long-term care expenses that are not otherwise covered as long as this care is a less expensive alternative to covered services under a policy (such as hospitalization).

Critical Illness Policies

Critical illness insurance (covered in chapter 6) provides a one-time lump-sum cash benefit if the insured is afflicted with a covered critical condition, and the insured can use these funds for whatever purpose he or she sees fit. This use might include family support, payment of nonreimbursed medical expenses, or payment for long-term care services. The specified conditions for which benefits are paid may result from injury, disease, or major surgery. The lump-sum benefits from such policies, assuming they are significant (such as $100,000), could help pay long-term care expenses for a limited period of time. However, the types of covered conditions are often restricted to no more than 10. Moreover, benefits in force after age 65 (if the policy is renewable after that age) are typically reduced by as much as 50 percent.

Specified Disease Insurance

Although benefits under specified disease insurance (covered in chapter 6) can be significant, they have limited applicability to long-term care because of the covered condition restrictions, the need for acute care rather than chronic care, and/or the limited nature of the benefits themselves.

Coverage under specified disease policies frequently extends limited benefits to care in certain long-term care settings, if related to a covered disease. Skilled-nursing facility care and home care may be covered, but benefits are usually less than $100 a day. In the case of skilled-nursing facility care, benefits are often paid only for a duration of care equal to that of a prior hospital stay for which policy benefits are paid. Benefits for home care also have a maximum duration, such as 2 weeks. However, expenses for hospice care in a hospital, hospice center, or a home may be paid up to $100 per day with a lifetime maximum of 180 days.

Substantial benefits under these policies are related to acute care, not to care for chronic illnesses and disabilities. For example, subject to policy limitations, benefits of up to $125,000 per calendar year may be available for the expenses of chemotherapy, $25,000 per year for bone marrow transplant expenses, or $600 a day for up to 30 days of hospital intensive care. These benefits are paid in addition to benefits provided by other insurance. If a primary program of medical benefits covers the expenses of these services, then the insured may use the specified disease policy's benefits for other purposes, including payment of long-term care services for a limited period.

Specified disease policies also frequently offer a first-occurrence benefit that pays a one-time lump-sum amount for each covered person who receives a diagnosis of internal cancer. This amount may range from $1,000 to $50,000 or more and could also help pay long-term care expenses to some extent.

NONINSURANCE SERVICE PLANS

noninsurance service plan

The *noninsurance service plan,* also known as a buying service or a buying club program, for the purchase of health care services is becoming increasingly common. This type of plan is also called a discount program, because its prominent feature is the assurance of a discount on the purchase of specified professional services and products from a designated list or network of providers and suppliers. For example, discounts may apply to services received from physicians, dentists, vision care providers, hearing specialists, dentists, optometrists, and to prescriptions and over-the-counter medications. These plans may also offer health assessments, access to health information, and assistance in locating health care services, often at no additional charge other than the membership fee. Depending on the services offered, the membership fee may be nominal, or it may be as much as several hundred dollars per year, sometimes with an initial application charge. Just as with discount stores that have membership fees, the savings will depend on the amount of services, the product purchased, and the size of the discount.

Organizations that offer noninsurance programs are adapting them more specifically to the market for long-term care services. Increasingly, they list home health care agencies, assisted-living facilities, and nursing homes as network participants. Discounts may range up to 10 percent at assisted-living facilities and up to 20 percent for home health care services and nursing homes.

These plans are often marketed to employees through their employer or directly to individuals. Insurers, through agreements with plan sponsors, may also offer them as an alternative when applicants for long-term care insurance are unable to qualify for coverage. Indeed, the Federal Long Term Care Insurance Program discussed in chapter 18 offers such an alternative as a noninsurance service package.

Noninsurance service plans may also extend the benefits of an existing long-term care insurance policy. If services are obtained at a discount, the daily, weekly, or monthly benefit payment will cover a greater portion of expenses and reduce the insured's out-of-pocket payments. Similarly, a policy with a pool of funds as a benefit maximum (unless the maximum is unlimited) can purchase more care if the charges for services are discounted than if they are not.

Some insurers are considering the use of discounts to encourage insureds to receive services covered under their long-term care policies from preferred providers. Few, if any, companies have marketed such a product, however, because location, reputation, and services offered—not price—typically dominate an insured's selection of long-term care providers.

FAMILY SUPPORT

For many individuals, long-term care needs are met with the support of family members, or even friends. In some cases, family members may act as caregivers themselves; in other cases, they may give financial support to provide the care. Families may offer this support because the relative who needs care has no other resources. They may also furnish the care because they feel it is their obligation.

One of the most important steps that any family can take to provide for any relative's future long-term care is to discuss this contingency in advance. In this way, all family members have an understanding of the potential magnitude of the situation and the role that each may have to play in the future.

Family Members as Caregivers

As mentioned in chapter 10, family members provide about 70 percent of home health care, often at great personal sacrifice to themselves. However, demographic, social, and economic factors are making it increasingly difficult for family members to provide this care. As the following examples illustrate, the availability of family members as caregivers and the acceptance of such care can vary.

Example 1:   Paul and Shirley have modest financial resources to pay for long-term care. They are both in their late 70s and beginning to show signs of failing health. Their four children all live nearby and are devoted to their parents. The children and their spouses have agreed that they will do everything possible to see that Paul and Shirley are cared for as long as possible in their home of 50 years. One daughter and a daughter-in-law, who do not work outside the home, are willing to provide some home care services during the day. Other family members are willing to help out at night and on weekends.

Example 2:   Claire, aged 85, receives home health care services from Medicare, but these services are now insufficient to meet the level of care required to remain in her apartment. She has one daughter who would like to be of assistance, but the daughter lives 2,000 miles away. Her other daughter, who lives nearby, is unwilling to take on caregiver responsibilities and suggests that her mother apply for Medicaid to provide care in a nursing home.

Example 3:   Albert, aged 75, is a lifelong bachelor and has no close living relatives. Most of his friends are older than he and could be of no assistance in caring for him at home.

Example 4:   Hortense, aged 87, is barely able to care for herself at home. Although her children are willing to provide some care, Hortense has made up her mind that she will not be a burden to them and refuses their assistance.

Financial Support

Family members may also have the means to provide financial resources to relatives who are in need of long-term care. The support may be in the form of paying for long-term care expenses or long-term care insurance premiums.

Example 1:   Carolyn, age 68, is concerned about her ability to finance any future long-term care needs. Even though she could afford to pay the premiums for a long-term care insurance policy, she has certain health impairments that make her uninsurable. However, both of her children are financially secure and can pay any long-term care expenses that she is unable to afford. In fact, her son has even established a trust that should be able to finance any portion of future nursing home costs that Carolyn is unable to pay.

Example 2:   George and Marlene, both in their late 60s, would like to buy long-term care insurance but are unable to afford payment of the entire premium. Their three children are unable to provide any care because of geographic location and their own family responsibilities. In addition, they cannot afford to finance the cost of prolonged care for their parents. Among the children, however, they are able to provide the additional $3,000 that their parents need each year to purchase long-term care insurance policies.

Continued Availability of Family Support

Just as financial resources can diminish over time, so can the availability of family resources, as the following examples illustrate.

Example 1:   Carmela, aged 94, has continued to live in her own apartment, despite many frailties of old age. This has been possible because of the assistance of her two children. However, her son recently died and her daughter now has the task of caring for a husband who suffered a stroke. The daughter cannot care for both her mother and husband.

Example 2:   Ryan's father, aged 95, is in a nursing home, and his mother, aged 92, is in an assisted-living facility. Although his parents accumulated substantial resources for their retirement, these assets are now largely depleted, and Ryan is paying a large portion of their expenses. Ryan, who is 68, worked past his normal retirement age to help finance their needs. A recent heart attack forced him to retire, and he no longer has the financial resources to be of much assistance to his parents after his own needs are met.

ASSETS

Many individuals have some—even significant—assets that can be used to finance long-term care. However, when determining the possible use of assets for this purpose, an individual or couple must answer three basic questions: Are the assets available for this purpose? Are the assets adequate? Is this the way that the individual or couple wants to use the assets?

Availability of Assets

In determining the availability of assets to finance long-term care expenses, it is necessary to ascertain the extent that the assets are needed for other purposes. As the examples below indicate, availability can vary significantly among persons who have similar amounts of assets.

Example 1: Joe and Beth, aged 67 and 65, respectively, recently sold their dry cleaning business and now have $1 million of assets, exclusive of their home and personal possessions. Their only retirement income is from Social Security, and they will need to invest most of their assets to provide them with the additional income necessary to have the comfortable lifestyle for which they have planned. Only limited assets will be available if one of them needs to enter a nursing home.

Example 2: Grant and Lindsay are also aged 67 and 65, respectively, and have $1 million of assets, exclusive of their home and personal possessions. They recently retired but have sizable pensions from their former employers. They have no need to use their assets to provide a retirement income and could use all their assets to finance long-term care expenses if the need arises.

In addition, assets may be unavailable because they cannot be easily liquidated.

Example: Jacques, aged 65, had a successful career as a businessman. Last year, he sold two-thirds of his business to his two sons and is living off the income from this sale. He still retains ownership of the remaining one-third of the business, and this asset comprises most of his $900,000 investment portfolio.

It is highly unlikely that anyone other than his sons would purchase this minority business interest. In addition, his sons went heavily into debt to buy their shares of the business and are not in a position to take on more debt at this time. Therefore, the business asset could not easily be turned into cash to pay long-term care expenses.

Adequacy of Assets

Although some seniors have sufficient assets to entirely finance their long-term care needs, most seniors do not. They have not saved enough. In some cases, this lack of savings may be a result of individuals living beyond their means. In many cases, however, there is simply insufficient income left for savings and investments beyond the expenses of raising and educating a family. And, as mentioned earlier, accumulated assets are often needed to generate income for normal living expenses during retirement. However, the assets that have been accumulated—unless they are needed for other purposes—can be used to finance at least a portion of future long-term care expenses.

As is discussed in more detail in chapter 16, an individual must estimate the future expenses that will be incurred if long-term care is necessary. These expenses will vary as a result of many factors, such as age, type of long-term care desired, and inflation projections. Once the potential expenses are determined, the individual must determine the resources that are available to finance these expenses. As previously discussed, these resources may come from many sources, such as income or family support. Moreover, an individual must determine the extent to which accumulated assets can be used to generate additional income to pay another portion of these expenses. Depending on an individual's preferences, this additional income may come from the earnings generated by these assets and/or a liquidation of principal. This process of comparing needs with resources will indicate whether an individual has unfilled needs that can be met through other means—such as the purchase of long-term care insurance.

Example 1:   Bryan is a 67-year-old bachelor who has a retirement income of $65,000 a year and $900,000 in accumulated assets. If he were to need nursing home care today, his income would finance the cost of that care in his community. However, Bryan is aware that nursing home costs are rising, and he feels he might need an income of $150,000 or more to finance such care in the future if he lives into his 90s like some of his relatives have. Considering that his assets will continue to grow, even if invested conservatively, Bryan's income and assets will be able to finance any future long-term care costs for many years. He could get by without long-term care insurance.

Example 2:   Jose and Maria, both aged 65, are able to live on their Social Security and pension income of $40,000. In addition, they have $250,000 in accumulated assets other than their home and personal possessions. Their financial advisor has indicated that these assets could generate about $20,000 in income if either of them needed long-term care. However, the cost of such care where they live is about $45,000 per person per year. They could not fully finance long-term care expenses for a lengthy period of time, particularly if both need care. They are candidates for long-term care insurance to make up this shortfall in their personal resources.

Just as with income, economic conditions may affect the value of assets and the income it can generate.

Example: When Irv and Rebecca retired 17 years ago, they felt they had sufficient assets to meet their future financial needs. Now that they are approaching 80, however, they realize that their conservatively invested assets have grown more slowly that the cost of long-term care. Furthermore, current economic conditions no longer make it possible to safely generate the investment income from these assets that they once had expected.

Desired Use of Assets

Some individuals have no qualms about using their accumulated assets to finance their future expenses—including long-term care. However, there are probably a larger number of individuals who would prefer to put their assets— or at least a portion of them—to different uses. As the following examples show, these uses might range from bequests to meeting special needs.

In each of these cases, the individuals could help finance their potential long-term care needs with long-term care insurance.

Example 1:	Jack and Pauline worked very hard to accumulate almost $700,000 by the time they retired. They do not want these assets lost to long-term care expenses. Rather, they wish to leave the assets to their four children.
Example 2:	Beryl could probably finance any future long-term care expenses as a result of a $1 million settlement from a lawsuit. Because she has no close relatives, Beryl would like to leave most of her assets to the church that has been her "family" for the last 40 years.
Example 3:	Cal and Betty have nearly $1 million in assets. They have a profoundly learning disabled son whom they have cared for at home for more than 40 years. Although he would be eligible for assistance in a state-funded facility if they could no longer provide care, they want him to receive care in a better facility. In addition, they do not want themselves or their son to rely on public assistance. Their desire is to use their assets for their son's care.
Example 4:	Rudy has $300,000 in assets that could be devoted to his long-term care needs. His preference, however, is to use these assets to help pay for the college education of his nine grandchildren.

RECONFIGURATION OF ASSETS

An individual's assets are not always in the optimal form to generate the funds necessary to finance long-term care expenses. However, there are many ways that assets might be reconfigured to better provide these funds. In some cases, this reconfiguration might take place at the time long-term care is needed. In other cases, the reconfiguration might occur in anticipation of such a need in the future, possibly in a way that also allows the individual to meet other financial objectives at the same time.

The remainder of this chapter looks at certain techniques that are sometimes used to reconfigure assets. These include

- entering continuing care retirement communities
- purchasing annuities
- accelerating life insurance benefits

- selling life insurance policies through viatical settlements
- converting home equity into income

It should be pointed out that these techniques might be used as an alternative to long-term care insurance, as a way to supplement long-term care insurance, or because an individual has no long-term care insurance as a result of inadequate planning or uninsurability. It should also be mentioned that each of these techniques has tax and financial planning ramifications and should be discussed with financial advisors and family members.

Continuing Care Retirement Communities

As mentioned in chapter 11, one type of supportive-living arrangement is the continuing care retirement community (CCRC). In the simplest sense, a CCRC offers all the types of living arrangements that an older individual or couple needs. Upon entering, the individual or couple occupies an independent living unit, but access is guaranteed to the assisted-living facility or nursing home portion of the facility if the need arises. There are, however, many variations of the CCRC, and the services and amenities vary among them.

CCRCs have increased in popularity in recent years, and estimates are that between 500,000 and 750,000 older Americans now reside in these facilities. The financial commitment to enter some CCRCs sponsored by religious and fraternal organizations may be within the means of even lower-income individuals, but most CCRCs require a significant monetary outlay. Depending on the type of living unit selected, the amenities, and the services provided, entrance fees typically fall in the range of $100,000 to $300,000 (and sometimes significantly more). Monthly fees per resident can range from $1,000 to more than $3,000.

The CCRC Contract

Upon entering a CCRC, a resident agrees to a contract that spells out the accommodations and services provided, the entrance fee, and the monthly fee, which is usually subject to annual increases. The contract also specifies the portion of the entrance fee that will be refunded if the resident leaves the facility for any reason—including death. Some CCRC contracts specify that a portion of the entrance fee will be forfeited for each month of occupancy. Other CCRC contracts specify that a portion, or all, of the entrance fee will be refunded. Other things being equal, the larger the portion of the entrance fee that will be refunded, the larger the monthly fee and/or the higher the entrance fee. The following are two examples of the many arrangements found.

Example 1:	Anne paid a fee of $100,000 to enter a CCRC. The fee is forfeited at the rate of 2 percent for each month of occupancy. If Anne decides to leave after 20 months of occupancy, she will receive a refund of $60,000. Her heirs will receive the same amount if she dies after 20 months. Once Anne has lived in the facility for 50 months, there is no refund.
Example 2:	Clyde and Irma are about to enter a CCRC and are considering the possible financial arrangements. The entrance fee is $250,000. They can elect to receive a 50 percent refund if they leave at any time for any reason. With this option, their per person monthly fee will be $2,000. If they elect an 80 percent refund, the monthly fee will be $2,600. And if they elect a 100 percent refund, the monthly fee will be $3,000. The refund is also paid to their heirs if Clyde and Irma die while residing in the facility.

The prior discussion is based on the typical form of CCRC. A few CCRCs operate on a rental basis and have no entrance fee. Some CCRCs are structured so residents can purchase their units as if the units were part of a condominium or cooperative. They can also sell their units to new residents who meet the facility's entrance criteria.

Just as refund provisions affect the cost of CCRC contracts, so does the extent to which coverage is included for nursing home care. A CCRC contract takes one of three approaches with respect to the provision of nursing home care. One approach, usually referred to as an extensive contract, stipulates that all levels of care will be provided at essentially the same monthly fee. The second type of contract, referred to as a modified contract, guarantees access to all levels of care, but the duration of covered nursing home care is limited. After that period has ended, the resident must pay for the cost of nursing home care but often at a discounted rate. The third type of contract, referred to as a fee-for-service contract, also guarantees access to all levels of care, but the resident must pay the cost of all required nursing home care.

Some Considerations

The decision to use a CCRC to meet the potential need for long-term care should take many factors into consideration. These factors include age at entrance, the CCRC's location, future costs, and the financial stability of the facility.

Age at Entrance. CCRCs typically have a minimum entrance age of 65 for an individual or at least one spouse in the case of a couple. Most residents, however, enter in their mid-70s. At the time of entrance, applicants are underwritten to determine whether they meet the physical requirements of being able to reside in an independent living unit for a period of time. Applicants who are currently receiving long-term care or who have conditions that make it likely that care will be needed very soon are denied entrance. As a result of this underwriting, an applicant may find that he or she has waited too long to use a CCRC. Therefore, anyone considering a CCRC for the future should have contingency plans if this alternative becomes unavailable. These plans might include the purchase of long-term care insurance.

Location. Individuals need to think seriously about the location of a CCRC. It is not unusual for individuals who retire to move to locations far away from their families and then return home when their health begins to fail. Similarly, older seniors who have not moved to a new location may want to relocate to an area where they have relatives. Even though their intention is not for their families to provide long-term care, they are looking for the emotional support and occasional assistance that close family members can offer. If they leave a CCRC, this relocation can result in a significant financial loss as well as a loss of their guaranteed access to future care.

Future Costs. As previously mentioned, monthly costs in CCRCs are typically subject to annual cost increases. Unfortunately, residents' monthly incomes are often largely fixed. Most CCRCs take this into account when they underwrite new applicants and require that applicants have enough income (or assets to generate income) to pay their future monthly fees and to furnish the other items of needed personal support. For example, a CCRC might require that an applicant have an income equal to 200 percent of the initial monthly fee.

If a CCRC uses a modified or fee-for-service contract, a resident may also be faced with higher monthly costs in the future because of the need for nursing home care. As a result, some of these CCRCs require that residents carry long-term care insurance to meet these potential costs.

Even when a CCRC carefully analyzes an applicant's financial situation, there will always be some residents who suffer financial reversals and are unable to make their monthly payments. Many CCRCs set aside some funds to provide limited assistance to these persons. Circumstances may still arise, however, where some residents can no longer afford to remain in a CCRC.

Financial Stability. CCRCs, like any other type of enterprise, can have financial difficulties. Some have had to raise fees significantly; others have even declared bankruptcy. In many cases, the difficulties have arisen as the residents have aged and the demand for nursing home care has increased.

Therefore, a CCRC's financial stability—both present and future—is of utmost importance.

For several reasons, CCRCs today tend to be in a significantly better financial situation than in the past. Actuarial estimates of future long-term care utilization are much more accurate. Close to 40 states also have legislation and regulations that apply to CCRCs, including standards for reserves to meet future costs. The nursing home and assisted-living portion of the facilities are subject to state and federal health care regulations. Finally, most CCRCs are accredited by the Continuing Care Accrediting Commission, which publishes a list of the facilities it accredits. The commission looks at financial resources and disclosure and other characteristics of a CCRC. These characteristics include governance and administration as well as resident life, health, and wellness.

Use of Annuities

annuity

An *annuity* is a series of periodic payments that begin at a specific date and continue throughout a fixed period or for the duration of a designated life or lives. Although a detailed analysis of annuities is beyond the scope of this book, a few words can be said about their variations. Any annuity can be characterized in the following ways:

- An annuity may be purchased with periodic premiums (an installment annuity) or with a lump-sum premium (a single-premium annuity).
- Benefits may commence in the distant future (a deferred annuity) or shortly after funding (an immediate annuity).
- Payments can be received for a specified period of time (an annuity certain) or for the duration of one life (a single life annuity). Payments may also be received for as long as the first of two or more persons lives (a joint life annuity) or until the last of two persons dies (a joint-and-last-survivor annuity).
- Payments may cease at the death of the last annuitant (a pure annuity), or some of the purchase price may be returned to a beneficiary (a refund annuity).
- Payments may be a fixed number of dollars (a fixed annuity), or they may vary with investment earnings of the annuity company (a variable annuity).

charitable gift annuity

Life insurers issue most annuities, but some organizations specialize in annuities only. In addition, there are charitable gift annuities and private annuities. A *charitable gift annuity* involves the transfer of money or other assets to a charitable or nonprofit foundation. The foundation then provides a contractually established income for the life of the donor. In most cases, this income is generally determined in part using an actuarial assumption that on average 50 percent of the value of the donated assets is returned to the annuitant. A *private annuity* is a transaction between two parties, but the person or organization that assumes the obligation for the annuity payments is not in the business of selling annuities.

Many individuals are concerned about the future financial well-being of themselves and their families. This has led to an increasing interest in financial planning for their retirement years and the creation of an estate for their heirs. No financial plan, however, is complete without considering long-term care needs, and the use of annuities often plays many roles in this planning. Although annuities, along with many other types of investment vehicles, are often used in the general process of wealth accumulation, this book does not contain a discussion of this aspect of financial planning. However, annuities can play a role in guaranteeing a lifetime income to meet long-term care expenses or pay long-term care insurance premiums. Annuities may also be used to fulfill long-term care needs of individuals and couples when long-term care insurance is not an available alternative and to meet long-term care needs of heirs. As with any financial product, there are many considerations that must be addressed when using annuities—including the annuity company's ability to meet its future obligations.

Guaranteeing a Stream of Income

For many individuals and couples, the ability to meet future long-term care needs depends on a steady stream of income that will last until death. As the following examples show, there are many ways that annuities might be used to generate this income.

Example 1:	Bill and Cathy are both in their early 60s. When they retire, they expect that their pension and Social Security income will be adequate to meet their basic living needs. In addition, they bought long-term care insurance policies 5 years ago. When they purchased the policies, they were concerned about their ability to pay the premiums after retirement. As a result, they used part of a small inheritance from Bill's mother to purchase single-premium deferred annuities for each of them. The annuities will provide an annual lifetime income, starting at age 65, equal to the premium payments for the long-term care insurance policy.
Example 2:	Hans recently retired at age 62 and had a significant amount of money in his employer's employee stock ownership plan (ESOP). He has no heirs to whom he wishes to leave anything, and his sole financial goal is to satisfy his own needs, including long-term care.

However, he is concerned about the possibility of his former employer's stock decreasing in value. By using the proceeds of his ESOP, he was able to purchase an annuity that pays him $170,000 per year for the rest of his life.

Example 3:   At ages 75 and 77, respectively, Henry and Gay have decided to move to a continuing care retirement community. One of their financial goals has been to leave a substantial amount of money to their church at their deaths. Now that their long-term care needs are met, they feel they can do this immediately. Through the use of a charitable gift annuity, they can give the church $1 million, while receiving a lifetime income of $71,000 per year from the annuity. This income will be more than adequate to pay their monthly resident's fees.

Example 4:   Nick and Gloria, aged 71 and 69, respectively, recently retired from the construction company that they founded 40 years ago. Almost all their assets were tied up in this business, and Nick and Gloria want to convert it into retirement income that can be used for their support, including long-term care. They entered into a private annuity with their daughter and son-in-law, whereby the daughter and son-in-law obtain the business and agree to pay Nick and Gloria $100,000 per year as long as both are alive. At the death of either Nick or Gloria, the survivor will get $60,000 per year for the remainder of his or her life.

Meeting Specific Long-Term Care Needs

Annuities can also be used to plan for specific long-term care needs, often when an individual is unable to qualify for long-term care insurance. In fact, some types of annuities are suited to this purpose.

One example is an annuity that contains a long-term care rider. With such a rider, the periodic payment increases when the annuitant is determined to need long-term care. For the most part, this involves satisfying the same criteria that trigger benefits under a long-term care insurance policy. These criteria are discussed in chapter 14. However, the additional monthly benefit is available only after the contract has been in force for a period of time, often 6 or 7 years. In addition, the benefit is usually paid for a limited number of months.

Eligibility for a long-term care rider is underwritten much less stringently than long-term care insurance. Coverage can often be obtained if an individual is in the early stages of a condition that may require long-term care in the distant future.

Example: Grace recently retired at age 63 and is interested in turning some of her assets into a lifetime income stream to supplement her retirement income. She was recently diagnosed with the very early stages of Parkinson's disease. Her physician has told her that her health will slowly decline, but it should be several years before she needs any type of long-term care. Although Grace cannot qualify for long-term care insurance, she is able to purchase a single-premium annuity that will guarantee her $2,000 of monthly income. The annuity has a rider that after 6 years increases this amount to $4,000 per month for a 36-month period if Grace satisfies the criteria for needing long-term care. Grace feels that the annuity payments and her other resources will be sufficient to meet her future needs, whether or not they involve long-term care.

Unlike life insurance for which underwriters are concerned with applicants dying too soon, underwriters of annuities are concerned with applicants living too long. In determining the annuity payments for a given outlay, there is an assumption about an insured's life expectancy. Individuals who need long-term care have life expectancies, on the average, that are of shorter duration. This factor is taken into consideration if an applicant

impaired risk annuity

purchases an *impaired risk annuity*. With such annuities, an applicant's health is considered in the underwriting process, and the annuity payments are increased (or the premium lowered) in relation to the shorter life expectancy. This type of annuity is frequently used as part of structured settlements that arise out of legal liability judgments.

Considerations When Using Annuities

As the previous examples have shown, annuities may be valuable in planning for long-term care needs. The use of annuities in financial planning is complex, however, and the ramifications of their use are not always considered or fully understood by consumers or even some financial advisors who recommend and sell these products. Proper financial and tax advice is essential.

Annuities often have significant tax advantages, such as the tax-deferred growth of funds during the accumulation period. However, several of the previous examples involve the conversion of other assets into annuities. Some of these transactions may trigger capital gains when the older assets are disposed of in the conversion process. Other transactions may actually have a beneficial tax impact. For example, the sale of an asset to buy an annuity may result in a capital loss that can be used to offset capital gains that would otherwise be taxed. The purchase of a charitable gift annuity may result in significant tax benefits in the form of charitable deductions.

The income and estate tax treatment of any death benefits must also be considered. A deferred annuity has a death benefit payable to the annuitant's beneficiary if the annuitant dies during its accumulation period. A refund annuity may also have a residual value that is paid to a beneficiary if an annuitant dies after benefits commence. Without proper planning, there may be some unpleasant surprises when the taxation of these death benefits becomes apparent to heirs.

Annuities often make fixed benefit payments over time. To the extent a fixed annuity is used to finance future needs, the available resources will not grow as inflation drives future costs higher. If a variable annuity is used, future increases in annuity payments are uncertain because of the volatility in the securities markets. It should be pointed out that some insurers sell annuities that are designed so that benefits increase from year to year, such as 4 percent per year on a compound basis. For the same dollar outlay, such an annuity will have lower initial benefit payments than a fixed annuity, but payments will increase over time and eventually be higher.

Annuities, like insurance, involve the law of averages. Although there are average life expectancies that are used to calculate premiums, some people live much longer than others. For those who outlive their life expectancies by many years, a life annuity was a great "investment" from a financial standpoint. However, when large amounts of money are used to purchase an annuity, little if any of these funds may go to heirs if the annuitant dies soon after the purchase. On one hand, the use of annuities to meet long-term care needs may free heirs from having to provide or finance care for a relative. On the other hand, it may also result in a smaller inheritance than other alternatives when the relative dies.

An annuity may be difficult to access to meet long-term care needs. In the case of a deferred annuity, there may be a substantial penalty for an early withdrawal of funds. Some annuities, however, do allow penalty-free withdrawals under certain circumstances, such as the need for long-term care.

The final consideration mentioned here is probably the most important—the security of the benefit payments. Private annuities are generally not secured, and defaults do occur. In the previous example about Nick and Gloria, what happens if the business fails because their daughter and son-in-law are not as good at business as Nick and Gloria were? Where will the funds then come from to support Nick and Gloria?

Even insurers that sell annuities have occasionally had financial difficulties and been forced into liquidation. Although annuitants usually receive something, it is typically in the form of reduced annuity payments or a lump-sum settlement that is inadequate to purchase a comparable annuity. It is important for a consumer to evaluate the company from which an annuity is purchased, not only in terms of the cost of the annuity, but also in terms of financial strength and reputation. The considerations with respect to annuity companies are essentially the same as those for long-term care insurers and are discussed in chapter 16.

Use of Life Insurance

An insured can reconfigure the asset value of a life insurance policy in a number of ways to yield funds that may be used to pay for long-term care. Life insurance policy provisions usually allow for policy loans, withdrawals, or policy surrenders. However, these alternatives often yield minimal funds because they are limited to the cash value of the policy, which is likely to be inadequate to pay the cost of long-term care for a significant period.

Accelerated benefits and viatical settlements, on the other hand, can yield significantly greater proceeds because they are based on a percentage (or in some cases all) of a policy's death benefit. Consequently, accelerated benefits and viatical settlements are the more likely alternatives to which some persons with life insurance policies may turn when seeking funds to pay for long-term care. Nevertheless, the use of these transactions is no substitute for long-term care insurance. Although no one should buy a life insurance policy just to obtain its proceeds to meet long-term care expenses, those who have policies should certainly be aware of the resources that can be made available. This use of a life insurance policy may be appropriate for someone who cannot afford long-term care insurance or does not qualify for it due to poor health. However, such a financial transaction also has its limitations.

First, these benefits are often available only if the insured is terminally ill and has a limited life expectancy. Many individuals who need long-term care services do not fit these criteria.

Second, the proceeds of a life insurance policy received through accelerated benefits or viatical settlements, even if substantial, may give the insured a false sense of security that long-term care needs are being met. In fact, the proceeds are very likely to be inadequate to cover prolonged periods of long-term care. For example, if an insured received $100,000, that amount would cover skilled care in a nursing home for no more than 2 years. Not surprisingly, the use of accelerated benefits or viatical settlements occurs most frequently when death is a near-term prospect rather than in chronic illness situations.

Third, the receipt of a life insurance policy's death benefit while the insured is still living diminishes or eliminates the resources available after the insured's death to meet the needs for which life insurance was purchased in the first place. If the policy was bought to pay estate taxes, retire a mortgage balance, and provide income for surviving family members, there may little or no money available to handle these financial needs. However, many of the purposes for which life insurance is initially purchased can diminish over time. Dependent children become independent adults, and major debts, such as a home mortgage are significantly reduced or paid off.

A characteristic that accelerated benefits and viatical settlements have in common is the tax-preferred status that may apply to the proceeds received by the insured under certain circumstances. The proceeds received by a terminally ill patient are tax free if a licensed health care professional certifies that the individual is expected to die within 24 months after the date of certification, even if death occurs later. The payment may also be tax free to those with chronic, but not terminal, illnesses if the proceeds are used to pay for long-term care services not covered by long-term care insurance. HIPAA's requirements for the determination of a chronically ill patient and tax-qualified long-term care benefits are also applicable and discussed in chapter 13.

Accelerated benefits and viatical settlements are both vehicles to obtain proceeds from the death benefits of a life insurance policy while the insured is still living, and both may have tax-preferred treatment of an insured's receipt of those proceeds. However, they are vastly different transactions. One involves receiving some policy proceeds in advance; the other involves the sale of the policy.

Accelerated Benefits

accelerated-benefits provision

Many insurers now include an *accelerated-benefits provision* in newly written life insurance policies as a standard feature and/or allow a policyowner to collect accelerated benefits from policies that do not contain an explicit provision. Under such a provision, an insured is entitled to receive a portion of his or her death benefit while still living if one or more of the following events, known as triggers, occur:

- diagnosis of a terminal illness or physical condition for which death is likely to occur within a specified number of months, usually 12 months or less
- occurrence of one of a number of specified medical conditions, such as dread diseases or catastrophic illnesses, that would result in a drastically limited life span with extensive or extraordinary medical treatment
- the need for extended long-term care in a nursing facility, at home, or in the community due to an inability to perform daily activities
- permanent confinement to a nursing home

The categories of triggering events and their specific definitions vary among insurers and are subject to state regulation. Most insurers, however, restrict the accelerated benefits trigger to a single event, which is most frequently terminal illness.

The amount of the accelerated benefits available is a percentage of the basic life insurance coverage and may range from 25 to 100 percent. In addition, many insurers limit the maximum benefit to a specified dollar amount. This amount varies widely among insurers and can be as low as $25,000 or as high as $500,000 or more. The proceeds can be distributed as monthly payments, which in turn reduce the cash value and death benefit of the policy each month. Any amount not accelerated is paid to the beneficiary upon the insured's death.

Other than the tax-qualified requirements discussed previously for those with chronic rather than life-terminating conditions, there are no limitations on how the accelerated benefit can be used. It may be used to pay medical expenses and nursing home care not covered by other insurance; it can even be used to prepay funeral expenses.

Example 1:	Jay, a 72-year-old widower, has insufficient income to pay the full cost of his home health care. He has two life insurance polices, each with a $50,000 death benefit and a cash value of $20,000. The policies were purchased several years ago, and neither has an accelerated-benefits provision. Jay can borrow the cash value or surrender the policies to receive $40,000. However, he would like to receive a larger amount. When he inquires about the possibility of obtaining an accelerated benefit, both insurers indicate that they offer such benefits but only if the insured is certified as having a life expectancy of 1 year or less. Because Jay does not meet this criterion, he then explores the possibility of a viatical settlement. Although some viatical companies are willing to buy his policies, he finds that they will offer only about $10,000 more for each policy than he can obtain through a policy loan or surrender.
Example 2:	Kay, aged 80, has incurred significant long-term care expenses, and her assets are nearly depleted. She has a $100,000 life insurance policy with a $30,000 cash value. Because she has been certified as having a life expectancy of less than 1 year, she can elect an accelerated benefit of 92 percent of the policy benefit ($92,000) rather than surrendering the policy for its cash value.

Viatical Settlements

viatical settlement

A *viatical settlement* is another arrangement that gives the insured a cash advance against all or a portion of the death benefit of a life insurance policy while the insured is still alive. Under the arrangement, the policyowner (who may be the insured or someone else, such as a spouse) typically sells the policy to obtain financial resources to pay for expenses at the end of the insured's life. These expenses may include payment of long-term care costs.

Typically, a viatical company purchases the policy at a percentage of the death benefit that ranges from 50 percent to 80 percent if the usual regulatory guidelines for the remaining life expectancy of terminally ill individuals are used. The viatical company becomes the owner and beneficiary of the policy and assumes responsibility to pay the premium required to maintain the policy in force.

Other factors also affect the amount of the proceeds. If a waiver-of-premium provision is in effect when a policy is sold, the viatical company incurs less expense and is in a position to provide the insured with a higher settlement percentage. The financial strength of the insurance company that issued the policy and that of the viatical company itself affects the amount of the settlement that the viatical company is willing and able to offer the insured.

When the insured dies, the viatical company or investor to whom the policy has been sold, not the original policyowner, collects the death benefit. Usually, although not always, the viatical company or investor makes a profit. The viatical settlement paid to the insured plus administrative expenses and premium payments, if any, are expected to be less than the death benefit received when the insured dies.

Viatical settlements have been a source of controversy. Although accelerated benefits are subject to state regulations, many viatical settlements have taken place in an unregulated environment. This has often led to the policyowner's receiving proceeds that are significantly less than justified by the insured's life expectancy and a reasonable profit for the viatical company or investor.

Some states now regulate the minimum proceeds that the policyowner receives in a viatical settlement and the types of persons who can be owners of a viatical company or solicit such transactions. However, regulations do not exist in every state. As a result, many financial advisors suggest that a viatical settlement should be considered only if the amount of the proceeds exceeds that of an accelerated benefit or if the insured does not qualify for an accelerated benefit.

Reverse Mortgages

For many seniors, their home represents their greatest single source of financial wealth. They have spent many years paying off a mortgage loan, while experiencing significant appreciation in home values. As a result, they have accumulated thousands of dollars in home equity—a significant personal resource. There is a spectrum of financial transactions that allow homeowners to reconfigure this resource to provide cash and/or income to meet the expenses of retirement and old age, including long-term care.

Traditionally, homeowners—either as individuals or as couples—have accessed their equity through a home equity loan or the sale of their home. Both transactions have drawbacks. A home equity loan creates a new repayment obligation that may cut into scarce spendable dollars and increase the risk of foreclosure. Selling one's home to meet expenses represents a major life disruption, and a new place to live must be found.

Homeowners may retain occupancy after the sale of their home through a sale-leaseback arrangement. Depending on the lease terms, they may also free themselves from such ownership responsibilities as maintenance and the payment of taxes and insurance. However, the homeowners are giving up ownership of their home and are subject to the lease terms that are unlikely to anticipate their changing needs.

Homeowners may also take advantage of the increased cost of housing by renting a part of their home to generate additional income or to obtain such services as home upkeep and personal care in exchange for rent. Although attractive in concept, rental arrangements also have drawbacks. They are temporary, unadaptable to changing circumstances, and frequently undependable. Moreover, rental income is often modest.

A relatively new financial transaction, known as a reverse mortgage, avoids the drawbacks of these alternatives. As explained later, however, this technique has some other limitations. A reverse mortgage is unsuited to a borrower who has little equity in a home, regardless of the home's value.

reverse mortgage

A *reverse mortgage* may be defined as a nonrecourse, first mortgage loan against a home's value that advances cash to the borrower who remains the homeowner. It requires no installment repayments, although such payments may be made to restore, in whole or in part, the amount of available cash. Proceeds from the sale of the home are used to repay the loan when the borrower no longer maintains the home as a principal residence.

The loan is a nonrecourse loan because the home is the only asset available to satisfy the repayment obligation, even if the amount of the loan exceeds the value of the home—a situation possible under circumstances that are explained later. All other assets, including investments, savings, and personal property, are unencumbered by this transaction and can continue to be used at the homeowner's discretion or left to heirs without regard to the mortgage loan liability.

A reverse mortgage is also a first mortgage loan because it has the priority right of repayment over any other loan against the home. Thus, the balance of any existing regular mortgage loan must be repaid as a condition for obtaining a reverse mortgage or repaid from its proceeds.

Loan Proceeds and Payout Options

Under a reverse mortgage, the amount of the cash payout to the borrower, known as the loan proceeds, depends on four factors:

- the age of the borrower
- the value of the home
- the borrower's equity in the home
- the expected level of interest rates

Generally, when interest rates are low, borrowers who are older and own more expensive homes with no mortgage receive higher loan proceeds than other borrowers. The age of the borrower, who usually must be at least 62 years old, is particularly significant because it affects the interest expense portion of the loan's total cost. Because they are expected to live fewer years and, therefore, incur less total interest expense until the loan is repaid, older borrowers are able to receive a greater portion of their home's value as loan proceeds. Often lenders allow up to three co-owners to become borrowers under a reverse mortgage, in which case the age of the youngest borrower determines the amount of the proceeds. Interest rates are usually adjustable annually.

Under a reverse mortgage, borrowers can elect one or a combination of the following three basic options to receive the payout of the proceeds from their home equity:

- The lump-sum option allows a borrower to receive the entire amount of the loan proceeds at one time.
- The credit-line option allows the borrower to draw the loan proceeds entirely, partially, or not at all, as future events unfold and needs arise.
- The monthly payment option provides the loan proceeds as a steady source of funds in a prescribed amount, somewhat like an annuity. Payments may be for a specific term or the borrower's tenure in the home. Under a tenure plan, monthly checks continue as long as the borrower maintains the home as a principal residence, even if the payments continue longer than expected and eventually exceed the value of the home.

Lenders offer variations on these three basic options based on the borrower's financial circumstances and needs. The credit-line and monthly payment options may be offered in a constant amount or at amounts that increase with the value of the home. Borrowers may choose to take part of the proceeds as a lump sum and part as monthly payments.

The payout option selected affects the total interest cost of the reverse mortgage, which in turn determines the amount of the proceeds the borrower receives; the greater the cumulative interest expense is, the lower the portion of a home's value is available as proceeds to the borrower. Thus, all other things being equal, the proceeds accepted as a lump sum, which incur immediate interest charges on the full amount, are likely to be less than cumulative proceeds received through monthly payments over the course of the borrower's tenure in the home.

The total cost of a reverse mortgage to the borrower can be difficult to calculate, especially under a monthly payment option. Federal law requires that lenders disclose the estimated total annual loan cost (TALC) of every reverse mortgage. The TALC is most useful for comparing one type of reverse mortgage to another because it combines the loan amount, interest, closing costs, points, and the monthly loan service fee into a single rate. Lenders are required to illustrate the TALC rate for their loans at the end of 2 years following closing, at the end of the borrower's life expectancy, and at a period 40 percent beyond life expectancy.

Example 1:	Marcia, an 83-year-old widow, has been able to live on her monthly Social Security benefits. She has no other income and her only asset, other than $5,000 in a bank account, is her home. Marcia realizes that she will need to rely on Medicaid if she ever has to go to a nursing home. She would like to remain in her home as long as possible, but her physical condition is making this more difficult. Marcia has found that she is eligible for a reverse mortgage that will pay her $500 per month. By taking the reverse mortgage, she will be able to afford assistance that will help her postpone the time when nursing home care will be needed.
Example 2:	Mark and Julie, both in their 70s, have sufficient retirement income to pay their normal living expenses. They have become aware of the cost of long-term care and realize that they have insufficient resources to pay for these costs if they both should need care. The cost of long-term care insurance policies, for which they are eligible, is beyond their financial means. However, they are eligible for a reverse mortgage on their home. The lump-sum proceeds will be enough to purchase paid-up long-term care insurance policies that, when used to supplement their other resources, should meet any future long-term care expenses.

Repayment

The obligation to repay the reverse mortgage loan typically occurs when the borrower or the last surviving borrower sells the home, moves, or dies. If the borrower does not live in the home as a principal residence for 12 consecutive months, even when due to illness, the loan becomes payable. The borrower, who remains the homeowner, can also trigger the reverse mortgage repayment obligation through a failure to pay property taxes, pay homeowners insurance premiums, or make necessary repairs. Generally, lenders have the option to use loan funds, if available, to pay these required expenses and add the amount to the balance owed.

Other borrower actions that could make a reverse mortgage immediately repayable are:

- bankruptcy
- abandonment of the home
- renting the home, even in part
- adding a new owner to the home's title
- changing the home's zoning classification

As a general rule, the amount of repayment is equal to the total amount of the loan advance paid out plus accrued interest cost and any fees that have been rolled into the loan, not to exceed the value of the home. A borrower who moves but wishes to retain ownership may repay the loan from other resources. If the home is sold, any proceeds remaining after satisfying the loan obligation belong to the borrower or, in the instance of death, to the borrower's heirs. (Note, however, that the loan amount and accumulated interest may exceed the home's value if the borrower continues to live in the house for a long enough period.) Heirs may wish to maintain the home in the family and pay off the reverse mortgage obligation with a traditional mortgage loan or by using life insurance proceeds, for example.

Sources

Reverse mortgages are available through lending institutions as well as state and local governments. Loans from state and local governments are often provided in lump-sum amounts for limited purposes, such as home improvement or the payment of property taxes. Under the term of these loans, borrowers typically must also qualify under income limitation requirements. Although lending institutions in the private sector make reverse mortgages broadly available, they most frequently do so in accordance with the requirements of the programs offered by the U.S. Department of Housing and Urban Development (HUD) and the Federal National Mortgage Association (Fannie Mae). The Federal Housing Administration (FHA) is part of HUD.

Both HUD and Fannie Mae provide reverse mortgages through approved lending institutions that may include banks, mortgage companies, credit unions, and savings and loan institutions as well as state and local housing authorities. HUD's reverse mortgage, known as a Home Equity Conversion Mortgage (HECM), is a federally insured private loan. HECM loan amounts, although they may be lower than other reverse mortgage alternatives, contain a growth feature that allows amounts under the line of credit payout option to increase as the home's value increases. In other respects, however, HUD and Fannie Mae reverse mortgage are similar; there are no limitations on the use of loan advances and no borrower income limits or qualifications. In addition, both programs offer the three loan advance payout options discussed previously. Both HUD and Fannie Mae place a limit on the loan amount. The basis of the HUD limit is the cost of housing in each geographical area; Fannie Mae uses the average home price in the United States as the basis for its maximum loan. Fannie Mae also sponsors a special program that allows seniors to use their reverse mortgage loans to make the transition from a larger home to a smaller one without a mortgage payment while drawing a monthly income.

Information on HUD-approved and Fannie Mae–backed reverse mortgages is available on their respective Web sites at www.hud.gov and www.fanniemae.com. AARP also provides information on reverse mortgages at www.aarp.org, under the link "Money and Work."

Payment for Long-Term Care

The loan advances from a reverse mortgage can be significant and may be used for long-term care. They are often sufficient to pay the long-term care insurance premiums for those who are insured or insurable. In the absence of long-term care insurance, the loan amounts may be enough to entirely pay for the cost of care for an extended period or for the purchase of an annuity to generate income, which together with other personal resources may be available for long-term care.

Like all personal resources, reverse mortgages have limitations when used to pay long-term care expenses. The loan advances may be less than expected and insufficient to cover the high cost of long-term care. For example, even at low interest rates, the proceeds a borrower aged 65 receives from a reverse mortgage on a $300,000 home may be no more than 55 percent under a credit-line option and less than $1,000 under a monthly payment option for the borrower's tenure. Moreover, estimates of long-term care expenses that served as the basis for determining an adequate amount and appropriate payment option today may be outstripped by inflation and/or the need for more extensive care in the future.

Also, the circumstances under which the reverse mortgage must be repaid are often unpredictable or inopportune. For example, a person may obtain a reverse mortgage to pay for long-term care at home, only to subsequently require nursing home care. Also, a person living in the home and using the reverse mortgage payments for a spouse's nursing home care may die unexpectedly or suffer a debilitating illness that also requires care outside the home. In both cases, repayment of the reverse mortgage is required. Any loan advances taken as monthly payments or a line of credit would cease at the very time they are most needed.

Development of
Long-Term Care Insurance

Chapter Outline

The remainder of this book is devoted primarily to long-term care insurance. This chapter begins with a brief discussion of the development of this relatively new form of insurance protection. It then discusses the influence the NAIC and HIPAA have had on the provisions that are in many policies today.

Chapter 14 contains an analysis of the policy provisions found in long-term care insurance policies.

Chapter 15 reviews the underwriting of long-term care insurance—a process that is more complex than for many other types of insurance.

Chapter 16 is devoted to the consumer and long-term care insurance. In that chapter, the marketplace is described by looking at consumers' attitudes toward long-term care insurance and examining their various purchase patterns. Many of the questions facing consumers are also analyzed. Should a policy be tax qualified or non-tax qualified? What are the appropriate types and levels of benefits? What provisions should be considered to minimize premium cost?, and so forth.

Chapter 17 covers the many hybrid products that combine long-term care insurance with life insurance or annuities. Group insurance is also discussed.

Finally, chapter 18 analyzes government's role in providing or encouraging long-term care insurance. Pending federal legislation is also briefly addressed.

DEVELOPMENT OF INSURANCE COVERAGE

It is common for insurance coverages to evolve over time. However, the evolution of long-term care products has been dramatic with respect to the magnitude of the changes and the speed with which these changes have occurred.

Early Policies

The long-term care policies in existence in the early 1980s were primarily designed to provide care during the recovery period following an acute illness. They seldom met the needs of persons who required long-term care for chronic conditions. The following provisions were characteristic of many of these policies:

- short benefit periods
- modest daily benefits
- a prerequisite for benefits in a skilled-nursing facility, often a prior hospitalization of 3 to 5 days
- a prerequisite of a higher level of out-of-hospital care before benefits could be received for a lower level of care. For example, custodial care might be covered, but only if a person received 3 to 5 days of skilled-nursing care in a nursing home.
- the exclusion of benefits for preexisting conditions
- the exclusion of benefits for care needed as a result of Alzheimer's disease or other organic brain diseases
- no benefits for home health care
- no inflation protection to meet higher long-term care costs in the future
- lack of guaranteed renewability provisions

In addition, the sale of early long-term care policies was often accompanied by improper sales practices. Consumers were led to believe that policies were much more comprehensive than they actually were. In effect, policyowners felt that they were purchasing "nursing home" insurance that would cover them anytime nursing home care was needed. Only when such care was needed did many of these policyowners realize that their coverage was very limited.

Finally, for many years, no favorable tax treatment was given to long-term care insurance. Premiums for coverage were not deductible, and employer-paid premiums under group plans resulted in taxation to employees.

Evolution of Coverage

Criticism of the early long-term care policies created considerable pressure for change. Consumer groups argued for more government regulation. The federal government conducted studies and held hearings, with the results painting a less than flattering picture of long-term care policies. Change itself, however, resulted primarily from the actions of insurance companies themselves and from the state regulators of insurance. But the threat of federal regulation was always present. The negative publicity about early long-term care policies (and also Medicare supplement policies) had a dampening effect on the public's acceptance of long-term care insurance. This led many insurance companies to modify their policies and companies entering the business to offer more comprehensive policies. At the same time, the National Association of Insurance Commissioners began to take an active interest in long-term care insurance. This culminated in the adoption of the Long-Term Care Insurance Model Act in 1987. In 1988, the NAIC Long-Term Care Model Regulations were issued to enable the states to implement the model act. The act and the regulations have been amended almost every year since. Sometimes these amendments changed previous act provisions; at other times, new issues were addressed.

All states now regulate long-term care insurance. Most states have adopted the model act, which is discussed in more detail later. However, the version in force in a given state is often not the latest NAIC version. The remaining states have adopted legislation different from the model act, although it may be similar to that recommended by the NAIC.

Considerable changes have also taken place at the federal level with passage of the Health Insurance Portability and Accountability Act in 1996. HIPAA provides favorable tax treatment to long-term care insurance contracts that meet certain standards. These contracts are referred to as *tax-qualified* policies. The requirements for such policies are described later in this chapter.

tax-qualified

Most insurance companies' long-term care policies have gone through many revisions. Although coverage is still not always complete, there is little comparison between the early policies and most of what is marketed today; policies have become more comprehensive over the last few years. For a while, premiums also tended to drop as competition intensified and as more credible statistics about long-term care claims became available. Currently, premiums for new business are increasing. Enhancements to policies, such as a lifetime benefit period and an automatic benefit increase, also require an additional premium increase.

non-tax-qualified

Most companies that write individual policies now issue only the tax-qualified contracts prescribed by HIPAA. Some companies issue both tax-qualified contracts and *non-tax-qualified* contracts. Although purchasers of these contracts do not receive the new tax advantages, the contracts usually include provisions that make it easier to qualify for benefits.

Effect of Changes on Existing Policyowners

As policies have evolved, insurance companies have been faced with the decision of how to treat existing policyowners. Until recently, many policy upgrades were also accompanied by reduced future premiums for the entire policy. At one extreme, companies made no effort to let existing policyowners know of these changes. If the policyowner found out, he or she might have been allowed to exchange an old policy for the newer form. However, the premium may or may not have been based on the original age of issue. If the conversion was based on the attained-age rates (the rates at the policyowner's current age), a higher premium might have resulted. In some cases, the policyowner could get the new policy only if current underwriting rules were satisfied. Finally, for some insurers, the policy provisions of the new policy, such as any preexisting-conditions provisions, were again applicable.

At the other extreme, many insurance companies took a more consumer-oriented approach. Policyowners with no claims history were automatically given the enhanced coverage at issue-age rates (the original-age cost) and without any policy restrictions.

Current enhancements to long-term care products usually result in an increased premium. Again, insurance company practices vary. Some companies allow the policyowner to add the enhanced benefits by paying the new premium based on the policyowner's original age of issue. Other companies may require evidence of insurability and use attained-age rates.

Where Are We Now?

Since the early 1980s, long-term care insurance has evolved from being virtually nonexistent to being an important form of insurance that now provides protection to about 6.2 million persons. Individual policies cover approximately 4.2 million lives, and about 2.6 million lives are covered by group plans.[1] The number of insurers with long-term care products is about 100. However, a relatively small number of companies account for the vast majority of the coverage; ten companies account for 81 percent of the new individual premium written in 2004. The group market is even more concentrated, with the top five writers accounting for 94 percent of the new premium in the same year.[2] The major providers of employee benefits now also make group products available.

Long-term care insurance can probably best be described as having grown from infancy to somewhere between the childhood and teenage years. Coverage will undoubtedly continue to evolve to meet consumer demands and expectations, and the largely untapped market for coverage will continue to grow as the American population ages.

NAIC MODEL LEGISLATION

Because of its widespread adoption by the states, it is appropriate to discuss the NAIC model legislation regarding long-term care. The legislation consists of a model act that is designed to be incorporated into a state's insurance law and model regulations that are designed to be adopted for use in implementing the law. This discussion is based on the latest version of the model legislation, which, as mentioned earlier, seems to be amended almost annually. Even though most states have adopted the NAIC legislation, some states may not have adopted the latest version. However, the importance of the model legislation should not be overlooked. With most insurers writing coverage in more than one state, it is likely that the latest provisions have been adopted by one or more states where an insurer's coverage is sold. Because most insurance companies sell essentially the same long-term care product everywhere they do business, the NAIC guidelines are often, in effect, being adhered to in states that have not adopted the legislation.

Before proceeding with a summary of the major provisions of the NAIC model legislation, it is important to make two points. First, the model legislation establishes guidelines. Insurance companies still have significant latitude in many aspects of product design. Second, many older policies that were written prior to the adoption of the model legislation or under one of its earlier versions are still in existence.

long-term care insurance

The model legislation states that *long-term care insurance* is any insurance policy or rider that is advertised, marketed, offered, or designed to provide coverage for not less than 12 consecutive months for each covered person in a setting other than an acute care unit of a hospital for one or more of the following: necessary or medically necessary diagnostic, preventive, therapeutic, rehabilitative, maintenance, or personal care services. This definition is broad enough to include policies or riders that provide coverage for long-term care in a single setting, such as the home, or a variety of alternative settings that range from the home to a skilled-nursing facility. The 12-month period has been the source of considerable controversy because, in effect, it allows policies to provide benefits for periods as short as 1 year. Many critics of long-term care insurance argue that coverage should not be allowed unless benefits are provided for at least 2 or 3 years. Statistics would seem to support their views. Approximately 55 percent of all persons currently in nursing homes have been there in excess of one year. This figure drops to about 30 percent for stays of 3 years or longer. On the average, the length of stay for persons currently in nursing homes has been about 2 1/2 years.[3] However, about 14 percent of stays exceed 5 years, and stays for such conditions as severe arthritis and Alzheimer's disease sometimes exceed 10 years.

The model act specifically states that the term long-term care insurance also includes group and individual annuities and life insurance policies or riders that directly provide or that supplement long-term care insurance. Long-term care insurance *does not* include an insurance policy that is offered primarily to provide any of the following:

- Medicare supplement coverage
- basic hospital expense coverage
- basic medical-surgical expense coverage
- hospital confinement indemnity coverage
- major medical expense coverage
- disability income or related asset-protection coverage
- accident-only coverage
- specified disease or specified accident coverage
- limited benefit coverage

In addition, long-term care insurance *does not* include life insurance policies (1) that accelerate the death benefit specifically for one or more of the qualifying events of terminal illness, a medical condition that requires extraordinary medical intervention, or permanent institutional confinement *and* (2) that provide the option of a lump-sum payment for the previous benefits if neither the benefits nor the eligibility for benefits is conditional upon the receipt of long-term care.

The act specifies, however, that any product advertised, marketed, or offered as long-term care insurance is subject to the act's provisions even if it is included in the previous list of policies or riders otherwise excluded from the definition of long-term care insurance.

The model legislation focuses on two major areas—policy provisions and marketing.

Policy Provisions

Many of the criteria for policy provisions pertain to definitions, renewal provisions, limitations and exclusions, prior levels of care, incontestability, inflation protection, and nonforfeiture benefits.

Definitions

Many words or terms cannot be used in a long-term care insurance policy unless they are specifically defined in the policy and are in conformity with the model legislation. Examples include activities of daily living (ADLs), adult day care, cognitive impairment, home health care services, mental or nervous disorder, personal care, and skilled-nursing care. These terms as defined are consistent with their use in other sections of this book.

Renewal Provisions

No policy can contain renewal provisions other than guaranteed renewable or noncancelable. With either type of provision, the insurance company cannot make any unilateral changes in any coverage provision or refuse to renew the coverage.

Under a guaranteed renewable provision, coverage is also continued by the timely payment of set premiums, but the insurance company is allowed to revise premiums on a class basis.

noncancelable

Under a *noncancelable* provision (very rarely used with long-term care insurance), premiums are established in advance and the insured has the right to continue the coverage in force by the timely payment of premiums. The term *level premium* can be used only with a noncancelable policy.

Limitations and Exclusions

Limitations and exclusions by type of illness, treatment, medical condition, or accident are prohibited, except in the following cases:

- preexisting conditions or disease. The definition of preexisting conditions, however, can be no more restrictive than to exclude a condition for which treatment was recommended or received within 6 months prior to the effective date of coverage. In addition, coverage can be excluded for a confinement for this condition only if it begins within 6 months of the effective date of coverage.
- mental or nervous disorders (but this does not permit the exclusion of Alzheimer's disease)
- alcoholism and drug addiction
- illness, treatment, or medical condition arising out of war, participation in a felony, service in the armed forces, suicide, and aviation if a person is a non-fare-paying passenger
- treatment provided in a government facility, unless required by law
- services for which benefits are available under Medicare or other governmental programs, with the exception of Medicaid
- services for which benefits are available under any workers' compensation, employer's liability, or occupational disease law
- services available under any motor vehicle law
- services provided by a member of the covered person's immediate family
- services for which no charge is normally made in the absence of insurance
- expenses for services or items available or paid under another long-term care insurance or health policy

In addition, the model legislation permits exclusions and limitations for services provided outside the United States and for legitimate variations in benefit levels to reflect differences in provider rates.

Prior Levels of Care

No policy can provide coverage for skilled-nursing care only or provide significantly more coverage for skilled care in a facility than for lower levels of care, such as custodial care.

Eligibility for benefits cannot be based on a prior hospitalization requirement, and eligibility for benefits provided in an institutional care setting cannot be based on the prior receipt of a higher level of institutional care.

A policy that conditions eligibility for noninstitutional benefits on a prior receipt of institutional care cannot require a prior institutional stay of more than 30 days.

Incontestability

A policy must contain a provision that makes the policy incontestable after 2 years on the grounds of misrepresentation alone. The policy, however, can still be contested after 2 years on the basis that the applicant knowingly and intentionally misrepresented relevant facts pertaining to the insured's health.

If the policy has been in force for less than 6 months, an insurer can rescind the policy or deny an otherwise valid claim upon a showing of a misrepresentation that was material to the insurer's acceptance of coverage. If the policy has been in force for at least 6 months but less than 2 years, the insurer can rescind the policy or deny an otherwise valid claim upon showing that the misrepresentation was both material to the insurer's acceptance of coverage and pertains to the condition for which benefits are sought.

The insurer cannot recover any benefits paid under a policy prior to the time a policy is rescinded.

Inflation Protection

Insurance companies must offer the applicant the right to purchase coverage that allows for an increase in the amount of benefits based on reasonable anticipated increases in the cost of services covered by the policy. The applicant must specifically reject this inflation protection if he or she does not want it. This provision does not apply to life insurance policies that provide accelerated benefits for long-term care.

Nonforfeiture Benefits

Insurance companies must offer the applicant the right to purchase a nonforfeiture benefit. If the applicant declines the nonforfeiture benefit, the insurer must provide a contingent nonforfeiture benefit that is available for a specified period of time following a substantial increase in premium rates. This provision, like the inflation-protection requirement, does not apply to life insurance policies that provide accelerated benefits for long-term care.

Marketing

Some of the provisions of the model legislation that pertain to marketing include outline of coverage, shopper's guide, 30-day free look, standards for appropriateness of coverage, limitations on post-claims underwriting, third-party notification of pending policy lapse, and policy replacement.

Outline of Coverage

An outline of coverage must be delivered to a prospective applicant at the time of the initial solicitation. Among the information it must contain is

- a description of the principal benefits and coverage provided in the policy
- a statement of the policy's principal exclusions, reductions, and limitations
- a statement of the terms under which the policy may be continued in force or discontinued
- a statement that the outline of coverage is a summary only, not a contract of insurance, and that the policy contains governing contractual provisions
- a description of the terms under which the policy or certificate may be returned and premium refunded
- a brief description of the relationship of the cost of care and benefits
- a statement whether the policy is intended to be federally tax qualified

Shopper's Guide

A shopper's guide must be delivered to all prospective applicants. The guide must either be in the format developed by the NAIC or one developed by the state insurance commissioner. In the case of agent solicitations, the guide must be presented prior to the presentation of an application or enrollment form. Shopper's guides are discussed in more detail in chapter 16. A few states also require that information on Medicare supplement policies be provided to applicants aged 65 or older.

30-Day Free Look

The policy must allow applicants to have a 30-day free look after the policy's delivery. During that time, an applicant may have the premium refunded if, after examining the policy, he or she is not satisfied for any reason. The policy is then void from its inception. A notice of this provision must be prominently displayed on or attached to the policy's first page.

Standards for Appropriateness of Coverage

Any entity that markets long-term care insurance, other than life insurance policies that accelerate benefits for long-term care, must develop and use suitability standards to determine whether the purchase or replacement of coverage is appropriate for the applicant's needs, and agents must be trained in the use of these standards. In addition, the agent and insurer must develop procedures to determine the following:

- the applicant's ability to pay for the proposed coverage and other relevant financial information related to the purchase of coverage
- the applicant's goals or needs with respect to long-term care and the advantages and disadvantages of insurance to meet these goals or needs
- the values, benefits, and costs of any existing insurance the applicant has when compared to the values, benefits, and costs of the recommended purchase or replacement

Limitations on Post-Claims Underwriting

**post-claims
underwriting**

An issue that has been of concern to regulators, consumers, and insurance professionals is *post-claims underwriting*. This practice occurs when an insurer does little underwriting at the time of the initial application for coverage. Then, after a claim is filed, the insurer obtains medical information that could have been obtained earlier and may rescind the policy or deny the claim based on this new information.

To control post-claims underwriting, applications for insurance must be clear and unambiguous so that an applicant's health condition can be properly ascertained. Except for policies that are guaranteed issue, the application must also contain a conspicuous statement near the place for the applicant's signature that says the following: "If your answers to this application are incorrect or untrue, the company has the right to deny benefits or rescind your policy."

If an application contains a question about whether an applicant has had medication prescribed by a physician, the application must also ask the applicant to list the medications that have been prescribed. If the policy is issued and the insurer knew, or should have known, at the time of application that the medications listed in the application were related to a condition for which coverage would normally be denied, it cannot rescind the policy for that condition.

The insurer is also required to obtain additional information on applicants aged 80 or older. This includes at least one of the following: a report of a physical examination, an assessment of functional capacity, an attending physician's statement, or copies of medical records.

Finally, a copy of the completed application must be delivered to the insured no later than the time of the delivery of the policy unless it was retained by the insured at time of application.

Third-Party Notification of Pending Policy Lapse

No policy can be issued until the applicant has been given the option of electing a third party to be notified of any pending policy lapse because of nonpayment of premium. The purpose of this provision is to eliminate the problem of policy lapse because a senile or otherwise mentally impaired person or a person with a loss of functional capacity fails to pay the premium.

Policy Replacement

If one long-term policy replaces another, the new insurer must waive any time periods pertaining to preexisting conditions and probationary periods for comparable benefits to the extent that the original policy had such provisions.

The model regulation also requires applications to contain questions as to whether the applicant has other long-term care insurance in force and whether a long-term care insurance policy is intended to replace any other medical expense policy or long-term care insurance policy in force. These questions include the following:

- Do you have another long-term care insurance policy?
- Did you have another long-term care insurance policy in force during the last 12 months? If so, with which insurer? If that policy lapsed, when did the lapse take place?
- Do you intend to replace any medical or health insurance coverage with this policy?
- Are you covered by Medicaid?

Agents must also list any other health insurance policies they have sold to the applicant that are still in force as well as any policies sold to the applicant in the past 5 years that are not in force.

If it is determined that a sale will involve a policy replacement, an insurer or its agent must furnish an applicant with a notice regarding the replacement of long-term care coverage and its potential disadvantages. The applicant retains a copy of the notice; the insurer retains another copy, signed by the applicant. In addition, the insurer replacing coverage must notify the existing insurer of the proposed replacement within 5 days of the earlier of the date of application or the date the policy is issued.

EFFECT OF HEALTH INSURANCE PORTABILITY AND ACCOUNTABILITY ACT (HIPAA)

The enactment of HIPAA in 1996 made the tax treatment of long-term care insurance more favorable. Because favorable tax treatment is given only if long-term care insurance policies meet prescribed standards, the nature of most long-term care insurance coverage has changed. In many cases, the imposition of federal standards resulted in broader coverage for consumers. However, Congress seemed to have been concerned with the revenue loss associated with this tax legislation. As a result, policies that were modified to comply with the federal standards sometimes actually provide more limited access to benefits than had been previously required in several states. Moreover, the amount of long-term care insurance premiums that can be deducted for income tax purposes is subject to limitations.

It should be emphasized that the long-term care changes in the act are primarily changes in the federal income tax code. States still have the authority to regulate long-term care insurance contracts. They have no obligation to bring state rules and regulations into conformity with these tax changes. However, all states allow tax-qualified contracts so that consumers can obtain the favorable federal tax benefits.

Requirements for Favorable Tax Treatment

To understand whether a long-term care insurance policy will receive favorable tax treatment under HIPAA, it is necessary to understand the meaning of several terms. These include qualified long-term care insurance contract, qualified long-term care services, and chronically ill individual.

Qualified Long-Term Care Insurance Contract

qualified long-term care insurance contract

The act provides favorable tax treatment to a *qualified long-term care insurance contract*. This is defined as any insurance contract that meets all the following requirements:

- The only insurance protection provided under the contract is for qualified long-term care services. The act does allow a contract to satisfy this requirement, however, if payments are made on a per diem or other periodic basis (such as $150 per day) without regard to the expenses incurred during the period to which the payments relate.

- The contract cannot pay for expenses that are reimbursable under Medicare or would be reimbursable except for the application of a deductible or coinsurance amount. However, this requirement does not apply to expenses that are reimbursable if (1) Medicare is a secondary payer of benefits, or (2) benefits are paid on a per diem or other periodic basis without regard to the expenses incurred during the period to which the benefits relate.
- The contract must be guaranteed renewable.
- The contract does not provide for a cash surrender value or other money that can be borrowed or paid, assigned, or pledged as collateral for a loan.
- All refunds of premiums and all policyowner dividends must be applied as future reductions in premiums or to increase future benefits. A refund in the event of the death of the insured or a complete surrender or cancellation of the contract cannot exceed the aggregate premiums paid under the contract.
- The policy must comply with various consumer protection provisions. For the most part, these are the same provisions in NAIC model legislation and already adopted by most states.

Under the act's provisions, a qualified long-term care insurance contract also includes the portion of a life insurance contract that provides long-term care insurance coverage by a rider or as part of the contract as long as the above criteria are satisfied.

Furthermore, the act allows any contract issued before January 1, 1997, that met the long-term care requirements in the state where the policy was issued to be considered a qualified long-term care insurance contract even though the contract does not meet the above requirements. If such a "grandfathered policy" undergoes a material change, however, the policy must then conform to the HIPAA requirements to retain this status. An example of a material change is the addition of a new covered service for which an increased premium is charged.

Although the term qualified long-term care insurance contract is used in HIPAA and the Internal Revenue Code, different terminology is often used for the sake of brevity. Thus, it is common to see these contracts referred to just as qualified contracts (or policies), TQ contracts (or policies), or tax-qualified contracts (or policies). The latter terminology is used in this book. Similarly, contracts (or policies) that are not tax qualified are referred to as non-tax-qualified or NTQ.

To further complicate the issue of terminology, the terminology for qualified contract is sometimes preceded by the word *federally* to clarify that HIPAA provides favorable tax treatment with respect to federal tax laws, not state tax laws. It is left to the reader to determine the tax treatment of long-term care insurance in his or her own state. It should be noted, however, that most states do not tax long-term care insurance benefits, and about half the states that levy income taxes provide some type of tax deduction or tax credit for the purchase of long-term care insurance.

Qualified Long-Term Care Services

qualified long-term care services

The act defines *qualified long-term care services* as necessary diagnostic, preventive, therapeutic, curing, treating, and rehabilitative services, and maintenance or personal care services required by a chronically ill individual and provided by a plan of care prescribed by a licensed health care practitioner.

Chronically Ill Individual

chronically ill individual

A *chronically ill individual* is one who has been certified by a licensed health care practitioner as meeting one of the following requirements:

- The person is expected to be unable to perform, without substantial assistance from another person, at least two activities of daily living (ADLs) for a period of at least 90 days due to a loss of functional capacity. The act allows six ADLs: eating, bathing, dressing, using the toilet, maintaining continence, and transferring into or out of a bed, chair, or wheelchair. A tax-qualified long-term care insurance policy must contain at least five of the six. (The Secretary of the Treasury in consultation with the Secretary of Health and Human Services is permitted to prescribe regulations so that a person who has a level of disability similar to the level of disability of a person who cannot perform two ADLs would also be considered chronically ill. However, no action has ever been taken in this regard.)
- Substantial supervision is required to protect the individual from threats to health and safety because of severe cognitive impairment.

licensed health care practitioner

For purposes of certifying an individual as chronically ill, a *licensed health care practitioner* is a physician, registered nurse, licensed social worker, or other person who meets any requirements prescribed by the Secretary of the Treasury. Recertification of an individual as chronically ill must occur at least every 12 months.

Federal Income Tax Provisions

This chapter concludes with a summary of the federal income tax provisions pertaining to long-term care insurance with respect to: individual purchases by persons other than the self-employed; individual purchases by persons who are considered self-employed; taxation resulting from employer-paid premiums; taxation of benefits; and the requirements of insurers.

Purchases by Individuals

A qualified long-term care insurance contract, typically referred to as tax qualified, is generally treated as accident and health insurance. With some exceptions, expenses for long-term care services, including insurance premiums, are treated like other medical expenses. That is, persons (other than the self-employed) who itemize deductions can include the cost of long-term care services, including insurance premiums, for purposes of deducting medical expenses in excess of 7.5 percent of their adjusted gross income. Deductions for long-term care services cannot be taken for payments made to a spouse or relative who is not a licensed professional with respect to such services. In addition, there is a cap on the amount of personally paid long-term care insurance premiums that can be claimed as medical expenses. The limits, which are based on a covered individual's age and subject to cost-of-living adjustments, are shown for 2006 in table 13-1. They are reduced by any amounts withdrawn on a tax-free basis from a consumer-directed health plan, such as an HSA.

TABLE 13-1 **Long-Term Care Deduction Limits**	
Age	**Annual Deduction Limit per Covered Individual**
40 or younger	$ 280
41–50	530
51–60	1,060
61–70	2,830
Older than 70	3,530

Purchases by the Self-Employed

The tax rules are similar for persons who are classified as self-employed. However, they are allowed to deduct long-term care premiums up to the amount shown in table 13-1 along with other medical expense premiums when determining adjusted gross income. Such an above-the-line deduction is much more favorable than including these premiums with other medical expenses subject to the 7.5 percent limitation. The overall medical deductions for insurance premiums used to determine adjusted gross income cannot exceed earned income from self-employment.

Taxation of Employer-Paid Premiums

An employer may choose to pay some or all of the long-term care insurance premiums for employees or retirees. If the employer is a C corporation, these premiums are deductible to the business and do not represent taxable income to the employees or retirees.

The situation is different if the employer is a sole proprietor, partnership, or S corporation. Any premiums paid by the business on behalf of the sole proprietor are included in the sole proprietor's income. Premiums paid on behalf of a partner or persons who own more than 2 percent of the stock of an S corporation are deductible at the business level, but they are included in the partner's or shareholder's gross income. However, all of these persons are subject to the tax rules for the self-employed and eligible for a tax deduction up to the applicable limits.

An employer cannot offer coverage through a cafeteria plan on a tax-favored basis. In addition, if an employer has a flexible spending account for unreimbursed medical expenses, any reimbursements for long-term care services must be included in the employee's income.

Taxation of Benefits

Benefits received under a tax-qualified long-term care contract are generally received tax free with one limitation. Under contracts written on a per diem basis, benefits are excludible from income in amounts up to $250 per day in 2006. (This figure is indexed annually.) Amounts in excess of $250 are also excludible to the extent that they represent actual costs for qualified long-term care services.

Insurer Requirements

Insurers are required to report the total value of long-term care insurance benefits received by a claimant, using IRS Form 1099-LTC. The claimant must then complete and file IRS Form 8853 with his or her tax return, even if the benefits are tax free.

NOTES

1. *Long-Term Care and Medicare Supplement, Executive Summary, Annual 2004,* LIMRA International, Inc., 2005, p. 2, and *U.S. Group Long-Term Care Insurance, Executive Summary, Annual 2004,* LIMRA International, Inc., 2005, p. 2.
2. Ibid.
3. *The National Nursing Home Survey, 1999 Summary*, Centers for Disease Control and Prevention (CDC)/National Center for Health Statistics (NCHS), June 2002.

14

Characteristics of Individual Long-Term Care Insurance

Chapter Outline

For many types of insurance, policy provisions are relatively standardized. For long-term care insurance, the opposite is true. Significant variations (and therefore differences in cost) exist from one insurance company to another. An applicant also has numerous options with respect to policy provisions.

The policy provisions covered in this chapter include the definition of the insured, eligibility for benefits, types of care covered, benefit variations, benefit amounts, period of benefits, restoration of benefits, inflation protection, exclusions, nonforfeiture options, premiums, renewability, and claims. The provisions and practices described represent the norm in that most policies fit within the extremes that are described. However, the norm covers a wide spectrum. This, coupled with the large number of options available to an applicant, makes the evaluation and comparison of long-term care insurance policies more difficult than the evaluation and comparison of most other types of insurance.

DEFINITION OF INSURED

Most long-term care insurance policies provide coverage for only one person and define the insured as the person named in the policy. However, some insurance companies issue joint policies on more than one individual. These joint policies usually involve a husband and wife but occasionally can include other family members as well. Most insurers will even issue joint policies to domestic partners who live together. In these cases, the insured will be defined as any of the persons listed in the policy.

The purchase of long-term care insurance is often a joint purchase by a married couple, and insurers encourage this action with premium discounts and favorable policy provisions. As a result, some insurers have a single application that both spouses can use. More often than not, however, an insurer's practice will be to issue each spouse a separate policy.

ELIGIBILITY FOR BENEFITS

benefit trigger

All tax-qualified long-term care insurance contracts use the same two criteria, each known as a *benefit trigger,* to determine whether an insured is chronically ill and eligible for benefits. The insured is required to meet only one of the two. The first criterion is that the insured is expected to be unable, without substantial assistance from another person, to perform at least two of either five or six of the ADLs that are acceptable under HIPAA for a period of at least 90 days due to loss of functional capacity. Most insurers use a benefit trigger of the inability to perform two or more of all six ADLs.

hands-on assistance

standby assistance

The definition of substantial assistance can vary among policies. Policies that have the most restrictive definition require actual *hands-on assistance.* This means that the insured must need actual physical assistance from another person to perform the ADLs. Other policies require only that the insured need *standby assistance,* which means that the insured requires the presence of another person within arm's length who can intervene to prevent physical injury. Standby assistance can also be defined to include cueing to accomplish an ADL. Cueing includes verbal prompting, gestures, and other demonstrations. In some policies, either hand-on assistance or standby assistance constitutes substantial assistance.

Although insurers are also allowed to use less restrictive definitions than those below, the six ADLs and their definitions under the NAIC model regulation are the following:

- bathing—washing oneself by sponge bath, or washing oneself in either a tub or shower (including the task of getting into or out of the tub or shower)
- continence—the ability to maintain control of bowel and bladder function; or, when unable to maintain control of bowel or bladder function, the ability to perform associated personal hygiene (including caring for a catheter or a colostomy bag)
- dressing—putting on and taking off all items of clothing and any necessary braces, fasteners, or artificial limbs
- eating—feeding oneself by getting food into the body from a receptacle (such as a plate, cup, or table) or by a feeding tube or intravenously
- toileting—getting to and from the toilet, getting on and off the toilet, and performing associated personal hygiene
- transferring—moving into or out of a bed, chair, or wheelchair

substantial supervision

The second criterion is substantial supervision required to protect an individual from threats to health and safety due to severe cognitive impairment. *Substantial supervision* is the continuous presence of a person directing and watching over another and may also be defined to include cueing. Most policies use the definition of cognitive impairment in the NAIC model regulation, which is a deficiency in a person's (1) short- or long-term memory, (2) orientation as to person, place, and time, (3) deductive or abstract reasoning, or (4) judgment as it relates to safety awareness.

Tax-qualified policies require that someone certify whether the insured is chronically ill. Some insurers use the broadest definition allowed by HIPAA and state only that certification must be by a licensed health care practitioner. As defined in chapter 13, this definition includes physicians, registered nurses, and licensed social workers. However, regulations allow insurers to use a subset of this definition. As a result, some insurers have more restrictive requirements. For example, they may require that the certification be from a physician or from a licensed health care practitioner employed by an organization with whom the insurer contracts.

medical necessity

Non-tax-qualified long-term care insurance contracts, on the other hand, may have more liberal eligibility requirements. Many of these contracts use the same benefit triggers that are in tax-qualified contracts except that there is no time period that applies to the inability to perform ADLs. A small number of non-tax-qualified contracts require only the inability to perform one ADL and/or use more than the six ADLs allowed by HIPAA. Finally, many non-tax-qualified contracts make benefits available if a third criterion—*medical necessity*—is satisfied. This generally means that a physician has certified that long-term care is needed, even if neither of the other criteria is satisfied.

TYPES OF CARE COVERED

There are many types of care for which benefits may be provided under a long-term care insurance policy. These can be broadly categorized as nursing home care, assisted-living care, hospice care, Alzheimer's facilities, home health care, respite care, caregiver training, care coordination, and alternative sources of care. A long-term care insurance policy may provide benefits for one, several, or all of these types of care. Most of these care settings have already been discussed in a general sense in chapter 11. The following discussion focuses on the specific provisions of long-term care insurance policies that apply when each of these types of care is covered.

Nursing Home Care

Nursing home care is a term that encompasses skilled-nursing care, intermediate care, and custodial care in a licensed facility.

bed reservation benefit

Policies that provide nursing home care often also provide a *bed reservation benefit*, which continues payments to a long-term care facility for a limited time (often 21 or 30 days per calendar year) if a patient temporarily leaves because of hospitalization or any other reason. Without a continuation of payments, the bed may be assigned to someone else and unavailable upon the patient's release from the hospital. Policies that cover care in assisted-living and/or hospice facilities (discussed in the following sections) often include a bed reservation benefit for those settings as well.

The definition of a nursing home (sometimes referred to as a nursing care facility) is very specific in long-term care insurance policies and varies somewhat among insurers. It usually includes the following requirements:

- The facility must be licensed or legally authorized.
- A doctor must be available to furnish care in case of an emergency.
- Nursing services must be provided 24 hours a day under the supervision of a full-time nurse.
- The facility must maintain records for all patients.
- The facility must have appropriate procedures to handle medications.

The definition is broad enough to include facilities that provide nursing care only as well as distinct units of other facilities (such as hospitals) that meet the definition. However, the definition excludes several types of facilities, such as places designed primarily for rest, the aged, drug addicts, alcoholics, the mentally retarded, treatment of the mentally ill, or education.

Assisted-Living Facility Care

Assisted-living facility care is provided in facilities that care for the frail elderly who are no longer able to care for themselves but do not need as high a level of care as is provided in a nursing home.

As with nursing homes, long-term care insurance policies have very specific definitions of assisted-living facilities. Again, definitions vary, but the following requirements are commonly included:

- The facility must be licensed, if required by the state in which it operates.
- The facility must serve a minimum number of residents, such as 5 or 10.
- The facility must serve meals and accommodate special dietary needs.
- Trained personnel must be on duty and ready to respond at all times to provide care.
- There must be formal arrangements for the services of a physician or nurse to provide medical care in case of an emergency.
- There must be appropriate procedures for handling medications.

Hospice Care

Hospices for the treatment of terminally ill persons are a recent development in the area of medical care. A hospice may be a separate facility, but this type of care can also be provided on an outpatient basis in the dying person's home. Most comprehensive long-term care insurance policies that provide benefits for hospice care make no distinction in the setting. However, some policies provide benefits only for care in a facility because Medicare provides home care benefits for those persons eligible for Medicare.

Alzheimer's Facilities

The states require long-term care insurance policies to cover Alzheimer's disease and related forms of degenerative diseases and dementia under the same terms as they cover other conditions that qualify an individual as chronically ill. Therefore, coverage is provided if an individual receives services in a nursing home, in an assisted-living facility, or at home—as long as the specific type of care is covered in the policy. Most policies, however, have some specific reference to Alzheimer's facilities. In some cases, they are included as part of the definition for assisted-living facilities. In other cases, they are referred to separately but defined as a facility that must meet the policy's definition of either a nursing home or an assisted-living facility.

Home Health Care

Home health care is much broader than just part-time skilled-nursing care, therapy, part-time services from home health aides, and help from homemakers. Benefits for home health care may also include one or more of the following:

- the purchase or rental of needed medical equipment and emergency alert systems
- modifications to the home, such as a ramp for a wheelchair or bathroom modifications
- adult day care (also called adult day services). As with nursing homes and assisted-living facilities, benefits are provided only for services from a facility that meets standards specified in the policy. When adult day care is included with home health care, the type of care is often referred to as home and community-based care.

homemaker companion

- a *homemaker companion*, who is an employee of a state-licensed home health care agency. The companion may assist with such tasks as cooking, shopping, cleaning, bill paying, or other household chores.
- payment for informal care when a covered person receives care in his or her home only from an informal caregiver
- payment of a transitional care benefit to assist a covered person to meet immediate needs resulting from the onset of loss of functional capacity

As with other types of care, long-term care policies are very specific about the forms of home health care that are covered.

Respite Care

Respite care, defined in a previous chapter, provides temporary relief to a primary caregiver from his or her responsibilities for a chronically ill person being cared for at home. The scope of coverage under a policy usually determines the services for which a respite care benefit may be paid. For example, a facility-only policy may pay for respite care in a nursing home, assisted-living facility, or hospice facility for a person who would otherwise be eligible for benefits in a facility, but is normally cared for at home. If the policy also covers home care, the services of a formal (and sometimes informal) caregiver at home or at an adult day care center may be paid. Limits, such as 30 times the amount of the daily benefit per calendar year, apply to respite care benefits.

Benefits for respite care and caregiver training, explained in the following paragraph, usually reduce a policy's overall benefits. In some ways, however, both of these types of benefits are independent of other policy benefits. Thus, for example, an insured person may receive benefits for respite care and/or caregiver training before becoming eligible to file a claim for facility and/or home care services.

Caregiver Training

caregiver training

Caregiver training is the instruction of an informal caregiver to provide needed assistance so that a chronically ill person can remain at home. Usually, family members, friends, and anyone who would normally live with an insured are eligible for such training as a benefit under a policy that covers this service. All policies that cover this service will limit the benefit; a lifetime benefit equal to 7 times the amount of the daily benefit is one example of such a limit.

Care Coordination

Many policies (either as a standard provision or an optional benefit) provide the services of a care coordinator who works with an insured, his or her family, and licensed health care practitioners to assess a person's condition, evaluate care options, and develop an individualized plan of care that provides the most appropriate services. The care coordinator may also periodically reevaluate ongoing plans of care and act as an advocate for the insured. Some long-term care policies mandate that the insured use the services of the care coordinator in order to receive benefits.

In many cases, the care coordinator is recommended by the insurance company but is not its employee or an employee of a care provider. If the recommended care coordinator is voluntarily used, additional benefits might be available to the insured, such as waiving elimination periods, increasing benefit levels, and not decreasing maximum policy benefits because of the cost of the care coordinator. When care coordination is provided, there may or may not be coverage if the insured or his or her family selects a care coordinator not recommended by the insurer.

Alternative Plans of Care

Many policies provide benefits for alternative plans of care, even though the types of care might not be covered in the policy. For example, a policy covering nursing home care only might provide benefits for care in an assisted-living facility if these benefits are an appropriate and cost-effective alternative to care in a nursing home. A policy provision permitting alternative plans of care also allows for adaptation to new forms of care. As a general rule, the alternative plan must be acceptable to the insurance company, the insured, and the insured's physician.

BENEFIT VARIATIONS

It is probably only a slight exaggeration to say that there are almost as many variations among long-term care policies as there are insurance companies writing the product. Much of this variation is related to the types of care for which benefits are provided. These benefit variations fall into three broad categories: facility-only policies, home health care policies, and comprehensive policies. Some insurance companies write only one type of policies; other insurance companies may write all three.

Facility-Only Policies

nursing home policy

facility-only policy

Many early long-term care policies were designed to provide benefits only if the insured was in a nursing home. This type of policy was frequently referred to as a *nursing home policy*. Such policies still exist, but they frequently also provide benefits for care in other settings, such as assisted-living facilities and hospices. The term *facility-only policy* is often used to describe this broader type of policy, and the term, in its most generic sense, also includes nursing home policies.

Home Health Care Policies

home health care policy

Home health care policies were originally developed to be used either as an alternative to nursing home policies or to complement such policies if more comprehensive coverage was desired. A *home health care policy* is designed to provide benefits for care outside an institutional setting. Some home health care policies also provide benefits for care in assisted-living facilities, and this is one area in which they often overlap with facility-only policies.

Although some insurers still write stand-alone home health care policies, many other insurers have exited this market and now write the coverage as part of a broader comprehensive policy.

Comprehensive Policies

comprehensive long-term care policy

Most long-term care policies written today can be described as comprehensive policies. A *comprehensive long-term care policy*, sometimes referred to as an integrated policy, combines benefits for facility care and home health care into a single contract. However, variations exist within this type of policy with respect to what is covered as part of the standard policy and what is an optional benefit that the applicant may select. For example, some policies cover almost all care settings as part of their standard benefits; other policies provide facility-only coverage as a standard benefit with home health care covered as an option for an additional premium.

Some Examples

The following examples of actual long-term policies in the marketplace illustrate some of the wide variations in benefits.

Example 1:   This policy is advertised as a nursing home policy. The policy provides coverage for

- nursing home care
- hospice-facility care
- a bed reservation benefit
- an alternative plan of care

Example 2:   The policy is advertised as a long-term care insurance policy providing facility benefits only. The policy provides coverage for

- nursing home care
- assisted-living facility care
- hospice-facility care
- a bed reservation benefit
- an alternative plan of care

Example 3:   The policy is advertised as a home health care policy and provides coverage for

- home health care
- adult day care
- a care coordinator

- caregiver training
- a homemaker companion
- respite care

Example 4: The policy is advertised as a home health care policy and provides benefits for

- home health care
- adult day care
- a care coordinator
- an alternative plan of care
- caregiver training
- respite care

Example 5: The policy is a comprehensive policy with standard benefits for facility care and optional benefits for home and community-based care. The standard benefits are for

- nursing home care
- assisted-living care
- hospice care
- a bed reservation benefit
- a care coordinator
- an alternative plan of care

Optional coverage includes a rider that provides benefits for

- home health care
- adult day care
- caregiver training
- a homemaker companion

Example 6: The policy is a comprehensive policy that provides benefits for

- nursing home care
- assisted-living facility care
- hospice care
- a bed reservation benefit
- home health care
- adult day care
- respite care
- an alternative plan of care
- caregiver training

- transitional care
- informal care
- a home health care coordinator

BENEFIT AMOUNTS

When purchasing long-term care insurance, the applicant selects the level of benefit he or she desires up to the maximum level the insurance company will provide. Benefits are often sold in increments of $10 per day up to frequently found limits of $200 or $250 or, in a few cases, as much as $400 or $500 per day. The benefit level selected is known as the daily benefit amount (DBA). Most insurance companies will not offer a DBA below $40 or $50. Some policies base benefits on a monthly (rather than daily) amount that can vary from $1,000 to $9,000 or more.

The same DBA is often provided for all levels of institutional care. Most comprehensive policies that provide home health care benefits once limited the daily benefit for home care services to one-half the DBA for institutional stays. However, many insurers now allow applicants to select home health care limits up to 100 percent of the DBA for institutional care; a few insurers even offer limits as high as 125 percent or 150 percent. If a policy provides home health care benefits only, the daily amount of that benefit is what the applicant selected.

Generally, the DBA for institutional care also determines the level of the other benefits that a long-term care policy may provide, as the following examples show:

- bed reservation—DBA for 21 days per calendar year
- respite care—60 percent of the DBA for up to 21 days per calendar year
- caregiver training—payment of up to 3 times the DBA per claim period
- informal care—25 percent of the DBA for up to 50 days per calendar year
- transitional care—one-time payment equal to 3 times the DBA

Policies pay benefits in one of two basic ways: reimbursement or per diem.

Reimbursement Policies

reimbursement basis

The majority of newer policies pay benefits on a *reimbursement basis*. These contracts reimburse the insured for actual expenses up to the specified policy limit. For example, a policy with a daily benefit amount of $200 will pay only $150 if that was the insured's actual charge for care. Tax-qualified policies that provide benefits on a reimbursement basis must be coordinated with Medicare except when Medicare is the secondary payer of benefits.

Home health care services may not be received every day of the week, and the cost of the services can vary on the days that they are received. Some insurers, at the time of claim, pay benefits on a weekly or monthly basis. Even though the insured must select a daily benefit amount, claims are paid as if the benefit is seven times this amount when a weekly basis is used.

Example: Francesca's long-term care insurance policy has a daily benefit of $100 for home health care services. On each day of the week, she receives care from a home health aide at a cost of $50 per day. On Mondays, Wednesdays, and Fridays, a nurse and a physical therapist also visit her. Their combined charges total an additional $90 on each of these days. Thus, Francesca's total home health care costs for the week are $620.

          If Francesca's policy pays benefits on a daily basis, she will receive her benefit maximum of $100 for Mondays, Wednesdays, and Fridays, and $50 for each of the remaining days of the week. Her total weekly reimbursement is therefore $500.

          However, if Francesca's policy pays a weekly benefit, she has an aggregate benefit amount of $700 that can be used anytime during the week. As a result, her entire expenses of $620 for the week will be reimbursed.

As the example illustrates, the payment of benefits on a weekly or monthly basis increases claim costs. Some insurers that pay claims in this manner do so automatically and build the extra claim costs into their basic rate structure. Other insurers may make this payment method a policy option for which the insured pays a higher premium.

Per Diem Policies

per diem basis   Some policies provide benefits on a *per diem basis* once care is actually being received. This means that benefits are paid regardless of the actual cost of care. In this case, a policy with a daily benefit of $200 will pay $200 even if actual long-term care charges for the day are only $150. Per diem contracts are seldom coordinated with any benefits that are payable under Medicare. If home health care benefits are provided, most per diem policies pay benefits regardless of the service provider. In such cases, benefits are paid even if care is provided by a family member at no charge. Some policies, however, define the type of service provider from whom care must be received.

Example:	Lynn, aged 70, recently entered a nursing home following a lengthy hospitalization. The cost of her care is $200 per day. Because she will need skilled-nursing care for a few months, Medicare will pay the cost of the first 20 days of care in full and provide an additional 80 days of benefits with a daily copayment. Lynn also has a tax-qualified long-term care insurance policy that will provide benefits of $150 per day after a 30-day elimination period.
	If Lynn's policy provides benefits on a reimbursement basis, no benefits will be payable as long as Lynn is collecting any benefits from Medicare. When Medicare payments cease after 100 days, Lynn requires only custodial care for a few more weeks. Beginning on the 101st day, she will collect $150 per day because her policy counts the days she was receiving Medicare benefits toward the elimination period.
	If Lynn's policy provides benefits on a per diem basis and if the policy is not integrated with Medicare, Lynn will collect a daily benefit of $150 beginning on the 31st day regardless of any Medicare reimbursement.

Note that per diem policies are sometimes referred to as indemnity policies even though the usual insurance meaning of indemnity implies payment of benefits for actual expenses up to policy limits. In this sense, reimbursement policies, not per diem policies, are actually policies of indemnity.

disability-based policy

A few insurers offer a variation of the per diem policy that pays benefits as long as the insured satisfies the policy's benefit triggers, even if no long-term care is being received. Such a policy is referred to as a *disability-based policy*.

PERIOD OF BENEFITS

To determine the period of benefits under a long-term care insurance policy, it is necessary to look at the elimination period and the maximum duration of benefits.

Elimination Period

elimination period

The applicant is required to select a period of time that must pass after covered long-term care services commence but before benefit payments begin. The majority of long-term care insurers refer to this period as an *elimination period.* However, some insurers call it a waiting period or a deductible period. Most insurers allow an applicant to select from three to five optional elimination periods. For example, one insurer allows the choice of 20, 60, 100, or 180 days. Choices are typically as low as 0 days or as high as 365 days. Some states limit the length of the elimination period to a maximum duration of 180 days, for example, although a few states allow longer durations, such as 2 years.

In a comprehensive policy, there is normally a single elimination period that can be met by any combination of days during which the insured is in a long-term care facility or receiving home health care services. The days of care that satisfy the elimination period need not be consecutive or associated with the same episode of care; all days of care accumulate until the elimination period is satisfied. However, some insurers require separate selections for facility benefits and home health care benefits. The two elimination periods may be for the same length of time, and days used for one elimination period may or may not offset days used for the other.

Some policies require the insured to meet the elimination period for each separate stay in a long-term care facility or each period of home health care. Under either approach, policies may or may not allow days that were applied to a prior elimination period, which was not satisfied, to be carried over to satisfy a new elimination period. Newer policies, however, typically do not require that more than one elimination period be satisfied during the insured's lifetime. The following are examples of varying provisions among policies with a single elimination period.

Example 1:   The policy requires the satisfaction of only one elimination period during the insured's lifetime but does not require that days used to satisfy the elimination period be consecutive. Assume Gary has a 90-day elimination period, is certified as chronically ill, and received services covered under his tax-qualified policy. Because he spent only 35 days in a nursing home before being discharged, he is ineligible for benefits because the elimination period was not satisfied. However, when he later enters a nursing home for an indefinite stay, there will be a period of only 55 days before he is eligible for benefit payments. If he leaves the nursing home after 55 days, there will be no additional elimination period for a subsequent stay in a long-term care facility or for home health care.

Example 2:   The policy requires the satisfaction of only one elimination period during the insured's lifetime, but it must be satisfied during the same time period for which the insured is certified as needing long-term care. Using the same facts as in example 1, Gary will not satisfy the elimination period during the first nursing home stay. Benefit payments will begin after Gary has been in the nursing home for 90 days during the second nursing home stay. If he is later discharged, there will be no additional elimination period for subsequent long-term care services.

Example 3:   The policy requires the satisfaction of a new elimination period for each period of long-term care if there is a gap of more than 6 months between periods of care. Using the same facts as in the previous example, Gary would satisfy the elimination period after he had been in the nursing home for 90 days during the second stay. If he were later discharged, a new elimination period would need to be satisfied for any subsequent long-term care services if the subsequent services begin more than 6 months after the discharge.

As mentioned in earlier chapters, Medicare may provide benefits for up to 100 days in a skilled-nursing facility. In addition, long-term care policies are permitted by the NAIC model legislation to exclude benefits for services that are provided under Medicare, and tax-qualified policies written on a reimbursement basis must generally have such an exclusion. Nevertheless, the vast majority of these policies allow an insured's Medicare-covered days in a skilled-nursing facility to be counted toward the elimination period. However, the long-term care insurance policies of a few insurers—frequently their older policies—do not permit these days to be counted.

There are several ways that home health care services can be counted toward the elimination period. Some policies count only those days when actual services are received for which charges are made and that will be covered after the elimination period is satisfied. If an insured receives services 3 days during the week, this counts as 3 days. If the insured's policy has a 60-day elimination period, benefit payments will not begin until the insured had been receiving services for 20 weeks (or 140 days). Some policies count each week as 7 days toward the satisfaction of the elimination period if services were received on any number of days in the week, even 1 day. In this case, the insured will start receiving benefit payments after 60 days have elapsed from the first service.

Another variation in reimbursement policies is for the insurer to start counting days toward satisfaction of the elimination period as soon as long-term care is certified as being necessary, even if services are received from someone who does not make a charge. Therefore, family members or friends could provide the services until the elimination period is satisfied, and the insurer will then start paying benefits for the services of a paid caregiver.

One final comment about the elimination period concerns its relationship to the requirement that tax-qualified policies cannot pay benefits for the inability to perform ADLs unless this inability is expected to last at least 90 days. Actually, despite what some people think, there is no relationship! If an insured is certified as being unable to perform the requisite number of ADLs for at least 90 days, benefit payments will start after the satisfaction of the elimination period, be it 0, 20, 60, or any other specified number of days. If the insured makes a recovery after the elimination period is satisfied but before the end of the 90-day period, the insured is fully entitled to any benefits received because the period was *expected* to be at least 90 days.

In some cases, an insured will not be eligible for benefits because a medical practitioner does not believe and will not certify that the insured will need care for as long as 90 days. If, in fact, the period of necessary care continues for 90 days or longer, the situation can be reevaluated and benefits paid retroactively from the end of the elimination period.

Maximum Duration of Benefits

benefit period

The applicant is also given a choice as to the maximum period for which benefits are paid, often referred to as the *benefit period*. This period begins from the time benefit payments start after satisfaction of the elimination period. In addition, the benefit period does not necessarily apply to each separate period for which long-term care services are received. Rather, it is a period that applies to the aggregate time benefits are paid under the policy. When the maximum benefits are paid, the policy will terminate. However, if benefits are only partially exhausted during a course of long-term care, they may be restored under certain circumstances, as explained later. Also, as explained later, the length of the benefit period may actually differ from the period chosen if a policy uses a pool-of-money concept. Some benefits— such as those for respite care, caregiver training, informal care, and transitional care—may not count toward the maximum benefit, however.

Most insurers require the applicant to select the benefit period, and they make several options available. For example, one insurer offers durations of 2, 3, and 5 years as well as lifetime benefits. Some comprehensive policies have separate benefit periods for stays in a long-term care facility and home health care. For example, if each of these periods is 3 years, an insured could potentially collect benefit payments for up to 6 years—3 years while receiving benefits at home and an additional 3 years after entering a long-term care facility.

There are actually two ways that the benefit period is applied in the payment of benefits. Under one approach, benefit payments are made for exactly the benefit period chosen. If the applicant selects a benefit period of 4 years and collects benefits for 4 years, the benefit payments cease. The other approach, most commonly but not exclusively used with reimbursement policies, uses a *pool of money*. Under this concept, there is an amount of money that can be used to make benefit payments as long as the pool of money lasts. The applicant does not select the amount in the pool of money; it is determined by multiplying the daily benefit by the benefit period selected. For example, if the daily benefit is $200 and the benefit period is 1,460 days (or 4 years), then the pool of money is $292,000 ($200 x 1,460). Several important points about this pool of money should be mentioned:

pool of money

- Daily benefit payments from the pool of money cannot exceed the daily policy benefits.
- Under comprehensive policies, the pool of money is typically determined by using the daily benefit amount for institutional care.
- Adjustments are made to the pool of money during periods of benefit payments to reflect any inflation protection that applies to the policy benefits. This increase may apply to the original pool amount or any balance remaining in the pool after a claim commences.

Example: Renee has a comprehensive long-term care insurance policy that provides benefits on a reimbursement basis for a benefit period of 4 years. Her daily benefit is $200 for care in a long-term care facility and $100 per day for home health care. The policy makes benefit payments using the pool-of-money concept. Assume that Renee is chronically ill and receives home health care for 2 years at a cost of $80 per day for 5 days each week after she satisfies her elimination period. At that time, her condition deteriorates and she enters a nursing home that has a daily cost of $230.

Under a pool-of-money concept, the amount available for Renee's benefit payments is $292,000, as previously calculated. During the 2 years (104 weeks) that Renee receives home health care, the policy will make benefit payments equal to the full cost of her care because it is less than $100 per day. This totals $41,600 ($80 x 104 x 5). Therefore, the pool of money is reduced by this amount to $250,400 by the time she enters the nursing home. The policy will then pay a daily benefit but only up to the policy limit of $200 per day. (The extra $30 per day is her responsibility.) Consequently, Renee can receive benefits for an additional 1,252 days ($250,400 ÷ $200). The net effect is that Renee will actually receive benefit payments over a period that is equal to almost 5 1/2 years. This period would be somewhat longer if an inflation increase had been assumed for the pool of money.

shared benefit

A few insurers use the concept of a *shared benefit* when a husband and wife are insured under the same policy or with the same insurer. Under this concept, each spouse can access the other spouse's benefits. For example, if each spouse has a 4-year benefit period and one spouse has exhausted his or her benefits, benefit payments can continue by drawing on any unused benefits under the other spouse's policy. In effect, one spouse could have a benefit period of up to 8 years as long as the other spouse receives no benefit payments. If the insurer uses a pool-of-money concept, a single pool that combines the benefits of both spouses is created, and either or both spouses can receive benefit payments from the pool. There are also other variations on this theme. An insurer might allow the transfer of any unused benefits to a surviving spouse's policy. Or an insurer might allow the spouses to purchase an extra benefit, equal to each spouse's separate benefit. If either or both spouses exhaust their individual benefits, this third benefit amount or pool can be accessed.

There is at least one insurer that offers a shared benefit when any related family members are insured under its policy.

RESTORATION OF BENEFITS

Some policies written with less than a lifetime benefit period provide for a restoration of full benefits if the insured previously received less-than-full policy benefits and has not required long-term care covered by the policy for a certain time period, often 180 days. In some cases, this provision is a standard part of the policy; in other cases, it is offered as a rider for an additional premium. If a policy does not have such a provision, the benefits for a subsequent claim are reduced by the benefits previously paid.

INFLATION PROTECTION

Most states require that a long-term care policy offer some type of automatic inflation protection. The applicant is given the choice to select this option, decline the option, or possibly select an alternative option. The cost of an automatic-increase option is usually built into the initial premium, and no additional premium is levied at the time of an annual increase.

As a result of the NAIC model act and HIPAA, the standard provision in almost all policies is a 5 percent benefit increase compounded annually over the life of the policy. Under such a provision, the amount of a policy's benefits increases by 5 percent each year over the amount of benefits available in the prior year. New benefit amounts are often rounded to the nearest dollar. A small number of insurers offer compound benefit increases that use other percentages (such as 6 percent), and at least one insurer has an option tied to actual price inflation.

A common alternative that many insurers make available is based on simple interest, with each annual automatic increase being 5 percent of the original benefit amount. Other options that are occasionally found are increases (either simple or compound) based on different fixed percentage amounts, such as 3, 4, or 6 percent. Note that each state can determine which alternative options that an insurer may offer.

The effect of an automatic increase in daily benefits can be dramatic, as table 14-1 indicates. However, such a provision is also accompanied by a significant premium increase.

future purchase option

If an automatic-increase option is not selected, some policies have a *future purchase option* (called a guaranteed purchase option by some insurers), which allows the policyowner to increase benefits without evidence of insurability on a pay-as-you-go basis at specified intervals, such as every 1, 2, or 3 years. Each benefit increase is accompanied by a premium increase based on attained-age rates for the additional coverage.

The amount of the periodic benefit increase under a pay-as-you-go option may be a fixed dollar amount, such as a daily benefit increase of $20

TABLE 14-1
Effect of Automatic Increase on $100 Per Day Benefit

End of Policy Year	No Increase	5% Simple Interest	5% Compound Interest
5	$100	$125	$128
10	100	150	163
15	100	175	208
20	100	200	265
25	100	225	339
30	100	250	432

every third year, or based on a specified percentage or an index, such as the CPI. Some insurers have an aggregate limit on the total amount of benefit increases or an age beyond which they are no longer available. Failure to exercise a periodic increase or a series of increases over a specified period typically terminates the right to purchase additional benefits in the future or to obtain them without evidence of insurability.

Inflation increases also affect the lifetime maximum benefit or pool of money under a long-term care insurance policy. In most cases, the inflation increase applies only to the amount of unused benefits.

It is important to note that increases in benefits can be inadequate to offset actual inflation in the annual cost of long-term care, which for certain periods has been more than 5 percent.

EXCLUSIONS

With some exceptions, most long-term care insurance policies contain the exclusions permitted by the NAIC model legislation. These exclusions are enumerated in chapter 13.

Some of the other areas where an insurer's exclusions might differ from the NAIC model legislation include the following:

- Most policies no longer have exclusions for nervous or mental disorders and treat them like any other condition with regard to the need for nursing home or home care. Typically, however, no coverage is provided if care is received in an institution licensed primarily for the care of patients with mental illness.
- Most policies do not exclude benefits for expenses or services covered under another policy. Rather, the issue of other insurance is a factor taken into consideration during the underwriting process.
- Policies written on a per diem basis seldom have an exclusion for services or expenses provided under Medicare. Policies written on a reimbursement basis do contain such an exclusion. For tax-qualified policies, the exclusion also applies to amounts Medicare does not pay because of its deductible and coinsurance provisions. For non-tax-qualified policies, the exclusion is usually only for actual duplicate coverage.
- Although most policies do not cover services or treatment received outside the United States, some insurers provide benefits while the insured is in Canada. A few insurers provide benefits for services or treatment received in any foreign country, but benefit levels might be reduced or the coverage period might be limited to a year or an even shorter period, such as 30 to 60 days.

- Some policies have a preexisting-conditions provision that specifies that benefits are not paid within the first 6 months for a condition for which treatment was recommended or received within 6 months of policy purchase. Other policies, however, have no such provision or state that the provision does not apply to preexisting conditions listed on the policy application. There is little need for such a provision because insurers are required in most states to underwrite at the time coverage is written and are not allowed to use post-claims underwriting. If the policy is underwritten properly at the time of application, claims within the usual preexisting-conditions period are unlikely to occur. Elimination periods for benefits often serve a similar purpose.
- Policies in a few states limit the use of a war exclusion.
- Many policies no longer contain an aviation exclusion.

NONFORFEITURE OPTIONS

nonforfeiture benefit

Most companies give an applicant for long-term care insurance the right to elect a nonforfeiture benefit. Indeed, the offering of such a benefit is required by some states, the NAIC model legislation, and the requirements for a federally tax-qualified policy. With a *nonforfeiture benefit*, the policyowner will receive some value for a policy if the policy lapses because the required premium is not paid in the future.

The most common type of nonforfeiture option, and the one almost always available in tax-qualified policies, is a shortened benefit period. With this option, coverage is continued as a paid-up policy, but the length of the benefit period (or the amount of the benefit if stated as a maximum dollar amount) is reduced. Under the typical provision, the reduced coverage is available only if the lapse is on or after the policy's third anniversary. The amount of the benefit is equal to the greater of the total premiums paid for the policy prior to lapse or 30 times the policy's daily nursing home benefit.

return-of-premium rider

Some policies offer a *return-of-premium rider*, under which a portion of the premium is returned, usually if a policyowner dies after a specified number of years. For example, one insurer's policy pays nothing if the insured dies before the policy has been in force for 5 full years. Fifteen percent of the total premiums paid are returned if the policy was in force for 6 years, 30 percent for 7 years, 45 percent for 8 years, 60 percent for 9 years, and 80 percent for 10 or more years. Other insurers may refund as much as 100 percent of the premiums paid. There are also some policies that refund all premiums paid if the insured dies before age 65; after age 65, the percentage of the premiums refunded gradually decreases to 0 over a period of time, such as 10 years. Depending on the insurer, any benefits paid while coverage was in force may or may not be deducted from the refund.

**contingent
nonforfeiture
benefit**

The NAIC model legislation and an increasing number of states that require an insurer to offer a nonforfeiture benefit also stipulate that a policy must contain a *contingent nonforfeiture benefit* (also called a contingent benefit upon lapse) if the policyowner does not purchase the nonforfeiture benefit. Some insurers also include this provision in their contracts even when it is not required. The provision gives the policyowner the right to elect certain options each time the insurer increases the premium rate to a level that results in a cumulative increase of the annual premium equal to or exceeding a specified percentage of the premium at the time of policy issue. The percentage is a sliding scale determined by the issue age. For example, the percentage is 130 if the policy was issued when the insured was 45 to 49 and 110 at issue ages 50 to 54. The figure continues to drop to 70 percent for an issue age of 60, 40 percent for an issue age of 70, and 20 percent for an issue age of 80. The options are a reduction in benefits to a level sustainable by the current premium or the conversion of the policy to a paid-up status with a shorter benefit period. The policyowner must be notified of the rate increase and of these options prior to the increase, usually either 30 or 45 days. However, the policyowner is not required to select either of these options and can continue to pay the higher premium and maintain the current policy benefits.

PREMIUMS

In discussing the premiums payable for a long-term care insurance policy, it is necessary to look at the premium-payment period, the mode of payment, and provisions for waiver of premium and a grace period. In addition, the provisions for reinstating a lapsed policy must be addressed.

Premium-Payment Period

The majority of long-term care insurance policies have premiums that are payable for life and determined by the insured's age at the time of issue. For example, a policy may have an annual cost of $800 at the time of purchase. Assuming the policy is guaranteed renewable, this premium will not change unless it is raised on a class basis. A few insurers, however, promise not to raise premiums for a specified period after a policy has been written, such as 3, 5, or 10 years. In the past, guaranteed renewable policies were often advertised as being "level premium." This is misleading because premiums may be (and in some cases have been) increased by class. As a result, the current NAIC model act prohibits the use of this term unless a policy is noncancelable, which means that rates cannot increase.

In recent years, insurers have increasingly begun to offer accelerated (or limited) premium-payment periods. These shorter periods, which result in higher annual premiums, are popular with many applicants who want to have their policies paid for prior to retirement. They are also popular in executive incentive packages if the employer pays all the premiums for an executive's long-term care insurance. Some of the options include the following:

- a single-premium option, which is a one-time payment
- a higher first-year premium and a reduced premium thereafter
- a paid-up-at-65 option under which the policyowner pays an annual premium until he or she reaches age 65
- a higher premium until age 65 and a reduced premium thereafter
- a shortened payment period, such as 5, 10, or 20 years

Once these premiums are paid, the policy is paid up and no subsequent premiums are required to keep it in force.

With premiums paid on an accelerated basis, the policyowner has a lot to lose if the policy terminates in a short period of time because of either death or cancellation. As a result, some states require that an accelerated payment period of a short length, such as 10 years or less, be accompanied by some type of return-of-premium rider or nonforfeiture benefit.

Mode of Payment

Premiums for long-term care insurance policies are normally expressed in terms of annual premiums. Regardless of the length of the premium-payment period, the policyowner is normally given the option of paying the annual premium in semi-annual, quarterly, or monthly installments.

Waiver of Premium

waiver-of-premium provision

Most long-term care insurance policies contain a *waiver-of-premium provision*, under which the policyowner does not have to pay premiums after the insured has begun to receive benefit payments or has received them for a period of time. While the premiums are being waived, the policy remains fully in force.

Unlike the similar provisions in life insurance and many other types of health insurance, there are a variety of conditions that might apply to the waiver-of-premium provision for long-term care insurance:

- Some policies begin waiving premiums at the time the elimination period has been satisfied. Other policies do not waive premiums until the insured has been collecting benefits under the policy for a period of time, such as 30, 60, or most commonly 90 days. Most, but not all, policies require that this period consist of consecutive days. Still a third possibility is that premiums will be waived after a specified period during which the insured has been receiving long-term care, regardless of the length of the elimination period. In this case, it might be possible for the premium waiver to begin before the elimination period is satisfied.

- Many comprehensive policies waive premiums if the insured is receiving benefit payments either in an institution or at home. Waiver of premium when care is received at home may have specific restrictions, however. For example, one insurer waives premiums after the insured has been confined in a long-term care facility for 90 days. Premiums are also waived after 90 days of benefits for home health care but only if the care had been received for at least 5 days per week. Further restrictions often apply to waiver of premium when covered services are received outside the United States.

- The waiver of premiums usually ceases when the insured is no longer receiving daily benefits under the policy. However, some policies waive the premiums for the life of the insured, even if the insured recovers from the condition that resulted in the need for long-term care.

- Some policies waive the premiums for both spouses if either spouse is receiving benefits as long as each spouse is insured with the same company. A few policies contain a provision, often called a survivorship benefit, that waives the premium for a surviving spouse after the other spouse dies as long as the company insured both spouses and the policy had been in force for a certain period of time, such as 10 years.

Grace Period

Most policies have a 31-day grace period. This means that the premium can be paid any time within 31 days after it is due; during this time, the policy will remain in force. If the premium is not paid within the grace period, however, the policy will lapse at that time unless an alternate premium payer has been named.

To prevent the inadvertent lapse of a policy, particularly by an elderly person, the NAIC model legislation requires that the applicant be given the option of designating a third party to receive notification of the cancellation of a long-term care insurance policy for nonpayment of premium. This designee is sometimes referred to as an alternate premium payer. The provision requires the insurer, after the premium is overdue by at least 30 days, to notify both the policyowner and the designee that (1) the premium is overdue and (2) the policy will lapse at the beginning of the 36th day after the notice is mailed unless the premium is paid prior to that time. (Note: Technically, the insured is given 30 additional days to pay the overdue premium after the notification is received. However, the mailing period for the receipt of the notification is deemed to be 5 days.)

Some insurers allow an applicant to name two or three alternate designees.

Reinstatement

Another provision to protect the insured is a requirement that an insurer reinstate a lapsed policy within a specified period following the lapse if the insurer receives proof that the insured was cognitively impaired or had a loss of functional capacity at the time the premium was due. The NAIC requires that this period be at least 5 months, but some insurers use a somewhat longer period. The reinstatement is retroactive to the date of lapse and made without the insured's having to show any evidence of insurability. However, any overdue premiums must be paid.

If a policy lapses for any other reason, reinstatement is at the insurer's option. Most policies provide that the policy can be reinstated if the insurer accepts the overdue premiums without an application. In most cases, however, the insurer will require a new application, and the applicant will again be subject to underwriting. If the insurer decides to reinstate the policy, the reinstatement date will be the date the insurer approves the reinstatement application. Policies also state that if no approval is received within a specified period of the receipt of the premium paid, such as 45 days, the policy will be reinstated at that time unless the policyowner has been notified that the application has been disapproved. Benefits are provided only for long-term care that is received on or after the date of reinstatement.

RENEWABILITY

Long-term care policies currently being sold are almost always guaranteed renewable, which means that an individual's coverage cannot be canceled except for nonpayment of premiums. Although premiums cannot be raised on the basis of a particular applicant's claim, they can (and sometimes are) raised by class.

Insurers are allowed to issue policies that are noncancelable, but very few policies of this nature are written because of the uncertain nature of future claim costs.

CLAIMS

At some point, many insureds will file claims under a long-term care insurance policy, which spells out the procedures that must followed. The insured's failure to follow any necessary procedures may jeopardize the receipt of benefit payments and the ability to bring legal actions against the insurance company if disputes arise. Claim provisions fall into several categories, including notification of loss, proof of loss, and the payment of benefits. In the following discussion, the term *insured* is used. However, in many cases, the insured will be incapacitated and the necessary duties of complying with claim provisions will fall to the insured's legal representative.

Notification of Loss

The insured must first notify the insurer that a claim is being made. Policies often specify that notification be within 180 days after a covered service starts or as soon as reasonably possible. In most cases, the notification will be by telephone, and policies often contain the telephone number to call. Many insurers also want written notification of a claim. Some insurers initially do little other than send the claim forms to the insured with instructions to have them completed and returned to the insurer. However, many insurers are proactive and work with the insured to see that all necessary paperwork is properly completed. At this time, the insurer often provides the services of a care coordinator to help evaluate the insured's needs and determine the best setting for care.

Proof of Loss

The insurer will require a written proof of loss. Most policies state that no claim will be paid unless a proof-of-loss form is filed within a specified time, often 1 year after the start of covered services, unless the insured is legally unable to do so. The proof of loss requires a physician or other licensed health care practitioner to certify that the insured meets the conditions to qualify for benefits. For a tax-qualified policy, this means that the insured meets the HIPAA definition for being chronically ill.

At various times during the claim-paying period, the insurer may require verification that the insured still satisfies the criteria for benefits. The insurer also reserves the right, at its own expense, to have the insured examined as may be reasonably necessary during the course of a claim.

Payment of Benefits

Once the elimination period is satisfied, benefits are payable as soon as the insurance company receives the required proof of loss. The insured is entitled to the benefit payments, but they can generally be assigned to others, such as providers of care. Assignment reduces the family's involvement in handling financial matters. However, benefit payments cannot be paid, assigned, or pledged as collateral for a loan.

15

Underwriting of Long-Term Care Insurance

Chapter Outline

Chapter 5 is devoted to the underwriting of medical expense insurance. The basic concept of underwriting described in that chapter also applies to long-term care insurance. However, there are some underwriting considerations for long-term care insurance that are either different or unique. These pertain to classification factors, selection factors, sources of information, final underwriting action, and underwriting policy changes.

CLASSIFICATION FACTORS

As mentioned in chapter 5, an underwriter must classify and select applicants for insurance. Age, underwriting class, marital status, and use of tobacco are particularly important for long-term care insurance.

Age

Age is an important factor in determining rates for long-term care insurance for two reasons. First, the older an applicant is, the sooner long-term care is likely to be needed. Second, the younger an applicant is, the longer the insurer is likely to collect premiums before a claim occurs.

Significant variations exist among insurance companies with respect to the age at which they will issue policies. At a minimum, a person between the ages of 40 and 79 is eligible for coverage from almost all insurance companies. Most companies also have an upper age in the range of 84 to 89, beyond which coverage is not issued. Restrictive policy provisions and very high premiums often accompany coverage written at age 85 or older when available.

Underwriting Class

Each insurer has one or more underwriting classes for long-term care insurance. Some insurers have a single class; all applicants are either accepted and charged the rate for that class or declined for coverage. Other insurers have a series of underwriting classes that have different rate structures. The insured's medical condition determines the class into which he or she falls. Even with several underwriting classes, there are still applicants who will be unacceptable to the insurer. As explained later, it is often the agent who determines the underwriting classification used when an application is initially submitted.

Marital Status

Most insurers offer a spousal discount. Experience has shown that long-term care claims from married persons are less frequent and of shorter duration than claims from single or widowed persons. This favorable claim experience results because many married couples take care of each other for as long as possible before long-term care services are needed. Some insurers give a spousal discount, which may be 20 to 30 percent or more, only if they insure both spouses; other insurers may also give a discount (10 percent, for example) to anyone who lives with his or her spouse.

Insurers may also apply these discounts to siblings who live together and/or to unmarried couples who have committed relationships.

Tobacco Use versus Nonuse

As mentioned in chapter 5, the use of tobacco is a significant health hazard. Not only does it affect medical expense claims, but it also results in an increased need for long-term care. Therefore, tobacco use may disqualify a person for an insurer's preferred rate class or require placement in a higher rate class.

SELECTION FACTORS

After an applicant is classified, the underwriter looks at other factors to determine whether the company should offer insurance to the applicant. For long-term care insurance, the major factor is medical condition. The insured's lifestyle and the existence of other insurance are also concerns.

Medical Condition

Medical history and current physical status, which constitute a person's medical condition, are basic indicators of the probability of future problems that may require long-term care services. As a result, medical evaluation of an applicant requires a great deal of underwriting skill and judgment. Evaluation begins with the applicant's and agent's statements on the application form. The evaluation may continue in one of several ways depending on the information in the application. The actual underwriting process is described in more detail in a later section of this chapter.

It is important to point out that long-term care insurance is a relatively new type of insurance, and many potential claims from existing policies have yet to occur. Therefore, the underwriter must use a greater degree of subjectivity and conservatism than is necessary for many other types of insurance for which decades of claim experience is available. As a result, significant variations exist among the underwriting standards of long-term care insurers with respect to the evaluation of medical conditions.

Insured's Lifestyle

There are certain lifestyle factors that tend to have a bearing on the frequency and severity of claims. Two of these—marital status and tobacco use—were mentioned earlier and are so significant that they affect the premium the insured pays. Other factors are more subjective. For example, an underwriter may want to know if an applicant lives in a house or condominium. Such persons are less likely to move to a long-term care facility than persons who rent an apartment. The same is true of single or widowed persons who have support from family and friends. Evidence also indicates that a person who works, drives, has hobbies, or participates in social, recreational, and volunteer activities is less likely to need long-term care in the near term than a person who leads a much less active lifestyle.

Duplicate Coverage

As mentioned in chapter 13, the NAIC model legislation requires the insurer to obtain information about any long-term care insurance currently in force or in force during the prior 12 months. In addition, the applicant must state whether the new policy is intended to replace an existing policy. Even without the NAIC requirements, many underwriters would still want information about duplicate coverage, because it may result in overinsurance and provide an incentive for the insured to profit from the utilization of benefits.

SOURCES OF INFORMATION

The underwriter must select those applicants that are within the insurer's range of acceptability, as determined by the insurer's underwriting objectives for the types of policies issued and the claims experience anticipated. In the process of determining insurability, the underwriter relies on many sources of available information. These fall into four broad categories:

- the application
- medical records
- telephone interviews
- face-to-face assessments

The Application

As with medical expense insurance, the long-term care insurance application is the basis for the underwriter's decision. Therefore, the application requires careful drafting to elicit truthful and complete answers from the applicant and the agent's accurate recording of all information.

Although the format of the long-term care insurance application varies among insurers, the application will contain the following to assist the underwriter in the selection process:

- applicant information
- coverage selection
- prequalification questions
- medical information
- medications taken (including starting date, dosage, and condition being treated)
- authorization to release medical information
- the agent's statement

Applicant Information

The data in this section serve primarily to identify the applicant and provide basic information, such as age, gender, birth date, address, phone number, Social Security number, and whether the spouse has long-term care coverage or is applying for coverage with the same insurer as the applicant.

The applicant must give the name, address, and phone number of his or her primary care physician. Information about the applicant's height and weight is also solicited. This is an indicator of general health; many insurers tell agents not to submit an application from someone who is significantly underweight or overweight.

Example 1:	The insurer will not write coverage on a male who is 6 feet tall and weighs more than 286 pounds or less than 113 pounds.
Example 2:	The insurer has two underwriting classes with weight ranges for each class. The insurer requires that a woman who is 5 feet 4 inches tall weigh between 92 and 174 pounds to be eligible for coverage in its classification that has the lowest premiums. The insurer will write coverage for a woman of that height who weighs up to 228 pounds but at a higher premium.

Questions may also be asked to determine such lifestyle information as home ownership, whether the applicant works or drives, and the types of activities with which the applicant is involved. More recently, applications contain questions that inquire about family medical history.

Coverage Selection

In this section, the applicant selects among the benefit options available under the policy and any available riders. He or she also selects the mode of payment. This section indicates the proposed underwriting classification and specifies the initial premium. To make these determinations, the agent must understand the applicant's health status and consult the insurance company's underwriting guide. The guide lists medical conditions for which the insurer requests the agent not to submit applications, and it identifies other medical conditions, along with the underwriting class within which they are acceptable for submission. The underwriting guide also frequently states that multiple medical conditions may affect the applicant's acceptability or the underwriting class in which the applicant might be placed. In such cases, it is often suggested that the agent contact the underwriting department before submitting an application.

Example:	The insurer has four underwriting classes; class 1 has the lowest premium, and class 4 has the highest. The insurer's lengthy underwriting guide lists many conditions that make an applicant unacceptable for coverage. A few of the conditions on this list are

cerebral palsy, personality disorders, Down's syndrome, continuous use of oxygen, senility, and active tuberculosis.

The underwriting guide also lists many medical conditions and the underwriting class within which a person with that condition can be submitted. For example, an applicant with diverticulitis may be submitted under class 1. An applicant with hyperthyroidism may be submitted under class 2. An applicant who had a kidney removed because of disease may be submitted under class 3. And a diabetic applicant who uses more than 75 units of insulin a day may be submitted under class 4.

Some conditions are acceptable under different classifications, depending on severity and treatment. An applicant with asthma falls into class 1 if there have been no hospitalizations and no medication is required, into class 2 if there have been no hospitalizations in the past 2 years and only a single nonsteroidal inhaler is used, into class 3 if there has been a hospitalization within the past 2 years or steroidal inhalers are used, and into class 4 if there have been frequent attacks or more than one hospitalization in the past 2 years.

Prequalification Questions

Most applications contain a series of between four and 10 questions designed to prequalify applicants for coverage. If an applicant answers yes to any of these questions, the applicant is not eligible for coverage from that insurer. In fact, agents are often told not to submit an application for these individuals. At a minimum, most insurers will ask questions like the following:

- Do you use any medical appliances, such as a wheelchair, walker, quad (four-pronged) cane, crutches, hospital bed, dialysis machine, oxygen, or stair lift?
- Do you require the assistance or supervision of another person or device to perform everyday living activities, such as walking, bathing, dressing, eating, getting in or out of a bed or chair, or using the toilet?
- Are you currently confined in a hospital or long-term care facility, or are you receiving any type of home health care?
- Have you ever been diagnosed or treated for Alzheimer's disease, dementia, senility, any type of organic brain disorder, or Parkinson's disease?

- Have you ever been diagnosed with or tested positive for acquired immune deficiency syndrome (AIDS), AIDS-related complex (ARC), or human immunodeficiency virus (HIV)?

The list will be much longer for insurers that have stringent underwriting standards.

Medical Information

This section of the application asks several questions. At a minimum, these questions pertain to specific medical conditions. Some insurers ask additional types of questions that might reveal a higher-than-average need for long-term care in the future. A yes answer to any question requires an explanation, including information about hospitals, physicians, treatment, and medication prescribed.

Example 1:	The insurer asks only three questions about medical condition:

- In the past 2 years, have you had or been treated for angina, asthma, atrial fibrillation, stroke, chronic lung disease, osteoporosis, or joint replacement?
- In the past 2 years, have you had heart or blood vessel surgery, angioplasty, or a pacemaker inserted?
- In the past 5 years, have you had or been treated for congestive heart failure, peripheral vascular disease, alcoholism, drug abuse, or neuropathy?

Example 2:	The insurer asks questions similar to those in example 1. Additional questions are also asked:

- Within the past 5 years have you been hospitalized, confined to a nursing home, or received home health care?
- Do you currently use, or have you used within the past 2 years, a cane, walker, or wheelchair?
- Have you ever had a policy for life or health insurance declined, rated up, modified, or postponed?
- Have you ever received disability benefits of any kind?
- Within the past 12 months have you needed assistance with shopping, cleaning, cooking, laundry, or transportation?

Medications

Insurers also want information about medications the applicant takes and in many cases ask the applicant to state the conditions for which they are taking medications. The agent is usually told not to submit an application if the applicant is taking certain medications. For the most part, these are medications for the conditions that also rule out coverage under the prequalification questions.

Authorization to Release Information

Authorization statements permit the underwriter to obtain required information from outside sources to the extent responses in the application require. Specifically, the applicant authorizes a blanket release of information from health care providers, other insurance companies, and other organizations (such as MIB Group, Inc.) that have relevant personal and medical information. The applicant is also notified of, and agrees to, follow-up telephone interviews and face-to-face assessments.

These authorizations usually have an effective time limit, such as 24 or 30 months from the date an application is signed.

The Agent's Statement

Each long-term care application contains a statement that the agent must sign. The types of questions in this statement include the following:

- Did you personally interview the applicant and witness his or her signature?
- Did you observe any physical or mental impairments with respect to memory, walking, or speaking? If so, explain.
- Did you observe any tremor? If so, explain.
- Did you review the applicant's current health coverage and determine that the proposed insurance is appropriate for the applicant's needs?

State regulations usually also require the agent to list any other health insurance policies he or she has sold to the applicant within the last 5 years, whether or not the policies are in force.

Medical Records

As with medical expense insurance, an underwriter will routinely request an attending physician's statement (APS) and may also request information from MIB Group, Inc.

Telephone Interviews

Telephone interviews are very commonly conducted with applicants for long-term care insurance. In addition to verifying information and clarifying responses, telephone interviews can also be used to measure an applicant's cognitive ability. With a few basic questions, a properly trained interviewer can evaluate an applicant's memory, ability to understand questions, and sense of time and place.

Face-to-Face Assessments

An underwriter may order a face-to-face assessment of the applicant, either at the underwriter's discretion or because underwriting guidelines call for the assessment if certain medical conditions are present or if the applicant is over a specified age. A paramedical company or case management company normally performs the assessment in the applicant's home.

A face-to-face assessment may be used to determine or clarify an applicant's medical history. It may also be used to ascertain an applicant's ability to perform activities of daily living or instrumental activities of daily living. For example, one insurer routinely uses the assessment to evaluate an applicant who has had a stroke, a limb removed, or a joint replacement.

Finally, a face-to-face assessment may be used to evaluate an applicant's cognitive ability through the administration of various tests developed for this purpose.

FINAL UNDERWRITING ACTION

Underwriting information is collected until the underwriter determines that there is enough information to make a final decision. If an insurer has only one underwriting class, the decision will be to accept the application or decline coverage.

The situation is more complex if the insurer has more than one underwriting class. The insurer may accept the application as submitted or decline coverage. The insurer may also offer to accept the application in another underwriting class at a higher premium. In addition, the insurer may write coverage but under different conditions than the applicant wanted. For example, the insurer might be willing to write facility-only coverage rather than a comprehensive policy. Or the insurer might insist on a longer elimination period, lower daily benefit, or reduced maximum benefit.

When coverage is denied, this does not necessarily mean that an applicant cannot obtain long-term care insurance. Coverage may be available from another insurer with less restrictive underwriting standards. Of course, the premium might be higher. There are also situations in which a declination of coverage results from a recent medical condition. If that condition is controlled for a period of time or disappears, the insured may then qualify for coverage.

Two final points are worthy of mention. First, underwriting long-term care insurance is often not a quick process. It takes time to gather information. For example, physicians may not view the completion of an APS for an applicant as a high-priority item. As a result, a wait of 30 days or more to receive an underwriting decision is not unusual and is not necessarily an indicator that coverage will be declined. Second, underwriting action is sometimes not taken because insufficient or incomplete information is received. After a period of time, such files are closed.

UNDERWRITING POLICY CHANGES

Reunderwriting often takes place if the insured wishes to make changes in a policy. For example, an insured might want to add home health care or increase the daily or maximum policy benefits. These actions require submitting a new application that will be underwritten in a manner similar to the original application. However, the underwriting decision affects only the terms and premiums under which the additional benefits are offered. A reduction in policy benefits will usually not require additional underwriting. However, some insurers may not allow certain benefit reductions, such as dropping an inflation rider.

As long-term care policies evolve, insurers may make any new benefits available to existing policyowners. It was once common for insurers to make these benefits available without evidence of insurability but possibly at an increased premium. Today, most insurers require the submission of a new application. Underwriting again takes place, and a policy with the new benefits is issued if the insured meets the insurer's current underwriting standards.

16

Consumers and Long-Term Care Insurance

Chapter Outline

Like many types of insurance, long-term care insurance is a consumer product. Consumers include the public at large, those who decline coverage (referred to later as nonbuyers), and those who purchase or are in the process of purchasing long-term care insurance. Just as with homeowners insurance, automobile insurance, and other health insurance products, consumers must perceive long-term care insurance as offering needed financial protection. In addition, the product must be affordable and understandable so that consumers can make intelligent choices among policies and policy options and be satisfied with their purchase.

Making long-term care insurance appealing to consumers is especially important because of the product's market challenge. Persons who are more able to pay the premiums and obtain coverage because they are working and younger perceive less need to protect themselves from the consequences of a financial risk they often believe is distant. Persons who feel a greater need for the insurance are frequently less able to pay premiums and obtain coverage because they are often retired, older, and more likely to have chronic medical conditions.

In the final analysis, success requires that, over time, long-term care insurance play a meaningful role in meeting the financial need of long-term care for many (if not most) Americans, especially those who are elderly. In the meantime, progress toward that goal can be measured by the growth in the number of policies issued and increases in covered services and benefit levels. On one hand, consumers need the availability of an easily understood process to select policies and policy features. On the other hand, consumers must be able to tailor the product to their specific needs, resources, and preferences. Unfortunately, these two objectives are often in conflict.

This chapter discusses consumers and long-term care insurance as they relate to consumer attitudes toward long-term care insurance, the purchasers and purchase patterns of available policies, and the decision-making process in the selection of coverage, benefits, and other policy features.

CONSUMER ATTITUDES

Long-term care insurance is a relatively new product developed to meet a real and growing risk that is gradually surfacing in the public's consciousness. Consumer attitudes toward long-term care insurance grow out of their perceptions of the potential need for long-term care and the means to pay for it as much as from their perceptions of the long-term care insurance products themselves. Surveys show that many consumers are significantly uninformed.

Considerable consumer education is required to increase public awareness of the likely need for long-term care, correct broadly held misconceptions on how to pay for it, and provide an understanding of the value of long-term care insurance. This education, essential to informed decision making, is ongoing; progress has been made in many areas. Indeed, as the following discussion points out, consumers are much more informed today than previously.

Perceptions of the Need for Long-Term Care

Unless individuals believe they are likely to need long-term care sometime in their lives and to be personally responsible for the high cost associated with it, they will not seek an insurance plan to protect themselves. Many Americans are not looking for a solution to a problem they do not perceive. Most people give the need for long-term care very little or no thought, and only 12 percent claim to give it a great deal of thought. Interestingly, over two-thirds are unconcerned or only somewhat concerned about affording long-term care in the future.[1] However, there are signs of growing awareness.

A recent survey reports an increased perception of the need for long-term care among nonbuyers, defined as those who chose not to buy long-term care insurance after a solicitation and presentation of policy details. From 1990 to 2000, the percentage of such nonbuyers who believed they had a greater than 50 percent chance of needing nursing home care in their lifetimes more than doubled, increasing from 27 percent to 55 percent. Comparable statistics for home health care went from 31 percent to 56 percent.[2]

(Note that many statistics in this chapter are based on surveys that use 2000 data. Many of these surveys are conducted at 5-year intervals, and new surveys with 2005 data should be available in 2006.)

Perceptions of Available Means of Payment

Consumers also have significant misconceptions about the financial aspects of long-term care, including its cost, sources of payment, and available insurance coverage.

Cost of Care and Sources of Payment

Americans, including many who profess at least some familiarity with long-term care services, often do not know what long-term care services cost. For example, a majority significantly underestimates the cost of nursing home care.[3] Not surprisingly, consumers also have a limited understanding of how long-term care costs are paid.

Most people believe Medicare covers nursing home stays for 3 months or more for age-related or other chronic conditions. In fact, Medicare does not cover extended nursing home stays for such conditions. Four in 10 erroneously believe Medicare covers assisted living.[4] In addition, nonbuyers of long-term care insurance are more than twice as likely as buyers to agree with the statement that . . . "the government will pay for the cost of long-term care if services are ever needed."[5]

However, some misconceptions are giving way to reality. The percentage of nonbuyers who cite their belief that Medicare and Medicaid will pay for long-term care services as an important or very important reason for not buying coverage has declined from almost 60 percent to less than 25 percent over the 10-year period from 1990 to 2000. Indeed, 85 percent of nonbuyers and more than three-quarters of other surveyed individuals who generally have less experience with long-term care policies agree with the following statement: "Whatever health reforms come about in the next few years, it is more likely that individuals will have to rely on themselves to plan and pay for long-term care."[6]

Perceived Insurance Coverage

Many Americans believe they have long-term care coverage, when in reality they do not. Surveys indicate that from 25 to 30 percent of Americans claim to have some type of long-term care coverage. On closer examination, only one-quarter of this group actually has coverage through a specific long-term care insurance policy or the availability of an accelerated death benefit. More than half (54 percent) of those claiming to have coverage mistakenly believe that their medical insurance pays for long-term care. Among the remainder of this group, there are erroneous assumptions about coverage under disability income insurance and Medicare supplement insurance, as well as Medicare and Medicaid.[7]

Because so many people mistakenly believe they are already covered for long-term care or simply do not know how long-term care services will be paid, one study concludes that this may explain, in large part, why the market for long-term care insurance has not grown more quickly than it has.[8]

Perceptions of Long-Term Care Insurance Policies

Industry reports document that there is a growing awareness of long-term care insurance policies. In 1995, approximately 40 percent of those surveyed from the general population were aware of insurers that offered long-term care policies. By 2000, that recognition level was over 60 percent. Significantly, in 2000, almost half of this group had been approached to buy long-term care insurance or had considered buying it, nearly twice as many as in 1995.[9]

Although awareness and even interest in long-term care and long-term care insurance is increasing, in most cases it is insufficient to motivate consumers to purchase the product. The reluctance to purchase long-term care insurance, even among those who are aware of it, has many reasons. Undoubtedly, many of these reasons are based on a lack of understanding about long-term care and the sources to pay for it. There are also other reasons that can generally be grouped as psychological/emotional considerations and practical considerations.

Psychological/Emotional Considerations

More than one industry report points out that many Americans are simply ignoring the long-term care issue, even when they are realistic about the likelihood of needing long-term care and being affected by its financial ramifications.[10] Researchers attempt explanations. Some believe that reluctance to purchase coverage continues to be a matter of awareness and that long-term care insurance is simply an undiscovered necessity for some people. Other researchers believe that many older adults are in denial. Indeed, some study participants expressly admit they are ignoring the issue.[11] Just the consideration of their dependency and the loss of dignity associated with long-term care may repel those who are healthy and physically active from thinking realistically about the protection being offered. More important, they do not see that coverage for these services makes any real difference to them in the quality of care they can expect to receive.

Another group of researchers observe that, in spite of more recent restrictions, Medicaid's rules remain generous and flexible, and typical middle-class elderly persons who need long-term nursing home care can qualify for public benefits even without elaborate Medicaid planning. Because Medicaid provides a safety net, it is argued that many individuals can effectively ignore the financial risk of long-term care. Thus, these researchers conclude that trying to overcome consumer reluctance to purchase long-term care insurance by emphasizing asset protection is misplaced. In the current Medicaid environment, only an emphasis on access to quality care that long-term care insurance provides can be effective.[12]

Practical Considerations

There are important practical considerations that make people reluctant to purchase long-term care insurance. Although cost is the biggest obstacle, there are other challenges, such as those related to confusion and credibility.

Cost. Cost in terms of premiums appears to be the greatest practical obstacle to the purchase of long-term care insurance. In many cases, consumers unfamiliar with actual long-term care insurance premiums overestimate the premiums by as much as 5 to 10 times because they assume the cost of care is the cost of coverage. Consumers in this category become more interested in coverage when informed of actual premiums.[13]

In addition, over 80 percent of nonbuyers, who by definition are presented with detailed policy information, consistently report that cost remains the most significant barrier to purchase. Less than 20 percent of nonbuyers would pay the premium for policies selling to their age group. Thus, typical nonbuyers are assumed to believe that the policy value is less than its cost, or they are not convinced of or do not understand the value of the policy relative to its cost.[14]

Confusion. Industry reports consistently identify what can only be labeled as confusion about evaluating policies and the many options and features that accompany them. In addition to the complexity of long-term care insurance, financial planning experts' mixed messages about its value and the timing of its purchase have heightened consumer confusion. There is reason to be optimistic, however, because this situation, while by no means satisfactory, is improving significantly. In 1990, 87 percent of nonbuyers indicated an important or very important reason in their decision not to buy long-term care insurance was confusion that prevented them from determining which policy was appropriate. By 2000, this figure had dropped by almost half to 46 percent.[15]

Credibility. The lack of trust consumers have in the integrity of insurers and their representatives relates to the issue of confusion. Here, too, there is reason to be optimistic because confidence is growing in the integrity of insurance companies that provide long-term care insurance. In 1990, over 70 percent of nonbuyers did not believe that companies would pay benefits as stated in the policy; in 2000, this figure had dropped to 44 percent.[16]

PURCHASERS AND PURCHASE PATTERNS OF AVAILABLE POLICIES

Over 6.2 million Americans currently have long-term care coverage.[17] Approximately 68 percent or 4.2 million persons obtain this coverage through individual policies of long-term care insurance. The balance are covered under group plans, which an employer or association group may sponsor.[18] Nearly 30 percent, a percentage that is growing, have employer-sponsored long-term care insurance plans, with around 2 percent covered under association group plans.[19] The characteristics of purchasers and their purchase patterns, reflected in the policy design features buyers select, reveal important insights into the consumer/purchaser attitudes toward long-term care insurance.

Purchasers

People with long-term care insurance coverage share many characteristics. They are typically older, more affluent, and more highly educated than the general population. They are also somewhat more likely to be married, and in the vast majority of cases, each spouse has coverage. About 56 percent of the population with long-term care insurance are women.[20]

In contrast to the general population (discussed earlier), people with long-term care coverage are significantly more realistic with respect to the need for long-term care and their personal responsibility to pay for it. Virtually all insureds agree that it is important to plan now for the possibility of needing long-term care services sometime in the future. As might be expected, they do not look to the government and other types of health insurance as major payment sources for long-term care services. Buyers generally have the same objectives in deciding to acquire long-term care coverage. Protecting assets, leaving an estate, preserving financial independence, and guaranteeing the affordability of needed services are their most important reasons for obtaining coverage.[21] Easing the long-term care burden on one's family and choice of long-term care providers are also important considerations.

Purchase Patterns of Individual Policies

Studies show that the purchase patterns of buyers of individual long-term care insurance policies vary by income and age. Changes in purchase patterns have occurred over time and are likely to continue. Employer-sponsored plans exhibit their own purchase patterns.

Table 16-1 presents the policy design choices and premiums paid by individual long-term care insurance buyers by income levels.

Not surprisingly, as income increases, individuals are more likely to buy policies at higher premium levels with greater coverage, benefit levels, and additional features. Elimination periods are an exception to this rule because they are longer for those at higher income levels, presumably because these insureds can more easily afford to pay for the initial periods of long-term care out-of-pocket. Table 16-2 profiles by age the same policy choices and premium levels in table 16-1.

Older buyers tend to purchase less coverage, lower benefits, and fewer optional features. Age and income factors are interrelated, and both are often present in many decisions. For example, older individuals pay a much higher premium than their younger counterparts, usually at a time in their lives when they are retired and their incomes are lower. Thus, those who lack home care coverage tend to be older insureds.[22] Older buyers also tend to select shorter benefit durations and/or lower daily benefit amounts and are less likely to buy the automatic inflation-protection feature. This may be a rational choice for these buyers, who expect to access benefits sooner than younger insureds and anticipate that inflation will be less of a problem.

Table 16-3 shows how purchase patterns change over time.

Overall, coverage, benefits, and the purchase of optional features have increased during the period shown in table 16-3—in some cases significantly. Despite this growth, premiums reflect a surprisingly small increase, averaging only 11 percent over the period from 1995 to 2000.[23] More recently, however, premiums are increasing more rapidly. In 2004, new insureds paid on average an annual individual policy premium of $1,924, a 6 percent increase over 2003. During the same period, all individual insureds paid $1,612, a 3 percent increase over the previous year.[24]

Variations for Employer-Sponsored Coverage

Purchasers who obtain coverage through employer-sponsored plans often choose policy characteristics that differ from those of individual buyers, largely because, on average, these purchasers are younger (in their 40s versus their 60s). Table 16-4 shows these differences. On average, new insureds with an employer-sponsored plan paid an annual premium of $522. The low and declining average annual premium for group coverage is undoubtedly due to the increasingly younger population of insureds under employer-sponsored plans.[25]

TABLE 16-1
Key Policy Design Parameters Chosen by Individual Long-Term Care Insurance Buyers, by Level of Income

Policy Features	Level of Income			
	Less than $20,000	$20,000–$34,999	$35,000–$49,999	$50,000 and Over
Benefit Duration				
Average	3.7 years	4.6 years	4.8 years	6.2 years
1–2 years	37%	22%	21%	9%
3–4 years	42	45	42	33
5–6 years	12	11	14	18
Lifetime	10	21	24	40
Nursing Home Benefit Amount				
Average	$95	$96	$98	$117
Up to $40	5%	4%	2%	2%
$41–$50	3	7	8	2
$51–$70	8	11	11	8
$71–$90	19	10	11	10
$91 and Over	66	67	68	80
Home Care Benefit Amount				
Average	$95	$92	$98	$113
Up to $40	5%	2%	1%	2%
$41–$50	7	11	10	6
$51–$70	10	13	7	6
$71–$90	15	14	13	13
$91 and Over	64	60	68	73
Percentage with Inflation Protection	31%	31%	37%	53%
Average Elimination Period	60 days	61 days	72 days	70 days
Percentage with Home Care	86%	80%	79%	95%
Average Annual Premium	$1,656	$1,675	$1,619	$1,860
Monthly Premiums				
Up to $50	6%	7%	10%	3%
$51–$75	22	18	15	14
$76–$100	7	15	18	15
$101–$125	24	13	14	16
$126–$150	12	12	8	12
$151 and Over	29	35	35	40

Source: Health Insurance Association of America.[26]

The younger ages of buyers of employer-sponsored coverage, combined with generally higher income levels, enable these buyers to purchase more comprehensive coverage, higher benefits, and more other features than individual buyers at less than half the individual premium.

TABLE 16-2
Key Policy Design Parameters Chosen by Individual Long-Term Care Insurance Buyers, by Age

Policy Features	Age Category			
	55–64	65–69	70–74	75 and Over
Benefit Duration				
Average	6.4 years	5.3 years	4.8 years	3.7 years
1–2 years	11%	18%	20%	31%
3–4 years	29	37	44	51
5–6 years	15	16	14	8
Lifetime	45	29	22	10
Nursing Home Benefit Amount				
Average	$117	$108	$104	$95
Up to $40	1%	1%	2%	6%
$41–$50	2	7	9	8
$51–$70	7	11	9	11
$71–$90	8	9	14	14
$91 and Over	82	72	66	61
Home Care Benefit Amount				
Average	$113	$105	$97	$95
Up to $40	1%	2%	4%	3%
$41–$50	5	6	9	8
$51–$70	8	7	11	11
$71–$90	12	12	15	15
$91 and Over	74	73	61	63
Percentage Choosing Inflation Protection	59%	46%	32%	14%
Average Elimination Period	62 days	69 days	72 days	66 days
Percentage with Home Care	92%	85%	85%	77%
Average Annual Premium	$1,213	$1,487	$1,829	$2,581
Monthly Premiums				
Up to $50	8%	7%	4%	2%
$51–$75	28	16	10	4
$76–$100	20	19	14	5
$101–$125	19	16	12	13
$126–$150	9	14	10	10
$151 and Over	17	28	50	66

Source: Health Insurance Association of America.[27]

CONSUMER DECISIONS

Consumers are faced with many decisions when purchasing long-term care insurance. Helping them make these decisions intelligently requires that insurance agents and other financial advisors have the knowledge to guide

TABLE 16-3
Individual Long-Term Care Insurance Policy Designs Selling in 2000, 1995, and 1990

Attributes of Policies	Percentage of 2000 Sales	Percentage of 1995 Sales	Percentage of 1990 Sales
Types of Policies Sold			
Nursing Home Only	14%	33%	63%
Comprehensive Policies	77	61	37
Home Care Only	9	6	—
Nursing Home Duration			
1–2 years	17%	24%	23%
3 years	23	20	12
4 years	14	18	15
5 years	11	6	12
6 years	5	2	5
Lifetime Benefits	30	30	33
Average Duration	5.5 years	5.1 years	5.6 years
Nursing Home Daily Benefit			
Up to $30	1%	1%	2%
$31–$59	5	12	25
$60–$89	17	40	51
$90–$119	43	38	18
$120 and Over	34	9	4
Average Daily Benefit	$109	$85	$72
Home Health Care Duration			
1 year	5%	20%	N/A
2 years	14	31	
3 years	22	21	
4 years	13	5	
5 years	10	10	
6 years	7	1	
Lifetime Benefits	30	12	
Average Duration	5.4 years	3.4 years	
Home Health Care Daily Benefit			
Up to $30	1%	3%	25%
$31–$59	8	26	60
$60–$89	17	33	13
$90–$119	41	31	2
$120 and Over	33	8	—
Average Daily Benefit	$106	$78	$36
Elimination Period			
0 days	23%	28%	25%
15–20 days	3	17	41
30–60 days	16	16	12
90–100 days	55	39	22
More than 100 days	3	—	—

Table 16-3 continues on next page.

TABLE 16-3 (continued)
Individual Long-Term Care Insurance Policy Designs Selling in 2000, 1995, and 1990

Attributes of Policies	Percentage of 2000 Sales	Percentage of 1995 Sales	Percentage of 1990 Sales
Percentage Choosing Inflation Protection	41%	33%	40%
Simple	17	14	N/A
Compound	22	15	
Indexed to Consumer Price Index	2	4	
Total Annual Premium			
Up to $500	5%	10%	19%
$500–$999	24	29	40
$1,000–$1,499	26	23	21
$1,500–$1,999	18	15	11
$2,000–$2,499	9	9	5
Greater than $2,500	18	14	4
Average Annual Premium	$1,677	$1,505	$1,071

Source: Health Insurance Association of America.[28]

consumers through the maze of questions that must be answered. These questions include the following:

- Is coverage appropriate?
- When should coverage be purchased?
- Is it better to purchase a tax-qualified policy or a non-tax-qualified policy?
- Is it better to purchase a per diem policy or a reimbursement policy?
- What types of coverage should be purchased?
- What is the appropriate amount of coverage?
- What is the best way to plan for future inflation?
- Is a nonforfeiture option needed?
- How should policies be compared?
- What are the considerations for switching policies?
- How should premiums be paid?
- How can insurers be evaluated?

Long-term care insurance is relatively expensive, and for many consumers the amount of premium they will pay is an important factor. As the following discussion addresses each of the above questions, it takes cost considerations into account when appropriate. The closing sections of this chapter summarize and expand upon these cost considerations.

TABLE 16-4

Policy Design Characteristics in the Long-Term Care Group and Individual Markets

Policy Characteristics	Group Market	Individual Market
Policy Type		
Nursing Home Only	3%	14%
Comprehensive		
(Nursing Home and Home Care)	97	77
Home Care Only	—	9
Average Daily Benefit Amount		
Nursing Home	$124	$109
Home Care	$ 79	$106
Average Elimination Period (NH & HC)	63 days	65 days
0 days	5%	23%
30 days	36	12
60 days	3	6
90 days	56	59
Average Benefit Duration	6.3 years*	5.5 years
Nursing Home Duration		
1–2 years	10%	17%
3–5 years	51	48
6–9 years	—	5
10 years to lifetime	39	30
Home Care Benefit Duration		
1–2 years	6%	19%
3–5 years	21	44
6–9 years	21	7
10 years to lifetime	52	30
Percentage with Inflation Protection**	88%	41%
Simple	—	17
Compound	40	22
CPI Indexed	—	2
Future Increase Options	48	—
Percentage with Nonforfeiture**	29%	Less than1%
Return of Premium	2	
Shortened Benefit	26	
Other	1	
None	71	
Average Annual Premium	$722	$1,677

Table 16-4 continues on next page.

In the final analysis, however, many of these questions do not have precise answers. The way in which they will be answered lies with the consumer's personal preferences.

TABLE 16-4 (continued)
Policy Design Characteristics in the Long-Term Care Group and Individual Markets

Source: Health Insurance Association of America.[29]

*Average benefit durations are calculated based on the total benefit cap and the chosen daily benefit amount. Because home care benefits were typically chosen as a percentage of nursing home benefits, the amount of time needed to exhaust the total benefit pool when using home care benefits is typically greater. For home care benefits, we calculate the average benefit duration to be 7.6 years.

Note: For the purposes of determining average policy duration, lifetime policy durations were set to 10 years. Elimination periods for the individual market were adjusted to fit the closed categories for the group market. Therefore, for the individual market, 0 days is equal to 0 days, 30 days is equal to 1–30 days, 60 days is equal to 31–60 days, and 90 days is equal to 61–100 days. The average elimination period reported for the individual market is only for nursing home benefits; however, the percentages represent both nursing home and home care benefits.

**It is important to note that this represents the percentage of enrollees with these particular policy design features. It is not possible to make a statement about whether the employee chose these options or if they were automatically included in the basic plan design chosen by the employer.

Note: All but one of the participating employers offered long-term care plans on a voluntary basis. Thus, employees were responsible for paying the entire premium if they chose to enroll. Only employees who chose to "buy up" from the employer-funded base plan were used for comparability.

Appropriateness of Coverage

The first major decision in purchasing long-term care insurance is to determine whether such coverage is appropriate to meet an individual's needs. From the standpoint of the insurer, the agent, and the financial advisor, this process is often referred to as suitability.

The NAIC Long-Term Care Insurance Model Regulation addresses the issue of suitability. The regulation requires any insurer marketing long-term care insurance to develop and use suitability standards and to train its agents to use the standards. These standards must take the following into account:

- the applicant's ability to pay for the proposed coverage and other financial information appropriate to its purchase
- the applicant's goals or needs with respect to long-term care insurance and the advantages and disadvantages of insurance to meet these goals and needs
- the values, benefits, and costs of any of the applicant's existing insurance compared to the values, benefits, and costs of the recommended purchase or replacement

The insurer or agent, if one is involved, must make a reasonable effort to obtain the preceding information. This includes the presentation to the applicant of a long-term care insurance *personal worksheet*. The information on the worksheet and the questions asked vary among insurers, based on their practices and state insurance regulations. Insurers in some states are allowed to use a brief worksheet that the applicant signs to acknowledge that he or she has considered the following information:

- the current and future obligations for keeping the policy in force
- the current costs of nursing home care, home health care, and community-based services in the area where the applicant lives
- the average use of services covered by the policy. For example, these include the average length of stay in a nursing home and the average number of home health care visits in a week.

Other states require the use of a much more comprehensive worksheet that is in line with what the model regulation recommends. Such worksheets contain information about the premium for the coverage being considered, the insurer's right to increase premiums, and the insurer's history of rate increases. Worksheets also ask the applicant to answer the following questions:

- How will you pay each year's premium—from income, from savings and investments, or with family help?
- Have you considered whether you can afford to keep the policy if the premium goes up by 20 percent?
- What is your annual income?
- How do you expect your income to change over the next 10 years—increase, decrease, or not change?
- Will you buy inflation protection? If not, have you considered how you will pay the difference between future costs and your daily benefit amount?
- What elimination period are you considering, and how do you plan to pay for your care during this period?
- Other than your home, what is the approximate value of your assets?
- How do you expect your assets to change over the next 10 years?

The applicant must sign a statement that the insurer or agent has reviewed the worksheet with him or her. In addition, the applicant must indicate that the answers to the questions describe the applicant's financial situation or that he or she chooses not to provide the information.

The insurer then compares the applicant's financial information with its suitability standards. For example, the insurer may have adopted standards that premiums should not exceed more than 7 percent of an applicant's income and that the applicant should have an annual income of at least $35,000 and assets (excluding a home and automobile) of at least $75,000. In addition, the applicant should be able to absorb an increase in future premiums of up to 30 percent.

If an applicant does not meet an insurer's suitability standards or does not choose to provide financial information, the insurer may decline the application or send the applicant a letter stating that the insurer has suspended the final review of the application. If the applicant believes the policy is what he or she wants, however, the applicant, within the next 60 days, can check the appropriate box on the letter and return it to the insurer. The insurer will then continue to review the application and issue a policy if the applicant meets its underwriting standards.

Although many persons who fail to meet the insurer's suitability standards could rely on Medicaid, there are still reasons to purchase long-term care insurance, including the following:

- the protection of assets and income, even though modest
- independence from the financial support of others
- the ability to choose where and how long-term care services are received
- the ability to avoid reliance on public assistance (Medicaid)
- peace of mind from knowing that long-term care needs are met

It is important to point out that many individuals who are unable to afford long-term care insurance may have family members who are willing to pay part or all of the cost. After all, it is these same family members who may otherwise be called upon to provide long-term care services if and when these services are needed.

Suitability standards focus on determining minimum standards for the appropriateness of long-term care insurance. There are individuals, however, for whom coverage might not be appropriate—for example, individuals who have purchased alternative types of coverage, such as residence in a continuing care retirement community. There are other individuals whose wealth makes it possible to self-fund their long-term care expenses. Nevertheless, as mentioned in chapter 12, these individuals may still have valid reasons for purchasing long-term care insurance. Finally, there are the very elderly for whom a short life expectancy and the very high cost of coverage make the purchase of long-term insurance financially questionable, assuming they are even eligible for coverage.

Time to Purchase Coverage

It can be argued that an individual is never too young to buy a long-term care insurance policy. Even a young person can need long-term care services as the result of an accident or illness. In addition, the younger an applicant is, the less likely it is that the applicant will fail to meet the insurer's under-writing standards.

Most purchasers of individual long-term care policies postpone buying coverage until they begin to near, or are past, retirement age. In some ways, this is understandable. At earlier ages, these persons still have the expenses of supporting a family and are more concerned with purchasing life insurance and disability income insurance to replace lost income should they die or become disabled.

Postponing the purchase of long-term care insurance, in addition to increasing an individual's likelihood of being uninsurable, also confronts him or her with increasing premium costs. For example, one insurer sells a tax-qualified, facility-only policy that has a $100 daily benefit, a 5-year benefit period, a 90-day elimination period, and a 5 percent compound inflation rider. The annual premium is $510 at age 50, $690 at age 55, $980 at age 60, $1,330 at age 65, and $2,000 at age 70. Moreover, as the following example shows, the situation is actually much more dramatic when the benefit amount needs to be adjusted for inflation.

Example:	Betsy, aged 50, purchased a tax-qualified comprehensive long-term care insurance policy that has an unlimited elimination period and a 5 percent compound inflation rider. Her annual premium is $1,100.
	Betsy's friend Rosemary, also aged 50, decides to wait until she turns 60 to purchase her policy even though she knows that the insurer's annual premium for an identical policy with a $100 daily benefit will be $1,900 for an insured aged 60. However, what Rosemary fails to realize is that in 10 years, Betsy's daily benefit will have increased to $163 because of the inflation rider. Therefore, a policy identical to Betsy's at that time will require Rosemary to pay a premium of $3,097 for a daily benefit of $163 at the rates for a 60-year-old. In addition, during that 10-year period, it is also possible that the insurer will make matters even worse for Rosemary by raising its premium rates.

The lower premiums at younger ages also make it financially easier for many applicants to elect broader benefits, as shown in table 16-4, which compares characteristics in the group and individual marketplaces. Note that the average annual premium is markedly lower for the group coverage. This is primarily due to the significantly younger average age at which coverage is purchased under group plans. As the table shows, this leads to insureds having higher daily benefits, shorter elimination periods, and longer benefit durations. There is also an increased likelihood that both inflation protection and nonforfeiture benefits are purchased.

Tax-Qualified versus Non-Tax-Qualified Policies

Since the passage of HIPAA, there has been disagreement over whether consumers should purchase tax-qualified or non-tax-qualified policies. However, most insurers now offer only tax-qualified policies, and these policies account for about 96 percent of long-term care insurance policies sold.[30] The two types of policies differ with respect to tax treatment and benefit triggers.

Tax Treatment

The primary reason for the predominance of tax-qualified policies seems to be their more favorable income tax treatment. As pointed out in chapter 13, a policyowner who itemizes deductions may be able to deduct a portion of the premium cost if medical expenses exceed 7.5 percent of his or her adjusted gross income. In addition, benefits are received tax free, with the possible exceptions of benefits from per diem contracts that exceed $250 per year (in 2006).

Premiums for non-tax-qualified polices are not deductible. Furthermore, there is uncertainty over the tax status of benefits received from non-tax-qualified policies. There is no specific provision in the Internal Revenue Code that allows for tax-free receipt of benefits. There are arguments that such a provision is unnecessary because the policies qualify as accident and sickness insurance, but not all tax experts agree with this position. To make matters worse, the IRS has so far not issued a ruling on this matter, and IRS employees' stated opinions have been inconsistent. With this uncertainty, many consumers naturally shy away from non-tax-qualified policies. Many agents are also reluctant to sell these policies because of the potential legal liability of selling a policy whose benefits are subject to such ambiguity. However, some advocates of non-tax-qualified policies note that an agent might be just as liable for not letting a client know about the existence of such policies.

Benefit Triggers

HIPAA requires specific benefit triggers for tax-qualified policies. Most non-tax-qualified policies have somewhat less restrictive benefit triggers that make it easier to qualify for benefits. As a result, insurers that offer both types of policies tend to have premiums that are 5 to 10 percent higher for non-tax-qualified policies.

Although the two types of policies may differ with regard to the number and types of ADLs that an insured must be unable to perform, the majority of non-tax-qualified policies use the same criteria as in tax-qualified policies. The major differences are in the time period for which an insured must be expected to be unable to perform ADLs and the use of a medical necessity trigger.

90-Day ADL Period. As mentioned in chapter 13, a chronically ill person for purposes of a tax-qualified policy must be expected to be unable to perform at least two activities of daily living for at least 90 days. Non-tax-qualified policies do not have this 90-day requirement.

Example:	Ian has a comprehensive long-term care insurance policy with a 20-day elimination period. He recently broke both his arms as a result of a freak accident. His physician certified that he would need help with several activities of daily living but only for the next 50 to 75 days.
	If Ian has a tax-qualified policy, he will not be eligible for benefits because his disability is not expected to last for at least 90 days. However, if he has a non-tax-qualified policy, he can start receiving benefits after 20 days.

Although advocates of non-tax-qualified policies often emphasize this distinction, there are those who point out that it is of little or no significance to most insureds. First, as shown in table 16-3, the majority of insureds are subject to elimination periods of 90 days or longer. For them, claim payments will begin at the same time under either type of policy. Second, as explained in earlier chapters, coverage for certain long-term care services of short duration is provided under Medicare and private medical expense insurance. (However, the coverage might not pay for the type or duration of care needed.) Finally, many insureds have the resources to pay for long-term care services for relatively short periods of time.

Medical Necessity. Perhaps a more significant distinction is that many non-tax-qualified policies use medical necessity as a benefit trigger. Such a benefit trigger is not allowed in a tax-qualified policy. From a consumer standpoint, there are individuals, particularly the frail elderly, who do not meet the benefit triggers of tax-qualified policies but who still require long-term care services.

Per Diem versus Reimbursement Policies

A consumer must decide whether to purchase a policy that pays benefits on a per diem basis or a reimbursement basis. Note, however, that most policies pay benefits on a reimbursement basis, and many insurers do not offer per diem policies.

In general, a per diem (or indemnity) policy will be 10 to 15 percent more expensive, particularly if the daily benefit is high and there is the possibility of its exceeding the actual costs that would be paid under a reimbursement policy. One advantage of a per diem policy is that if the insured receives a benefit in excess of the cost of long-term care services, he or she can use this additional money to pay extra costs associated with such services. These costs might include payments to informal caregivers, payments for prescription drugs, or family support because of lost wages. The latter, however, is better provided under some type of disability income insurance. The insured could also save the money to pay for future long-term care services that might exceed the daily benefit.

Another advantage of a per diem policy is that the claims process tends to be somewhat simpler and faster. With a reimbursement policy, the insured must submit actual invoices to the insurer in addition to verification that he or she qualifies for benefits. With a per diem policy, it is only necessary to show that eligibility for benefits has been satisfied.

In addition to a per diem policy's higher premium, benefits are subject to federal income taxation if they exceed more than $250 per day (in 2006) and are used for anything other than the payment of qualified long-term care services.

Type of Coverage

Only a few years ago, most buyers of long-term care insurance policies purchased coverage only for care in facilities like nursing homes. As shown in table 16-3, there has been a significant change in recent years, with a large majority of buyers now selecting comprehensive policies. The public has become more aware of the need for long-term care services in the home environment and wants protection for this need even though it may increase the cost of a facility-only policy by 60 to 70 percent.

There are situations in which a facility-only policy may still be appropriate, however. It is a viable alternative if cost is a consideration, particularly if there are family members or others who will provide necessary services in the home. It may also be an appropriate choice if an insured has some resources that could be used to pay for home health care services before nursing home care becomes necessary.

There are also situations in which a stand-alone home health care policy may be a logical option. For example, an individual with limited resources may wish to remain at home for as long as possible. Once the person needs nursing home care, he or she may have no qualms about relying on Medicaid. Residents of continuing care retirement communities sometimes purchase stand-alone policies so they can obtain care in their independent-living units rather than having to move to the facility's assisted-living portion.

Amount of Coverage

The decision about the amount of long-term care coverage to purchase actually involves a series of decisions about the size of the daily benefit, the elimination period, and the benefit duration. Such factors as an applicant's age, income, assets, and tolerance toward financial risk also influence the decision. There are no precise answers. Each situation is unique, and the final amount of insurance selected in many cases is a balance between what the applicant feels is appropriate and what he or she can afford.

At one extreme, an individual could purchase a policy with a daily benefit equal to the cost of long-term care services (and appropriate increases for inflation), a 0-day elimination period, and lifetime benefits. However, such a policy would be unaffordable to many applicants and is also unnecessary. Virtually all applicants have some resources that can be used to finance at least a portion of their long-term care needs. As explained in chapter 12, these resources may also include accumulated assets and financial support from family members.

Daily Benefit

The first step in selecting the proper daily benefit is to find out the cost of care in the geographic region where care might be received. It should be noted that this might be a different region from where an applicant currently lives. For example, an applicant may feel that the city where a child lives might be a more appropriate location for long-term care if it is needed.

The average daily cost for nursing home care varies significantly from one geographic region to another. For example, one study of nursing home costs shows that in 2005 the average cost was $203 for a private room and $176 for a semiprivate room.[31] However, there are significant cost differences among regions, with the average daily cost of a private room averaging $115 in Shreveport to over $500 in Alaska. Even within regions, the variations from the average cost are sometimes greater than 50 percent. Although an applicant might prefer to be in the most expensive nursing home in town, he or she might be able only to afford insurance that will pay for care in a less expensive facility. Although published averages are helpful, they are no substitute for relying on an agent who is familiar with local nursing home costs. It may also be helpful to actually visit nursing homes to determine if they are acceptable and to obtain their rates. Nursing home rates can also be obtained from the local area agencies on aging, which were established by the Older Americans Act.

Other statistics in the same study show that the hourly cost of home health care provided by a home health aide working for a licensed home care agency was $19. Again, there are significant variations from one region to another and within regions. Even with these figures in hand, an estimate must be made about the need and frequency of home health care services. For example, if around-the-clock care is needed, the cost of home health care can exceed the cost of nursing home care. Most insurers, agents, and financial planners recommend that the daily home health care benefit be equal to somewhere between 75 and 100 percent of the daily nursing home benefit. As shown in table 16-3, individual policies are near the 100 percent figure ($106 versus $109). Note, however, that reducing the percentage of home health care benefits to 80 percent of nursing home benefits will usually lower the premium about 10 percent. A decrease from 100 percent to 50 percent often results in a premium saving of 25 to 30 percent.

The next step to determine the appropriate daily benefit is to subtract the daily costs that the applicant has determined can be made from other resources.

It should be pointed out that the cost of long-term care insurance is essentially proportional to the daily benefit chosen. All other things being equal, a policy with a daily benefit of $200 per day will cost twice as much as a policy with a daily benefit of $100.

Elimination Period

As shown in table 16-4, applicants for both individual and group long-term care insurance policies have elimination periods that average just over 60 days. Averages are deceiving, however, because many applicants elect an elimination period of either 90 days or 30 days or less. If all other factors are equal, an increase in the elimination period from 20–30 days to 90–100 days will usually result in a premium saving of between 10 and 20 percent. It is necessary to balance this saving in premium against the potential cost that an insured must assume if he or she needs long-term care. For example, with a 90-day elimination period, the insured would have to pay $18,000 before benefits commence if nursing home costs are $200 per day. This figure may increase substantially by the time an insured needs long-term care several years in the future, whereas the insured's available resources remain stable or decrease during retirement years. Although the premium saving for the longer elimination period is significant, so is the potential out-of-pocket cost.

Benefit Duration

As indicated in chapter 1, the average stay in a nursing home is 2.5 years. Although different statistics are often cited, it appears that somewhere between 10 and 20 percent of nursing home stays exceed 5 years. As table 16-4 indicates, many insureds have a benefit duration that exceeds 5 years, but an even larger percentage do not. If these persons have long-term care needs that exhaust their benefits, they will need to liquidate their assets, rely on financial support from relatives, and possibly apply for Medicaid.

Ideally, a policy would have an unlimited benefit period, but the realities of cost often dictate otherwise. Many long-term care experts feel that, at a minimum, a person should have a benefit period somewhere in the neighborhood of 4 to 6 years. However, even that might be unaffordable to some insureds. As a general rule, the cost to increase a benefit period from 2 to 4 years is approximately 50 percent. Going from a 2-year benefit to a lifetime benefit requires a premium increase in the range of 70 to 80 percent.

Inflation Protection

The amount of long-term care insurance coverage may be perfectly appropriate at the time a policy is purchased. The initial amount of coverage may be inadequate in the future, however, because of the effect of inflation on long-term care costs.

Example:	Five years ago when she retired at age 65, Sylvia purchased a long-term care insurance policy with a $100 per day nursing home benefit. The policy included no increase in benefits for inflation. At that time, the benefit amount was equal to the average cost of nursing home care in her community. However, nursing home costs there have risen at a rate of 6 percent over the last 5 years, and the average nursing home cost is now $133 per day. If this inflation rate continues, daily nursing home costs will increase to $179 in another 5 years and to $240 in 10 years. Sylvia's assets are currently insufficient to cover this increase in nursing home costs if she has a nursing home stay of more than a few months.
	Sylvia's twin sister, Salvia, bought a similar long-term care insurance policy at the same time. However, Salvia purchased a policy with a 5 percent compound inflation rider even though the extra premium meant that she would have to manage her retirement expenses more carefully than her sister would. After 5 years, Salvia's daily benefit has risen to $128. (See table 14-1 in chapter 14.) It will continue to rise to $163 in another 5 years and to $208 in 10 years. Although Salvia's benefit has failed somewhat to keep up with the actual increase in costs, she is in a better position than her sister to make up the shortfall out of her assets because the difference is much smaller.

This example illustrates two very important points. First, protection against the effects of inflation may be a determining factor in whether an individual's long-term care protection adequately meets future needs. Second, the inflation protection in many policies may not keep benefit limits in line with the real inflation in long-term care costs.

There may be some policyowners who feel that they have other resources to offset the effects of inflation. Although this may be true in some circumstances, many policyowners may change their minds when the true magnitude of inflation's effects is explained to them.

There are two ways to plan for inflation in long-term care costs. One is to purchase some type of automatic benefit increase; the other is to periodically purchase additional benefits. The characteristics of these types of inflation increases are described in chapter 14.

Automatic Benefit Increases

The election of an automatic benefit increase results in a significantly higher premium, and the magnitude of this increase varies widely among insurers. However, the increased premium remains level over the life of the contract unless an insurer increases rates by class. The cost of adding automatic inflation protection varies by insurer because of such factors as age and the particular type of plan selected. The authors of this book randomly picked three different comprehensive long-term care insurance policies from three different insurers and found that premiums increased by the factors in table 16-5 if 5 percent compound inflation protection was included. For example, a factor of 2.0 indicates that a policy with the inflation protection would be twice as expensive as a policy without it.

TABLE 16-5
Increase for 5 Percent Compound Inflation

Age	Insurer 1	Insurer 2	Insurer 3
40	3.3	2.5	2.0
55	2.4	2.0	1.9
65	2.0	1.5	1.8
75	1.6	1.4	1.6

Insurer 2 was the only insurer in table 16-5 that also offered a 5 percent simple inflation option. The factors for this option are 1.9, 1.6, 1.4, and 1.3, respectively. Unfortunately, benefits will eventually fall significantly behind those of a policy with 5 percent compound inflation protection, as shown in table 14-1 in chapter 14. However, a simple inflation option does result in a lower premium and may provide adequate future protection if an insured has (or expects to accumulate) other resources that can be also be used to finance future cost increases if long-term care is needed or if the insured has a very short life expectancy.

Future Purchase Options

Many insurers allow insureds to increase benefits periodically on a pay-as-you-go basis without evidence of insurability. This means that the initial premium will be much lower than that of a policy with an automatic benefit increase. However, each election of a benefit increase raises the premium, and the price for the increased benefit is determined by the insured's attained age. Eventually, the premium will surpass that of a policy written with an automatic benefit increase, and these increases will grow steadily larger.

As indicated in table 16-4, future (or guaranteed) purchase options have not been popular in the individual marketplace. This is largely due to the age of applicants. Many of these persons, who are in or near retirement, are unwilling to face large premium increases at a time when they will be living on fixed incomes. If they can afford to purchase inflation protection, they prefer the more predictable premiums of a policy with an automatic inflation increase.

The situation is very different in the group insurance market, where coverage is being purchased at a significantly lower average age. These applicants often feel that they will have future wage increases to pay their additional premiums, at least for several years. Upon retirement, however, insureds with a future purchase option will face ever-increasing age-rated premiums with incomes that are likely to be lower.

There are some drawbacks to purchasing additional benefits in the future. At some point, the cost of these increases may become unaffordable. Furthermore, some insurers place an aggregate limit on the amount of benefit increases or have an age limit beyond which benefit increases cannot be purchased. Finally, the failure to purchase a specified number of either consecutive or cumulative scheduled benefit increases typically terminates the right to exercise future benefit increases without evidence of insurability.

Nonforfeiture Benefits

In addition to deciding what, if any, type of inflation protection to include in a long-term care insurance policy, an applicant must decide whether to elect some type of nonforfeiture benefit. As shown in table 16-4, less than 1 percent of purchasers of individual policies elect such an option. There are several reasons for this. One reason is cost. For example, including a shortened benefit period option will typically increase premiums by 20 to 40 percent, depending on the insurer and the insured's age at which the policy is purchased. A refund-of-premium rider to a non-tax-qualified policy may increase premiums by 50 percent or more if 100 percent of the premiums are refunded. Applicants who are on tight budgets are probably better off if they use their limited resources to purchase an adequate benefit amount and include inflation protection.

Another reason most purchasers do not elect a nonforfeiture option seems to be that most applicants purchase long-term care insurance to meet future needs and do not plan to let a policy terminate later in life—a time when they are much more likely to need coverage. Therefore, they see little value in a nonforfeiture benefit, particularly when they realize the extra premium required. Moreover, they are not used to receiving any type of benefit when most other types of insurance terminate.

Finally, some financial planners question whether a nonforfeiture option makes good financial sense. They argue that if the policyowner can afford such an additional premium, he or she would be better off in the long run to invest the additional premium. In this way, additional funds will be available in the future whether a policy terminates or not.

It should also be noted, as shown in table 16-4, that purchasers of group coverage are much more likely to have a nonforfeiture benefit. These purchasers tend to be considerably younger than purchasers in the individual marketplace and, therefore, have significantly lower premiums. This, coupled with the fact that these buyers are typically working (because most group coverage is provided under employer-provided benefit plans), makes the cost of a nonforfeiture benefit more affordable.

Policy Comparisons

Consumers and financial services professionals are often faced with the daunting task of comparing long-term care insurance policies. Although most consumers are not interested in comparing every available policy, they are often presented with proposals from more than one agent or more than one proposal from a single agent. If the agents or insurers have done a proper evaluation of their client's needs, the policies will have many similarities, but there will also be differences. Thus, a systematic approach to compare the policies is needed. Note, however, that an agent's presentation of too many policies to a client can be overwhelming and may actually discourage the client from purchasing coverage. As a result, many agents are trained to ask probing questions at the onset of the sales process so that a limited number of policies can be presented, based on such factors as affordability and client needs.

Several insurance companies, consumer groups, and financial publications have prepared what are referred to as checklists or worksheets for this purpose. Perhaps the best known of these is the worksheet in the NAIC's *A Shoppers Guide to Long-Term Care Insurance*. This worksheet is reproduced in figure 16-1.

Switching Policies

Policyowners are sometimes faced with the situation in which they would like a "better" long-term care insurance policy—possibly because their existing policy has less-than-adequate benefits or more restrictive policy provisions than are currently available in the marketplace. Should they

(Text continues on page 385.)

FIGURE 16-1
How to Compare Long-Term Care Insurance Policies

Fill in the information below so that you can compare long-term care insurance policies. Most of the information you need is in the outline of coverage provided in the policies you are comparing. Even so, you will need to calculate some information and talk to the agent or a company representative to get the rest.

Insurance Company Information	Policy 1	Policy 2
1. Name of the insurance company's agent		
2. Is the company licensed in your state?	yes/no	yes/no
3. Insurance rating service and rating		
What levels of care are covered by this policy?		
4. Does the policy provide benefits for these levels of care?		
• Skilled nursing care?	yes/no	yes/no
• Personal/custodial care?	yes/no	yes/no
(In many states, both levels of care are required.)		
5. Does the policy pay for any nursing home stay, no matter what level of care you receive?	yes/no	yes/no
• If not, what levels aren't covered?		
Where can you receive care covered under the policy?		
6. Does the policy pay for care in any licensed facility?	yes/no	yes/no
• If not, what doesn't it pay for?		
7. Does the policy provide home care benefits for:		
• Skilled nursing care?	yes/no	yes/no
• Personal care given by home health aides?	yes/no	yes/no
• Homemaker services?	yes/no	yes/no
• Other _____?	yes/no	yes/no
8. Does the policy pay for care received in:		
• Adult day care centers?	yes/no	yes/no
• Assisted living facilities?	yes/no	yes/no
• Other settings? (List)		
How long are benefits paid and what amounts are covered? (You may be considering a policy that pays benefits on a different basis, so you may have to do some calculations to determine comparable amounts.)		
9. How much will the policy pay per day for:		
• Nursing home care?	$	$
• Assisted living facility care?	$	$
• Home care?	$	$
10. Are there limits on the number of days or visits per year for which benefits will be paid? If yes, what are the limits for:	yes/no	yes/no
• Nursing home care?	days	days
• Assisted living facility care?		
• Home care? (days or visits?)		
11. What is the length of the benefit period that you are considering?	years	years

FIGURE 16-1 (continued)
How to Compare Long-Term Care Insurance Policies

12. Are there limits on the amounts the policy will pay during your lifetime? If yes, what are the limits for:	yes/no	yes/no
• Nursing home care?	$	$
• Assisted living facility care?	$	$
• Home care? (days or visits?)	$	$
• Total lifetime limit	$	$

How does the policy decide when you are eligible for benefits?

13. Which of the "benefit triggers" does the policy use to decide your eligibility for benefits? (It may have more than one.)		
• Unable to do activities of daily living (ADLs)	yes/no	yes/no
• Cognitive impairment (Older policies may discriminate against Alzheimer's; newer ones don't.)	yes/no	yes/no
• Doctor certification of medical necessity	yes/no	yes/no
• Prior hospital stay	yes/no	yes/no
• Bathing is one of the ADLs	yes/no	yes/no

When do benefits start?

14. How long is the waiting period before benefits begin for:		
• Nursing home care?	days	days
• Assisted living facility care?	days	days
• Home health care?	days	days
• Waiting period—service days or calendar days	service days	calendar days
15. Are the waiting periods for home care cumulative or consecutive?		
16. How long will it be before you are covered for a pre-existing condition? (Usually 6 months)	months	months
17. How long will the company look back in your medical history to determine a pre-existing condition? (Usually 6 months)	months	months

Does the policy have inflation protection?

18. Are the benefits adjusted for inflation?	yes/no	yes/no
19. Are you allowed to buy more coverage? If yes,	yes/no	yes/no
• When can you buy more coverage?		
• How much can you buy?	$	$
• When can you no longer buy more coverage?		
20. Do the benefits increase automatically? If yes,	yes/no	yes/no
• What is the rate of increase?	%	%
• Is it a simple or compound increase?		
• When do automatic increases stop?		
21. If you buy inflation coverage, what daily benefit would you receive for: Nursing home care:		
• 5 years from now?	$	$
• 10 years from now?	$	$

FIGURE 16-1 (continued)
How to Compare Long-Term Care Insurance Policies

Assisted living facility care:		
• 5 years from now?	$	$
• 10 years from now?	$	$
Home health care:		
• 5 years from now?	$	$
• 10 years from now?	$	$
22. If you buy inflation coverage, what will your premium be?:		
• 5 years from now?	$	$
• 10 years from now?	$	$
• 15 years from now?	$	$
What other benefits are covered under the policy?		
23. Is there a waiver of premium benefit? If yes:	yes/no	yes/no
• How long do you have to be in a nursing home before it begins?		
• Does the waiver apply when you receive home care?	yes/no	yes/no
24. Does the policy have a nonforfeiture benefit? If yes, what kind?	yes/no	yes/no
25. Does the policy have a return of premium benefit?	yes/no	yes/no
26. Does the policy have a death benefit?	yes/no	yes/no
If yes, are there any restrictions before the benefit is paid?	yes/no	yes/no
27. Will the policy cover one person or two?	one/two	one/two
Tax-qualified status		
28. Is the policy tax-qualified?	yes/no	yes/no
What does the policy cost?		
29. What is the premium excluding all riders?		
• Monthly	$	$
• Yearly	$	$
30. What is the premium if home care is covered?		
• Monthly	$	$
• Yearly	$	$
31. What is the premium if assisted living is covered?		
• Monthly	$	$
• Yearly	$	$
32. What is the premium if you include an inflation rider?		
• Monthly	$	$
• Yearly	$	$
33. What is the premium if you include a nonforfeiture benefit?		
• Monthly	$	$
• Yearly	$	$
34. Is there any discount if you and your spouse both buy policies?	yes/no	yes/no

---

FIGURE 16-1 (continued)
How to Compare Long-Term Care Insurance Policies

• If yes, what is the amount of the discount?	$	$
• Do you lose the discount when one spouse dies?	yes/no	yes/no
35. What is the total annual premium including all riders and discounts?		
• Total monthly premium	$	$
• Total annual premium	$	$
36. When looking at the results of questions 29 through 35, how much do you think you are willing to pay in premiums?	$	$

Source: *A Shopper's Guide to Long-Term Care Insurance*, Worksheet 2: How to Compare Long-Term Care Insurance Policies, © 2005, National Association of Insurance Commissioners. Reprinted with permission of the NAIC. Further reprint or distribution to clients, customers, or any other entity strictly prohibited without written permission of the NAIC.

---

terminate the old policy and switch to a new policy? Such a change must be made with a careful and thorough determination that the new policy is better than the old policy and that the insured will qualify for the new policy. The difference in premiums must also be considered because the new policy will be written at attained-age rates that may be higher than those used for the old policy. In addition, an old policy should never be terminated before a new policy is actually issued. An insured must also be aware of any preexisting-conditions provision in the new policy, whereby benefits otherwise payable under the old policy would be denied. Finally, the insured must take into account any difference in the tax status of the old and new policies.

There are many reasons for considering a new policy. For example, an insured may wish to increase the daily benefit, add inflation protection, or add home health care. It is always prudent to determine if the existing insurer will raise its benefits at a lower cost than the additional premium for a new policy. Such increases in benefits require evidence of insurability, and the additional premium is usually based on attained-age rates. The rates that apply to the original benefits, however, will remain at the old issue-age level.

As mentioned in chapter 13, insurers have continued to enhance their newer policies, and the ability of and cost to existing insureds to obtain these benefits varies among insurers. However, it is always worth the effort to explore the possibility of upgrading an older policy before replacing it with a newer policy. In some cases, replacing an older policy may be justified; in other cases, it may not.

A final alternative to switching policies is to purchase an additional policy. For example, an insured with an acceptable facility-only policy may have decided that he or she would like benefits for home health care. The insurer, however, may be unwilling or unable to add this coverage for reasons that include jeopardizing a grandfathered policy's tax status or state laws that no longer allow issuing the home health care rider formerly used with the policy. Rather than purchasing a new comprehensive policy, the insured may find that it is less expensive to buy a separate home health care policy. An additional policy may also be a viable alternative if an insured is unable to increase daily benefit amounts under an existing policy.

Premium Payments

One of the final steps in the purchase of long-term care insurance is the determination of how to pay the premium. There are three basic options: Pay it over the applicant's lifetime, pay it periodically over an accelerated period, or pay it in a single lump sum. The most appropriate method is the one that best fits the applicant's financial circumstances and attitude toward uncertainty. A large majority of insureds have elected to pay premiums over their lifetimes.

Lifetime Payments

Most applicants elect to pay their premiums over their lifetime in annual, semiannual, quarterly, or monthly installments. The periodic payment is level and predetermined, but it might increase if the insurer raises premiums on a class basis. The insurer bills the insured unless an election is made at some point to have payments made automatically from a bank account—an approach that is often required if payments are made monthly.

Premiums for long-term care insurance are initially expressed as annual amounts; modal factors are used to determine the amount of less frequent payments. For example, one insurer's modal factor (identical to that of many other insurers) for semiannual payments is 0.52. This means that semiannual payments of $520 are required if the policyowner elects this mode of payment rather than a single annual premium of $1,000. The result is that the policyowner pays an additional premium of $40 to postpone payment of $500 for 6 months—an effective interest rate of 16.7 percent.[32] The modal rates for quarterly and monthly payments are 0.27 and 0.09, respectively. These result in quarterly payments of $270 and monthly payments of $90. In either case, the policyowner is paying $80 per year to make premium payments less than annually.

A policyowner who writes periodic checks for long-term care premiums should realize the high cost of paying premiums more than once a year. If resources are available, a single annual check is financially prudent unless the policyowner is earning a significant return on his or her investments.

An insurer's rate structure assumes that premiums are paid at the beginning of the year. Clearly, the company's investment earnings are decreased if the receipt of these funds is postponed, and levying a charge for this postponement is appropriate. It is also important to point out that a major portion of the additional charge is to compensate the insurer for the costs of sending bills and processing premium payments more than once a year.

Accelerated Payments

Some insurers allow applicants to make premium payments over limited periods of time, such as 10 years or until age 65. After that time, no more premium payments are required to keep coverage in force. In addition, an insured will not be subject to any rate increases that an insurer might impose for policies that are still in the premium-payment period. Such options are increasingly popular with younger purchasers of long-term care insurance who want a paid-up policy by the time they retire, possibly with a lower income than they had during their working years. Other purchasers like the peace of mind that having a paid-up policy will give them.

The major drawback to accelerated payments is cost. For example, one insurer offers 55-year-old applicants a policy that will be paid up at age 65 if they make periodic premium payments for 10 years that are 2.1 times the annual premium payments for a policy with a lifetime payment period. This factor is 2.3 at age 45 and 1.9 at age 65. Needless to say, many applicants are unable to afford such increased premiums. Moreover, accelerated payments are likely to cause otherwise tax-deductible premiums to exceed the annual deduction limits identified in chapter 13. The loss of a tax advantage for premium amounts above these limits effectively serves to increase a person's premium costs even further.

As a result, some financial planners feel that the applicant would be better off by investing this additional premium and would need only modest return to generate enough income to make premiums payments for life.

One final point is worthy of mention. Premiums during an accelerated-payment period, like those paid over an insured's lifetime, can be made in annual or less frequent modes.

Single Payments

Some insurers allow an applicant to purchase a paid-up policy with one single payment at the time of purchase. If an applicant has liquid resources that are not earning a sufficient return, this will enable him or her to avoid future premiums and rate increases.

Again, a major obstacle to this option is cost. For example, the insurer mentioned previously charges a premium at age 55 that is 16.8 times as much as a premium paid over the insured's lifetime. The policyowner also loses potential future income tax deductions if the policy is tax qualified. Furthermore, the insured's estate will be reduced if the insured dies in the near future unless the policyowner purchased some type of nonforfeiture or return-of-premium option. As mentioned earlier, such an option would have resulted in a significant further increase in the premium.

Evaluating Insurers

In addition to comparing and evaluating the provisions of long-term care insurance policies, it is important for a consumer to ensure that he or she is purchasing a policy from a reputable company at an appropriate price. In many cases, the consumer will rely on the advice of an insurance agent or financial planner who specializes in long-term care insurance and is perhaps in a better position to make this evaluation. The evaluation should focus on three basic considerations: financial strength, reputation, and cost.

Financial Strength

Probably the single most important criterion in evaluating an insurer is financial strength. Because the basic function of an insurer is to pay claims, care must be taken to select only those insurers that are most likely to have the financial strength to do so if and when the need arises. In light of past insolvencies and near insolvencies among insurers, this claims-paying ability cannot simply be taken for granted.

Detailed financial information can be obtained from the annual reports that insurance companies must file with state insurance departments. These reports are public information. Although an evaluation of this information is beyond most individuals' ability, it has been performed by several rating organizations that publish the financial history, ratings, and analyses of individual insurers. These organizations include A.M. Best Company, Fitch Ratings (formed by a merger of Duff & Phelps and Fitch IBCA), Moody's Investors Service, Standard & Poor's, and Weiss Ratings. A few words of caution are in order with respect to reliance on ratings assigned by these organizations, however. First, the criteria and methodology differ among the rating organizations, so an insurer may receive different ratings from different organizations. Second, a rating of A, which many people associate with excellence, may not be particularly good. For example, Best's has two ratings higher than A, and Standard & Poor's has five ratings higher than A. Third, some rating agencies seem to be more generous in their ratings than others. Fourth, not all insurers are assigned ratings by all of the rating organizations. In light of all of these differences, it is probably wise advice to choose insurers that have very high ratings from at least two or three of the rating organizations.

These ratings may be available from state insurance departments, public libraries, the Internet, or insurer brochures.

Reputation

With approximately 100 insurers writing long-term care insurance, there is no reason to purchase coverage from any insurer that has other than a good reputation. Reputation arises from many factors. For example, are current customers satisfied with the insurer? What is the insurer's reputation for fair and prompt claims settlement? How are insureds treated when the insurer introduces new or improved policies? What commitment and experience does the insurer have with long-term care insurance products? Does the insurer have a reputation it wants to protect and thus may be willing to "do the right thing"?

A good insurance agent or financial planner, through experience and interaction with colleagues, should have a feel for an insurer's reputation within the insurance industry. Another source of information is the records about consumer complaints that state insurance departments receive. There are also consumer publications that periodically evaluate insurers on the basis of costs, claims handling, consumer satisfaction, and other factors.

It should be noted, however, that reputation is of little value if an insurer does not have adequate financial strength. Unfortunately, a few insurers that were once highly regarded have become insolvent.

Cost

Many earlier sections of this chapter mentioned the effect of cost on various consumer decisions, focusing primarily on how alternative choices might affect an overall premium. It is also important to look at the variations among insurers for similar policies. One recent survey compared 42 policy forms from 30 insurance companies with respect to cost under varying assumptions.[33] Table 16-6 shows the premium variations for policy forms from 10 of these companies at selected ages for one particular set of policy assumptions. The comparison is based on the insurer's best preferred rates for a single-life comprehensive policy with the following characteristics:

TABLE 16-6
Premium Comparisons among Insurers

	Age 55	Age 60	Age 65	Age 70
Insurer 1	$1,474	$1,923	$2,629	$3,961
Insurer 2	1,594	2,025	2,475	3,544
Insurer 3	1,646	2,032	2,481	3,251
Insurer 4	1,713	2,162	2,868	4,371
Insurer 5	2,019	2,643	3,490	5,359
Insurer 6	2,088	2,784	3,792	5,688
Insurer 7	2,181	2,786	3,703	5,335
Insurer 8	2,229	2,661	3,260	4,387
Insurer 9	2,339	2,860	3,686	5,077
Insurer 10	2,550	3,052	3,870	5,113

- $100 daily benefit for both facility care and home health care
- lifetime benefit
- 90-day elimination period
- 5 percent annual compound inflation increase

As this table shows, there are substantial premium variations among insurers, and the array of companies from lowest to highest premium is not the same at different ages. In addition, the same pattern of price variation by insurer may differ significantly for other policy assumptions.

Cost comparisons must be used with care for several reasons. First, it is important that they are for identical policies, and any two policies are rarely identical. This fact is even indicated by the survey from which the above premiums were taken. For example, do the policies in the above example all apply the same elimination period in the same manner, or do they all have the same provision for preexisting conditions? Does waiver of premiums apply if the insured receives any long-term care services, or does it require that the insured be in a facility? Are the policies comparable in their provision of a bed reservation benefit or care coordination? Or will an applicant be acceptable at the best preferred rates from each of these insurers?

Second, what is the financial strength of each of these insurers? Low premiums may be an indication that an insurer has inadequate reserves or is trying to increase revenue in the short run because of a poor financial position.

Third, are the levels of service from the insurers the same? For example, an insurer with a low premium may have the reputation of being very strict in its claims-paying practices.

Last, but not least, what is the likelihood of future premium increases? Insurers with premiums that are among the lowest might be new to the business and have little experience in pricing long-term care insurance policies, or they might be using a low premium as a method for increasing market share. In either case, they may increase premiums in the future and make policies unaffordable for some insureds. It is worth asking an insurer about past rate increases; some states also provide this information. Some insurers with low premiums have a reputation for frequent price increases, while other insurers with somewhat higher premiums have infrequent or no increases because of more realistic pricing assumptions.

All of this is not to say that price differentials are not important. However, they must be analyzed with care.

A Final Example

The effect of cost on consumer decisions has been woven throughout much of this chapter. However, the discussion has focused on the way in which one factor, such as the length of the elimination period or the inclusion of inflation protection, affects the final premium. As this final example illustrates, an insured must often make several decisions before the final selection of a long-term care insurance policy.

Example:

Fred, aged 65, has decided that he needs long-term care insurance. Five years ago, he and his wife sold their small jewelry store and were able to retire comfortably. Their plans of a leisurely life during retirement years were soon shattered when Fred's wife had a serious stroke. For 3 years, Fred was able to care for her at home with the assistance of professional caregivers. After she was totally paralyzed 2 years ago by a second stroke, Fred found it necessary to put her in the nursing home where she recently died.

Having spent almost $250,000 to provide his wife with the best care possible, Fred is fully aware of the effect that long-term care can have on a family's assets. He wants to make sure that any long-term care expenses he might incur will not further deplete the $500,000 in remaining assets that he and his wife spent a lifetime accumulating and intended to leave to their children and grandchildren.

Fred has contacted a well-respected insurance agent whom he has known for several years and asked her to help him find a long-term care insurance policy that meets his objectives. Fred has indicated that he would like a policy that provides these benefits:

- a daily facility benefit of $150. A top-quality nursing home in Fred's town will cost about $250 per day, but Fred feels he can afford to pay $100 from his Social Security and retirement income.
- a home health care benefit of $150 per day
- a lifetime benefit period
- a 20-day elimination period
- 5 percent annual compound inflation protection

Fred's agent calculates that such a policy will have an annual premium of $5,060. Fred feels that this is somewhat more than he can pay without withdrawing funds from his assets and asks her what can be done to reduce the premium to about $4,000 per year. She comes up with the following alternatives:

- If Fred lowers the daily benefit to $130 per day, the premium will drop to $4,380. A further decrease to $120 per day will result in a premium of $4,050. Fred decides to consider this option.

- If Fred decreases the home health care benefit to 50 percent of the facility benefit, the premium will drop to $4,130. Fred realizes how costly home health care can be and doesn't like this option.

- If Fred elects a 5-year benefit period, the premium will drop to $4,135. For a 4-year benefit period, the premium will be $3,800. Fred is aware of some patients in his wife's nursing home who had been there for as long as 10 years and doesn't like this option either.

- If Fred increases the elimination period to 90 days, the premium will drop to $4,150. The premium for a 180-day elimination period will further decrease the premium to $3,750. Fred is willing to think about a 90-day elimination period, but he feels that 180 days is too long.

- If Fred changes the inflation protection from compound interest to simple interest, the premium will drop to $4,260. Fred hopes to live for many more years and realizes the effect that inflation will have on long-term care costs. This option doesn't appeal to him.

Fred decides to take a day or two to think about his options. He calculates that the longer elimination period will increase his out-of-pocket costs by $10,500 (70 days times $150) over what they would otherwise be if he needs long-term care. He also calculates that the lower benefit amount of $120 will increase his annual out-of-pocket costs by $10,950 (365 days times $30). Fred realizes that these additional out-of-pocket costs will come from his accumulated assets. He also understands that he could afford the benefits he originally desired if he were willing to reduce his assets by about $1,000 per year to pay the $5,060 premium.

Fred finally decides that the policy with the $5,060 premium is the most appropriate choice. Its benefits will make it more likely that his family will provide the level of care he wants if he is unable to make decisions for himself.

NOTES

1. *Long-Term Care Insurance: An Undiscovered Necessity*, American Council of Life Insurance, 1999, and Roper Organization Survey of 1990 Americans, 1998, figures 12, 13, and 15.
2. *Who Buys Long-Term Care Insurance in 2000? A Decade of Study of Buyers and Nonbuyers*, prepared for the Health Insurance Association of America by LifePlans, Inc., October 2000, p. 23.
3. *The Costs of Long-Term Care: Perceptions Versus Reality*, AARP, Washington, DC, December 20, 2001, Executive Summary, p. 5, and Report, p. 22.
4. Ibid., Report, pp. 26, 36.
5. *Who Buys Long-Term Care Insurance in 2000? A Decade of Study of Buyers and Nonbuyers*, prepared for the Health Insurance Association of America by LifePlans, Inc., October 2000, p. 21.
6. Ibid., pp. 35, 40.
7. *The Costs of Long-Term Care: Perceptions versus Reality*, AARP, Washington, DC, December 20, 2001, Executive Summary, p. 5, and *Long-Term Care Insurance: An Undiscovered Necessity*, American Council of Life Insurance, 1999, and Roper Organization Survey of 1990 Americans, 1998, figure 10.
8. *Who Buys Long-Term Care Insurance in 2000? A Decade of Study of Buyers and Nonbuyers*, prepared for the Health Insurance Association of America by LifePlans, Inc., October 2000, p. 22.
9. Ibid., p. 41.
10. *Long-Term Care Insurance: Consumer Perceptions*, a report by LIMRA International, Inc., Windsor, Connecticut, and the Health Insurance Association of America, Washington, DC, 2002, p. 3, and *Long-Term Care Insurance: An Undiscovered Necessity*, American Council of Life Insurance, 1999, and Roper Organization Survey of 1990 Americans, 1998, figure 13.
11. *Long-Term Care Insurance: Consumer Perceptions*, a report by LIMRA International, Inc., Windsor, Connecticut, and the Health Insurance Association of America, Washington, DC, 2002, pp. 3, 4.
12. *The Myth of Unaffordability: How Most Americans Should, Could, and Would Buy Private Long-Term Care Insurance*, Center for Long-Term Care Financing, Seattle, WA, September 1, 1999, pp. iv, 11, 35.
13. *Long-Term Care Insurance: Consumer Perceptions,* a report by LIMRA International, Inc., Windsor, Connecticut, and the Health Insurance Association of America, Washington, DC, 2002, p. 3.
14. *Who Buys Long-Term Care Insurance in 2000? A Decade of Study of Buyers and Nonbuyers*, prepared for the Health Insurance Association of America by LifePlans, Inc., October 2000, pp. 3, 34, 39.
15. Ibid., p. 34.
16. Ibid., p. 3.
17. *Long-Term Care and Medicare Supplement, Executive Summary, Annual 2004,* LIMRA International, Inc., 2005, p. 2, and *U.S. Group Long-Term Care Insurance, Executive Summary, Annual 2004,* LIMRA International, Inc., 2005, pp. 2–4.
18. Ibid.

19. Ibid.
20. *Who Buys Long-Term Care Insurance in 2000? A Decade of Study of Buyers and Nonbuyers,* prepared for the Health Insurance Association of America by LifePlans, Inc., October 2000, p. 16, and *Who Buys Long-Term Care Insurance in the Workplace? A Study of Employer Long-Term Care Insurance Plans,* prepared for the Health Insurance Association of America by LifePlans, Inc., October 2001, p. 14.
21. Ibid., pp. 2–3, and Ibid., pp. 3–4.
22. *Who Buys Long-Term Care Insurance in 2000? A Decade of Study of Buyers and Nonbuyers,* prepared for the Health Insurance Association of America by LifePlans, Inc., October 2000, p. 27.
23. Ibid., p. 23.
24. *Long-Term Care and Medicare Supplement, Executive Summary, Annual 2004,* LIMRA International, Inc., 2005, p. 2.
25. *Long-Term Care and Medicare Supplement, Executive Summary, Annual 2004,* LIMRA International, Inc., 2005, p. 2, and *U.S. Group Long-Term Care Insurance, Executive Summary, Annual 2004,* LIMRA International, Inc., 2005, p. 3.
26. *Who Buys Long-Term Care Insurance in 2000? A Decade of Study of Buyers and Nonbuyers,* prepared for the Health Insurance Association of America by LifePlans, Inc., October 2000, p. 26.
27. Ibid., p. 27.
28. Ibid., p. 24.
29. *Who Buys Long-Term Care Insurance in the Workplace? A Study of Employer Long-Term Care Insurance Plans*, prepared for the Health Insurance Association of America by LifePlans, Inc., October 2001, p. 19.
30. *Long-Term Care and Medicare Supplement, Executive Summary, Annual 2004,* LIMRA International, Inc., 2005, p. 2.
31. *MetLife Market Survey of Nursing Home & Home Care Costs,* September 2005, MetLife Mature Market Institute, p. 2.
32. To determine the annual percentage rate, assume that the insured has initially paid $520 of the $1,000 premium in advance and is financing the other $480 for 6 months. Therefore, $40 of the second semiannual payment represents the interest for this loan.
33. "Seventh Annual Long-Term Care Survey," *Broker World,* July 2005.

Group and Hybrid Products

Chapter Outline

In earlier chapters of this book, the focus is primarily on policies sold directly to individuals that provide long-term care insurance only. However, there are two other types of products in the long-term care insurance marketplace. The most significant of these is the group products that are part of employer-sponsored and association plans.

Readers may wonder about the relevance of employer-sponsored plans to seniors. Proper planning for long-term care needs often begins during working years. In addition, many employer-sponsored plans include retirees and parents of employees as persons eligible for coverage. There are also hybrid products that combine long-term care insurance with life insurance or annuities.

GROUP PRODUCTS

Insurance products initially developed for the individual insurance marketplace are often followed by products designed for the group marketplace. The same is true for long-term care insurance, where group products have been existence since the late 1980s. The first products were custom designed for a few large employers. Standardized products were soon designed for the group market, and today these products are available to groups of almost any size. Over 2.0 million persons with long-term care coverage obtained their protection through the group market under the plans of over 6,500 employers and 100 association groups.[1] This represents over 30 percent of persons with long-care coverage.[2] The percentage has been growing, helped in part by the introduction of the plan for federal employees (described in chapter 18) and its influence on other employers. Despite this growth, the percentage of group members who purchase coverage when it is available remains relatively modest. Participation rates may range from 20 to 50 percent; rates of 5 to 15 percent are more common. The highest enrollment rates generally occur when there is strong communication, sponsorship, and endorsement by the employer.

This discussion of group long-term care products first looks at the types of products available and the groups that use them. It then examines the ways in which these products differ from policies sold in the individual marketplace.

Types of Products

Although group long-term care products are often referred to in a generic sense as group insurance, there are actually two types of group products—group insurance and mass-marketed policies of individual insurance. Insurers that offer other types of group life and health insurance tend to issue group insurance contracts. Insurers that specialize in the individual market—often life insurers—tend to write mass-marketed individual insurance products. Some insurers that have historically written both group and individual life and health insurance may offer both types of long-term care insurance products. Large groups with several thousand employees are more likely to use group insurance products, and very small employers are more likely to use mass-marketed individual insurance products. Between these two extremes, both types of products are common. For the most part, the available coverage is similar, regardless of the type of product.

Group Insurance

group insurance

Group insurance is a method of providing insurance protection to members of a group. It is characterized by a group contract, group underwriting, and possibly experience rating.

master contract

Group Contract. A group insurance contract provides coverage to a number of persons under a single insurance contract issued to someone other than the insured persons. The contract, referred to as a *master contract*, provides benefits to a group of individuals—such as employees or association members— who have a specific relationship to the policyowner. Although these individuals are not actual parties to the master contract, they can legally enforce their rights and are often referred to as third-party beneficiaries of the insurance contract.

certificate of insurance

An insured covered under a group contract receives a *certificate of insurance* as evidence of coverage. A certificate is not an actual insurance contract but a summary of the coverage provided under the master contract.

In individual insurance, the coverage of the insured normally begins with the inception of the insurance contract and ceases with its termination. With group insurance, individual members of the group may become eligible for coverage long after the inception of the contract, or they may lose their eligibility status long before the contract terminates. However, if an insured loses group coverage, he or she often has the right to continue coverage on an individual basis.

Group Underwriting. Group insurance is accompanied by some degree of underwriting of a group itself. The degree of underwriting (and possibly premium rates) will vary to the extent that members of the group are also subject to underwriting. If members of the group are individually subject to full underwriting, there is minimum underwriting of the group as a whole. At the other extreme, the group is looked at much more closely if members can obtain coverage on a guaranteed-issue basis. Underwriting of group products is examined in more depth later in this chapter.

Experience Rating. If a group is sufficiently large, the actual experience of a group is a factor in determining the premium rates charged. However, such experience is determined on a class basis and applies to all insureds in that class. With the newness of long-term care insurance and the long time needed to obtain meaningful claims data, actual group experience currently has little effect on group long-term care insurance. Rather, any rate changes by an insurer are likely to be the same for all its group contracts.

Mass-Marketed Individual Insurance

mass-marketed individual insurance

worksite marketing

voluntary benefits

The second type of group product is not true group insurance but individual polices of insurance sold through a sponsoring organization, such as an employer or association. Generically, this type or arrangement is referred to as *mass-marketed individual insurance*, because the insureds receive individual policies of insurance. It is also often referred to by other names. For example, the term *worksite marketing* is often used for coverage that is made available as part of an employee-employer relationship. The term *voluntary benefits* is also often used to refer to situations in which the insured pays the entire premium. Other names that are sometimes seen include sponsored group discount programs and multilife discount programs.

Types of Groups

Approximately 92 percent of the long-term care insurance coverage under group arrangements is obtained through employer-sponsored plans that employers make available to their employees.[3] The remainder of the coverage is obtained under plans of association groups and affinity groups that make coverage available as a member benefit. Examples of these types of groups include the U.S. Chamber of Commerce, AARP, banks, service clubs, and alumni associations.

Comparisons with Individual Products

The following comparison of group and individual long-term care products focuses primarily on the plans sponsored by employers because this is by far the most common type of organization for which group products are used.

For the most part, the coverage available under group products is similar to the coverage under policies sold in the individual marketplace. However, there are some differences with respect to who purchases coverage and the types of coverage they purchase. In addition, there are some variations in and unique features of group products, including tax qualification, eligibility, premium payments, cost, benefits, underwriting, and portability. Before proceeding, however, it should be pointed out that group products—particularly those written for large groups—may be designed as a result of negotiation between an employer and an insurer. In addition, collective bargaining may have had significant influence. As such, numerous variations are possible.

Purchasers of Group Products

It was pointed out in chapter 16 that the purchasers of coverage under employer-sponsored plans tend to have a younger average age than the average age of purchasers of coverage in the individual marketplace. This was an unexpected and surprising phenomenon to insurers when they started selling coverage to this market. The lower age naturally resulted in a significantly lower annual premium for these insureds. These purchasers also tend to select a somewhat higher level of benefits than purchasers in the individual marketplace do. The average daily benefit is higher, and the average duration of benefits is longer. There is also a greater likelihood that these insureds have inflation protection and nonforfeiture benefits.

Two reasons probably account for these differences. First, purchasers of employer-sponsored coverage have lower premiums because of their ages, and they will continue to have wages for several (and possibly many) more years. As a result, they can afford better benefits. Second, as explained later, there may be slightly fewer options available to group members, and these options tend to be structured to offer certain types of coverage. For example, an employer's plan may automatically include inflation protection or may not have an option for a 0-day elimination period.

Tax Qualification

The group products currently available are tax qualified and as such meet all the requirements imposed by HIPAA. The products are also subject to the provisions of the NAIC model act and regulations.

Eligibility

An employer-sponsored plan may be available to all employees who meet specified employment criteria, such as being full-time, being actively at work, and having worked for the employer for a minimum period of time. Eligibility may also be limited to certain classifications of employees, such as management, salaried personnel, or employees with more than 3 years of service.

As long as an employee falls within an eligible classification, group coverage is available for the employee and/or spouse as long as the insurer's underwriting criteria are satisfied. Many plans also extend eligibility to retirees and other family members, such as adult children, parents, parents-in-law, grandparents, grandparents-in-law, or siblings.

Plans vary as to when an eligible person may apply for coverage. When a group plan is first installed, eligible persons must usually elect coverage within a defined enrollment period. To minimize adverse selection, eligible persons who initially declined coverage are often unable to enroll until the next open enrollment period, which might be on an annual basis or as infrequently as every 2 or 3 years. In addition, an employee who had initially been subject to guaranteed-issue underwriting will usually be subject to a more stringent level of underwriting. Under some plans that use the same level of underwriting as in the individual marketplace, however, an eligible person may be allowed to enroll at any time. A newly hired employee and any eligible relatives may be allowed to enroll as soon as the employee has satisfied any eligibility requirements, or the eligible persons may have to wait until the next open enrollment period.

Premium Payments

The majority of group programs are voluntary benefit plans with the employee (and other covered persons) paying the full cost of coverage. Depending on the plan, premiums may be payable for the employee's life or over the employee's working years.

Some employers pay a portion of the cost but usually for only an employee's coverage. The employer's contribution may be a percentage of the cost (such as 25 or 50 percent) or a specified dollar amount (such as $200 per year). However, it is more likely that the employer will provide a base amount of coverage, and the employee will be able to purchase additional benefits by paying the full cost of the added coverage. This arrangement is often referred to as a *buy-up plan.*

buy-up plan

Example: Alida's employer recently installed a group long-term care insurance plan. The employer pays the full cost of a base amount of comprehensive coverage for all eligible employees, who are defined to include any-one who works full-time and has at least 3 years of service with the employer. The benefit amount is $75 per day after a 90-day elimination period, and the benefit duration is 2 years.

Employees are given an option to increase the daily benefit amount to $100, $125, or $150 per day. In addition, they can increase the benefit duration to 5 years or their lifetime. An employee who elects higher benefits must pay the full cost of the additional coverage through payroll deductions, and the additional coverage above the base amount is subject to underwriting.

There are several methods by which insurers can collect employee premiums, and the way used may be a particular insurer's practice or a result of negotiation with the employer. If the employer pays any portion of the cost, the employer typically collects any employee premiums through payroll deduction and remits them to the insurer along with the employer contribution. Payroll deduction is also commonly used when the employees pay the full cost of coverage. This option is popular with employees and will probably lead to increased participation in group long-term care insurance plans. In some cases, employees are billed directly in the same manner as if they had purchased coverage in the individual marketplace.

When payroll deduction is used, an employee can usually elect to have the deduction include the cost of a spouse's coverage. The cost of coverage for other eligible family members is usually paid on a direct-bill basis, even if the employee pays the premium.

Retirees may be billed directly or allowed to have the premium deducted from pension payments they receive from the employer.

Cost

The cost of employer-provided coverage tends to be 5 to 15 percent less expensive than coverage purchased in the individual marketplace. Two major factors account for this lower cost. First, employers often provide, or at least assist with, many administrative services that would otherwise be the insurer's responsibility. These responsibilities generally include some or all of the following: communicating the plan to employees, handling enrollment procedures, collecting premiums on a payroll-deduction basis, and maintaining certain records. Second, agents or brokers' commission rates tend to be lower for group products than for individual products. This is a result of the larger overall premiums for group arrangements and the assistance the employer and company representatives often provide to encourage plan enrollment.

Just because the cost of coverage in the group marketplace may be less than the cost of individually purchased coverage, it should not be assumed that group coverage is always the best purchase for a consumer. As mentioned in chapter 15, there are significant price variations among insurers. If a high-cost insurer provides the group coverage, a person may be able to find less expensive coverage in the individual marketplace. In addition, the person may be able to design a benefit package to better fit his or her specific needs by purchasing coverage elsewhere.

Benefits

Some employer-sponsored plans offer as wide an array of benefit choices as in the individual marketplace. However, most plans simplify the decision process by limiting the available options from which an employee must select. This simplification may be to allow choice among several specific benefit options or choice among a limited number of predesigned benefit packages. Regardless of the approach, the available options are usually determined by negotiation between the employer and the insurer.

Choice among Benefit Options. Under this approach, an employee may have to make several benefit choices, but the options for each are limited. The following are some of the choices that employees often face:

- type of coverage. Most employer-sponsored plans provide comprehensive coverage. However, an employee may occasionally be allowed to select either comprehensive coverage or facility-only coverage. Home health care policies are seldom offered in the group marketplace.
- elimination period. Many plans offer only one elimination period, most commonly 90 days. A few plans offer additional choices, but elimination periods of fewer than 30 days or more than 180 days are infrequent.
- benefit amount. Most plans offer at least two or three daily benefit amounts, such as $100, $150, or $200. These amounts should approximate the cost of coverage where employees reside.
- benefit duration. Again, most plans offer two or three options, such as 2 years, 4 years, and 6 years. Some plans may also offer lifetime benefits.
- inflation protection. An insurer must offer inflation protection to the employer, who may decide to (1) not make it available under the plan, (2) require that it be part of any benefit package an employee designs, or (3) allow individual employees to make the decision

whether to purchase the coverage. In most cases, the employer elects one of the last two alternatives.

- nonforfeiture benefits. As with inflation protection, the employer decides whether this coverage is made available. In most cases, the benefit is either not available or the choice is passed on to employees.

Prepackaged Benefit Options. Some plans limit employee choice by having a series of (most commonly three) prepackaged benefit options. These options are often referred to as low, medium, and high to reflect the level of benefits and the cost. The low option offers the lowest level of benefits and lowest cost, while the high option has the highest level of benefits and the highest cost. Tables 17-1 and 17-2 show two such prepackaged plans.

TABLE 17-1
Prepackaged Benefit Options

	Low	Medium	High
Type of policy	Comprehensive	Comprehensive	Comprehensive
Elimination period	90 days	60 days	30 days
Daily benefit amount (80% for home health care)	$100	$150	$200
Benefit duration	3 years	6 years	Lifetime
Inflation protection	No	Yes	Yes
Nonforfeiture benefits	No	No	Yes

TABLE 17-2
Prepackaged Benefit Options

	Low	Medium	High
Type of policy	Facility only	Comprehensive	Comprehensive
Elimination period	90 days	90 days	90 days
Daily benefit amount (all care settings)	$150	$150	$200
Benefit duration	3 years	5 years	Lifetime
Inflation protection	Yes	Yes	Yes
Nonforfeiture benefits	No	No	No

Underwriting

There are several levels of underwriting that may apply to employer-sponsored groups. These levels include guaranteed issue, modified guaranteed issue, simplified issue, and full underwriting. From the standpoint of applicants, employees are often subject to less stringent underwriting than their family members. Adverse selection tends to be less of a problem with employees, because they tend to be healthier as a result of their being actively at work.

guaranteed-issue underwriting

Guaranteed Issue. Insurers occasionally use *guaranteed-issue underwriting* for employees. This means that coverage is provided for all employees who apply for it. Although this is the most liberal underwriting from the employees' standpoint, it also means that underwriting the group is much more stringent than when the insurer uses the underwriting methods discussed later.

Insurers generally use guaranteed-issue underwriting only if the group meets certain criteria that minimize adverse selection. These criteria, which are also common to group underwriting for other types of insurance, often include several or all of the following:

- The group is large enough in size.
- A high minimum number or percentage of employees applies for benefits.
- Eligibility is limited to full-time employees, possibly with a minimum length of service with the employer.
- The employer pays some or all of the premium costs.
- The employee has minimal choice in selecting the level of benefits.
- The group has a stable employment history.
- The group is in an industry that is not considered high risk for claims.
- The employer is able to handle its administrative responsibilities for the plan.
- The employer will actively endorse the plan and communicate it to employees.

Guaranteed-issue underwriting is seldom used for applicants other than employees. It is also often accompanied by a higher premium than other levels of underwriting.

modified guaranteed-issue underwriting

Modified Guaranteed Issue. With *modified guaranteed-issue underwriting*, the insurer accepts most applicants. However, some medical questions are asked on the application, and the answers to these questions may result in the declination of the application. These questions are often aimed at determining whether the applicant has recently received long-term care services or requires assistance with any activities of daily living. Questions may also ask whether the applicant has certain specified medical conditions, such as Parkinson's disease, multiple sclerosis, cancer, or AIDS. As long as there are no unsatisfactory answers to these questions, no further medical information is requested and coverage is issued.

There may also be some underwriting of the group itself but on a less stringent basis than if guaranteed-issue underwriting is used. Modified guaranteed-issue underwriting may also be limited to employees.

simplified-issue underwriting

Simplified Issue. With *simplified-issue underwriting* (sometimes referred to as short-form underwriting), the insurer tends to ask more medically related questions than are used with modified guaranteed-issue underwriting. Only if the answers to these questions are unsatisfactory does the insurer request further medical information—such as an attending physician's statement—or further medical assessments.

Simplified-issue underwriting might be used for all applicants, or it might be used for all applicants other than employees when the employees are subject to less stringent underwriting.

Full Individual Underwriting. In some cases, a group plan will use the same underwriting as in the individual marketplace (sometimes referred to as long-form underwriting), which is discussed in chapter 15. This type of underwriting is most likely to be used in the group marketplace when the size of the group is very small and for persons other than employees.

Portability

If an insured is no longer eligible for employer-sponsored coverage, he or she can elect to continue coverage. If the insured's coverage is in the form of an individual policy paid through payroll deductions, the insured needs only to make arrangements with the insurer to pay the premium on a direct-bill basis.

continuation of coverage

If the coverage is under a group policy, the NAIC model regulations require that the insurer provide the insured with a basis for continuation or a conversion provision. Under a *continuation of coverage*, the insured retains coverage under the group contract but pays premiums directly to the insurer. Under a conversion provision, the insured is issued an individual policy that must be identical or substantially equivalent to the group coverage. The premium for the converted policy is based on the rates for the individual policy at the insured's attained age when the original group coverage was obtained.

HYBRID PRODUCTS

hybrid product

As the sales of long-term care insurance grew in the 1990s, several insurers began to introduce insurance contracts that combined long-term care insurance and either life insurance or annuities into a single policy. Such a policy, which is called a *hybrid product* in this book, is also referred to by several other names, including a linked policy, blended policy, combination policy, and package policy. A few insurers experimented with riders for life insurance and disability income policies that guarantee the insured's ability to purchase long-term care insurance at a future date without evidence of insurability. The authors are unaware of the current availability of such riders, however.

The sales growth for these policies has been quite modest, and most companies' marketing efforts seem to be less intense than was once the case. This slow growth is due to several factors. First, many hybrid products were designed to take advantage of the high interest rates and the continually increasing stock market values of a few years ago. Lower interest rates and a declining stock market have made these products less attractive. Second, hybrid products combined complex long-term care polices with complex types of life insurance and annuities. The resulting products were often difficult for agents to understand and to explain to clients and their financial advisors. Third, many financial advisors view long-term care insurance as meeting a different need than life insurance or annuities and feel that separate products should be used for each need.

Despite these impediments to the growth of hybrid products, there are circumstances where their use is appropriate. However, not all the tax ramifications are clear—particularly with regard to withdrawals from single-premium products—and competent tax advice is recommended before their purchase.

Life Insurance Hybrids

Life insurance hybrid products can take the form of most types of cash value policies. However, most policies that have been sold are universal life insurance, including variable universal life insurance. Premiums can be paid in any mode, but most sales involve the payment of a single premium.

Purchasers of this type of policy tend to be persons of moderate-to-high net worth who transfer assets from traditionally low-yielding investments, such as money market accounts and certificates of deposit. They also tend to be persons who feel that their heirs should receive something (that is, a death benefit) from their long-term care coverage to the extent that they do not use the benefits. In addition, they prefer to keep control of their own financial options, they like the tax-favored nature of life insurance, and they want to avoid ongoing premium payments. The discussion below looks at the nature of universal life insurance, the character of the long-term care insurance element, and an example of one insurer's policy.

Universal Life Insurance

A detailed discussion of universal life insurance is beyond the scope of this book, and the following is only a brief explanation of a moderately complex form of life insurance.

Universal life insurance is an interest-sensitive policy that, unlike traditional cash value life insurance, divides the pure life insurance protection and the cash value accumulation into separate and distinct components. The insured is required to pay a specified initial premium for the amount of coverage desired. After a deduction to cover state premium taxes and administrative expenses, the premium is used to create a cash value account. Each month, deductions are made from this account to pay for the life insurance protection and—in the case of a hybrid product—for the long-term care protection. Interest is also credited to this account on a monthly basis. The process continues each month on an ongoing basis.

The insured receives an annual statement that shows policy values and any transactions that have taken place during the year. The statement is provided on a monthly basis if the insured is receiving long-term care benefits.

Some of the common characteristics of hybrid universal life insurance policies include the following:

- There is a guaranteed interest rate, usually in the range of 2.5 to 4 percent, which is credited to the cash value. However, the insurer typically pays a somewhat higher initial interest rate. This interest rate remains in effect for a minimum period of time, often 1 year. After that time, the insurer can adjust the interest rate on a quarterly or semiannual basis, subject to the minimum guarantee.

  At the time a policy is purchased, the benefits are determined on the basis of the current interest rate being credited. If this interest rate changes, the projected cash value may also change. If it decreases, the cash value may become insufficient to pay the required insurance and expense charges. In such cases, the insured is often given the option of paying an additional premium to bring the policy cash value back to its projected level so that the original policy benefits can be maintained. Alternatively, the insured may elect to reduce the amounts of the death benefit and monthly long-term care benefit.

  Any growth in the cash value is on a tax-deferred basis. If the cash value grows beyond the total premiums paid, however, any deductions for the long-term care insurance protection may represent taxable income. (Tax experts and insurers disagree on this issue, and there is no definitive IRS opinion.) If the insured is under age 59 1/2, there is also a penalty tax if the deductions are treated as withdrawals.

- Charges for the insurance protection are also usually subject to guarantees for a period of time, but these charges may change. As with interest rates, any changes affect a policy's cash value and possibly its benefits.

- The policyowner is usually allowed to take policy loans from the cash value. There is an interest charge for these loans, and any loan is subtracted from the policy's death benefit. An outstanding loan may also result in the lapse of a policy if the loan exceeds the cash value.

- The policyowner is also usually allowed to take partial surrenders of the cash value. However, there may be a surrender charge, particularly in early policy years. Any surrender reduces the amount of insurance proportionately.

- When a policy is paid with a single premium, there usually is a lifetime money-back guarantee. If the insured surrenders the policy for any reason, the amount received upon surrender is never less than the premiums paid minus any amounts paid as long-term care benefits. Any withdrawal from a single-premium policy—whether it is a policy loan, long-term care insurance premium, or cash value withdrawal—is subject to income taxation.

For an insured who wishes to be more speculative, some insurers have variable universal life insurance policies. Instead of a periodic interest rate with a guaranteed minimum, the insured elects to have the cash value invested in one of several different types of investment funds. This subjects the cash value and insurance benefits to a greater possibility of fluctuation.

Long-Term Care Coverage

The long-term care coverage under hybrid life insurance policies is designed to be tax qualified and is subject to most of the same HIPAA and state regulations that apply to stand-alone long-term care insurance policies. These products, however, are considered life insurance policies or riders that accelerate long-term care benefits and, as such, are sometimes treated differently under state regulations. For example, the insurer does not have to offer a nonforfeiture option because the cash value tends to serve this function.

The coverage under hybrid policies is comparable to that under comprehensive policies sold on a stand-alone basis. Depending on the insurer, the benefit may be paid on a per diem or reimbursement basis. The insured has some of the choices available to purchasers of stand-alone policies. There also, however, tend to be several differences:

- The amount of the long-term care benefit is a function of the amount of life insurance protection purchased. Conversely, the benefit amount selected dictates the amount of the life insurance that must be purchased.
- Benefit periods are often limited to 2, 3, or 4 years. However, some insurers make lifetime benefits available.
- There is typically no choice of elimination period. The usual period in these policies is 90 days.
- There is usually no option for automatic inflation increases. Rather, the insured can elect each year to increase both the death benefit and long-term care benefit by 5 percent of the amount of the prior year's coverage. The additional coverage is at the insured's attained age at the time of the election and must be paid with an additional lump sum if the original policy was purchased with a single premium. Failure to exercise an annual option results in the forfeiture of the right to elect additional coverage in the future.
- There is no nonforfeiture option.

Simplified issue is sometimes used for younger issue ages and small amounts of coverage. However, full individual underwriting is used for most coverage. Rates vary by the same classification factors as discussed in chapter 15 for stand-alone policies—age, gender, underwriting class, and possibly use of tobacco.

Example:	The contract is a universal life policy, and the insurer requires a minimum single premium of at least $10,000. The policy also includes a long-term care insurance benefit that in the aggregate is double the life insurance death benefit. The long-term care coverage provides benefits on a reimbursement basis from a pool of money, and the benefits can be used for all types of long-term care. Benefits can be increased by 5 percent each year by the payment of an additional lump-sum premium.

Helen wishes to purchase this policy at age 60 and have 4 years of benefits at $200 per day. She wants total long-term care benefits of $292,000 (1,460 days times $200). If Helen fits into the insurer's best underwriting classification, her lump-sum premium is $52,000. For this premium, she also receives a $146,000 death benefit.

If Helen decides to purchase the policy and dies without needing the long-term care benefit, her beneficiary will receive the $146,000 death benefit. If she receives up to $146,000 in long-term care benefits before her death, her beneficiary will still receive a $146,000 death benefit.

If Helen's long-term care benefits are greater than $146,000, the excess will be deducted from the death benefit. For example, assume she receives $200,000 in long-term care benefits. Then the death benefit will be reduced by $54,000 ($200,000 minus $146,000) to $92,000. This policy, like the policies of many other insurers, has a minimum death benefit equal to 10 percent of the life insurance benefit. Therefore, her beneficiary will always receive at least $14,600.

Note that the previous benefit amounts would have been different if Helen had purchased any additional benefits, received any policy loans, or made any withdrawals. |

Annuity Hybrids

As mentioned in chapter 12, annuities may be used to finance long-term care expenses with impaired-risk underwriting or through contract provisions that increase payments when annuitants need long-term care. These are not hybrid products, however, because the contracts themselves do not provide any type of long-term care insurance.

Only a small number of insurers sell hybrid annuity contracts. As with the hybrid life insurance contracts, these annuities are usually purchased with a large single premium by persons who have moderately high income and net worth and want to transfer assets from some other source.

There are probably almost as many variations of these hybrid annuities as there are insurers offering them. The following are two examples of such contracts.

Example 1: With one insurer's annuity, the annuitant funds a deferred annuity with a single premium equal to the deferred annuity's face amount. This premium also buys an additional amount of long-term care protection equal to twice the annuity premium. As with any long-term care protection, there is a specified level of benefits. The annuity fund grows tax deferred at a fixed rate of interest, and the annuitant has all the usual annuity options. If the annuitant has long-term care expenses, the first benefit payments are considered a liquidation of the annuity. After the annuity is liquidated, the remaining long-term care benefits come from the long-term care portion of the contract. If the annuitant dies before receiving any long-term benefits from the contract, a death benefit equal to the original deposit is paid to a beneficiary.

Example 2: With another insurer's annuity, the annuitant purchases a deferred variable annuity. The initial deposit is split between two accounts—one for the annuity and the other to fund the desired long-term care benefit. The insured has the choice of several options for each account, and the final annuity amount and long-term care benefits depend on investment results. This insurer's product provides two totally separate benefits. If the annuitant withdraws annuity benefits, there is no effect on the long-term care benefits. Similarly, if the annuitant uses long-term care benefits, the annuity account remains unaffected. There is a guaranteed death benefit under the contract so that the insured's beneficiary always receives an amount at least equal to the annuitant's initial investment.

Guaranteed Purchase Options

A very small number of insurers have recently introduced riders that can be added to life insurance or disability income policies to guarantee the insured's right to purchase long-term care insurance in the future without evidence of insurability. However, the riders, for which there is a premium charge, are underwritten at the time of issue and are available only to applicants who meet the insurer's standards at that time. These riders, which are referred to by such names as *guaranteed purchase option* or guaranteed insurability rider, are likely to be introduced by other insurers if they find acceptance in the marketplace.

guaranteed purchase option

The rider of one insurer allows the insured to purchase a long-term care insurance policy at any 5-year age interval starting at age 25 (or older if the policy was purchased at a later age) and continuing until age 60. However, the option cannot be exercised unless it has been in force for at least 2 years. The option can be exercised only once, and when it is exercised the insured can purchase any individual policy that is then being sold by the insurer. The only restriction on benefits is that there is a maximum daily benefit available. This limit varies from $110 to $220, depending on the geographic region in which the insured resides. Exercising the option has no effect on the policy to which it is attached; the insured can continue that policy in force.

NOTES

1. *U.S. Group Long-Term Care Insurance, Executive Summary, Annual 2004*, LIMRA International, Inc., 2005, p. 2.
2. Ibid., and *Long-Term Care and Medicare Supplement, Executive Summary, Annual 2004*, LIMRA International, Inc., 2005, p. 2.
3. *U.S. Group Long-Term Care Insurance, Executive Summary, Annual 2004*, LIMRA International, Inc., 2005, pp. 2 and 3.

18

The Government and Long-Term Care Insurance

Chapter Outline

Government typically assumes the role of an insurance regulator. As explained in chapter 13, that role also extends to long-term care insurance. More recently, government has taken on the role of counselor in ways that relate to long-term care insurance. Seldom, however, does government assume the role of an advocate of insurance products as it does in the case of long-term care insurance. Government in that unusual role, a subject of this chapter, is evident in the following:

- the Federal Long Term Care Insurance Program
- partnership programs for long-term care
- pending legislation

In addition, the federal and state governments, recognizing their stake as the major purchasers of long-term care services, have restructured the traditional Medicare and Medicaid programs to create alternatives that provide long-term care more effectively. These alternatives, initially established as demonstration projects, are designed to meet the needs of the chronically ill and frail elderly in home and community settings rather than in nursing homes. Social managed care plans and programs of all-inclusive care for the elderly are prominent alternative government-sponsored models.

GOVERNMENT AS COUNSELOR

The emerging role of government as counselor with regard to long-term care insurance is evident in the State Health Insurance Assistance Program and in the Long-Term Care Consumer Awareness Campaign.

State Health Insurance Assistance Program

State Health Insurance Assistance Program (SHIP)

Each state has a *State Health Insurance Assistance Program (SHIP)* that receives money from the federal government to give free local health insurance counseling to people with Medicare. Generally, SHIP counselors assist Medicare beneficiaries with their questions about benefits, claim denials and appeals, complaints about care or treatment, and selecting an appropriate Medicare plan. Significantly, among its other specific responsibilities, SHIPs offer guidance about the purchase of long-term care insurance. Medicare's Web site at www.medicare.gov identifies and provides contact information for each state's SHIP by following the home page search tools under helpful phone numbers and Web sites. The home page also provides links to information on long-term care services and options to pay for them, including long-term care insurance.

Long-Term Care Consumer Awareness Campaign

Long-Term Care Consumer Awareness Campaign

The *Long-Term Care Consumer Awareness Campaign* is a multistage project established as a cooperative effort between several participating states and agencies of the federal government to increase awareness among the public of the need to plan for long-term care.

The objective of the campaign, called "own your future," is to measure the effect that increased awareness of long-term care needs among retirees and near-retirees will have on their increased planning and use of private-sector options, including long-term care insurance, to pay for long-term care. The campaign's fundamental premise is that the burden of public financing of long-term care services under Medicaid will decline with the increased use of private-sector payment options.

Recent campaign activities encompassed a comprehensive media and direct mail campaign to residents aged 50 to 70 in participating states. SHIP counselors and staff members of local area agencies on aging with training in long-term care planning and finance options responded to the expected increase in the public requests for information on planning for long-term care needs. Upcoming campaign activities may include education of private employers on the importance of providing access to long-term care insurance coverage for their employees and extending long-term care insurance coverage to state employees. Further information on the next stage of the campaign and its program of activities is available at www.ltcaware.info.

THE FEDERAL LONG TERM CARE INSURANCE PROGRAM

The Long-Term Care Security Act, signed into law in September 2000, authorizes the U.S. Office of Personnel Management (OPM) to negotiate with private insurers to offer long-term care insurance to a group collectively referred to as the federal family. This group includes federal and postal employees and annuitants (generally retirees and surviving spouses), members and retired members of the uniformed services, and qualified relatives. Although the federal government is by far the largest employer to offer long-term care insurance, it is not the only government employer to do so; more than 30 states currently offer or are in the process of offering long-term care insurance to their employees and/or retirees.[1]

In December 2001, OPM negotiated a 7-year contract with Metropolitan Life Insurance Company and John Hancock Life Insurance Company to insure the Federal Long Term Care Insurance Program (FLTCIP). These two companies formed Long Term Care Partners, LLC (known as the LTC Partners), a jointly owned entity whose sole purpose is to administer the FLTCIP. OPM maintains continuing oversight of the program and must approve any premium increases (although none are anticipated) and benefit changes. At the end of the 7-year period, OPM will negotiate a renewed contract or a new contract with other carriers. Complete information on the FLTCIP, including a premium calculator, is available from OPM's Web site (www.opm.gov/insure/ltc) and the LTC Partners' Web site (www.ltcfeds.com).

The following sections summarize the FLTCIP with respect to its implications for long-term care insurance, eligibility, enrollment and underwriting, benefit design, other policy features, and premiums.

Implications for Long-Term Care Insurance

Many in the insurance industry viewed the creation of the FLTCIP as a positive development that could serve to promote long-term care insurance.

First, the passage of the Long-Term Care Security Act addresses many long-standing sources of consumer reluctance to purchase long-term care insurance. In effect, the federal government is telling the members of its own federal family that the likelihood of needing long-term care is real, and they should consider a program to pay for it because current government and private medical insurance programs are insufficient. Enactment of the new law also implies that a government-sponsored and paid-for social insurance program to provide long-term care for all Americans is unlikely in the foreseeable future.

Second, the federal government, as the nation's largest employer, becomes a model for other employers and encourages them to establish employer-sponsored long-term care insurance programs. The significant education program during the open-enrollment period (referred to as the open season) with thousands of educational meetings, satellite broadcasts, and videos also serves to raise the awareness of employees outside the federal program of their need for long-term care coverage and the possibility that their employers could offer it.

Finally, the action further validates the professional standing of insurance companies and their agents in their work to provide long-term care insurance to their clients.

Eligibility

The FLTCIP provides coverage on a voluntary basis, and participants pay 100 percent of the premium. The federal family, as previously defined, is eligible for participation. Qualified relatives as specified in the legislation are spouses, adult children (who are at least 18 years old), parents, parents-in-law, and stepparents. Although the law provides authority to designate other groups as qualified relatives (for example, grandparents, brothers and sisters, and foster children), there are currently no plans to do so. Each eligible person individually has the right to enroll in the program. Consequently, a federal employee's spouse may enroll even if the employee does not.

A fully extended federal family could number as many as 20 million members. However, active federal employees, postal workers, and members of the uniformed services; retirees; and spouses of both active and retired members of the federal family—a total of about 8 million persons—form the core of the eligible population. Current enrollment exceeds 200,000.

Enrollment and Underwriting

Eligible members of the federal family may apply for coverage at any time by completing one of two forms, an abbreviated underwriting application or a full underwriting application. Use of the abbreviated underwriting application is limited to newly hired or newly eligible federal or postal employees and those who have recently joined the uniformed services and their spouses.

The main advantage of the abbreviated form is that it allows applicants to obtain coverage at a less stringent level of underwriting that is equivalent to a modified guaranteed-issue basis as described in chapter 17. (Spouses are required to answer slightly more questions than are employees or uniformed service members.) However, if these applicants select the lifetime benefit option, more medically related questions must be answered and simplified-issue underwriting is used.

In addition, under the abbreviated form, those applicants who are unable to qualify for the coverage requested may apply for an alternative benefit plan that provides facility-only coverage with a 180-day waiting period, a 2-year benefit period, and a higher premium. If these applicants are denied coverage as initially requested or through the alternative plan, they may purchase a noninsurance service package. The service package, which is available for a small fee, provides access to a care coordinator, general information and referral services, and access to discounted networks of long-term care providers and services. The alternative benefit plan is unavailable to applicants required to use the full underwriting form who do not qualify for coverage, although they may purchase the noninsurance service package.

Benefit Design

The standard benefit program provides reimbursement benefits up to the selected benefit amounts. There is a choice of two types of tax-qualified options: facility-only coverage or comprehensive coverage. The coverage is also fully portable. If an insured leaves federal employment, is no longer a member of the uniformed services, or gets divorced, he or she may maintain the policy at the same premium as long as premium payments continue.

The following discussion summarizes the daily benefit amount, benefits for covered services, weekly benefits, benefit period, elimination period, inflation protection, and prepackaged plans.

Daily Benefit Amount

All enrollees must select a daily benefit amount within the range of $50 to $300 at $25 increments. This amount is also a factor in determining the weekly benefit, if selected, and the maximum lifetime benefit.

Benefits for Covered Services

The facility-only option and the comprehensive option each provide reimbursement of actual charges incurred for covered services, as indicated in table 18-1.

TABLE 18-1
FLTCIP Covered Services under a Facility-Only Option or a Comprehensive Option

Services	Daily Reimbursement
Nursing home, assisted-living facility, or hospice facility	100 percent of the daily benefit amount
Bed reservation benefit	100 percent of the daily benefit amount—limited to 30 days per calendar year
Caregiver training	100 percent of the daily benefit amount—lifetime limit of 7 times the daily benefit amount
Respite services in a facility	100 percent of the daily benefit amount—limited to 30 times the daily benefit amount per calendar year

Enrollees who select the comprehensive policy also receive the benefits for covered services indicated in table 18-2.

TABLE 18-2
Additional FLTCIP Covered Services under a Comprehensive Option

Services	Daily Reimbursement
Home health care services by formal caregivers	75 percent of the daily benefit amount
Home health care services by informal caregivers who do not normally live in the enrollee's home	75 percent of the daily benefit amount—benefits limited to 365 days for family members
Hospice care at home	100 percent of the daily benefit amount
Adult day care center	75 percent of the daily benefit amount
Respite services at home or adult day care center	100 percent of the daily benefit amount—limited to 30 times the daily benefit amount per calendar year

Weekly Benefits

Enrollees who select the comprehensive option may also choose a weekly benefit amount that is equal to seven times the daily benefit amount selected. Thus, the reimbursements levels in tables 18-1 and 18-2 would provide a weekly benefit amount in place of the indicated daily benefit amounts. Weekly benefit levels are encouraged because they adapt to varying daily expense levels that may be incurred over the course of a week.

Benefit Period

Enrollees may choose a 3-year, 5-year, or lifetime benefit period. The benefit period and the daily benefit amount selected form a pool of money known as the lifetime maximum benefit to be used for covered services. As explained in chapter 14, under this approach, the policy pays benefits until the pool of money is exhausted—a process that may take longer than the 3-year or 5-year benefit period if the insured does not receive covered services every day or if benefits paid are less than the daily or weekly benefit amount. Benefits paid reduce the pool of money, dollar for dollar. When the pool is gone, the insurance ends. If the enrollee selects the lifetime benefit period, the pool of money ends with the life of the insured.

Elimination Period

Enrollees must select either a 30-day or 90-day elimination period—a requirement that must be satisfied only once in a lifetime. Because the elimination period consists of only the days when covered services are actually received, a 90-day elimination period, for example, lasts longer than 90 calendar days unless covered services are received every day. The elimination period need be satisfied only once in a lifetime. There is no elimination period for hospice care, respite services, and caregiver training. Receipt of these services does not count toward the satisfaction of the elimination period.

Inflation Protection

Enrollees may choose one of two inflation-protection features:

- automatic-increase option. The daily benefit and the remaining portion of the pool of money automatically increase by 5 percent each year over the benefit levels available in the prior year (compounded annually). Premiums are designed (but not guaranteed) to remain level for life, even when benefits increase. The automatic compound inflation option is recommended for purchasers who are not likely to need benefits for many years.

- future-purchase option. The benefit and the remaining portion of the pool of money automatically increase every other year based on the consumer price index (CPI) for medical care or another agreed-upon inflation index. However, unlike the automatic-increase option, premiums increase as benefits increase. The enrollee may decline the increase in benefits and premiums. Three refusals to accept the every-other-year-increases condition any subsequent benefit increase on satisfactory evidence of insurability.

A unique feature of the FLTCIP is the ability to move from the future-purchase option to the automatic-increase option without evidence of insurability.

Prepackaged Plans

Although enrollees may customize their benefit packages, there are also four alternative prepackaged plans to assist them in making choices among the program's many options. One prepackaged plan provides facility-only coverage with a $100 daily benefit amount, a 3-year benefit period, and a 90-day waiting period. The other prepackaged plans are comprehensive programs with different combinations of daily benefit amounts (either $100 or $150), varying benefit periods (3 years, 5 years, or unlimited), and a 90-day waiting period. Inflation options are available under all prepackaged plans.

Other Policy Features

Other features that apply to all policies include care coordination and referral services, alternative plans of care, care abroad, contingent nonforfeiture benefit, limitations and exclusions, and third-party review of disputed claims.

Care Coordination and Referral Services

The program requires a licensed health care practitioner, who is selected by the insured and approved by the program, to serve as a care coordinator. The care coordinator assesses and approves the need for long-term care services and develops a cost-effective plan of care to make efficient use of the pool of money. The care coordinator may also provide information, make referrals, and arrange for care. The care coordinator's services are provided at no cost to insureds. Qualified relatives who are not enrolled may also purchase these services.

Alternative Plans of Care

A care coordinator can authorize benefits for services and products that are not specifically defined as covered services. The services must meet the enrollee's needs and be cost effective. For example, a comprehensive plan can pay benefits to maintain a person at home, such as making the home wheelchair accessible.

Care Abroad

If the enrollee selects a 3-year or 5-year benefit period, charges for covered services received outside the United States are covered up to 80 percent of the daily benefit allowance for up to 80 percent of the maximum lifetime benefit. The remaining 20 percent of the lifetime maximum benefit is available for services received in the United States. If the enrollee selects the lifetime benefit period, the benefit period outside the United States becomes 10 years with a maximum lifetime benefit equal to 3,650 days (10 years) multiplied by 80 percent of the daily benefit amount. If the insured returns to the United States, benefits remain unlimited.

Contingent Nonforfeiture Benefit

The FLTCIP includes a contingent nonforfeiture benefit. If the insurer increases premiums beyond a specified percentage, an enrollee can choose to stop paying premiums and elect a policy with a shortened benefit period. There are no other nonforfeiture options.

Limitations and Exclusions

The federal long-term care insurance coverage has the usual contract provisions and exclusions with the notable exceptions that acts of war are not excluded; nor are mental or nervous conditions. However, there is a catastrophic coverage limitation that may reduce benefits if an event or series of events (including war) affect a significant number of enrollees and threaten to undermine the federal program's financial stability.

Third-Party Review of Disputed Claims

If the program's appeals committee upholds a claim denial, the insured may request an independent third-party review. The result of the review is final and binding on the parties.

Premiums

This section discusses program premiums and compares them with other policies.

Program Premiums

The law requires that FLTCIP participants pay 100 percent of the premiums and that premiums reflect the cost of benefits provided. Premiums do not differ by enrollee class, such as active employee or member of the uniformed services, spouse, or parent. Premiums are based on age when the coverage is purchased and the benefits selected. There are no spousal or family discounts.

Three options are available for payment of premiums—automatic bank withdrawal, federal payroll/retirement annuity deduction, and direct billing. Federal employees and annuitants and active and retired members of the uniformed services may pay the premiums for any qualified relative even if they themselves do not apply for or are denied coverage.

A waiver of premium applies after the insured satisfies the selected waiting period. However, after recovery, the insured must resume the payment of premiums.

Comparison with Other Policies

By law, FLTCIP premiums must reflect the cost of benefits provided. OPM estimates these premiums to be as much as 20 percent lower than premiums for other available standard-issue policies. Reasons that OPM cites as keeping premiums low include its negotiating role, economies of scale, and direct purchase that eliminates the agent/broker-system distribution costs (no commissions). Nevertheless, some other policies can be quite competitive based on a premium comparison.

Several factors might make other insurers' policies competitive to the FLTCIP's from a cost standpoint. Among them are the FLTCIP's absence of preferred rates, the lack of spousal or family discounts, and the inclusion of a rich package with such extra benefits as caregiver training and payment to informal caregivers. In addition, the absence of substandard ratings may deny coverage to those who would otherwise qualify outside of the FLTCIP.

Long-term care policies issued under the FLTCIP may appear similar to policies purchased outside the program. However, there is a fundamental difference: FLTCIP policies are governed by federal law and are exempt from any state or local laws, including insurance regulation and premium taxation. The difference has several important implications. First, coverage, benefits, and other policy provisions available under the FLTCIP are identical in whichever location an applicant purchases a policy. Second, as mentioned earlier, there is binding arbitration for disputed claims.

And third, the program's rate stability and financial solvency are protected by OPM, not state insurance commissioners. OPM is also responsible for monitoring FLTCIP performance, auditing the program, and anticipating financial problems. OPM and LTC Partners must agree to any rate increases. In addition, the General Accounting Office must evaluate the program and may audit it as well. The program's funds can be used only for program expenses, including administration. These funds must be maintained and accounted for separately from the funds of the LTC Partners' companies for any of their other lines of business.

Example:

Harvie and Mary Beth, having completed fulfilling careers, consider themselves fortunate to leave their respective employers for a secure and busy retired life. With two of their friends recently requiring nursing home care, they have become aware of the need for long-term care insurance. Jason, their insurance agent for many years, presented them a plan from a reputable insurance company and suggested three options for covered services and benefit levels, each of which generally meets their needs.

As they were considering these options, Mary Beth received a notice that her former employer is now sponsoring a long-term care insurance plan as a voluntary benefit for which active and retired employees and their spouses are eligible. Coincidentally, during a casual conversation, Gwendolyn, Harvie and Mary Beth's daughter who works for the Treasury Department, points out that they are also eligible for the Federal Long Term Care Insurance Program (FLTCIP) as qualified relatives. Gwendolyn shows her parents how to use the premium calculator on the federal Web site to determine the premiums that match as closely as possible the plan options they are considering.

They have decided to analyze these alternative plans as well as the options from Jason.

PARTNERSHIP PROGRAMS FOR LONG-TERM CARE

The partnership programs for long-term care are alliances between certain state governments and insurance companies to encourage the sale of approved long-term care policies. The goals of these programs are to protect people from being impoverished by long-term care expenses and to avoid their immediate dependence on Medicaid. These programs also provide further evidence of government's advocacy of long-term care insurance. Indeed, the states that currently have partnership programs make a concerted effort to inform and counsel their residents about the value of purchasing long-term care insurance.

Partnership programs are summarized with respect to their impetus, program development, state requirements, program types, and limitations. The removal of a federal legislative impediment to widespread expansion beyond the original partnership states is also discussed.

Impetus

Many middle-class people in nursing homes qualify for Medicaid by spending virtually all of their assets on long-term care or by transferring the assets to put themselves in a state of poverty. The result has been a staggering financial burden on Medicaid that endangers its mission to care for the poor in many states. The cycle of spending down to Medicaid dependence can be broken if more middle-class Americans—especially those of more modest means who are likely to spend down to qualify for Medicaid—could be broadly encouraged to purchase long-term care insurance.

The potential savings to the Medicaid program are obvious. If the policy's benefits prove sufficient to meet the cost of care, a person with long-term care insurance may not have to rely on Medicaid at all. Moreover, a comprehensive policy provides resources to care for someone at a much lower cost at home. If the person was on Medicaid, higher nursing home costs might be incurred.

States, in return for the potential cost savings generated by reducing Medicaid dependence, are willing to offer an incentive for the purchase of long-term care insurance. Policymakers agreed that an effective incentive from the state is to allow people who purchase long-term care insurance to qualify for Medicaid while maintaining a higher-than-usual personal asset level. As a result, purchasers of long-term care insurance with significant assets can still qualify for Medicaid without having to spend down those assets.

Program Development

In 1987, the Robert Wood Johnson Foundation funded a study by the state of Connecticut. The study concluded that collaboration between insurers and the state could help reduce the burden on the Medicaid program through the use of private long-term care insurance. The foundation subsequently awarded program development grants to four states: California, Connecticut, Indiana, and New York. The resulting and continuing programs in these four states, known as the partnership programs,[2] became operational in the early 1990s. The Department of Health and Human Services granted the required approval or waivers that permitted these states to change the Medicaid asset spend-down requirements. Purchasers of long-term care insurance policies under these programs could then maintain some or all of their assets and still qualify for Medicaid without having to spend down their assets to levels typically required for Medicaid eligibility.

State Requirements

Insurers participating in the partnership programs are required to meet the state's requirements for qualified policies and reporting.

Requirements for Qualified Policies

Insurance companies that participate in partnership programs must develop special products to qualify for approval in each state. The plans, which may be individual or employer sponsored, must meet HIPAA standards for tax-qualified policies. The state's approval further boosts consumer confidence in purchasing the plan. Policy requirements of most partnership programs, which were considered innovative a decade ago when they were first introduced, include the following:

- availability of both facility-only and comprehensive policies
- minimum and maximum benefit amounts and durations
- inflation protection
- single lifetime elimination period
- a care coordinator or consultant, often from a state-approved or state-required agency, to assist in planning for care and obtaining appropriate services
- protection against policy lapse due to nonpayment of premium through waiver of premium and notification of a specially identified third party in the event of the insured's failure to pay the premium
- state role in the claims process to ensure prompt payment and review of denials
- agent training in partnership policies

Some states require insurers to offer upgraded partnership products when new products are issued in the nonpartnership market. At least one state (California) requires any new policy enhancements also to be offered to current partnership policyowners.

An important objective of partnership programs is to encourage purchase of coverage by individuals of modest means. To keep the cost of partnership policies affordable, the state programs may allow shorter benefit durations than otherwise allowed by state regulations. For example, California and Indiana allow the sales of policies with benefit durations of 1 year, and Connecticut allows sales of policies with a 2-year benefit duration. Purchase of policies with shorter duration periods has ranged from 30 percent to more than 50 percent of partnership policies sold in some years.

Reporting Requirements

Partnership states require insurers to report activity on program-approved policies regularly. The reporting requirements encompass the following:

- new insureds, both individual and employer sponsored
- insureds who have changed or dropped coverage

- claimants, including those assessed for benefit eligibility and those meeting elimination periods
- applicants denied coverage

The partnership states have developed a single uniform data set and streamlined their requirements to ease reporting by insurers that participate in more than one state. In addition, the states themselves can more easily track partnership program progress.

Program Types

Two basic partnership models were developed—the total-assets model and the dollar-for-dollar model.[3] Both models have minimum requirements on the amount of coverage that a consumer is required to purchase. As with all Medicaid recipients, insureds who become eligible for Medicaid must contribute their income toward the cost of care.

Total-Assets Model

The total-assets model adopted by New York requires that participants select a minimum daily benefit amount for 3 years of nursing home care and 6 years of home health care, or a combination of the two. When total minimum benefits are exhausted (even if policy benefits are greater), the insured's income determines Medicaid eligibility, regardless of assets. Because New York's minimum coverage requirements, which are high compared to other partnership states, may discourage enrollment of middle- and lower-income persons, the state has considered implementing a hybrid arrangement that incorporates a dollar-for-dollar model for the purchase of less extensive coverage.

Dollar-for-Dollar Model

The dollar-for-dollar model also allows consumers to protect their assets through the purchase of a partnership policy that has a state-approved level of coverage and benefits. When policy benefits are utilized, an amount of assets equal to the benefits that were paid for long-term care services is disregarded in determining financial eligibility for Medicaid. In general, the minimum policy must cover at least one year in a nursing home at a minimum daily benefit amount. Three states—California, Connecticut, and Indiana—initially adopted this model. Indiana later changed to a hybrid arrangement that combines a total-assets model for coverage amounts above an annually increasing threshold level with a dollar-for-dollar model for coverage levels below the threshold amount.

Limitations

A person with a partnership policy has all the advantages of long-term care insurance discussed throughout this textbook. The limitations of the program occur if those with approved policies qualify for Medicaid under the partnership program. Although assets are protected as enrollees turn to Medicaid to pay for their care, they must keep in mind the Medicaid shortcomings discussed in chapter 9.

In addition, as mentioned previously, although assets are protected, income is not. Program beneficiaries must therefore spend essentially all their income, allowing certain limited amounts for the support of a spouse who continues to live at home. This standard Medicaid requirement effectively eliminates participation in partnership plans by high-income persons.

Although insureds under this program may receive their insurance benefits in any state, their assets are protected only in the state where they purchased their partnership-program-eligible policy. This is currently a major drawback as many people relocate at or during retirement for leisure living or to be near family. However, with the approval of the Department of Health and Human Services, Connecticut and Indiana have established reciprocity of program benefits between them, whereby residents with partnership policies in one state who relocate to the other are eligible for asset protection in the determination of Medicaid eligibility. If many states implement partnership programs, reciprocity among them would be a significant advantage, creating a further incentive to purchase coverage under the program.

Program Experience

Initially, nonpartnership long-term care polices had lower premiums than partnership policies because they did not have to meet the stricter requirements that states mandated. The resulting lower-than-expected sales of long-term care insurance under the partnership programs prompted the four states and their insurers to narrow the differences between the two types of policies. Subsequently, California and Connecticut, two states that made notable changes, realized significant increases in partnership policy enrollment. Available data, however, remain insufficient to confirm the effectiveness of partnership programs in relieving the long-term care cost burden on Medicaid. Current studies do not answer such key questions as whether the policies are purchased by people who otherwise would not buy insurance, whether the partnership polices are a substitute for other long-term care insurance polices, or if participants would have used Medicaid regardless of their long-term care insurance. The answers to these questions require continued evaluation of purchasers of long-term care coverage who use their insurance benefits and/or exhaust them to the point where they become Medicaid eligible. Nevertheless, available data are encouraging.

Over 25 insurance companies participate in partnership programs in one or more of the original four partnership states. Since the inception of the program through 2003, the combined sales of the partnership-approved policies in these states exceeded 180,000, with approximately 148,000 policies remaining in force. Of the over 2,000 insureds who received long-term care benefits, fewer than 90 have accessed or applied for Medicaid. The data indicate that those participants who needed Medicaid made substantial contributions to their own care through their long-term care policy benefits prior to accessing Medicaid.

To achieve Medicaid cost savings, partnership programs seek to encourage enrollment of persons at middle and lower-middle income levels because they are generally less likely to purchase long-term care insurance and more likely to become Medicaid eligible by spending down their assets. Thus far, available data from the partnership states indicate that the program encourages upper-middle income persons to obtain long-term care insurance—but they are already the most common buyers of this type of insurance. More promising for the program's effectiveness is the result that shows the purchasers of partnership policies are, on average, measurably younger than long-term care insurance purchasers in general.[4]

Removal of a Federal Legislative Impediment

The Deficit Reduction Act of 2005 (DRA) removed a long-standing impediment to the expansion of partnership programs beyond those implemented in the initial four states.

The Omnibus Budget Reconciliation Act of 1993 (OBRA) effectively eliminated an important feature of state partnership programs approved by the Department of Health and Human Services after May 14, 1993. Any partnership program approved after that date was no longer able to exempt amounts from Medicaid's estate recovery requirements for individuals who applied to Medicaid after exhausting their private long-term care insurance benefits. Even though a new partnership program could continue to allow a participant to retain greater asset amounts upon application for Medicaid, the state was required to recover Medicaid's long-term care expenditures from the participant's estate, including the previously protected assets. Thus, the asset-protection component of any new partnership program would be in effect only while the participant was alive. This requirement effectively removed the asset-protection incentive essential to consumer interest in any long-term care insurance policy that a new state partnership program might offer.[5]

DRA restored the ability of states to obtain a Medicaid plan amendment that allows exemption from the estate recovery requirement for qualified partnership programs. However, these partnership programs may exempt only the amounts of the insurance benefits made to or on behalf of an individual under a long-term care policy that meets the requirements specified in the law. Thus, while the act grandfathers programs approved prior to OBRA, new qualified partnership programs must use the previously described dollar-for-dollar model (not the total assets model) to determine the amount of assets exempt from estate recovery. The standards for long-term care policies offered through qualified partnership programs under DRA are consistent with the practices of the four active programs and conform to NAIC and HIPAA requirements.

DRA also promotes the expansion of state partnership programs through new initiatives:

- a national clearinghouse of information to educate consumers on long-term care
- standards for uniform reciprocal recognition of long-term care polices offered through states with qualified partnership programs
- an annual report to Congress by the secretary of health and human services on qualified partnership programs

PENDING FEDERAL TAX LEGISLATION

According to an industry survey, an important government reform that would lead nonbuyers to consider buying long-term care insurance is the ability to deduct premiums from personal income tax.[6] Pending federal legislative proposals would grant improved tax-preferred status to long-term care insurance and directly addresses this area. Such proposals evidence legislative support for the growth of long-term care insurance.

As explained in chapter 13, HIPAA allowed qualified long-term care policies to enjoy tax-preferred status for the first time. Under more recent legislation, premiums for long-term care insurance up to HIPAA's age-based limit reduce taxable income if paid through a health savings account or an Archer medical savings account. Nevertheless, the tax treatment of long-term care insurance falls short of what is accorded other accident and health insurance policies. Specifically, long-term care coverage cannot be offered through a cafeteria plan on a tax-preferred basis, and any reimbursement drawn from an employee's flexible spending account for unreimbursed long-term care expenses (other than medical expenses) must be included in the employee's income. The pending proposals would eliminate these exceptions, thereby giving long-term care expenses and long-term care insurance premiums and benefits the same tax preferences as medical expenses and premiums for medical expense insurance.

Indeed, some proposals would make premiums paid for long-term care insurance directly deductible in whole or in part from gross income. This deduction, which could be taken without itemizing, is known as an "above-the-line" tax deduction. Supporters of such proposals point out that currently there is little actual tax benefit for premium payments because most people do not have medical expenses, even including long-term care insurance premiums, that exceed 7.5 percent of adjusted gross income. Other proposals feature tax credit for premiums and for caregiver expenses to help families pay for supplies, home improvements, and other services to keep a family member at home.

ALTERNATIVE GOVERNMENT-SPONSORED MODELS

Since the 1980s, the federal government in cooperation with state governments encouraged the development of alternative models using restructured Medicare payments and Medicaid payments to better meet the needs of the chronically ill and frail elderly. Two examples of these types of alternative government-sponsored models are social managed care plans and programs of all-inclusive care for the elderly.

Social Managed Care Plans

social managed care plan (SMCP)

A *social managed care plan (SMCP)* (formerly known as a social health maintenance organization) is an organization that provides the full range of medical benefits typically offered to Medicare beneficiaries by Medicare Advantage plans. It also provides a required prescription drug benefit and, more significantly, chronic care services. The additional chronic care services include care coordination, short-term nursing home care, and a full range of home and community-based services that include homemaker services, personal care services, adult day care, respite care, and medical transportation. Other services may include eyeglasses, hearing aids, and dental benefits. In short, membership in a SMCP offers Medicare enrollees benefits that are not provided through traditional Medicare or most other alternative senior health plans.

SMCPs are discussed with respect to current sites, chronic care services provided, payment, and program transition.

Current Sites

There are currently four SMCPs. These plans are located in Portland, Oregon; Long Beach, California; Brooklyn, New York; and Las Vegas, Nevada.[7] Total enrollment is estimated at more than 100,000.

Chronic Care Services Provided

SMCPs enroll a broad spectrum of Medicare beneficiaries. They focus their home and community-based services on those members who are at greatest risk of being admitted to a nursing home or who have significant health care needs. Approximately 20 percent of enrollees fall into this category. All SMCPs use a "health status form" to screen new members for risk factors that indicate frailty and functional impairments. They subsequently screen each member annually. Case managers assess members who appear to be at risk for complications that could lead to a hospital or nursing home stay (including those referred directly by providers). They conduct an in-person comprehensive assessment to determine whether members are eligible for extra services. Members who are at risk receive these services to help them to stay in the community and reduce the risk of complications.

Payment

SMCPs receive capitated payments and accept risk for their members, just like Medicare Advantage plans. However, they are paid more than Medicare Advantage plans because of two features of the payment method. First, the SMCPs receive the Medicare Advantage plan rate augmented to cover the expanded benefit package of community care and care coordination that SMCPs provide. Second, SMCP payment is further adjusted for additional risk factors that indicate differences among members in need of services. This adjustment is known as a frailty factor.

Like many Medicare Advantage plans, SMCPs usually charge premiums to their Medicare-eligible enrollees. SMCPs do not charge premiums if the enrollee is eligible for Medicare and also qualifies for Medicaid.

Program Transition

A study by the Centers for Medicare & Medicaid Services determined that there is no evidence that SMCPs have improved member outcomes uniquely. As a result, the Secretary of Health and Human Services is in the process of changing the status of SMCPs from demonstration projects to Medicare Advantage plans. This phased transition is planned for completion by the end of 2007.

Upon completion of the transition, it is anticipated that the risk adjustment methodology applicable to all Medicare Advantage plan payments will be sufficiently accurate to compensate SMCPs for the higher cost of their frail patients. In addition, SMCPs would no longer be required to offer the expanded benefit package mentioned previously. They could, however, choose to continue such benefits through improved efficiency or by charging their members additional premiums.

Programs of All-Inclusive Care for the Elderly

programs of all-inclusive care for the elderly (PACE)

Programs of all-inclusive care for the elderly (PACE) are optional benefit programs under both Medicare and Medicaid that focus entirely on older people who are frail enough to meet their state's Medicaid eligibility standards for nursing home care. The PACE model was tested through the demonstration projects that the Centers for Medicare & Medicaid Services began in the mid-1980s. The programs have now been made permanent. PACE providers are not-for-profit private organizations or public entities that are primarily engaged in providing PACE services.

Programs bring together comprehensive medical and social services that can be provided at an adult day care center and at home for someone who otherwise might be in a nursing home. Nursing home services are also provided for those who ultimately must rely on them. For most enrollees, however, the comprehensive service package permits them to continue living at home while receiving services rather than being institutionalized. PACE is available only in states that have chosen to offer PACE under Medicaid.

The following sections describe PACE programs' eligibility and enrollment, long-term care services, sources of payment, and permanent status.

Eligibility and Enrollment

Eligible individuals participate through voluntary enrollment. Participants must be at least 55 years old, live in the PACE service area, be able to live separately in the community with the support of PACE services, and be certified as eligible for nursing home care by the appropriate state agency.

There are 25 PACE program sites, and each site has about 200 enrollees with an average age over 80. New programs may be added each year. PACE programs are available in the following states: California, Colorado, Maryland, Massachusetts, Michigan, Missouri, New York, Ohio, Oregon, South Carolina, Tennessee, Texas, Washington, and Wisconsin. About 80 percent of applicants are Medicaid enrollees.

Long-Term Care Services

The PACE service package must include all Medicare benefits and any Medicaid services that the state provides. PACE offers and manages all the medical, social, and rehabilitative services that enrollees need to (1) preserve or restore their independence, (2) remain in their homes and communities, and (3) maintain their quality of life. A team of doctors, nurses, and other health professionals assess participant needs and develop care plans. The team also delivers all services, which are integrated into a complete health care plan. Generally, social and medical services are provided in an adult day care center setting but may also include in-home and other referral services that enrollees may need, such as medical specialists, laboratory and other diagnostic services, and hospital care. If a participant needs to be placed in a nursing home, PACE provides that service and maintains care by regular evaluation and monitoring of the enrollee's condition.

Adult day care centers—which are at the heart of the PACE programs—must provide primary care services, social services, restorative therapies, personal care and supportive services, nutritional counseling, recreational therapy, meals, and transportation. Services are available 24 hours a day, 7 days a week, 365 days a year.

Sources of Payment

PACE providers receive a fixed monthly capitation per enrollee from Medicare and Medicaid during the contract year, regardless of the services an enrollee may need or changes in his or her health status. The capitation is considered payment in full, and the PACE providers assume full financial risk for participants' care without limits on amount, duration, or scope of services.

Under the Medicare program, the monthly capitation rate paid to the PACE provider equals the risk-adjusted Medicare Advantage rate that is also paid to SMCPs, as described previously. However, PACE payments also include, when applicable, an adjustment for frail enrollees and those with end-stage renal disease. Under the Medicaid program, the monthly capitation is negotiated between the PACE provider and the state Medicaid agency. It is based on an estimate of how much Medicaid would pay for PACE enrollees under the traditional Medicaid program and in alternative settings.

Enrollees may be individuals who are entitled to Medicare, individuals who are eligible for Medicaid, or both, or neither. If a person qualifies for both Medicare and Medicaid, Medicaid pays its portion of the monthly PACE premium and Medicare pays the rest. The PACE program becomes the sole source of services for Medicare- and Medicaid-eligible enrollees. Medicare-eligible participants who do not qualify for Medicaid pay monthly premiums equal to the Medicaid portion of the capitation amount, but no deductibles, coinsurance, or other type of Medicare or Medicaid cost-sharing applies. Medicaid pays the entire capitation amount for Medicaid-eligible enrollees who do not qualify for Medicare. Although it is unusual for a PACE enrollee to be ineligible for both Medicare and Medicaid, such a person would be responsible for the entire monthly payment.

Permanent Status

In 1999, the Centers for Medicare & Medicaid Services published regulations to implement legislation that established PACE as a permanent part of the Medicare program. This legislation limits the growth of PACE programs, but it is not anticipated that new programs will exceed the limit imposed. This limit is 220 programs in 2006 and will increase by 20 programs each year thereafter.

NOTES

1. The Minnesota Department of Employee Relations conducted a *Survey of States that Offer Long-Term Care Insurance to Employees and/or Retirees*. The survey, updated in August 2003, identified 31 states that offer such long-term care insurance programs. The California program, self-insured through a trust established by the California Public Employees Retirement System (CalPERs), is by far the largest of these programs with over 170,000 enrollees. With the exception of the program in Alaska, which like that in California is self-funded, all other state programs are insured.

2. Detailed information on the specific partnership programs is available from each state's Web site as follows: California (www.dhs.ca.gov/cpltc), Connecticut (www.CTpartnership.org), Indiana (www.IN.gov/fssa/iltcp), and New York (www.nyspltc.org).

3. Program descriptions are taken from University of Maryland Center on Aging, Partnership for Long-Term Care, Overview, pp. 4 and 5, from its Web site at www.inform.umd.edu/aging.

4. The discussion on program experience is based on *The Long-Term Care Partnership Program: Issues and Options,* George Washington University School of Public Health and Health Services, December 2004.

5. States other the original four states with active programs have shown interest in partnership programs.

   Because its plan amendment was approved before the OBRA legislative deadline, the Iowa partnership program can offer asset protection with an exemption from estate recovery under Medicaid. Massachusetts is also not subject to the estate recovery conditions of the legislation, but its partnership program provides no up-front protection of assets upon application for Medicaid. Illinois and Washington also undertook partnership program initiatives, but both programs are subject to the estate recovery requirement. All these programs experienced little or no insurer interest.

   An estimated 21 states drafted or passed enabling statutes and regulations for partnership programs. However, these programs were not implemented because of the estate recovery requirement.

   With DRA's enactment, the above-mentioned states and other states may pursue active implementation and/or establishment of partnership programs for long-term care insurance.

6. *Who Buys Long-Term Care Insurance in 2000? A Decade of Study of Buyers and Nonbuyers,* prepared for the Health Insurance Association of America by LifePlans, Inc., October 2000, p. 38.

7. Three additional SMCPs specifically target members with end-stage renal disease but are less applicable to the chronic needs of the Medicare population as a whole.

Glossary

abbreviated underwriting • *See* modified guaranteed-issue underwriting.

ABN • *See* Advance Beneficiary Notice.

accelerated-benefits provision • a life insurance policy feature that allows the policyowner to receive a portion of the death benefit while the insured is still living if one or more specified events, known as triggers, occur. The trigger is typically a singular event involving the need for health care services; the most common event is the diagnosis of a terminal illness or physical condition for which death is likely to occur within 12 months or less. *Compare* viatical settlement.

accidental death and dismemberment (AD&D) insurance • a policy or a rider to a policy that designates a dollar benefit (the *principal amount*) that is payable at the insured's accidental death. Payment of all or part of the principal amount is also made in the event of the accidental loss of a hand, foot, and/or eye, or at a degree of complete and irreversible paralysis of the limbs.

accident-only coverage • a policy or a rider to a policy that provides coverage singly or in combination for death, dismemberment, disability, or hospital and medical care caused by accident. *See also* accidental death and dismemberment (AD&D) insurance.

activities of daily living (ADLs) • physical functions that are the basic and necessary tasks of everyday life and usually include eating, bathing, dressing, using the toilet, maintaining continence, and transferring into or out of a bed, chair, or wheelchair. *Compare* instrumental activities of daily living (IADLs).

acute care • medical care received for a relatively brief time for a severe episode of illness, an accident or other trauma, or recovery from surgery. Acute care is usually given in a hospital.

Administration on Aging (AOA) • an agency within the U.S. Department of Health and Human Services created by the Older Americans Act (OAA) that funds assistance and services for older persons and their caregivers

adult day care center • a care setting that provides social, medical, and rehabilitative services to persons with physical and mental limitations who normally reside in their own homes but are unable to remain at home during the day. Such centers, also known as adult day centers and adult day health centers, allow family caregivers to be away from home during the day.

Advance Beneficiary Notice (ABN) • a notice that a physician, other medical provider, or supplier is required to give a Medicare beneficiary if they think Medicare will not pay for an item or service

adverse selection • the tendency for those who know that they are highly vulnerable to loss to be more likely to purchase insurance to cover that loss

433

agent's statement • a declaration in an insurance application signed by the agent attesting that the agent personally interviewed the applicant, determined the appropriateness of the coverage, witnessed the applicant's signature, and reported all available information and observations relative to the applicant's insurability

aggregate maximum • the overall amount of benefits payable under a policy for all covered services on behalf of each insured as long as the policy is in force. *Also known as* lifetime maximum.

aging in place • a term frequently used to summarize the approach to placement in the care continuum under which the care setting and the level of services provided best meet the care recipient's needs while maintaining a maximum degree of independence and as normal a living situation as possible

allowable charges • a basis on which benefits are determined under a medical expense policy. Once a deductible is satisfied, the benefit payment is a percentage of the remaining allowable charge.

alternate premium payer • a designee authorized by the long-term care insurance policyowner under a provision for third-party notification of policy lapse

Alzheimer's facility • a facility with a high level of staffing and other capabilities to provide the social interaction, close monitoring, and significant personal assistance individuals with Alzheimer's disease need. An Alzheimer's facility may be a stand-alone facility but most frequently is a separate unit of a nursing home or assisted-living facility devoted to this type of care.

amendment • *See* rider.

ancillary medical expense insurance • a policy that provides coverage and benefits for health care services that historically were considered incidental to medical care. Examples include dental, vision, hearing, and prescription drug services. Policies that offer this type of insurance are often called limited benefit policies.

annuitant • a person who receives the periodic payment from an annuity • for purposes of federal benefit programs, retired federal government and postal employees—more specifically, the retirees who qualify to receive a pension in the form of a retirement annuity

annuity • a financial contract that typically provides a series of periodic payments beginning at a specific date and continuing throughout a fixed period or for the duration of a designated life or lives

annuity certain • an annuity in which payments are received for a specified period of time

application • a form that is the basis for an underwriter to make a decision to provide requested coverage. It includes an identification of the insured, coverage and benefit selections, an insurability declaration (if necessary), authorizations and notifications, the agent's statement, and the applicant's signature.

Archer medical savings account (MSA) • a tax-preferred personal savings account established with a qualified high-deductible health plan that conforms to provisions of the Health Insurance Portability and Accountability Act. Authorization for new accounts terminates at the end of 2005 unless the date is extended. Account holders may roll over balances into recently authorized health savings accounts (HSAs).

area agencies on aging (AAAs) • public or private nonprofit agencies, designated by a state under the Older Americans Act (OAA) to address the needs and concerns of all older people in local communities

assisted-living facility • a supportive-living arrangement for elderly residents who, despite some degree of impairment, remain independent to a significant degree but require continuing super-vision and the availability of assistance on an unscheduled basis. *Compare* independent housing.

association plan • an insurance benefit program established through an affiliation of independent members with a professional, industry, or other noninsurance relationship or as a construct by insurers (known as a discretionary or trust plan) to provide coverage to individuals who are unaffiliated other than for the purpose of obtaining insurance

attained-age rate • a premium rate for a policy or policy change that is based on the insured's age at the time the policy is written or the change is made. *Compare* issue-age rate.

attending physician's statement (APS) • a statement that asks the physician to provide infor-mation to an insurer about an applicant's dates of treatment, length of treatment, tests ordered, medications prescribed, and the degree of recovery or control achieved for medical conditions

authorization to release information • a statement or series of statements signed by an applicant for insurance that approves the release of the applicant's financial and/or and medical information to the insurer by individuals and organizations

automatic-increase option • a provision in a long-term care insurance policy designed to offset the effects of inflation by increasing benefits over the life of the policy by a stated percentage applied annually to either the initially selected benefit (simple) or the amount of benefits available in the prior year (compound). The cost of an automatic-increase option is usually built into the initial premium, and no additional premium is levied at the time of an annual increase. *Compare* future purchase option.

basic hospital and medical-surgical insurance • medical expense insurance that has fixed or limited benefits per period of illness or injury, such as a maximum amount per day for a specified number of days of inpatient hospital confinement, a fee schedule for surgeon services, and dollar maximums for physician visits. Basic hospital and basic medical-surgical coverages may be marketed separately, but are frequently combined in a single policy.

bathing • washing oneself by sponge bath, or washing oneself in either a tub or shower (including the task of getting into or out of the tub or shower)

bed reservation benefit • a long-term care insurance policy benefit that continues payments to a long-term care facility for a limited time (such as 20 days) if a patient temporarily leaves because of hospitalization or any other reason. Without a continuation of payments, the bed may be assigned to someone else and unavailable upon the patient's release from the hospital.

benefit period • under a long-term care insurance policy, the period after satisfaction of the elimination period for which benefits are paid. It may be used as a factor to be multiplied by the daily benefit amount to produce a pool of money available for payment of benefits. A benefit period may be unlimited, in which case the daily benefit amount is available for the insured's lifetime.

benefit trigger • under long-term care insurance policies, a criterion that determines whether an insured is chronically ill and eligible for benefits

blended policy • *See* hybrid product.

brand-name drug • a drug manufactured and marketed under a trademark by a specific pharmaceutical company

buy-up plan • a group insurance contract in which the employer purchases a base amount of coverage for each employee and the employee is able to purchase additional coverage by paying the added cost

cafeteria plan • a benefit program that permits employees to design their own benefit packages by purchasing benefits with a prescribed amount of employer dollars. Additional benefits can often be purchased on a payroll-deduction basis.

cancelable • a contract in which the insurance company reserves the right to terminate coverage at any time (and perhaps for any reason) during the term of coverage by notifying the insured. *Compare* noncancelable; guaranteed renewable; nonrenewable for stated reasons only; optionally renewable.

capitation • a payment mechanism in which payment to a health care provider is made per subscriber per month without regard to services rendered

care continuum • a progression of care from less intensive to more intensive as the care delivered moves from family members to professionals and from the home setting to supportive-living arrangements based on the needs of the care recipient and the availability and capacity of family and other caregivers

care coordinator • a health care professional, often a social worker, who assesses an elderly patient with some degree of physical or cognitive impairment to determine the care needs and to develop a care plan to meet those needs. *Also known as* a care manager *or* care planner.

care manager • *See* care coordinator.

care planner • *See* care coordinator.

care setting • an environment in which long-term care services may be rendered to care recipients. Home health care and supportive-living arrangements are categories of care settings.

caregiver training • training of a family member or friend to provide care so that a person can remain at home

carve-out benefit • a certain class of services that is separated from a medical/surgical benefit plan and supplied under an alternative arrangement, usually involving a network of specialized providers, to achieve more effective care and/or efficiency. *See also* specialty benefit and service organization.

case management • a program of coordinated health care services for disproportionately high-cost patients with the goal of improving continuity, quality, and outcomes and lowering expenses through cost-effective resource utilization. *Also known as* large or catastrophic case management.

catastrophic high-deductible policy • a policy with a very high deductible that operates as an umbrella major medical plan to provide benefits after an extraordinary amount of medical expenses has been incurred, such as $50,000, or an underlying principal plan reaches its maximum

Centers for Medicare & Medicaid Services (CMS) • part of the U.S. Department of Health and Human Services that is responsible for the administration of the Medicare and Medicaid programs

centers of excellence • health care facilities that provide highly specialized care, such as organ transplants, and are designated as the providers of choice for such care under a contract with a health benefit plan

certificate of insurance • a summary of the coverage provided under the master contract that an insured receives as evidence of coverage

charitable gift annuity • an annuity that involves the transfer of money or other assets to a charitable or nonprofit foundation, which in turn provides an income for the life of the donor

chronic condition • a disease or disorder that develops slowly and persists for a long period of time, often the remainder of a person's life, although the condition is generally not immediately life threatening

chronically ill individual • a definition used in long-term care insurance policies for someone who meets the criterion for benefit eligibility, known as a benefit trigger, due either to a loss of functional capacity or a need for substantial supervision to protect the individual from threats to health and safety because of severe cognitive impairment. Tax-qualified policies require a licensed health care practitioner to certify the individual as chronically ill and that the loss of functional capacity involves the need for substantial assistance for a period of at least 90 days to perform at least two of the five or six activities of daily living specified in the Health Insurance Portability and Accountability Act. That assistance may be hands-on and/or standby assistance.

classification factors • information on which premium rate categories are based. Examples include family class, age, gender, geographic area, and smoking/nonsmoking status.

CMS • *See* Centers for Medicare & Medicaid Services (CMS).

COBRA • legislation passed in 1985 as part of the Consolidated Omnibus Budget Reconciliation Act that requires group health plans to allow employees working for companies with 20 or more employees to extend their current health insurance coverages at group rates for up to 36 months following a qualifying event that results in the loss of coverage for a qualified beneficiary. For retirees, the normal COBRA period is 18 months.

cognitive functions • activities that pertain to the mental processes of comprehension, judgment, memory, and reasoning

coinsurance • the percentage of covered expenses under a major medical plan that will be paid once the deductible is satisfied. The most common coinsurance percentage is 80 percent. *Also known as* percentage of allowable charges. *Compare* percentage participation.

combination policy • *See* hybrid product.

community rating • the practice of using the same rate structure for all enrollees in a medical expense plan, regardless of both their past or potential claim experience and whether coverage is written on an individual or a group basis

community spouse • the non-Medicaid dependent spouse of a person who applies for or is a recipient of Medicaid benefits

community-based services • a category of services provided by community groups under contract with area agencies on aging (AAAs) that includes employment services, senior centers, congregate meals, adult day care services, and volunteer opportunities

community-sponsored programs • various services provided by local volunteers, community groups, charities, churches, and government agencies that support family caregivers and enhance a care recipient's ability to remain at home

comprehensive long-term care insurance policy • a long-term care insurance policy that combines benefits for facility care and home health care services into a single contract. *Also known as* an integrated policy. *Compare* facility-only policy; home health care policy.

conformity-to-statute provision • a stipulation in a policy that any provision in conflict with any statute of the state where the policyowner lived when the policy was issued is amended to conform to that state statute

consumer-directed health plan • a medical expense plan that attempts to give members a strong reason to use health care services with the same prudence and economy they would use when paying any expense with their own money. These plans commonly feature a high-deductible health plan and an annual deposit of funds to a tax-favored savings account for the payment of health care expenses unreimbursed by the plan.

continence • the ability to maintain control of bowel and bladder functions or, when unable to do so, the ability to perform associated personal hygiene (including caring for a catheter or a colostomy bag)

contingent benefit upon lapse • *See* contingent nonforfeiture benefit.

contingent nonforfeiture benefit • a provision in some long-term care insurance policies whereby, if cumulative annual premiums increase beyond a specified level, the insured may elect to have reduced benefits sustainable by the current premium or a paid-up policy with a shorter benefit period

continuation of coverage • continued coverage under a group contract by an insured who is no longer a member of the group, with the insured paying the premiums directly to the insurer. *Compare* conversion provision.

continuing care retirement community (CCRC) • a facility that offers the full continuum of supportive-living arrangements and is obligated to provide access to housing and defined long-term care services at each level of care for the life of the resident. *Also known as a* life-care facility.

contract • a binding or legally enforceable agreement between two or more parties for the provision of goods or services through an exchange of value

conversion provision • a provision in a group insurance plan that gives an employee whose coverage ceases the right to convert to an individual policy without providing evidence of insurability. The conversion policy may or may not be identical to the previous group coverage.

copayment • a fixed-dollar amount that the insured must pay for a covered service. *Also known as a* copay. *Compare* percentage participation.

corridor deductible • a deductible amount under a supplemental or catastrophic major medical policy that is imposed after the payment of benefits under a basic plan of coverage

coverage gap • under Medicare prescription drug plans, the range in which the beneficiary must pay the full cost of prescription drugs. Under a standard benefit structure, the gap begins after a beneficiary has incurred $2,250 of expenses and continues until the plan begins paying again after total drug costs reach $5,100. *Also called* doughnut hole.

creditable prescription drug coverage • prescription drug coverage under other plans that is deemed to be equivalent to or better than the standard benefit plan for Medicare prescription drug coverage

creditable qualifying coverage • prior coverage under a group plan

critical illness insurance • supplemental medical expense insurance that provides a one-time lump-sum cash benefit if the insured is afflicted with a covered critical condition. The specified conditions for which benefits are paid may result from injury, disease, or major surgery. *Also known as* serious illness insurance.

cueing • a form of standby assistance that involves verbal prompting, gestures, and other demonstrations to assist someone to accomplish an activity of daily living

custodial care • assistance given to a person who has a limited ability to conduct his or her routine daily activities because of deficiencies in physical and/or cognitive functions. Persons without professional medical skills or training can usually provide custodial care. *Also known as* personal care.

daily benefit amount (DBA) • the dollar amount selected by the insured as the benefit level for each day of covered services under a long-term care insurance policy that is paid either on a per diem or reimbursement basis depending on the terms of the policy. The amount may differ by type of service. *Compare* weekly benefit.

daily money manager (DMM) • assists clients who, for any reason, may have difficulty conducting their routine personal financial affairs. DMMs, in effect, serve as long-term caregivers when they assist a person with physical and/or cognitive disabilities, usually precipitated by aging, that inhibit the ability to manage one's own finances.

DBA • *See* daily benefit amount.

declaration • a factual statement identifying the specific person, property, or activity being insured and the parties to the insurance transaction. A declaration also provides descriptive information about the insurance being purchased.

declination of issue • the decision to refuse coverage

deductible • the initial amount of covered medical expenses that an individual must incur before he or she receives benefits under a medical expense plan

deductible period • *See* elimination period.

deferred annuity • an annuity with which benefits commence at a future date

dementia • a progressive mental disorder characterized by confusion, disorientation, and loss of intellectual capacity, memory control, and judgment

dental benefit plan service-level groupings • four groupings of professional treatment categories: level I—preventive and diagnostic services; level II—basic services, including fillings, as well as endodontic, periodontic, and oral surgery services; level III—major services, including major restorations (crowns, inlays, onlays, veneers) and prosthodontic procedures (dentures, bridges); level IV—orthodontic services (benefits usually limited to dependent children under age 19 or older if a student)

dental HMO • a prepaid managed care plan that provides dental care services to insureds in a defined geographic area. It accepts responsibility for the delivery of services (not just the payment), pays a fixed periodic payment to dentists based on the number of insureds, and is organized under state law as a dental HMO.

dental PPO • a managed care arrangement between a plan and a panel of dental providers whereby the providers agree to accept a negotiated payment (usually less than their customary fees) in anticipation of a higher volume of patients

dependent • a category of insured under a medical expense policy that usually includes a policyowner's husband or wife and unmarried children under a specified age (such as 19 or older if a full-time student), including adopted children

DHMO • *See* dental HMO.

dietitian • a professional trained in the application of the principles of nutrition to the planning and preparation of foods to promote health and treat disease

disability-based policy • a long-term care insurance policy with a per diem basis of payment that provides benefits even if no care is being received as long as the insured satisfies the policy's benefit trigger

disability income insurance • a form of health insurance that provides periodic payment when the insured is unable to work as a result of illness or injury. Disability benefits may be offered in conjunction with medical expense policies.

discharge planning • the process used to decide what a patient needs for a smooth transition from one level of care to another

discount program • *See* noninsurance service plan.

disease management • a continuous program of care conducted across a broad range of settings affecting the course of chronic illnesses (such as emphysema, asthma, diabetes, and heart disease) that incorporates the use of care guidelines by physicians and self-care education of patients. The goal of disease management is to eliminate or reduce the frequency and severity of critical episodes associated with a chronic illness, thereby reducing costs as well.

dollar-for-dollar model • a type of partnership program for long-term care in which the purchase of an amount of coverage through an approved policy allows an equal amount of the insured's assets to be disregarded (protected) in determining financial eligibility for Medicaid if the insurance benefits become exhausted

domiciliary care • rehabilitative and long-term care that involves a minimal level of medical care that excludes skilled-nursing care but often includes homemaker and chore services, as well as respite care

doughnut hole • *See* coverage gap.

dread disease insurance • *See* specified (dread) disease insurance.

dressing • putting on and taking off all items of clothing and any necessary braces, fasteners, or artificial limbs

dual eligibles • persons who are eligible for Medicare and any level of Medicaid assistance

durable medical power of attorney • a document that appoints someone else to make decisions about a person's health care in the event of medical incapacity

eating • feeding oneself by getting food into the body from a receptacle (such as a plate, cup, or table), by a feeding tube, or intravenously

elder rights • a category of services for older individuals that includes legal assistance, elder abuse prevention programs, and ombudsmen services for complaint resolution

elder-care locator • a nationwide toll-free telephone service to help older adults and their caregivers find local services. Part of this service is available on the Internet.

elimination period • a period of time that must pass after covered long-term care services commence but before benefit payments begin

Employee Retirement Income Security Act • *See* ERISA.

end-stage renal disease • permanent kidney failure requiring dialysis or transplant

endorsement • *See* rider.

entire contract provision • a required policy provision stating that only those items actually included in a policy, including any riders or attachments, are part of the contract of insurance

ERISA • a federal act protecting the interests of both participants in employee benefit plans and their beneficiaries

estate recovery • a state's program to recoup from the estates of certain Medicaid beneficiaries the cost of the Medicaid benefits they received

exclusion rider • a provision in an insurance contract stating that the insurer will not pay for a medical expense resulting from a particular medical problem (such as a back disorder) or an unusually hazardous occupation or avocation (such as automobile racing). *Also known as a waiver.*

exclusions • items that the insurer does not intend to cover

extension of coverage • if an insured person is confined in a hospital or skilled-nursing facility because of covered injuries or sickness on the date insurance ends, coverage for that person is extended, but not past the date that the continuous confinement ends. Benefits are extended only for those conditions that cause the confinement and are payable during the extension on the same basis as if coverage did not end. Some policies further limit the extension to a maximum number of months (such as 3 or 12) from the date coverage otherwise ended or the eligibility date for other coverage. *Also known as* extension of benefits

extra premium • an additional premium paid by the insured to garner full protection. Extra premiums are used in cases where medical conditions are too difficult to define to be covered adequately by an exclusion rider (such as nervous disorders) or where the stated condition has too many complications that would have to be excluded (such as obesity, hypertension, or diabetes).

facility-only policy • a policy that provides benefits for care in a nursing home and other settings, such as an assisted-living facility and hospice. *Compare* comprehensive long-term care insurance policy; home health care policy.

Federal Long Term Care Insurance Program (FLTCIP) • a program authorized under federal legislation to provide long-term care insurance to federal and postal employees and annuitants, members and retired members of the uniformed services, and qualified relatives. The program is sponsored by the U.S. Office of Personnel Management (OPM) and administered by Long Term Care Partners, LLC, under contract with OPM.

field underwriter • a term used to describe the insurance agent and his or her role in the underwriting process

first mortgage • a claim on real property, usually as security for a loan, that has a priority right of satisfaction over any other mortgage loan that may exist on the same property

fixed annuity • an annuity for which payments are a fixed number of dollars

flexible spending account (FSA) • a cafeteria plan account, usually funded by before-tax salary reductions by employees. Monies can be withdrawn from the account to pay unreimbursed medical expenses.

FLTCIP • *See* Federal Long Term Care Insurance Program.

formal caregiver • an individual who provides care as a profession or occupation and earns a living by rendering services to long-term care recipients. Formal caregivers include physicians, nurse caregivers, other licensed medical personnel, and nonlicensed personnel. *Compare* informal caregiver.

formulary • a plan's or pharmacy benefit manager's list of drug products that are preferred for dispensing to covered persons when appropriate. The list contains both generic and brand-name drugs.

fraud • an active intent to deceive or intentionally mislead another person. In order to constitute fraud, intent must be shown, and the information concealed or misrepresented must be relied upon by and injure the other party. *See also* misrepresentation.

free-look period • a period of time, typically 30 days, after a policyowner receives a policy, during which the policyowner may return the policy for a full refund of any premium paid and the policy is void from its inception

FSA • *See* flexible spending account (FSA).

full individual underwriting • the most stringent form of underwriting. It requires the most extensive information of the applicant regarding medical history and current medical condition. This type of underwriting is typically used in the individual marketplace, but it may also be used in the group marketplace when the size of the group is very small and for persons other than employees who are eligible for group coverage. *Also known as* long-form underwriting. *Compare* guaranteed-issue underwriting; modified guaranteed-issue underwriting; simplified-issue underwriting.

future purchase option • a provision in a long-term care insurance policy designed to offset the effects of inflation by allowing the policyowner to increase benefits (by $10 per day, for example) without evidence of insurability at specified intervals, such as every 1, 2, or 3 years. Each benefit increase is accompanied by a premium increase based on attained-age rates for the additional coverage. *Compare* automatic-increase option.

generic drug • a drug product that is chemically equivalent to a brand-name drug whose patent has expired

geriatric care manager • *See* care coordinator.

geriatric physician • a physician who specializes in the treatment of the aged

grace period • a required policy provision that gives an insured a specific number of days beyond the due date to pay each premium. States usually require a 31-day grace period for most policies.

group contract • *See* master contract.

group insurance • a method of providing insurance protection to members of a group that is characterized by a master contract, group underwriting, and possibly experience rating

group insurance contract • an arrangement for insuring a number of identified persons under a single master insurance policy that is issued to someone other than the persons insured

group underwriting • underwriting that evaluates the insurability of applicant employer groups that are organized for job, profession, or industry reasons. *Compare* individual underwriting.

guaranteed insurability rider • *See* guaranteed purchase option.

guaranteed purchase option • for long-term care insurance, *see* future purchase option • a rider that can be added to a life insurance or disability income policy to guarantee the insured's right to purchase long-term care insurance in the future without evidence of insurability. These riders, for which there is a premium charge, are underwritten at the time of issue and are available only to applicants who meet the insurer's standards at that time.

guaranteed renewable • a renewal provision in an insurance contract whereby the insurance company cannot make any unilateral changes in any coverage provision or refuse to renew the coverage. The insured has the right to continue coverage by the timely payment of premiums that the insurer may revise periodically for broad classes of insureds. *Compare* noncancelable.

guaranteed-issue underwriting • the most liberal form of group underwriting in which coverage is provided for all employees who apply for it. However, the insured group must satisfy certain insurer criteria to minimize adverse selection. *Compare* full individual underwriting; modified guaranteed-issue underwriting; simplified-issue underwriting.

guaranty fund • a state fund to pay claims of insolvent insurers. It is usually funded by assessments of other insurers licensed in the state.

hands-on assistance • actual physical assistance received from another person to perform activities of daily living

health insurance • includes policies that cover injury or sickness and encompasses medical expense, disability income, and long-term care insurance

Health Insurance Portability and Accountability Act (HIPAA) • *See* HIPAA.

health maintenance organization (HMO) • a health plan of comprehensive medical benefits that emphasizes preventive services and the cost-effective use of medical care for an enrolled population living in a specific geographic area. An HMO is a "managed" health plan because of its contracts with a network of hospitals and physicians and other health professionals. These contracts require provider agreements and payment arrangements that promote appropriate utilization and contain costs of the services rendered to enrollees. Generally, enrollees must receive services from network providers to obtain their benefits under the health plan. In addition, access to specialists, testing, and therapies frequently require a referral from a primary care physician.

Health Maintenance Organization Act • a federal act passed in 1973 that introduced the concept of the federally qualified HMO. *See also* health maintenance organization (HMO).

health reimbursement arrangement (HRA) • a type of personal savings account from which unreimbursed medical expenses can be paid. An HRA can be established only by an employer for its employees. An employer may allow a former employee to spend down the unused balance after retirement but is not required to do so.

health savings account (HSA) • a type of tax-preferred savings account or fund that a person with a qualified high-deductible health plan may establish to pay for certain medical expenses. HSAs are similar to Archer MSAs but have more liberal funding and qualified health plan requirements.

high-deductible health plan • *See* high-deductible major medical insurance.

high-deductible major medical insurance • a major medical policy with a deductible of $1,000 or more. There are specified deductibles that are required when these policies are used as part of certain consumer-directed health plans, such as health savings accounts.

high-risk pool • a mechanism, operated as a not-for-profit association, to broadly share the risk of above-standard financial losses for the benefit payments of comprehensive medical insurance offered to individuals whose preexisting health conditions denied them standard coverage in the private market

HIPAA • federal legislation for the primary purpose of making medical insurance more available, particularly when an employed person changes jobs or becomes unemployed. However, the legislation contains other provisions related to health care data standards and privacy, as well the requirements for the tax-preferred status of long-term care insurance policies that are described as contracts.

HMO • *See* health maintenance organization (HMO).

home and community-based services • under the Medicaid program, a special category of services that states may provide with approval from the Centers for Medicare & Medicaid Services to keep beneficiaries from being institutionalized. Unlike other Medicaid services, these additional services may be targeted to specific populations (such as the developmentally disabled and the mentally disabled) and to certain geographic areas.

home care agency • company that provides little medical care but specializes in home health aides (nursing assistants) and nonlicensed personnel, such as homemakers, companions, and chore workers, who may maintain and repair a home. *Compare* home health care agency.

home health care • a setting that encompasses virtually any home environment outside of a nursing home in which the care recipient resides and receives care

home health care agency • company that specializes in medical and/or custodial care of the elderly and disabled in the home environment. Many of these agencies employ a range of formal caregivers that frequently include nurse caregivers, other licensed medical personnel, and nonlicensed personnel. *Compare* home care agency.

home health care policy • a long-term care insurance policy designed to provide benefits only for care outside an institutional setting, although some policies may provide benefits for care in assisted-living facilities. *Compare* comprehensive long-term care insurance policy; facility-only policy.

homemaker companion • an employee of a state-licensed home health care agency who may assist with such tasks as cooking, shopping, cleaning, bill paying, or other household chores

hospice care • a system of treatment designed to relieve the discomfort of a terminally ill individual and to maintain the quality of life to the extent possible throughout the phases of dying

hospital • frequently defined in policies providing hospitalization benefits as "an institution licensed, accredited, or certified by the state which (1) is accredited by the Joint Commission on Accreditation of Healthcare Organizations; (2) provides 24-hour nursing service by registered nurses; (3) mainly provides diagnostic and therapeutic care under the supervision of physicians on an inpatient basis; and (4) maintains permanent surgical facilities or has an arrangement with another surgical facility supervised by a staff of one or more physicians"

hospital confinement indemnity insurance • a type of supplemental medical policy featuring cash benefits in the event of hospitalization and/or surgery resulting from illness or injury

HRA • *See* health reimbursement arrangement.

HSA • *See* health savings account (HSA).

hybrid product • an insurance contract that combines long-term care insurance and either life insurance or annuities into a single policy. *Also known as a* linked policy, blended policy, combination policy, or package policy.

immediate annuity • an annuity for which benefits commence one payment interval from the date of purchase

impaired risk annuity • an annuity for which an applicant's health is considered in the underwriting process and the annuity payments are increased (or the premium lowered) in relation to the shorter life expectancy

incontestable clause • a required policy provision that limits an insurer's right to rescind a policy to 2 years (3 years in some states) with respect to any misstatement made by the insured on the application

indemnity • a concept which means that the insured is entitled to payment only to the extent of financial loss or legal liability—in other words, the insured should remain in the same financial position that existed prior to a loss and should not profit from the loss

indemnity (fee-for-service) contract • in medical expense insurance, a policy under which an insured has considerable freedom in choosing providers of care. Claims are generally paid on the basis of charges billed by providers with few attempts to control costs.

indemnity policy • in long-term care insurance, a designation often applied to a long-term care insurance policy with a per diem basis of payment even though the usual insurance meaning of indemnity implies payment of benefits for actual expenses up to policy limits. *Also known as a* per diem policy.

independent housing • a wide range of supportive-living arrangements that include senior apartments, home sharing, and accessory apartments in which residents do not require constant supervision and are free to go and come as they please. Nonmedical support services that can be scheduled, such as meals, housekeeping, and laundry, are usually available. Assistance with some routine daily activities, such as bathing, dressing, and grooming, may be purchased as separate services.

independent living • *See* independent housing.

individual market • the market for health insurance coverage offered to individuals other than in connection with a group plan

individual medical expense insurance • a personally purchased contract of health insurance that provides insureds with the financial resources to pay for or gain access to medical services required by illness, injury, or the maintenance of well being

individual underwriting • underwriting that evaluates the insurability of each applicant separately. *Compare* group underwriting.

informal care • voluntary assistance, usually in the form of personal or custodial care, provided without pay to a long-term care recipient by a person without formal education and training in long-term care

informal caregiver • a person who provides informal care. Informal caregivers include immediate family members, other relatives, friends, neighbors, and volunteers. *Compare* formal caregiver.

infusion therapy • the introduction of fluids, electrolytes, or drugs directly into a vein, tissue, or organ to improve a patient's condition

in-home services • a category of services provided by community groups that includes meals-on-wheels, housekeeping, chore services, telephone reassurance, friendly visiting, energy assistance and weatherization, emergency response systems, home health services, personal care services, and respite care

injury • defined as "accidental bodily injury independent of disease, bodily infirmity, or other cause sustained while this policy is in force"

inspection report • the results of an investigation of an insurance applicant conducted by an independent agency that specializes in such investigations

installment annuity • an annuity purchased with periodic premiums

instrumental activities of daily living (IADLs) • necessary and routine activities of life that require a greater degree of skill, judgment, and independence than activities of daily living (ADLs) and include shopping for personal items, managing money, using the telephone, preparing meals, managing medication, and doing housework. *Compare* activities of daily living (ADLs).

insurance • defined broadly to include arrangements that provide benefits for losses and/or services via insurance companies, Blue Cross–Blue Shield plans, self-funded programs, and such managed care organizations as health maintenance organizations (HMOs)

insurance commissioner • the head of the state insurance department, an authorized administrative office that both issues and enforces rules and regulations. The state's governor usually appoints the insurance commissioner, although in a few states the commissioner is an elected official.

integrated policy • *See* comprehensive long-term care insurance policy.

interim medical expense insurance • coverage that is purchased only for a specific period of time. Interim medical expense insurance includes temporary, international travel, and student policies.

intermediate care • medical care services that may be provided or available perhaps 2 to 4 days per week. Intermediate care may be provided in a nursing home, an intermediate-care unit of a nursing home, or at home. *Also known as* intermediate-nursing care.

intermediate-nursing care • *See* intermediate care.

internal limit • *See* separate service maximum.

international travel medical policy • an interim medical expense insurance policy for persons who are traveling abroad

Internet • a global arrangement of computer networks that provides users with the ability to access and exchange information with any other computer that has access to the system

intranet • interconnected computers and networks within an organization and/or connecting an affiliated set of clients

issue-age rate • a premium rate for a policy change that is based on the insured's age at the time a policy was issued rather than at the time the change is made. *Compare* attained-age rate.

joint life annuity • an annuity for which payments are received for as long as the first of two or more persons lives

joint-and-last-survivor annuity • an annuity from which payments are received until the last of two persons dies

licensed health care practitioner • for purposes of certifying a person as chronically ill under the Health Insurance Portability and Accountability Act requirements for tax-qualified long-term care insurance contracts, a physician, registered nurse, licensed social worker, or other person who meets any requirements prescribed by the Secretary of the Treasury

life-care facility • *See* continuing care retirement community (CCRC).

lifetime maximum • *See* aggregate maximum.

limitations • restrictions on the extent of coverage or benefits

linked policy • *See* hybrid product.

living will • a document that addresses what should be done when a person is clearly in a terminal medical condition

Long Term Care Partners, LLC • the organizational entity formed by Metropolitan Life Insurance Company and John Hancock Life Insurance Company for the sole purpose of administering the Federal Long Term Care Insurance Program. *Also known as* LTC Partners.

long-form underwriting • *See* full individual underwriting.

long-term care • the broad range of medical, custodial, social, and other care services that assist people who have an impaired ability to live independently for an extended period

Long-Term Care Consumer Awareness Campaign • a pilot project established as a cooperative effort between a number of participating states and agencies of the federal government to increase the awareness of the need for long-term care and to measure the impact of planning and the use of private-sector options, including long-term care insurance, to pay for such care

long-term care insurance • any insurance policy or rider that is advertised, marketed, offered, or designed to provide coverage for not less than 12 consecutive months for each covered person in a setting other than an acute care unit of a hospital for one or more of the following: necessary or medically necessary diagnostic, preventive, therapeutic, rehabilitative, maintenance, or personal care services

loss ratio • claims divided by premiums

LTC Partners • *See* Long Term Care Partners, LLC.

lump-sum benefit • in a specified disease or critical illness policy, a benefit that pays a one-time amount for each covered person who receives a diagnosis of a covered disease or condition or undergoes a covered medical event

major medical insurance • a medical insurance policy designed to provide substantial coverage for most types of medical expenses arising from hospital, other facility, and physicians' services, as well as diagnostic tests and therapies, regardless of setting. Benefit structure commonly uses deductibles, coinsurance payments, out-of-pocket limits, and aggregate and separate service maximums.

managed care • a health plan or insurance policy that tries to manage cost, quality, and access to health care; frequently used as a generic term applicable to HMOs, preferred-provider organization (PPO) arrangements, and major medical policies with managed care features

mandated benefit • a benefit, beyond routinely available benefits, that a medical insurance plan must offer or provide as required by law

mandated option law • legislation, usually a state statute, that requires insurers to offer mandated benefits in an insurance plan for purchase by consumers at their discretion. Thus, if consumers decline the mandated benefits, policies may be sold without them. *Compare* mandated benefit.

mandatorily eligible • under the Medicaid program, the categories of persons who must automatically qualify for benefits. They include certain families with dependent children, children under age 6, and pregnant women, as well as recipients of Supplemental Security Income (SSI).

mass-marketed individual insurance • a type of insurance product sold as individual polices of insurance through a sponsoring group, such as an employer or association

master contract • an insurance contract that provides benefits to a group of individuals (such as employees or association members) who have a specific relationship to a group policyowner

maximum per calendar year • an annual limit on total benefit payments imposed by some policies in addition to the aggregate (lifetime) maximum. *See also* aggregate maximum.

McCarran-Ferguson Act • a federal law that exempts insurance from certain federal regulations to the extent that individual states actually regulate insurance. It also stipulates that most other federal laws are not applicable to insurance unless they are specifically related to the business of insurance.

Medicaid • a federal/state public assistance or welfare program that provides health care benefits based on need. Each state has its own rules that must meet federal guidelines. In return, the federal government finances the major portion of each state's program. At the federal level, Medicaid is administered by the Centers for Medicare & Medicaid Services (CMS), which is part of the U.S. Department of Health and Human Services.

Medicaid planning • the process of rearranging a person's financial resources to make that person eligible for Medicaid while sheltering the financial resources for use by a spouse, children, or others

medical expense insurance • a health insurance contract that pays for or provides access to medical care services required by illness or injury, usually of an acute nature. Coverage may include benefits in long-term care settings.

Medical Information Bureau • *See* MIB Group, Inc.

medical necessity • a benefit trigger in a non-tax-qualified long-term care insurance policy under which a physician certifies that long-term care is needed, even if no other criteria are satisfied

medically needy • under the Medicaid program, a category of eligibility that states may establish for persons who have too much income to qualify as members of the mandatorily eligible or other categorically needy groups but who are determined to be unable to afford needed medical care

medical provider statement • a written report from a hospital or a physician that has provided medical services to the applicant. The underwriter asks for this statement if the application discloses any serious or questionable medical history.

medical services • the spectrum of health care provided by institutions, such as hospitals and other acute and nonacute facilities, and health care professionals, such as doctors and other licensed practitioners. Includes diagnostic and therapeutic services whose goal is to restore or maintain health

medical-event benefit • in a specified disease policy, a benefit paid if an insured has inpatient care, surgical procedures, nonsurgical treatments (such as radiation and/or chemotherapy), or skilled-nursing care. *See also* upon-diagnosis benefit; *compare* lump-sum benefit.

Medicare • a social insurance program of health benefits for most persons aged 65 or older, although certain younger persons are also eligible for benefits. The program is administered by the Centers for Medicare & Medicaid Services (CMS), which is part of the U.S. Department of Health and Human Services.

Medicare Advantage • the program administered by the Centers for Medicare & Medicaid Services that allows Medicare beneficiaries to enroll in certain HMOs, PPOs, and other approved options as alternatives to receiving their benefits under the original or traditional Medicare program; formerly called Medicare+Choice. *Also known as* Part C of Medicare.

Medicare carve-out • a medical expense plan that reduces benefits to the extent that they are provided under Medicare

Medicare cost plan • a Medicare Advantage plan that is structured as a point-of-service plan

Medicare managed care plan • a Medicare Advantage plan that is structured as an HMO

Medicare Part A • the part of Medicare that covers hospitalization, confinement in certified skilled-nursing facilities, home health care, and hospice care under certain circumstances. *Also known as* hospital insurance.

Medicare Part B • the part of Medicare that covers most physicians' services as well as medical items and services not covered under Part A. Part B premiums are deducted from participants' Social Security or railroad retirement benefits.

Medicare Part C • *See* Medicare Advantage.

Medicare Part D • the part of Medicare that, as of 2006, makes prescription drug coverage available to Medicare enrollees. *See* Medicare prescription drug plans.

Medicare Prescription Drug, Improvement, and Modernization Act of 2003 • federal legislation affecting Medicare and other health care areas. Among its major provisions are a Medicare drug discount card program through 2005 followed by drug coverage in voluntary prescription drug plans (Part D of Medicare). It also strengthens and expands alternatives to traditional Medicare through Medicare Advantage and authorizes tax-preferred health savings accounts (HSAs).

Medicare prescription drug plans • private prescription drug plans in which Medicare participants can voluntarily enroll. The plans must meet certain standards established by Medicare, and beneficiaries must pay a monthly premium.

Medicare secondary rules • regulations that specify when Medicare will be secondary to an employer's medical expense plan for disabled employees and active employees over age 65

Medicare SELECT • a type of standard Medicare supplement insurance policy in which the beneficiary must use the insurance plan's designated hospitals and doctors for nonemergency services to be eligible for full supplemental insurance benefits

Medicare Summary Notice (MSN) • a notice to beneficiaries that explains the services and supplies that were billed to Medicare during a 30-day period

Medicare supplement • an approach by which an employer gives retired employees benefits to supplement Medicare. This coverage is not necessarily the same as individual Medicare supplement insurance.

Medicare supplement insurance • individual medical expense insurance designed to fill the deductible, coinsurance, and copayment gaps in Medicare's benefits for covered services that would otherwise result in out-of-pocket expenses for beneficiaries. However, in a few instances benefits in addition to those provided under Medicare are provided. *Also known as* medigap.

Medicare+Choice • *See* Medicare Advantage.

medigap • *See* Medicare supplement insurance.

medsup insurance • *See* Medicare supplement insurance.

MIB Group, Inc. • a not-for-profit association of insurance companies that exchanges information among its members relevant to underwriting life, health, disability income, and long-term care insurance

misappropriation • the unlawful keeping of funds belonging to another

misrepresentation • a false statement made by an applicant to an insurer at the time of or prior to the formation of a contract. *See also* fraud.

misstatement of age • an optional policy provision stating that, if the insured's age has been misstated, all benefits payable under the policy shall be at a level that the premium paid would have purchased at the correct age. In medical expense insurance, this provision may allow payment of the additional premium at the correct age if the insured understated the age but remains eligible for coverage. If the covered person is ineligible for coverage at the correct age, then the misapplied coverage is rescinded and any applicable premium is refunded.

MMA • *See* Medicare Prescription Drug, Improvement, and Modernization Act of 2003.

mode of payment • the frequency with which premium payments are made, such as annually, semiannually, quarterly, or monthly

modified guaranteed-issue underwriting • a form of group underwriting in which some medical questions are asked on the application to determine whether the applicant has recently received care, requires assistance, or has certain medical conditions. Although the insurer accepts most applicants, the answers to these questions may result in the declination of some applicants. *Compare* full individual underwriting; guaranteed-issue underwriting; simplified-issue underwriting.

modified issue • the decision to provide insurance with certain modifications to standard coverage, such as an exclusion rider, an extra premium, a change in benefits, or some combination of these options

moral hazard • the perverse human tendency that increases the frequency and severity of a loss because insurance is in force

morbidity statistics • the incidence of sickness and disability

MSA • *See* Archer medical savings account (MSA).

MSN • *See* Medicare Summary Notice.

NAIC • *See* National Association of Insurance Commissioners (NAIC).

National Association of Insurance Commissioners (NAIC) • a voluntary association of all state insurance commissioners. The organization's specific objectives are the development of uniform regulatory policy and the coordination of regulations of multistate insurers.

National Association of State Units on Aging • a national nonprofit membership organization of 57 state and territorial government agencies on aging founded to respond to the needs of a diverse aging population

Newborns' and Mothers' Health Protection Act • a federal act that prohibits insurers from restricting hospital benefits to less than 48 hours for both mother and newborn following a vaginal delivery and 96 hours following a cesarean section

noncancelable • a renewal provision in an insurance contract whereby the insurance company cannot make any unilateral changes in any coverage provision or refuse to renew the coverage. The insured has the right to continue the coverage in force by the timely payment of premium rates that are established in advance and cannot be changed. *Compare* guaranteed renewable.

nonforfeiture benefit • a provision in an insurance policy whereby the policyowner will receive some value for a policy that lapses if the premium is not paid in the future

noninsurance service plan • a program for the purchase of specified professional services and products at a discounted price from a designated list or network of health care providers and suppliers. *Also known as a* discount program.

nonlicensed personnel • individuals employed to provide long-term care recipients with personal care services of a nonmedical nature. In the home setting, these nonlicensed personnel are called homemakers, companions, and chore workers.

nonrecourse loan • a loan arrangement in which the lender bases recovery of the amount loaned only on the asset that secures the loan with no encumbrance of the borrower's other assets or resources. In the case of a reverse mortgage, the asset is the borrower's home.

nonrenewable for stated reasons only • a type of policy in which the insurer is permitted to refuse to renew the policy for conditions specifically listed in the policy. *Compare* guaranteed renewable; noncancelable; optionally renewable; cancelable.

non-tax-qualified • a type of long-term care insurance contract that fails to meet certain standards of the Health Insurance Portability and Accountability Act for favorable tax treatment. *Compare* tax-qualified.

notice of claim • a claim provision in a policy requiring that the insured provide written notice to the insurer within 20 days of loss or as soon as is reasonably possible

nurse caregiver • a registered nurse, licensed practical or vocational nurse, or nurse assistant (aide) who is responsible for the medical treatment of actual or potential health problems with the goal of rehabilitating a care recipient or stabilizing his or her medical condition

nursing home • a state-licensed facility that provides skilled, intermediate, and custodial care services. The care recipient's condition determines the combination and extent of services provided.

nursing home policy • a type of long-term care insurance policy that is designed to provide benefits only if the insured is in a nursing home. *Compare* facility-only policy.

occupational therapy • treatment to enhance the capabilities of persons who have physical, social, and emotional deficits arising from injury, illness, emotional disturbance, congenital or developmental disability, or aging

Older Americans Act (OAA) • legislation that created the Administration on Aging (AOA) and authorized grants to states for community planning and service programs in the field of aging. As amended, the act also provides grants to area agencies on aging (AAAs) to meet local needs and provide support programs for the elderly, especially those who are in greatest economic and social need.

open-enrollment period • the time during which coverage can be obtained under an employee benefit or government plan and during which the evidence-of-insurability requirement is lessened or waived.

optionally renewable • an insurance contract in which the insurer reserves the right to refuse to renew coverage at each policy anniversary date, either for specified reasons or for any and all reasons. *Compare* noncancelable; guaranteed renewable; nonrenewable for stated reasons only; cancelable.

original Medicare program • Medicare's traditional pay-per-visit/service benefit arrangement under Part A and Part B

other categorically needy • under Medicaid, a category or class of individuals and families who receive Medicaid benefits despite income levels that disqualify them as mandatorily eligible

out-of-pocket limit • the maximum sum of all payments by an insured for the amounts remaining after the coinsurance benefits for the allowable expenses of covered services in a yearly benefit period. *Also known as* stop loss.

PACE • *See* programs of all-inclusive care for the elderly.

package policy • *See* hybrid product.

palliative care • therapy designed to reduce pain or discomfort but not to produce a cure

paramedical examination • a medical examination of an applicant by trained personnel other than a physician

Part A • *See* Medicare Part A.

Part B • *See* Medicare Part B.

Part C • *See* Medicare Advantage.

Part D • *See* Medicare Part D.

partial advance funding • the funding method used for Medicare. Taxes are more than sufficient to pay current benefits and also provide some accumulation for future benefits.

partnership programs for long-term care • alliances between certain state governments and insurance companies to encourage the sale of approved long-term care policies. The goal of these alliances is to protect individuals from impoverishment by long-term care expenses that would result in their immediate dependence on Medicaid.

pay-as-you-go option • *See* future purchase option.

per-cause deductible • a deductible amount that must be satisfied for each separate accident or illness before medical benefits are paid

percentage of allowable charges • *See* coinsurance.

percentage participation • the percentage of covered medical expenses that remains unpaid after the coinsurance benefit payment of a medical expense policy and that must be paid by the insured. *Compare* copayment; coinsurance.

per-day or per-service benefits • benefits that require specific services to be rendered in order to receive a cash benefit that may have little or no relation to specific charges

per diem basis • a method of paying benefits under long-term care insurance policies in which the insured receives a specified daily or weekly benefit amount regardless of the actual cost of care. *Compare* reimbursement basis.

period of benefits • *See* benefit period.

persistency • the length of time an insurance contract remains in force

personal care • *See* custodial care.

personal care services • in general, services that assist with activities of daily living and instrumental activities of daily living • under Medicaid, the optional services that states may provide to assist persons with physical and cognitive impairments so they may remain in their homes and communities

personal worksheet • a form containing questions to help ensure that an insurance applicant has considered certain relevant information before buying insurance. For long-term care insurance, these questions cover (1) the current and future obligations for keeping the policy in force, (2) the current costs of nursing home care, home health care, and community-based services in the area where the applicant lives, and (3) the average use of services covered by the policy.

physical therapy • treatment of physical impairments through the use of special exercise, application of heat or cold, and other physical treatment modalities

physician • a licensed health professional who has earned a degree of Doctor of Medicine or Doctor of Osteopathy at an approved medical school and completed National Board Examinations, usually with postgraduate training through a hospital internship or residency program or further training in a specialty

physician examination • a medical examination of an applicant conducted by a physician. A physician examination is used if a paramedical exam yields uncertain or unfavorable results. Insurers may also require a physician examination because of the amount of coverage applied for, the applicant's age, or the need for more specific details of medical history.

point-of-service (POS) option • a hybrid arrangement that combines aspects of a traditional medical expense plan with HMO coverage. At the time of medical treatment, a participant can elect whether to receive treatment for specified services within the plan's network or outside of the network. However, full benefits are paid only for services received within the network. *Also known as a* point-of-service (POS) plan.

policy • a written insurance contract

policy form • a standardized contract that an insurer offers to its policyowners. In many states, it must be filed with the insurance department.

policyowner • an insurance applicant becomes a policyowner when the contract of insurance is formed

pool of money • maximum available benefits under a long-term care insurance policy calculated by multiplying the daily benefit by the benefit period to create a total amount of funds from which benefit payments may continue as long as the funds lasts. If the benefit period is unlimited, the pool of money ends with the life of the insured.

portability • under HIPAA, portability means that preexisting-conditions limitations for medical insurance are defined and, once satisfied, may not serve to deny, limit, or delay the issuance of a qualified person's group or individual medical coverage or the renewal of that coverage as required by the act. *See also* Health Insurance Portability and Accountability Act (HIPAA).

post-claims underwriting • an insurer practice of rescinding a policy or denying a claim based on medical information obtained at the time a claim is filed that could have been obtained and included in the underwriting process at the time the insured completed the application for insurance. State regulations attempt to minimize this practice.

PPO • *See* preferred-provider organization (PPO).

precertification • *See* prior authorization.

predetermination • *See* prior authorization.

preexisting condition • any condition, including illness or injury, not fully disclosed on the application that occurred within a specific time period prior to the policy's effective date, and either (1) for which symptoms existed that would cause a prudent person to seek diagnostic care or treatment, or (2) for which medical advice, treatment, or service was recommended by or received from a physician

preferred drug list • *See* formulary.

preferred-provider organization (PPO) • a managed health care plan or the feature of a health benefit plan that makes available to insureds an identified network of participating providers or selected providers to obtain cost-effective medical services. The providers may or may not bear a financial risk for the utilization and cost of health services that is reflected in the payments they receive under the plan. PPO arrangements may be formal or informal.

premium • the price charged for a period of coverage provided by an insurance policy • in health insurance, a specified amount of money paid for coverage by an insured that the insurer draws on to pay benefits for the covered expenses of insureds who incur them

premium-conversion plan • a cafeteria plan account that permits an employee to elect a before-tax salary reduction to pay his or her premium contribution to an employer-provided medical expense plan

premium-only plan (POP) • *See* premium-conversion plan.

premium tax • levied by the state, it usually equals 2 to 3 percent of gross premiums collected by an insurance company

prequalification questions • a series of questions at the beginning of an insurance application intended to immediately ascertain the ineligibility of an applicant for insurance and relieve the applicant from the need to complete the application and the agent from the need to submit it

pretreatment estimate • *See* prior authorization.

primary caregiver • the informal caregiver, usually a family member, with overall responsibility for a person's long-term care

principal medical expense insurance • a plan that provides substantial benefits for the major portion of the expenses for needed health care services and generally constitutes the policyowner's or beneficiary's fundamental program of medical expense protection. *See also* major medical insurance, managed care, basic hospital and medical-surgical insurance, interim medical expense insurance.

prior authorization • the process under an insurance plan for the review of a proposed course of treatment. For example, under a dental benefit program, the insured's dentist is asked to complete and submit a written request for preauthorization of benefits for major services and orthodontia that describes the diagnosis, the proposed treatment, and the cost. *Also known as* predetermination, precertification, *or* pretreatment estimate.

private annuity • an annuity arrangement in which the person or organization that assumes the obligation for the annuity payments is not in the business of selling annuities

private fee-for-service plan • a traditional insurance benefit plan (such as major medical) offered as an alternative to original Medicare that determines prospectively the payment rate of providers accepting the plan without placing them at financial risk for the utilization of services. Providers are allowed to bill beyond what the plan pays (up to a limit), and the beneficiary is responsible for paying whatever the plan does not cover and any additional premium the plan requires.

probate • the judicial process for the proof and registration of a deceased person's will and administration of a deceased person's estate

programs of all-inclusive care for the elderly (PACE) • optional benefit programs provided jointly by Medicare and Medicaid that focus entirely on older people who are frail enough to meet their state's Medicaid standards for nursing home care. The PACE service package must include all Medicare services and Medicaid services covered by the state plus all the medical, social, and rehabilitative services that enrollees need to (1) preserve or restore their independence, (2) remain in their homes and communities, and (3) maintain their quality of life.

proof of loss • a written statement that details the specifics of loss. The specifics are spelled out in policies and vary by line of business. In medical expense insurance, the completion of a claim form acceptable to the insurer that contains or attaches the health care provider's bill for services usually constitutes proof of loss. Under managed care arrangements in which the health care provider bills the health plan directly, the provider's claim satisfies the contract's proof of loss requirements.

provider-sponsored organization (PSO) • a managed care plan established by doctors and/or hospitals that have formed their own program for the delivery and payment of health care services and deliver a substantial portion of services through their own or affiliated provider systems

pure annuity • an annuity with which payments cease at the death of the last annuitant

qualification period • a stipulated interval from the first diagnosis of a covered medical condition to the date when benefits become payable, which may vary by diagnosis as in the case of critical illness insurance. It is similar to an elimination period.

qualified beneficiary • as defined under COBRA, any employee, or the spouse or dependent child of that employee, who on the day before a qualifying event was covered under the employee's group health plan

qualified long-term care insurance contract • any long-term care insurance contract that meets the requirements of the Health Insurance Portability and Accountability Act (HIPAA) for favorable tax treatment or any long-term care insurance contract issued before January 1, 1997, that remains materially unchanged and met the long-term care requirements in the state where the policy was issued even if it does not meet other HIPAA requirements. *Also known as a* tax-qualified policy.

qualified long-term care services • services that must be covered for a long-term care insurance policy to be a tax-qualified insurance contract under the Health Insurance Portability and Accountability Act. Required services are necessary diagnostic, preventive, therapeutic, curing, treating, and rehabilitative services, as well as maintenance or personal care required by a chronically ill individual and called for by a plan of care prescribed by a licensed health care practitioner.

qualifying event • as defined under COBRA, an event (such as termination of employment, reduction in hours worked, or death) that triggers the eligibility of a qualified insured to elect continuing coverage

reasonable and customary fee • the lesser of the actual charge, the fee most often charged by the provider for the same service or supply, or the fee most often charged in the same area by providers with similar training and experience for comparable service or supplies

rebating • the return of any part of the premium (except as dividends) to the policyowner by the insurer or agent as a price-cutting sales inducement. Rebating is prohibited under the Unfair Trade Practices Act.

receipt • official acknowledgment of payment made with an application for insurance. Insurers may issue a conditional receipt, a binding receipt, or a temporary insurance agreement (TIA).

recision • revocation of a policy by the insurer

refund annuity • an annuity for which some of the purchase price may be returned to a beneficiary

regulation • defined broadly to include legislation and administrative regulations as well as decisions of the courts that affect the business of insurance

rehabilitative services • care and treatment intended to restore an individual to normal functions after a disabling disease, injury, or incapacitation

reimbursement basis • the dominant method of paying benefits under newer long-term care policies that reimburse the insured for actual expenses incurred up to the specified daily or weekly benefit amount. *Compare* per diem basis.

reinstatement provision • a provision in an insurance contract that sets forth procedures for allowing an insured to request a policy to be restored to full effectiveness should a premium not be paid by the end of the grace period

replacement • the canceling of one policy and replacing it with another policy. States have rules that must be followed by insurers and agents who are aware that a replacement is taking place.

representation • a statement made by an applicant to an insurer at the time of or prior to the formation of a contract

respiratory therapy • treatment that maintains or improves the breathing function through the administration of medications and oxygen and/or the use of ventilator equipment

respite care • a form of long-term care provided by informal or formal caregivers to relieve a primary caregiver from the physical and emotional stress of caring for a family member over a long period of time and/or to allow the primary caregiver to have some personal time. Respite care can be relatively brief or extended in duration.

respite caregiver • an alternative caregiver who relieves a primary caregiver to allow the primary giver to have some time off

restoration of benefits • a provision or rider in some long-term care policies written with less than a lifetime benefit period that provides for a reinstatement of full benefits if the insured previously received less than full policy benefits and has not required long-term care covered by the policy for a certain time period

return-of-premium rider • a policy provision under which a portion of the premium is returned to the policyowner or beneficiary, usually if an insured dies after a specified number of years

reverse mortgage • a nonrecourse first mortgage loan against a home's value that advances cash to the borrower who remains the homeowner. It requires no installment repayments, and proceeds from the sale of the home are used to repay the loan when the borrower no longer maintains the home as a principal residence.

rider • a provision, also called an endorsement, in an insurance policy that can clarify, restrict, or expand coverage

right of examination • *See* free-look period.

risk • the possibility of undesired and unintended loss

sandwich generation • persons who at the same time are caring for their own children as well as aging parents or relatives

SCHIP • *See* State Children's Health Insurance Program (SCHIP).

secondary caregiver • an informal caregiver other than the primary caregiver

separate service maximum • benefit limit applicable to specific services, such as organ transplants, substance abuse and dependency, mental illness, home health care, infertility treatment, and skilled-nursing home care. *Also known as* internal limit.

serious illness insurance • *See* critical illness insurance.

shared benefit • a long-term care insurance policy provision that allows a husband and wife insured under the same policy or with the same insurer to access each other's unused benefits

SHIP • *See* State Health Insurance Assistance Plan (SHIP).

shopper's guide to long-term care insurance • a publication produced by government agencies, consumer groups, or insurers and other financial institutions to help consumers understand long-term care insurance and to assist them in the decision to buy a policy. The National Association of Insurance Commissioners (NAIC) publishes the best known of these guides.

sickness • often defined as "illness, disease, or complications of pregnancy which first manifest themselves after the effective date of coverage"

simplified-issue underwriting • a form of group underwriting in which the insurer tends to ask more medically related questions than are used with modified guaranteed-issue underwriting. Only if the answers to these questions are unsatisfactory does the insurer request further medical information—such as an attending physician's statement—or further medical assessments. *Also known as* short-form underwriting. *Compare* full individual underwriting; guaranteed-issue underwriting; modified guaranteed-issue underwriting.

single life annuity • an annuity in which payments are received for the duration of one life

single-premium annuity • an annuity purchased with a lump-sum premium

skilled care • medical care services that may be provided or available 24 hours a day or on a daily basis. The most common setting for skilled care is in a nursing home that is classified as a skilled-nursing facility. *Also known as* skilled-nursing care.

skilled-nursing care • *See* skilled care.

skilled-nursing facility • an institution, usually a nursing home, or part of an institution that meets the accreditation criteria required for reimbursement of skilled-nursing care provided to Medicare and Medicaid patients. *See* skilled care.

SMCP • *See* social managed care plan.

social adequacy • a principle of social insurance programs under which beneficiaries receive a minimum floor of coverage, regardless of their economic status, individual equity, or need. Coverage above the minimum floor is a personal responsibility.

social care • services that help maintain an individual's personal interactions and identity as a member of a community

social managed care plan (SMCP) • an organization that offers a Medicare plan alternative with the full range of medical benefits typically offered to Medicare beneficiaries by Medicare Advantage plans, including a prescription drug benefit plus chronic care services. Social managed care plans target their services to enrollees who are at greatest risk of being admitted to a nursing home to help them remain at home and stay in the community.

social insurance • government-run or government-regulated insurance programs designed primarily to solve major social problems that affect a large portion of society. Distinguishing characteristics are emphasis on social adequacy, compulsory employment-related coverage, partial or total employer financing, benefits prescribed by law, and benefits as a matter of right.

social worker • an individual with advanced education in dealing with social, emotional, and environmental problems associated with physical or cognitive impairments

specialty benefit and service organization • an independent business that provides health care services and management within a limited area of health plan benefits. Its services, often called *carve outs,* usually involve access to a specialty network for behavioral health care, chronic condition and disease management, rehabilitation after catastrophic injury, or transplant surgeries. *See also* carve-out benefit.

specified (dread) disease insurance • supplemental medical insurance that provides per day, per service, expense-incurred, and/or lump-sum benefit payments upon the occurrence of medical events or diagnoses related to the treatment of a disease named in the policy. Although specified disease insurance for cancer only continues to be a prevalent form of this type of coverage, many policies cover cancer and as many as 30 or more other dread diseases.

speech-language pathologist • a professional with advanced training and education in human communications, its development, and its disorders. Individuals with these skills measure and evaluate language abilities, auditory processes, and speech production and treat those with speech and language disorders.

spousal discount • a reduction in otherwise applicable premium rates based on anticipated lower average claim expenses of those who live together in committed relationships and take care of each other before needing long-term care services

SSI • *See* Supplemental Security Income (SSI).

stand-alone plan • a Medicare prescription drug plan that is available to persons enrolled in original Medicare

standard issue • the decision to approve an insurance application as applied for. Most insurers approve 70 to 80 percent of their applications on this basis.

standby assistance • the presence of another person within arm's length who can intervene to prevent physical injury or help with the completion of a task

State Children's Health Insurance Program (SCHIP) • a federal program established by the Balanced Budget Act of 1997 that gives grants to states to provide health insurance coverage to uninsured children who are 18 years old or under and are ineligible for Medicaid

State Health Insurance Assistance Plan (SHIP) • a state program that gets money from the federal government to give free health insurance counseling and assistance to people with Medicare

state high-risk health insurance plan • a high-risk pool established through a not-for-profit association under state legislation that offers comprehensive medical insurance benefits to individuals whose preexisting health conditions deny them standard coverage

step therapy • the practice in prescription drug plans under which approval for higher-cost medications is contingent upon an individual first trying lower-cost, often well-established, drugs to see if they are effective

stop loss • *See* out-of-pocket limit.

student medical expense policy • *See* interim medical expense insurance.

subrogation • a process by which an insurer assumes the legal rights its insured has against a third party responsible for a loss

substantial supervision • the continuous presence of a person directing and watching over another; may also be defined to include cueing

suitability • the process of finding insurance solutions that are appropriate for the needs and wants of consumers

supplemental accident insurance • a medical insurance policy that provides a specified dollar benefit (such as $500 or $1,000) for medical expenses incurred as a result of an accident. When offered in conjunction with a principal policy of medical expense insurance, supplemental accident insurance policies pay benefits without regard to otherwise applicable deductible, copayment, or other self-pay amounts, with covered expenses continuing to apply to the annual deductible.

supplemental medical expense insurance • a policy intended to augment and possibly extend insurance protection to expenses uncovered under a principal policy. *See also* hospital confinement indemnity insurance; specified (dread) disease insurance; critical illness insurance; Medicare supplement insurance.

Supplemental Security Income (SSI) • benefit payments available under the Social Security Program to certain persons with limited incomes and financial resources. This group includes persons aged 65 or older as well as the blind or disabled.

survivorship benefit • a policy provision that waives the premium for a surviving spouse after the other spouse dies. It is used in situations in which a company insures both spouses and the coverage is in force for some period of time, such as 10 years.

TALC • *See* total annual loan cost (TALC).

tax-qualified • the type of long-term care insurance contracts that meet certain standards of the Health Insurance Portability and Accountability Act for favorable tax treatment. *Compare* non-tax-qualified.

temporary medical policy • *See* interim medical expense insurance.

temporomandibular joint dysfunction • *See* TMJ dysfunction.

term life insurance • a form of insurance in which the death proceeds are payable in the event of the insured's death during a specified period; however, nothing is paid if the insured survives to the end of that period

therapist • a trained medical specialist who commonly performs physical, respiratory, infusion, or occupational therapy

third-party notification of policy lapse • a long-term care policy provision whereby the policyowner designates another person to receive notification of the imminent cancellation of a policy for nonpayment of premium

three-tier copayment or deductible structure • a managed health care plan benefit feature that requires members to pay one of three out-of-pocket amounts for services, such as hospital services, or products, such as prescription drugs, depending on their cost to the health plan. *Refer to* copayment; deductible.

time limit on certain defenses • a required policy provision that restricts an insurer's right to rescind or void a policy because of nonfraudulent misstatement to 2 years (3 years in some states). However, if the misstatements were fraudulent, the time limit does not apply. *Compare* incontestable clause.

TMJ dysfunction • in dental treatment, any procedure that affects the way the teeth meet and changes the relationship of the temporomandibular joint is considered treatment of TMJ dysfunction. Because TMJ dysfunction is difficult to diagnose and there is little professional consensus on its appropriate treatment, TMJ dysfunction claims can be costly and subject to abuse.

toileting • getting to and from the toilet, getting on and off the toilet, and performing associated personal hygiene

total annual loan cost (TALC) • a calculation of the cost of a reverse mortgage that combines the loan amount, interest, closing costs, points, and monthly loan service fee into a single rate. Under federal law, lenders are required to illustrate the TALC rate for their loans at the end of 2 years following closing, at the end of the borrower's life expectancy, and at a period 40 percent beyond life expectancy.

total-assets model • a type of partnership program for long-term care in which consumers may purchase an approved long-term care insurance policy at a specified benefit level. It results in none of the insured's assets being considered in determining financial eligibility for Medicaid if the insurance benefits become exhausted.

transferring • moving into or out of a bed, chair, or wheelchair

transitional care benefit • payment to assist a person in meeting immediate needs resulting from the onset of loss of functional capacity

TROOP • stands for true-out-of-pocket costs; sometimes used to describe the out-of-pocket costs that an individual must incur before a Medicare prescription drug will pay 95 percent of covered drug costs

twisting • a form of misrepresentation in which an agent may induce a policyowner to cancel disadvantageously the contract of another insurer in order to take out a new contract

underwriting • an insurer's classification of applicants and their selection for insurance coverage

unfair discrimination • under the Unfair Trade Practices Act, the insurer's ability to decline coverage and to underwrite and rate individuals applying for or seeking to renew health insurance is limited. Specific regulations also address gender, marital status, blindness, physical or mental impairment, and AIDS.

universal life insurance • an interest-sensitive insurance policy that, unlike traditional cash value life insurance, divides the pure life insurance protection and the cash value accumulation into separate and distinct components. The insured is required to pay a specified initial premium for the amount of coverage desired that is used to create a cash value account. Some universal life policies have long-term care riders attached, in which case deductions are made from the account to pay for this protection.

upon-diagnosis benefit • in a specified disease policy, a benefit paid in a single lump sum upon the initial diagnosis of the covered disease, often with an incremental payment for each month the policy has been in force. *See also* medical-event benefit.

variable annuity • an annuity with which payments vary with investment earnings of the annuity company

veterans' benefits • a program of the U.S. Department of Veterans Affairs, often referred to as the VA, that provides a broad spectrum of assistance and services to military veterans, such as health care services that include some types of long-term care

viatical settlement • an arrangement that provides the insured with a cash advance against all or a portion of the death benefit of a life insurance policy while the insured is still alive. Under the arrangement, the policyowner (who may be the insured or someone else, such as a spouse) typically sells the policy to obtain financial resources to pay for expenses at the end of the insured's life. *Compare* accelerated-benefits provision.

voluntary benefits • group or individual insurance products, usually made available by an employer, that an employee may purchase by paying 100 percent of the premium. *Also known as* employee-pay-all benefits, list billing arrangements, and worksite benefits.

waiting period • *See* elimination period.

waiver • *See* exclusion rider.

waiver-of-premium provision • a medical expense policy provision under which the insured, in the event of a total disability, does not have to pay premiums for the duration of the disability to maintain the policy in force • a long-term care policy provision under which the policyowner does not have to pay premiums after the insured has begun to receive benefit payments or has received them for a period of time. While the premiums are waived, the policy remains fully in force.

weekly benefit • a benefit amount, usually applicable to home care benefits, that is determined by multiplying the insured's selected daily benefit amount by 7. Some insurers calculate the weekly benefit at the time of claim when several occasions of service occur on various days during a week. Other insurers offer a weekly benefit as an option, usually at a higher premium.

wellness • the state of being in good health

Women's Health and Cancer Rights Act • a federal act that mandates that any policy providing medical and surgical benefits for mastectomy must also provide coverage for reconstruction of the breast on which the mastectomy was performed, surgery and reconstruction of the other to achieve a symmetrical appearance, and prosthesis and physical complications of all stages of mastectomy, including lymphedemas

workers' compensation • insurance that provides coverage for earnings lost due to occupational injuries and also pays for medical treatment for such injuries

worksite marketing • the process of selling group or individual insurance coverage to persons through their place of employment

Index